Dry Grain Farming Families

By the same author

Migrant Cocoa-Farmers of Southern Ghana: a study in rural capitalism (1963)
Studies in Rural Capitalism in West Africa (1970)
Rural Hausa: a village and a setting (1972)
Population, Prosperity and Poverty: rural Kano 1900 and 1970 (1977)

Dry Grain Farming Families

Hausaland (Nigeria) and Karnataka (India) compared

POLLY HILL

Fellow of Clare Hall, Cambridge

CAMBRIDGE UNIVERSITY PRESS

CAMBRIDGE

LONDON NEW YORK NEW ROCHELLE

MELBOURNE SYDNEY

Published by the Press Syndicate of the University of Cambridge
The Pitt Building, Trumpington Street, Cambridge CB2 1RP
32 East 57th Street, New York, NY 10022, USA
296 Beaconsfield Parade, Middle Park, Melbourne 3206, Australia

First published 1982

Printed in Great Britain
at the University Press, Cambridge

Library of Congress catalogue card number: 81-21610

British Library Cataloguing in Publication Data

Hill, Polly
A dry grain agrarian system: Hausaland
(Nigeria) and Karnataka (India) compared.
1. Nigeria – Rural conditions 2. Nigeria –
Economic conditions 3. Karnataka (India)
– Rural conditions 4. Karnataka (India)
– Economic conditions
I. Title
330.954'87 HC437.K/

ISBN 0 521 23370 4 hardcovers
ISBN 0 521 27102 9 paperback

WP

Contents

Contents

Tables

Figures

Plates

Preface

This book was written accidentally. Prevented by immigration restrictions from working in Nigeria for longer than three months, in 1977 I decided on the spur of the moment to seek my fortune in south India instead, despite my entire unfamiliarity with that continent. The idea of comparative inter-continental work had not occurred to me until I had spent some time in the Karnataka (south Indian) villages, when I realised, to my surprise, that I was in a rather familiar environment in terms of the kind of enquiry on rural economic inequality and individual poverty which I was again resolved to undertake.

As this book attempts a radical assault on prevailing orthodoxy, I doubt if it could have been written by an ordinary member of a university department, such as I had once been myself, for in close academic communities only those of high status are acceptable non-conformists – which is not to deny that one department may include two violently opposed schools of thought.

A cardinal intellectual error of our times seems to amount to a belief in a 'standard condition' of under-development in tropical food-farming societies, for how otherwise can one account for the belief that so much prevailing orthodoxy on matters such as economic inequality and the causes of severe poverty has universal validity, despite the flimsiness of the empirical basis? My contrary contention is that there is so much variability within the rural tropical world that hardly any doctrines below the highest level of generality have universal application, and that it is only by emphasising the significance of heterogeneity that we can hope to make proper intellectual progress. That being so, our first task, whether as economic anthropologists or as (those rare birds) field economists, must be that of identifying and analysing, *by means of fieldwork*, the more important (in terms of the sizes of the populations involved) of the various agrarian systems which exist in the tropical world. It seems to me that the number of important systems may be quite manageably small – say ten or twenty rather than a thousand; and that one of them might prove to be the particular dry grain mode which is the subject of this book.

I hope that I have provided sufficient background information for the book to be comprehensible to students with no prior knowledge of West Africa or south India, thus enabling the formulation of this hypothetical dry grain mode to be assessable within a world context. The book has many other purposes. It is, for example, a practical demonstration of the advantages of setting the socio-economic problems of rural India within a wider world. Indian studies are presently such a specialised field that I found that it was positively advantageous to enter the villages with all the beliefs and prejudices that I had acquired as a long-term West Africanist – my approach being necessarily different from that of a trained Indianist.

Most third world people being country dwellers, I find it appropriate to follow my own inclination of *looking at the world as a whole from within the countryside*. But I have, unfortunately, been unable to avoid a constant switching between the past and present tenses: sometimes I seem to be inside a village as I write, sometimes I merely remember being there. In this connection I have to stress that my comparison is based on conditions as I myself found them in the villages – that it would have been quite impracticable to have taken account of developments in rural Hausaland since 1968.

Since I have already produced two books on rural Hausaland, to which there are many cross-references, I here provide much more detail on the Indian than the Hausa villages. (Even so, limitations of space have forced me to omit much Indian material, archival and other, which is in my files.) In order to enhance the readability of the main text, which is mainly concerned with the inter-continental comparison, part of this detailed material has been relegated to appendices, some of which are primarily statistical.

I shall, of course, be criticised by those who note that my deeply pessimistic conclusions are little relieved by practical suggestions of palliatives. This is deliberate and does not imply a hard heart – indeed, like every other concerned amateur, I have some strong views on 'what ought to be done'. Our present dire ignorance of tropical rural life can be alleviated only by fieldwork which, together with the associated archival work, background reading, analysis of field material and writing, is arduous indeed, leaving no time for other work. While as fieldworkers we do our utmost to provide policy makers with findings which are relevant to their needs, their task must be different from ours, and they should not expect us to step into their shoes. If they do, our ignorance (especially about the most impoverished regions which lack irrigation systems) will continue to be so profound that we shall lack all comprehension of how ignorant we are.

POLLY HILL
July 1981

Acknowledgments

I could not have written this book without the constant encouragement and practical assistance of Dr Christopher Gregory of Clare Hall at every stage; he gave much time to detailed criticism of the numerous drafts through which the chapters passed, as well as valuable bibliographic help and many fresh ideas. Without his support I would have lacked the strength to withstand the scepticism which the very idea of this comparative enterprise aroused in most people. I am also particularly grateful to Dr Susan Bayly, also of Clare Hall, for her constructive criticism of my drafts based on her intimate knowledge of south India, and for much friendly discussion and advice both before and after I went to India; and to Dr Christopher Baker who gave valuable assistance before his greatly regretted removal from Cambridge to Thailand.

Prof. Joan Robinson, Dr Murray Last, Dr Keith Hart, Dr A. F. Robertson, Dr Francesca Bray, Dr Charles Ross, Dr C. A. Bayly and Dr Peter Skalnik read and criticised most or some of the draft chapters at various stages. I am most grateful to them all and must, of course, insist that they and the others named hold no responsibility for any of my conclusions. I must also thank Prof. Meyer Fortes, Dr Sunanda Sen, Dr J. R. Hood, Prof. Michael Lipton and my daughter Mrs Susannah Burn.

On arriving in Bangalore it was my great good fortune to recruit two university graduates, Mr A. V. Diwakar and Mr B. A. Gopal, as my full-time assistants. As it had always been my intention to work in several villages simultaneously, we each continued to live in Bangalore, proceeding daily in the direction of one or other village in an ancient car, which broke down repeatedly. As a statistician, who now works with the Population Centre, Indian Population Project, Bangalore, Mr Diwakar was responsible for compiling the household 'genealogies' and for collecting village statistics generally; his work was excellent, his experience invaluable. Mr Gopal, who acted as my interpreter and constant guide and friend, fortunately spoke each of the three necessary mother tongues (Telugu, Kannada and Tamil) – he was much appreciated by villagers of all castes, almost being regarded as one of themselves. The dreadful task of unravelling the village land revenue statistics fell jointly on Mr Gopal and myself; we suffered greatly from the working conditions then endured by two of the three Village Panchayat Secretaries with whom we worked. We are indeed grateful to these three officials for much help and advice and for their tolerance of our peculiar ways.

We made so many friends in the Anekal villages that I can thank only a few of them by name. We are especially grateful to those who allowed us to sit in their houses for days on end, almost as though we lived there, especially to Sri H. A. Mallareddy of Hullahalli, and his mother Smt Bayyamma, in whose glassed-in verandah we spent hundreds of hours talking to our special friends among the large Harijan population of that village. We also enjoyed much hospitality from the households of ex-patel Madappa of Mahantalingapura (with whom we enjoyed exploring the hinterland of his village), of ex-Shanbhog V. R. Subbrayappa of Vabasandra, of Sri Krishnareddy of Srirampura and of Sri R. Subbramaiah, retired schoolmaster of Bukkasagara. I am especially grateful to the several Harijan village servants (*thotis*) who were my particular friends, among them Thotis Chikkamuniswamy and Papanna of Hullahalli and Thoti Muniappa of Bukkasagara with whom we must have spent the equivalent of several weeks walking round the farmland and nearby villages. Nor can I resist thanking Contractor Mallareddy of Hullahalli and Priest Lokappa of Bukkasagara.

On the official level I am grateful to Smt Negarathnammanni, then Tahsildar (head official) of Anekal Taluk; to the Special Deputy Commissioner of Bangalore District for granting permission for access to the village records; and to the Archivist of the Karnataka State Archives for permission to consult the records as well as to the staff for much fetching and carrying of bulky papers. I must also thank Prof. M. N. Srinivas and other members of the Institute for Social and Economic Change at Bangalore for welcoming me when I first arrived.

The work in India was undertaken during my tenure of the six-year Smuts Readership in Commonwealth Studies at Cambridge University. I am grateful to the Managers of the Smuts Fund for granting me additional funds in support of my Indian fieldwork. I must also acknowledge financial support from the Leverhulme Trust while I was writing the book. I doubt whether I should have sustained the ordeal of persisting with the book had the Cambridge University Press not offered me positive encouragement at all stages.

Finally, I must praise the unique academic atmosphere provided by my college Clare Hall, a truly international institution which never ceases to amaze me.

Abbreviations and conventions

AKs and ADs	At appropriate points I refer to members of the Adikarnataka and Adidravida castes as AKs and ADs, but other caste names in the Anekal villages have not been abbreviated.
Book references	The title of any publication is given only for its first mention; thereafter reference should be made to the author's name in the book list.
Currency	In 1977–8 the rate of exchange between the rupee and the £ sterling fluctuated somewhat; I have taken it to be Rs 14 to the £.
Rounding	As the use of decimal points in my statistical tables would have given a spurious sense of accuracy, I have rounded all percentages to the nearest integer with the result that they do not always total 100.
Tables	Nil is indicated by –, . . . signifying inappropriate or irrelevant.
Vernacular words	I have endeavoured to reduce the number of vernacular words to a minimum. Although several languages were spoken in the Anekal villages, all vernacular words for those villages are Kannada – apart, of course, from all-India words connected with such matters as land revenue and tenure.

INTRODUCTORY CHAPTER

The Need to Engage in the Field Experience

As a fieldworker who has long studied agrarian systems and economic inequality in the tropical third world, more recently with particular reference to the causes of severe impoverishment, I have suffered much condescension since about 1970 owing both to my unfashionable methods of field enquiry and to my inability to formulate logically coherent conceptual systems of any general appeal. Now that I have widened my scope to include a district of south India (my earlier work for a period of fourteen years from 1953 had been confined to West Africa), I have ventured to write this book as a practical demonstration of the possibilities of formulating, on the basis of detailed fieldwork, a set of coherent hypotheses relating to a specific type of rural under-development which has recently come into existence in certain very densely populated dry grain zones in both West Africa and south India – as doubtless in certain other regions of these and other continents. There is a crying need for *systematic categorisation of types of rural under-development in the tropical third world*, and I hope that in identifying and analysing this particular 'dry grain mode' I shall have done something to encourage other fieldworkers to identify other modes.

The conditions associated with the existence of this dry grain mode are summarised at the beginning of Chapter II, which serves as an introduction to Chapters III to XI – the remaining chapters being historical. In this introductory chapter I try, in a general way, to justify the use of detailed field enquiries in the tropical third world, without regard to my own success, or otherwise, in adopting such procedures.

The long and agonising process of detailed exploration in the field has as its aim the formulation of certain general principles – it should not be seen as an old-fashioned kind of nature study pursued as an end in itself, but as a necessary preliminary to socio-economic analysis and the pursuit of theory. But partly because the problems facing the rural third world are rightly seen as so urgent, intellectual standards are commonly thrown to the winds: despite extreme ignorance of rural conditions, the formulation of policy takes priority, followed by analysis and theory generally – description and classification (much of which ought to be statistical) trailing far far behind, if it is there at all. From bitter experience I know that a fieldworker who fails to give priority to policy questions is invariably accused of lack of compassion.

This contemporary contempt for proper field enquiry emanates from a great many quarters, some of them unexpected, and has resulted in some unholy alliances between, for example, marxists and apolitical ('conventional') historians, both of whom are apt to assume that there is a large body of proven received wisdom of sufficient consistency and universality to require no testing in the field – whereas I myself doubt whether any such 'wisdom' has universal validity. Much of this orthodoxy is based on simple evolutionary notions, such as the inevitability of recent 'cash crop revolutions' and the belief that rural inequality necessarily derives from the urban world. It takes account of the wide extent of extreme poverty, but has little real conception of its depth.

Partly in the hope of improving their standing in relation to economists, whom they regard with unnecessary awe, economic anthropologists, whether they be marxists or not, are apt to emphasise their theoretical rectitude by denouncing their enemies, in the manner of M. Bloch:

> The criticism which marxists and others would make of empiricism is not so much that it is wrong but that it is impossible; this means that there are theoretical postulates present in the work of all social anthropologists and that these have political significance[1]

Since such a fear of field enquiries is shared by economists, who are nowadays especially terrified of the dangers of wasting money by pursuing work of no practical utility, I now counter Bloch's statement by listing a set of general postulates which taken together, and in no particular logical order, might help to justify the experience of field enquiry.

A list of general postulates relative to methodology

1. There *are* theoretical postulates present in the minds of all trained fieldworkers – they are unavoidable.
2. Some, but not all, of these postulates are necessarily unconscious.
3. Some, but not all, of these postulates have political significance: the full array is necessarily unascertainable.
4. The postulates themselves are, to some degree, necessarily transformed by the 'work process' involving the three stages of fieldwork, analysis of material and writing (with all that that involves); we do not know what we have found out until we read what we have written.

[1] From the introduction by M. Bloch to *Marxist Analyses and Social Anthropology*, ed. M. Bloch, 1975, p. xiii.

5. The 'findings' and the transformed postulates therefore, become, to some degree, inextricably confused; at least this means that one travels with a revised set of postulates on the next expedition to the field.
6. Theoretical systems are not, in themselves, therapeutic – as the field experience ought to be; whether one adopts a theoretical approach or not, there is no hope of expunging one's unconscious postulates or of ensuring that they fit one's conscious theoretical apparatus of thought; entire purging is impossible and no one can render themselves classless.
7. Whether we happen to be marxists or not, our unconscious postulates, which cannot be wholly eradicated by theoretical training, are necessarily to some degree ethnocentric; by denying this, in the sense that we condemn others (though not ourselves) for their ethnocentrism, we falsify our work.
8. Part of our susceptibility to the criticisms of others is due to the fear that they perceive our unconscious postulates whereas, by definition, we cannot do so ourselves; by adopting a wholly theoretical framework which, by definition, is supposed to oust unconscious postulates, theoreticians vainly hope to reduce their vulnerability.
9. Anthropological fieldworkers may or may not ultimately come to have a better understanding than their readers of such of their erstwhile unconscious processes as have ultimately surfaced; however, the threefold work process to which they necessarily submit themselves may give them some advantages in appreciating their earlier naivety. (Is naivety necessarily ethnocentric?)
10. Yes, the psychoanalysts have taught us that we are all creatures whose preconceptions are partly based on our unremembered experiences; one and all, marxists, amarxists and non-marxists, we are necessarily to some degree ethnocentric and class-centric and there is a limit to which our preconceptions may be modified, even with the help of therapists. (As elitists, indigenous fieldworkers in third world countries are apt to be greatly hampered by their class-centrism.)
11. The deliberately ahistorical approach of many theoreticians, which will be discussed below, renders them peculiarly ethnocentric; maybe the past lies in the future, but the unconscious mind is far too inventive to tolerate a vacuum.
12. It is, also, arguable that marxists are among the most emotional (and hence subjective?) of all investigators, if only because they find themselves obliged to identify various classes of actual 'villain' in the village – however, 'subjective' has an old-fashioned ring in this general context and is best avoided.
13. An exploratory field approach essentially relies on the testing of hypotheses in the field; although one would not know it at the time, unconscious as well as conscious hypotheses are certain to be tested.
14. The testing approach is much facilitated if resort to history is possible.
15. 'The general and particular interact and modify each other at every level. Nothing important is a matter of chance, but nothing can be seen to be caused by a single factor.'[2]

[2] A citation from a review by B. Crick of *Politics and History* by R. Aron, *The Observer*, 22 April 1979.

16. The more unfamiliar the field, the more appropriate the method of submitting oneself to experiencing the realities of the unknown; educated 'experts', whether Westerners or members of the third world, know far less about third world rural economies than they think and owing to their alienation from the countryside they become increasingly prejudiced – this is particularly true of north Americans who usually refer to third world cultivators as 'small farmers'.
17. The fact, insofar as it is a fact, 'that our thinking is determined by our social position is not necessarily a source of error. On the contrary, it is often the path to political insight.'[3]

Abandoning these polemics, I now get down to more banal matters. I start by identifying the various world establishments which are apt to disdain the use of inductive field methods in studying socio-economic matters in the rural tropical world.

The *first* is the general establishment of Western academic economists, whose ideological outlook is reflected in the fact that it seldom encourages its graduate students to undertake such inductive fieldwork[4] – this being in great contrast to various establishments of Western historians which, in the past fifteen years or more, have successfully emulated social anthropologists in both India and Africa. Why should the economists, who are so severely rent by political dissension, at least find themselves in agreement on this subject? I pose this question because I cannot answer it but can only roam around it. Perhaps economists do not want to understand 'the peasantry', which is regarded as outmoded or withering away, but only to transform its way of life – for is not industry 'the engine of growth'? Perhaps they think that all work resembling economic anthropology, with its apparently obsessive concern with unnecessary detail, is invariably devoid of practical value? Perhaps they suppose that they have already developed a sufficient body of received doctrine? These are mere random thoughts on a subject which seems to receive little attention. Ought the relationships of economists to the power structure of modern capitalism to be more clearly delineated?

The *second* establishment consists of official grant-awarding authorities, including the British Social Science Research Council and its counterparts elsewhere, which are all too apt to require their applicants to forecast their conclusions when outlining their research projects and to demand that

[3] *Ideology and Utopia* by K. Mannheim, 1936, cited in *Caste, Class and Power: Changing Patterns of Stratification in a Tanjore Village* by A. Béteille, 1971, p. 12.

[4] This is subject to the qualification that such institutions as the School of Oriental and African Studies in London or the West African Studies Centre in Birmingham are apt to encourage socio-economic fieldwork. See the list of 'Thesis Titles for Degrees in the United Kingdom 1977/8 and 1978/9', *Economic Journal*, March 1979.

work should be 'useful'. But if one does not know what is not known, how does one know what might be useful? I think that it is owing to false analogies with the experimental methods of scientists (proper), who enjoy far more general prestige than social scientists, that it is thought that a set of detailed pre-packed assumptions, identifying the main socio-economic variables, should be taken to the field by the innocent applicant, as though it were a camera.

Third, there are the specialised agencies of the United Nations, such as the FAO, which seldom support *intensive* socio-economic studies affecting agrarian systems and never integrate them with projects such as vast irrigation schemes, until it is far too late. Our ignorance is as great today as in 1968 when Myrdal reported that an accurate statistical picture of the numerical strength of the main 'social groups' in farming communities could not be produced for any South Asian country.[5]

Myrdal identified our *fourth* group of anti-inductivists, certain elitists in the third world, when adding that:

> The fact that rigorous enquiries – even those obliged to improvise somewhat arbitrary conceptual categories – have not been sponsored officially must be partly ascribed to the vested interests in concealment among the upper strata, both in rural and in urban areas.[6]

After spending nearly a year in south Indian villages I certainly agree that:

> the numerical strength of the various social groups in the village, and the area of land each commands, may well be said to be among the best guarded secrets of the South Asian economies.[7]

And our ignorance of West African rural economies is far more profound.

Among the numerous reasons which account for the consensus of the four establishments I pick out the following. *First* is the failure to realise that we are so ignorant of the economic condition of man in rural tropical regions that we do not know how ignorant we are. *Second* (a connected point) was the precipitate and premature way in which economists started 'teaching under-development' soon after the second world war, despite their own profound ignorance; many of their early hypotheses about rural conditions, based on little if any evidence, have since hardened into truths. *Third* is urban bias and the failure to realise that the great bulk of the population in most third world countries will continue to rely on agriculture for many years to come. *Fourth* is the inherent belief in the essential reliability of official statistics[8] relating to rural conditions which

[5] *Asian Drama* by G. Myrdal, 1968, p. 1056.
[6] *Ibid.*
[7] *Ibid.*, p. 1056.
[8] See Appendix to this Chapter.

has been assiduously fostered by UN and governmental agencies and by third world countries themselves, notably India; it is no exaggeration to say that as the statisticians' power to manipulate the figures increases, so their lack of interest in the quality of the 'raw data' declines. The insistence that official statistics keep us basically well informed, in terms both of the identification of the salient variables and their fluctuations, is one of the fundamental intellectual immoralities of our time – it is, of course, regarded as one of the main justifications for dispensing with intensive fieldwork by individuals, although this may be the only means by which the basic defects in the raw material can be exposed.

Fifth is the wish not to offend officials in the third world by implying that they share our ignorance of rural conditions. Visiting experts usually have a touching and sincere belief in the omniscience of the officials they happen to encounter and are often unaware that urban bias is even more pronounced in the third world than in the West; unconscious colonial attitudes on both sides result in an inversion of former roles, the expert being over-subordinate. *Sixth* is the unfortunate respectability of the 'questionnaire approach' in villages, which necessitates identifying the salient variables in advance. *Seventh* is the poor quality of many village surveys which have been undertaken by indigenous economists since the last war, especially in India; it is true that the villages are far too often treated as isolates, both in space and time. *Eighth* is the genuine contempt which most 'technical experts', such as agronomists and irrigation engineers, feel for anthropologists and other students of rural life, on the grounds both that they lack expertise, their methods being no more than 'glorified commonsense', and that they pursue their work for its own sake, irrespective of its usefulness to the under-privileged.

Finally, there is a failure to realise that it is not the function of the fieldworker himself to produce a body of doctrine which will influence the course of events, but rather to provide relevant data for the use of those who construct the influential analytic systems. But if the fieldworkers' findings appear irrelevant to the mainstream of current thought they are always wholly ignored.[9] So unless one is prepared to sit down indefinitely in an intellectual backwater it is essential to concentrate on broad subjects which might be expected to appeal to the policy maker – whose servant one is in the last resort. That is one reason why I, for my part, concentrate on the matter of economic inequality, hoping that my findings will have some

[9] See *British Economic Thought and India 1600–1858: A Study in the History of Development Economics* by W. J. Barber, 1975, pp. 207 *et seq.*, on Richard Jones's failure to offer economists acceptable analytical criticism of the Ricardian master model.

slight relevance to the passionate worldwide debate – but I have experienced a singular lack of success so far. I fear that the only fieldworkers whose findings have impact are those like C. Geertz who in *Agricultural Involution*[10] combined the three functions of investigation, analysis and policy formulation in an appealing and succinct manner. Fieldworkers must continue to hope that they may be permitted a narrower scope – that division of labour may ultimately prove acceptable, their findings being useful to theoreticians and policy makers.

My list of general postulates relative to methodology at least implies that the distinction between theoretical and field methods is not as straightforward as is nowadays often supposed, for both of them rely on the testing of conscious and unconscious (preformulated and unformulated) hypotheses in the field – if the theoreticians ever get there. Perhaps most theoreticians would dispute this, on the grounds that they are concerned to validate laws not hypotheses. But what could be the point of going to the field to test axioms of universal validity, such as the following, which I have arbitrarily formulated for present purposes:

> *Laissez-faire* rural economies in the third world, in which most exchange transactions, including transactions in land, involve cash, are necessarily such that the rich constantly tend to benefit at the expense of the poor, whatever their conscious intentions, to the extent that non-radical official intervention, designed to improve the situation of the poor will necessarily fail to reverse the general tendency.

It is the theoreticians who have confused the issue by assuming, as Victorian political scientists did not, that the two methodologies are entirely distinct.

In 1890 John Neville Keynes, the father of John Maynard Keynes, offered the following outline of the deductive method in political economy, which consisted of three steps:

> It is necessary, first to determine what are the principal forces in operation, and the laws in accordance with which they operate. Next comes the purely deductive stage, in which are inferred the consequences that will ensue from the operation of these forces under given conditions. Lastly, by a comparison of what has been inferred with what can be directly observed to occur, an opportunity is afforded for testing the correctness and practical adequacy of the two preceding steps, *and for the suggestion of necessary qualifications.* [My italics][11]

[10] Subtitled *The Processes of Ecological Change in Indonesia*, 1963.
[11] *The Scope and Method of Political Economy* by J. N. Keynes, 1890, pp. 212–13.

As J. N. Keynes proceeds to add:

> It will be observed that only one of these three steps – namely the middle one – is strictly speaking deductive. The so-called deductive method in its complete form is thus seen to be not an exclusively deductive method. It . . . is still aided and controlled by induction.[12]

It will be noted that to the fieldworker the weakness of such a deductive method is that it provides no opportunity for the formulation of new, testable, hypotheses, such as had not been anticipated, but which had emerged in the course of the work, but only for 'the suggestion of necessary qualifications'. If these qualifications are inconsistent with the 'laws' formulated in the first stage, then presumably the deductive method has failed?

Owing to the false belief that under-development in the tropical rural world is a standard condition with certain necessary salient features (and also to the associated belief that all members of any particular rural community are apt to have similar economic responses),[13] many deductivists and textbook writers sought, from the 1950s onwards, to identify these features in the simplest possible terms so as to enhance their universality. The list of common presumptions, which underwent constant swings of fashion, makes very sad reading owing to the crudity of the ideas involved and the speed with which they suddenly seemed outmoded. I deal with a few of them here.[14]

The presumption of amorphousness and homogeneity is well illustrated by the following citation from a very respectable textbook by H. Myint:

> A peasant family could have produced a much larger agricultural output than it was actually producing . . . . *But it chose not to do so* [my italics] for the simple reason that every other peasant family could do the same.[15]

In the 1950s it was commonly presumed[16] by textbook writers that Asian and African cultivators were (unfortunately) all too apt 'to choose leisure'

[12] *Ibid.*, p. 213.

[13] Whereas the economic behaviour of the poorer people is often the mirror image of that of the richer.

[14] I am not here concerned with the obsolete debate instigated by the Polanyi school since it is evident that the kind of tropical rural economies to which this book relates are necessarily regulated to some extent by 'market principles'.

[15] *The Economics of the Developing Countries* by H. Myint, 1964, p. 43. The generalisation referred to the 'thinly populated peasant societies' of Asia and Africa.

[16] But not by P. T. Bauer and B. S. Yamey in *The Economics of Under-Developed Countries*, 1957, who insisted, p. 86, that there appeared to be 'no ceiling to economic development imposed by inflexibility in habits of consumption in many, perhaps most, under-developed countries'.

when, in their own interests, they ought to be working – an idea which was respectably dressed up in terms of a backward sloping supply curve of labour. (That this notion was later ousted by a belief in the over-responsiveness to the price mechanism on the part of all cultivators, reflected the post-colonial need to presume that the erstwhile 'native' was more like ourselves than we had thought.)

An associated idea was that peasants preferred leisure because their range of 'wants' was so limited. This was given particular cachet by G. M. Foster in 'Peasant Society and the Image of Limited Good',[17] who based himself on fieldwork in Mexico. The article is altogether invalidated by the assumption that the 'peasant community' was a closed system, for if 'peasant' has any proper application to third world rural economies it must refer to cultivators who are, in some straightforward sense, economically subservient to the capitalists of the wider world; nor do the formal qualifications of the premiss, that it is made for the purposes of analysis and argument only, give the work any pertinence.[18] On the one hand censorious outsiders are always apt to deplore crippling 'bride prices' and deep indebtedness; on the other hand, there is the contrary presumption of 'limited wants' – which is deeply offensive to those of us who have witnessed extreme poverty in the field.

Myint was also responsible for developing the 'vent for surplus' theory of international trade in relation to third world countries[19] – a concept which ultimately stemmed from Adam Smith. But why should such a theory, which states that exporting led to no decline in other forms of economic activity, necessarily be of general application, when circumstances are so variable? Whereas detailed fieldwork has convinced me that the original growth of Ghanaian cocoa exporting represented a large net gain to the rural population concerned (partly because food-farming was basically the responsibility of women), the same was by no means necessarily true of the early years of groundnut exporting from northern Nigeria, the main effect of which may have been (for all we know) to deprive the local population of much needed dietary fats and proteins in the form of groundnut oil.

* * *

17 *American Anthropologist*, April 1965, pp. 293–315.

18 The author's 'image of limited good' even assumes that 'peasants' believe that such attributes as friendship and love (as well as wealth) 'exist in finite quantity' and are 'always in short supply'. *Ibid.*, p. 296.

19 'The "Classical Theory" of International Trade and the Underdeveloped Countries' by H. Myint, *Economic Journal*, June 1958, pp. 317–37. For criticism of this theory see 'The Vent-for-Surplus Model and African Cash Agriculture to 1914' by J. Hogendorn, *Savanna*, June 1976.

In the course of this book, I shall call in question the conventional usages of several fundamental economic terms such as *subsistence* and *surplus* (the latter in certain contexts) on the grounds that they incorporate and conceal implicit assumptions which it is our particular function to investigate. It is the very words whose meanings appear to be the most obvious which particularly impede our enquiries. But I deal now with the semantics of *peasant* which, readers will note, is employed nowhere in this book – and with no resultant circumlocutions.

Very abruptly in the 1960s *peasant* became the vogue word, denoting virtually all the inhabitants of the rural tropical world. Prior to that date we anthropologists had distinguished between farmers (or cultivators), farm labourers, artisans, traders and other groups – but suddenly they all became subsumed under *peasant*. The operation reminded me, in mirror image, of the moment when, virtually overnight, the word 'native' had been removed from all the exhibits in the (then) Imperial Institute, being replaced by 'African', 'Indian' and so forth – and rightly so, for *peasant* in its contemporary usage in the tropical third world *is* the semantic successor to *native,* incorporating all its condescending and derogatory racial overtones, especially among town-dwellers in the third world. We anthropologists had previously managed quite well without that Eurocentric word and it seemed odd that its use should suddenly have become compulsory.

In stating my numerous objections to the use of this emotive word, I lay primary stress on the power that it has to conceal the extremities of individual poverty. While *peasant* is necessarily very derogatory in many contexts, it also has cosy connotations: it does not readily conjure up a situation where a high proportion of the population rather resembles an under-employed, landless rural proletariat. In literature and tradition a peasant is a hardworking, suffering man who tills his own small plot with a little success – not a propertyless man who is nearly always hungry.

The other main objection to *peasant* is its power to confirm our aboriginal ideas of an amorphous (undifferentiated) tropical peasantry, despite the extraordinary efforts that began in the 1970s to qualify the word appropriately. Considering the political leanings of those who were most insistent on employing *peasant*, it is astounding that so little heed was paid to the warnings uttered by Lenin in *The Development of Capitalism in Russia*[20] on the dangers of obscuring differentiation by the use of notions relating to average peasants of various categories. Lenin himself noted[21]

[20] Vol. 3 of the Collected Works of V. I. Lenin. Originally published in 1899.
[21] English translation of the second edition, p. 173.

that local people themselves referred to the differentiation of the peasantry as 'depeasantisation'.

It is, therefore, my strong and solemn opinion that students of rural economic inequality in the tropical third world negate their own work by employing *peasant*, however earnestly they may seek to qualify the word. (And outside specifically political contexts, *rural community* is usually preferable to *peasantry*.) In circumstances where nearly everyone in a village has some connection with agriculture or the care of livestock, the definitional difficulties of distinguishing peasants from non-peasants lead to ridiculous convolutions and no agreement, especially where, as so commonly in West Africa, most adult men and women also have a non-farming occupation. *Peasant* also leads to an under-estimation of the significance of farm-labouring: thus T. Shanin in his introduction to his influential *Peasants and Peasant Societies* insists that a fundamental component of the definition is that 'The family, and nearly only the family, provides the labour on the farm'[22] – thus rendering a decrepit widow with no dependants who occasionally employs farm labourers into a capitalist farmer?

Of course it may be entirely justifiable to employ *peasantry* in political contexts, if only because such usage reflects the genuinely derogatory attitudes of educated elites;[23] but were a writer like myself to abandon the use of *farmer* or *cultivator* in favour of *peasant* when examining economic inequality and the structure of agrarian systems *from a stance within the village* this would confuse the reader – and is, anyway, quite unnecessary.

A further objection to *peasant* resides in its evolutionary connotations: built in is the thought that in the tropical third world there must have been a time *not long ago* when those who are peasants today were in some earlier evolutionary phase. I find that it is always presumed that pre-colonial West African cultivators were '*pre-peasants*', so when one insists that richer farmers in pre-colonial Hausaland commonly bought farm slaves for cash in order to increase their production of grain for sale, one is met with incredulity. So this is an appropriate point at which to emphasise that students of agrarian systems who work in the field attach much importance to an historical approach: that an appeal to history is part of the procedure of testing hypotheses – and that archival, as well as oral sources are useful.

22 *Peasants and Peasant Societies: Selected Readings*, ed. T. Shanin, 1971, pp. 14–15.

23 It is significant that the only Hausa word which one might equate with peasant is *talaka*, literally 'poor man'; its plural form *talakawa* (peasantry) is employed by villagers themselves when they contemplate their subordination to townsmen.

Field anthropologists are now agreed that systems and relations of production must be studied in historical perspective.

But anti-historical postures are increasingly adopted by theoreticians, such as Hindess and Hirst, who themselves admit that their *Pre-capitalist Modes of Production*[24] 'will appear to many people, historians and others, to be a contradictory enterprise':

> How can a book about pre-capitalist modes of production be abstract and anti-historical?[25]

Yet despite their repudiation of 'history', which goes undefined, they make much reference to past events and relations, for instance to farm-slavery. Their so-called 'Comment', which follows, irons out the variations between different farm-slavery systems, as does their reference to *the* slave mode:

> Slavery is (*sic*) not the most efficient system of augmentation of the labour-power of a peasant farm. The chattel slave is a capital investment and must be maintained, although the farm's demand (*sic*) for labour-power is uneven. Casual wage-labour is a more satisfactory form of augmentation of the farm's labour-power when it is needed.[26]

What possible justification can there be for including such an appeal to history in an anti-historical book? Unassailable *theoretical* comment though it is supposed to be, I have to insist that it has no application to farm-slavery in Kano Emirate in Hausaland where the alternative of casual wage-labour did not exist; where it would have been a less efficient system than slave-labour had it existed; and where the chattel slave did not have to be 'fully maintained' by his owner, since he was permitted, indeed encouraged, to work for part of the time on his own account.

British political economists of the last century usually regarded the appeal to economic history as being mainly statistical, involving long-term movements in prices, wages and other indices. Richard Jones,[27] on the other hand, who was greatly admired by Marx,[28] considered that inductive procedures in relation to the study of land tenure must be supported by qualitative distinctions based on 'bringing together the accounts of all countries and all ages'. In opposing Ricardo's deductive approach to rent he classified types of rent into 'certain large classes', 'according as they exist

[24] By B. Hindess and P. Hirst, 1975.

[25] *Ibid.*, p. 308. [26] *Ibid.*, p. 138.

[27] See *Literary Remains: consisting of lectures and tracts on political economy of the late Rev. Richard Jones*, ed. W. Whewell, 1859.

[28] Thus Chap. 24 of Marx's *Theories of Surplus Value*, Part III, is devoted to Jones's work. (But Marx had no taste for Jones's plea for inductive methods.)

in different nations'.[29] In other words, he set himself against the deductivists by risking the supposition, which is necessary for inductivists, that the process of qualitative classification does not imply the existence of an infinitude of types – the search for 'certain large classes' being indeed the main aim.

> If we wish to make ourselves acquainted with the economy and arrangements by which different nations of the earth produce or distribute their revenues, I really know but of one way to attain our object, and that is to look and see.
>
> If we want to understand the subjects of wages or rent for instance, and take the trouble to observe how the various nations of the earth employ and pay their labourers or distribute to the landowners their share of the produce of the soil, we shall necessarily gain much information in our progress.[30]

But, as I have already noted,[31] Jones failed to persuade his generation of the need to go into the field – Marx himself having 'no taste for Jones's plea for careful study of individual peasant economies'.[32] There were few who noted that many of Jones's conclusions were 'entirely at variance with the doctrines of the *a priori* school'.[33] Since Jones's time economists have, unfortunately, made little progress in identifying the types of conceptual apparatus 'appropriate to understanding and improving the economic condition of the poorer countries'.[34]

I have already referred to the worldwide conspiracy which forces us to accept the inherent reliability of official socio-economic statistics relating to the rural third world. In all seriousness we are informed by the FAO that the production of cassava (manioc) in Africa has risen by $x\%$ since the previous year although the acreage under this crop is never known with any reliability in any country, nor (which is worse) the period during which it remains unharvested in the ground.[35] In an Appendix to this chapter, as well as at many other points in this book, I discuss some of the defects in official Indian socio-economic statistics relating to the countryside. My purpose is not to discredit those responsible for collecting, processing, collating and disseminating these statistics, least of all the humble workers at grass roots level who are often given impossible tasks, but to draw attention to the need for unofficial fieldworkers to try to comprehend the meaning and reliability of the statistics at village level,

[29] Citations from the Preface by Whewell, 1859, p. xi.
[30] Whewell, 1859, pp. 568–9.
[31] Footnote 9 above.
[32] Barber, 1975, p. 228.
[33] Whewell, 1859, p. xi.
[34] See Barber, 1975, p. 234.
[35] The point being that cassava can be stored for long periods in the ground – and immediately rots when harvested.

with special reference to the practicability of data collection on elusive subjects such as daily-paid labour employment or the age classification of livestock.

One of my particular reasons for insisting that we are 'far more ignorant than we know' has to do with the poorly developed techniques for mapping the farmland owned or cultivated by individual farmers, taking account of the nature of the rights exerted. Although UN agencies, such as the FAO, profess an interest in improving the quality of agricultural and demographic statistics in the rural third world, the need for mapping farm-holdings, with the aid of those specialist statisticians the surveyors, is nearly always overlooked. In relation to agricultural development the lack of maps of land ownership is every bit as serious as any lack of demographic statistics would be – those who undertake large-scale irrigation works in West Africa usually learn this, to their cost, when it is far too late. It is true that the development of aerial photography in third world countries during the past few decades has resulted in much scientific analysis of land use; but such work usually lacks all socio-economic content. Only private research workers, and they but seldom, use aerial photographs for the mapping of individual farmholdings. The results are sometimes surprising.

It is this matter of *surprise* which provides so much of the justification for submitting oneself to the field experience. It is not merely that we hold no questionnaire in our hands, but that the salient variables which we are engaged in chasing are apt to change their identities overnight so that we are in a constant state of back-tracking and self-contradiction. The plight of the theoretician in this regard is well summed up by Jones:

> We must get comprehensive views of facts, that we may arrive at principles which are truly comprehensive. If we take a different method, if we snatch at general principles, and content ourselves with confined observations, two things will happen to us. First what we call general principles will often be found to have no generality; we shall set out with declaring propositions to be universally true, which, at every step of our further progress, we shall be obliged to confess are frequently false.[36]

Jones considered that the Ricardians had presumptuously taken up:

> The more fascinating employment of laying down those maxims of imposing generality, which seemed to elevate the enquirer at once into the *legislator of his subject* [my italics], and gift him, as if by some sudden manifestation of intellectual power, with an instant command over its remotest details.[37]

[36] Whewell, 1859, p. 569.

[37] *An Essay on the Distribution of Wealth and on the Sources of Taxation*, by R. Jones, 1831, p. xxiii.

He insisted that the principles determining the position and progress of large bodies of the human race, in unfamiliar circumstances, could be learnt only by an appeal to experience.

> He must, indeed, be a shallow reasoner, who by mere efforts of consciousness, by consulting his own views, feelings and motives, and the narrow sphere of his personal observations, and reasoning *a priori* from them expects that he shall be able to anticipate the conduct, progress and fortunes of large bodies of men, differing from himself in moral or physical temperament, and influenced by differences, varying in extent and variously combined in climate, soil, religion, education and government.[38]

But Jones had little influence in the longer run. The founding father of neo-classical economics, W. S. Jevons, threw Jones overboard when he observed that the science of economics is peculiar in that:

> its ultimate laws are known to us immediately by intuition, or, at any rate, they are furnished to us ready made by other mental or physical sciences.[39]

So far as the rural tropical world is concerned economics has remained peculiar ever since, for it is still true that

> The final agreement of our inferences with *a posteriori* observations ratifies our method.[40]

Field enquiry continues to be condemned as involving too much detail:

> The circumstances of a nation are infinitely complicated, and we seldom get two or more instances which are comparable.[41]

As Jevons held (p. 21) that economics could only be rendered into an 'exact science' with the aid of numerical data, it seems appropriate to attach an Appendix referring to the poor quality of official socio-economic statistics relating to the Indian countryside to this particular chapter. In these dire circumstances the only respectable course is to go and look for oneself.

I conclude this polemical Introduction, very abruptly, with a citation from Marx which refers to the relationship between Ricardo ('the master') and James Mill. For might it not likewise be held to refer to the relationship between Marx (the master) and those of his present-day disciples who oppose the field experience?

[38] *Ibid.*, p. xv.
[39] *The Theory of Political Economy* by W. S. Jevons, 1871; the citation is drawn from p. 18 of the 4th edition of 1911.
[40] *Ibid.*, p. 18. [41] *Ibid.*

> Mill was the first to present Ricardo's theory in systematic form, even though he did it only in rather abstract outlines. . . . With the master Ricardo what is new and significant develops vigorously amid the 'manure' of contradictions out of the contradictory phenomena. The underlying contradictions themselves testify to the richness of the living foundation from which the theory itself developed. It is different with the disciple. His raw material is no longer reality, but the new theoretical form in which the master has sublimated it.[42]

APPENDIX TO INTRODUCTION

Defects in official socio-economic statistics relating to the Indian countryside

In this book I draw attention to many defects in official socio-economic statistics relating to the Indian countryside – some of which are generally familiar, a few receiving no mention. Starting with some remarks about the general causes of 'bad statistics', I then list some of the main defects in the Indian statistics. Lacking space, I resist the temptation to quote from C. Dewey's excellent and witty exposé '*Patwari* and *Chaukidar*: Subordinate Officials and the Reliability of India's Agricultural Statistics',[43] except from his section 'Crop Yields: The Impossible Average'.

In this intellectually corrupt age, it is in the interest of all concerned with manipulating statistics relating to the rural tropical world, from the officials in the specialised agencies of the UN downwards (and it is a long, long, downward ladder), to assume that the collectors of the basic statistics at the ground level are honest, professional, hardworking, with a real knowledge of agrarian conditions – whereas they are more likely to be under-trained, forced into corruption, overworked, ignorant, bored, under-paid and genuinely unconvinced of the value of what they are doing.[44] But the fact that the basic statistics are essentially, inherently, unreliable is not so much the fault of village-level officials as of those who ask them to perform impossible tasks, such as to collect statistics of household income, expenditure and indebtedness, which are unascertainable even by their informants the householders – who are obliged to guess. We are faced with a massive defect in the ideology of our times; everyone believes that, given sufficient statistical manipulation, guessed figures (i.e. plausible figures) are bound to be transformed into 'useful data'; no one emphasises that bad figures are apt to be dangerous not neutral in their impact since they reflect many prejudices which are

[42] *Theories of Surplus Value*, Part III, by K. Marx, p. 84.

[43] In *The Imperial Impact: Studies in the Economic History of Africa and India*, eds. C. Dewey and A. G. Hopkins, 1978.

[44] A university-educated statistician told me that he sincerely believed he was justified in guessing the remaining figures after he had collected material from what he thought was a sufficient number of informants to establish a 'pattern of plausibility'.

themselves responsible for economic stagnation. Bad statistics are as much a cause of stagnation as bad sanitation.

Official over-optimism about the attainment of crop 'targets' may lead to preposterous inflation of figures. For certain taluks in North Arcot one of the authors of *Green Revolution?* found[45] that usage of high-yielding varieties of paddy was 13% compared with the official figures, for the same taluks in the same year, of between 39% and 48%. This he denoted 'top–down targetry in agricultural administration', the belief being that all concerned will work harder to achieve the target if:

> Statistics derived from some senior imagination are disaggregated down the hierarchy with sufficient authority to induce those at the bottom to try, or try harder, to turn them into reality.[46]

In a more general reference to the unreliability of official statistics relating to agriculture, R. Chambers and B. H. Farmer state that in both India and Sri Lanka:

> Survey methodology itself may generate a spurious finding of widespread direct contact between extension staff and individual farmers.[47]

In the following list of some defects in Indian[48] statistics I refer to the main pages, if any, on which the particular defect is discussed below.

(1) *The confusion between farm-holdings and farm-plots*

South Indian, like West African, vernaculars have no word for the farm-holding which consists of the set of farm-plots cultivated by any farmer – a plot being thought of as a 'farm'. For this, and other reasons, farm-plots and farm-holdings are often confused statistically. See, in particular, pp. 53 *et seq*.

(2) *The inevitable defects in the village land records*

See, in particular, Appendix II (1).

(3) *Lack of correspondence between 'the village land' and the total area cultivated by the villagers*

Much of the land cultivated by the inhabitants of any particular village lies outside the 'village land', and much of the 'village land' is cultivated by outsiders. See Chapter III.

(4) *The size-distribution of farm-holdings*

For reasons (1) to (3), among others, most official statistical tables relating to the

[45] *Green Revolution? Technology and Change in Rice-growing Areas of Tamil Nadu and Sri Lanka*, ed. B. H. Farmer, 1977, p. 162.

[46] *Ibid.*, p. 162. [47] *Ibid.*, p. 414.

[48] Statistics of this type are almost entirely lacking in northern Nigeria.

size distribution of farm-holdings are suspect – few have any explanatory notes. See, in particular, p. 244.

(5) *Average crop yields*

Since crop yields vary so greatly both from year to year and as between different cultivators, reliable averages are exceedingly hard to ascertain and are apt to be basically uninteresting. Dewey points out the tautology formerly involved in ascertaining average yields:

> In order to discover what average yields were, settlement officers had to know what average yields would be, in order to select 'representative' plots.[49]

In Chapter VIII I throw doubt on the reliability, at least within a certain range, of the statistics which purport to show an inverse relationship between yield and size of holding.

(6) *The population of villages*

If the Karnataka census is representative, as I think it is, the official statistics of the size-distribution of Indian villages based on decennial population censuses are highly misleading. This is because new settlements, some of which may be quite large, coming into existence since 1871, are invariably enumerated with older settlements, from which they had usually not emanated. See Chapter X, pp. 202–3.

(7) *The census definition of a 'cultivator'*

The Karnataka census definition of a cultivator runs as follows:

> A person is a *cultivator* if he or she is engaged in cultivation by oneself (*sic*) or by supervision or direction in one's capacity as the owner or lessee of land held from Government or as a tenant of land held from private persons or institutions for payment of money, kind or share.

Does this mean that dependent members of joint households who work under the authority of the household head, and who never own or rent land, do not count as cultivators? Although nearly all women members of farming households in the Anekal villages undertake cultivation, the 1971 census recorded the figure as 2%. On the other hand, in the case of dependent sons a fair proportion were evidently regarded in the census as cultivators.

(8) *The census definition of an 'agricultural labourer'*

The census definition of an agricultural labourer runs as follows:

[49] Dewey and Hopkins, eds., 1978, p. 301. See, also, the interesting discussion in 'Trends in the Agricultural Performance of an Indian Province: The Bombay Presidency, 1900–1920' by N. Charlesworth in Chaudhuri, *et al.* (eds.), 1979.

> A person who works in another person's land for wages in money, kind or share and does not have right of lease or contract on the land on which he or she works is regarded as an *agricultural labourer.*

The obscure wording of this definition would seem to deny the possibility that a person might work both on a farm-*plot* which he owns *and* for wages on a plot owned by another – this being the position of most male Harijans in the Anekal villages and of many other small land-holders. (Again, there is a failure to distinguish *plot* and *holding*.) But the census figures for the Anekal villages suggest that men who own or cultivate any farmland, however small the area, as well as their sons, do not normally declare themselves as labourers to the census enumerators.[50] As for female labourers, I think that the recorded number may be of the order of a tenth of the correct figure, were labourers to be defined as those who do more work for wages than on their own farmland. The census figures are indeed incomprehensibly low bearing in mind that in the *Final Report* of the (All India) *Rural Labour Enquiry 1963–5*[51] it is recorded (p. 121) that in 1964–5 as many as 43% of all agricultural labourers in Mysore agricultural labour households (defined as those which derived 'a major portion' of their annual income from labouring) were women.

(9) *Statistics of household income and indebtedness*

Most Indian village (as well as urban) surveys include tables purporting to relate to the distribution of household income. But householders, other than salary earners, seldom have any occasion to think in terms of annual income – and if asked by an investigator to do so will be bound to guess. See, in particular, pp. 67–8.

As for statistics of household indebtedness, they are invariably suspect. Debt ebbs and flows within the village, lubricating the village economy – and nearly all householders, other than some of the most impoverished, are debtors, though whether net debtors or not, they usually would not know.

(10) *Maps*

Since rural statistics are often derived from maps, it needs to be recorded that all contemporary Indian printed maps, other then those, like road maps, on a very small scale, are unobtainable anywhere in the world; neither libraries nor individuals may purchase them, they are state secrets.[52]

50 So ambiguous is the definition of a labourer, that it is possible that enumerators thought no cultivator should be classified as such.

51 Government of India. No date, but the preface is dated 1973.

52 Since this was written the Survey of India has lifted (1981) its restriction on the sale of maps, although supplies have not yet reached British libraries. Maps on the scale of 1:50,000 are, apparently, to be made available, except for a broad coastal band varying between about 50 and 100 miles in width.

(11) *Cultivated areas*

If the example of the village of Nanjapura is a reliable guide – see Appendix III(2) – the statistics of areas of cultivated land provided in the 1971 census are very seriously out of date, being based on maps of village farmland which had been compiled many years earlier. (The maps for the other Anekal villages were likewise out of date.)

(12) *The National Sample Survey*

Many of the 300 or so reports of the Indian Government's National Sample Survey relate to subjects on which most informants would have been bound to have guessed their replies to the point-blank questions put to them by officials wielding questionnaires. With the best will in the world most rural householders cannot provide accurate figures relating, for instance, to size of farm-holding, crop yields and production, crop disposal, annual income, indebtedness and so forth. It is on the basis of their personal experience of comparing guessed figures with those ascertained by other means, that anthropological fieldworkers know this to their cost, and those who assume otherwise are ignorant of the realities.

CHAPTER I

Background Material: The Two Regions and the Eight Localities

This chapter, which is descriptive, straightforward, summary and brief, is designed to provide sufficient background socio-economic material on contemporary rural conditions in the three research areas under comparison – Batagarawa and Dorayi in Hausaland (northern Nigeria) and six villages in Anekal Taluk in Karnataka (south India) – for readers, who may have no special knowledge of either region, to experience some sense of locality before embarking on the subsequent, detailed analysis of comparative agrarian systems. (See Figs. I(1) and I(2).)

Among the many pitfalls in comparative work of this unconventional kind is that of constantly slipping from one level of geographical generality to another – of referring to 'Hausaland' at a point where one has the peculiarities of a certain village in mind. So I start by presenting a reference table listing 'layers of geographical generality' for each region. Although my exposition throughout this book will necessarily involve a good deal of switching between layers, I shall reduce reference to particular villages to a minimum, for many of them have rather difficult polysyllabic names.[1]

My fieldwork in rural Hausaland was undertaken in 1966, 1967 (mostly in Batagarawa) and in 1971–2 (mostly in Dorayi), a total period of more than two years, including the time spent consulting the Nigerian National Archives at Kaduna.[2] My fieldwork in villages in Anekal Taluk, Karnataka State, was carried out between September 1977 and August 1978, when I also consulted the Karnataka State Archives at Bangalore.[3] It happens that each of my eight research localities lies within twenty miles of the largest

[1] The Karnataka names are less confusing when one realises that the very common terminations such as *pura* and *halli* mean 'village'.

[2] My main publications following this work are given in the List of References. The full titles of my two books are *Rural Hausa: A Village and a Setting* (1972), which includes a long (134 pages) 'Commentary' which provides much classified information on rural Hausaland generally and a full bibliography; and *Population, Prosperity and Poverty: Rural Kano, 1900 and 1970* (1977). These books are hereinafter referred to as Hill (1972) and Hill (1977).

[3] See Hill (1979) and Hill (1980).

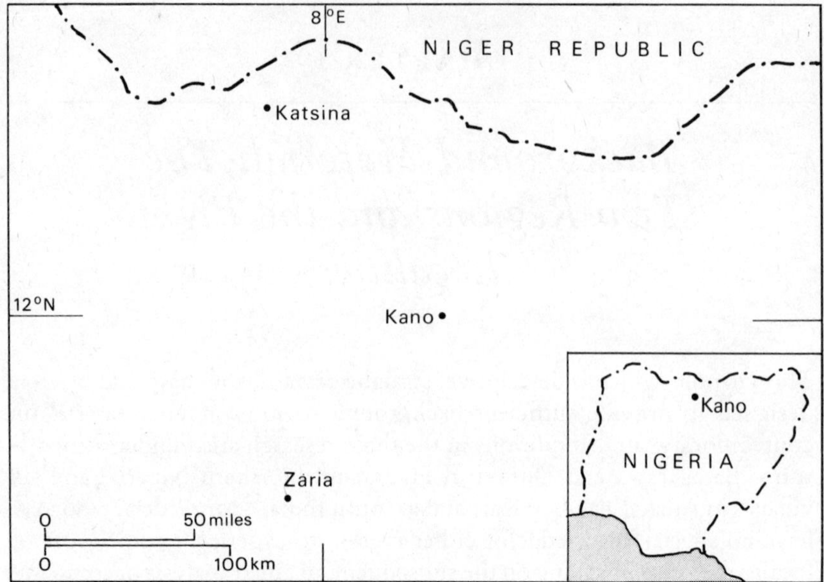

Fig. I(1) Outline sketch of part of northern Nigeria showing Katsina and Kano cities and the frontier with the Niger Republic. See p. 23 for the situation of Batagarawa and Dorayi in relation to the two cities.

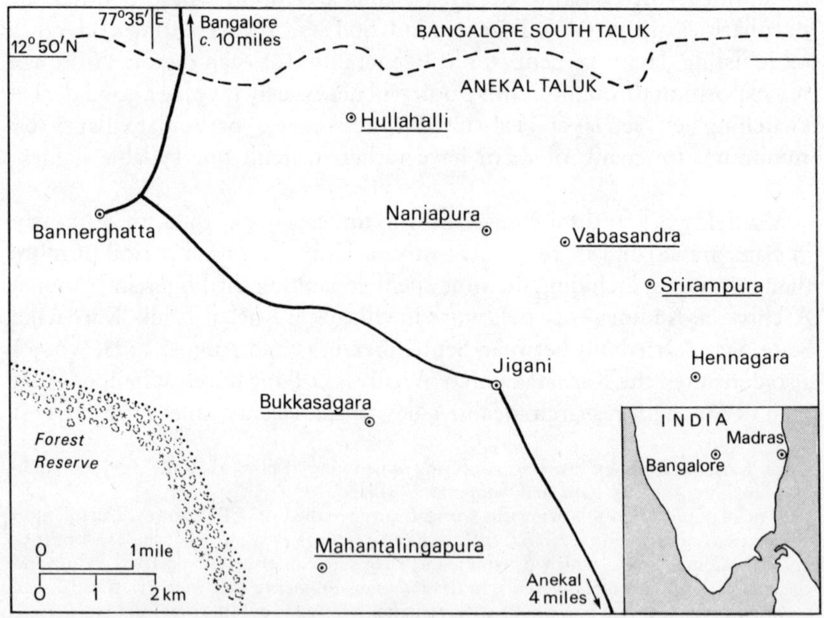

Fig. I(2) Outline sketch of part of Anekal Taluk showing: the six research villages (names underlined); the boundary with Bangalore South Taluk; the only two market towns in the area (Jigani and Bannerghatta); the position of Hennagara, near where the great annual cattle fair is held; the only motor road of any importance; and the approximate boundary of a forest reserve. See, also, Fig. III(1).

1. *Rural south India*
(Exclusive of Kerala and the mountainous Western Ghats – the Malnad)

2. *The Maidan* (non-mountainous area) *of south-eastern Karnataka*
(But only where river and channel irrigation are lacking)

3. *Rural Bangalore District*
(Excluding the city of Bangalore, which had a population of about 1½ million in 1971 (and some 2 million today), as well as 21 other urban centres, the population of rural Bangalore District was about 1½ million in 1971)

4. *Anekal Taluk*
(The smallest but one of the eleven Taluks of Bangalore District, Anekal had a recorded population of 129,600 in 1971, including two towns with a total population of 17,304)

5. *The six villages in Anekal Taluk*
(With a total population of 2,692 in 1978, according to my own count, the villages all lay off motor roads, some 15 to 20 miles south of the centre of Bangalore city, in three different Village Panchayats, the most distant being Mahantalingapura, near a large Forest Reserve)

Bukkasagara, pop. 604
*Hullahalli**, pop. 604
*Mahantalingapura**, pop. 477
Nanjapura, pop. 484
*Srirampura**, pop. 286
Vabasandra, pop. 237

*Ex-*jodidar* villages

1. *Rural West Africa*
(With particular reference to Nigeria and Ghana and to the northern savannah, which includes Hausaland, rather than the southern forests; excluding the northern Sahel, bordering the desert)

2. *Northern Nigerian Hausaland*
(For a full bibliography relating to rural Hausaland see Hill (1972). Some Hausa people live in the Francophone Niger Republic to the north of Nigeria)

3. *Rural Katsina and Kano Emirates*
(The total population of these two Emirates has never been known at all precisely, but may have been of the order of three times that of Bangalore District in 1971 – perhaps more than 10 million, of whom (say) one million lived in Kano and Katsina cities)

4. *The Kano Close Settled Zone*
(This irregularly shaped, densely populated, rural farming zone around Kano city, may have had a population of some 2½ million in 1971. See Hill (1977), Ch. III)

5. *Batagarawa*
(A nucleated village, 6 miles south of Katsina city, surrounded by 26 dispersed homesteads, with a total population in 1967, according to my own count, of 1,395; the capital of Mallamawa District. See Hill (1972))

Dorayi
(An arbitrarily named farming area of dispersed settlement, south of and very near to the walls of Kano city, which had a population, according to my own count, of 3,499 in 1972. See Hill (1977))

city in the State or Emirate in which they are situated; but as I now provocatively assert (and as I shall demonstrate later), they were not unduly anomalous rural areas for this reason. Accidental and practical considerations determined their choice. Batagarawa was the home village of my valued assistant, now Alhaji Sabi'u Nuhu, who indirectly arranged for a large, traditional style, walled mud compound[4] to be specially built for me in 1967 on a large vacant site in the centre of the village, close to the mosque; I there greatly enjoyed the status of *uwar gida* – mother of a house. In 1971–2 I was resolved to work, for comparative purposes, in the much more densely populated Kano Close Settled Zone, a farming area of dispersed settlement around Kano city, and I found myself reluctantly obliged to select 'Dorayi' for two cogent practical reasons, although it was closer to Kano city than I had originally wished. As my motives for choosing Dorayi have been curiously misunderstood by many reviewers of Hill (1977), I take this opportunity of stating that my decision was due entirely to the existence of a certain up-to-date aerial photograph which enabled me to map the farmland.[5]

As for the six Anekal villages, these were deliberately selected, one by one, after studying the only reasonably up-to-date map of Anekal Taluk that was available[6] and making preliminary visits; many of the villages I visited were rejected as unsuitable for a variety of methodological and practical reasons – in two cases because they were quite exceptional in being single-caste villages with very high rates of commuting to Bangalore city for specialised wage-labour on stone dressing or construction sites. As my technique necessitated obtaining a great variety of information for each household, not for a mere sample, I was obliged to select rather small settlements in both regions.

POPULATION

The Hausa, most of whom live in the savannah of northern Nigeria,[7] are

[4] Complete with its own entrance hut, kitchen, thatched sleeping hut, mud-roofed 'office', store room, 'bathroom', well, garden and large yard open to the sky.

[5] In Hausaland there are no official farm maps, so students of economic inequality have to resort to making their own. The particular choice of Dorayi was due to the use of henna hedges as farm boundaries which, unlike the boundaries in many other areas, were clearly visible on the photograph. (The area of dispersed settlement which I arbitrarily denoted 'Dorayi' consisted of one entire 'Village Unit' and 4 contiguous 'Hamlet Areas' – see Hill (1977), p. 76.)

[6] This small and uninformative sketch map on the scale of c. 2½ miles to the inch is included in the two *District Census Handbooks (1971)* for Bangalore District. On the lack of modern printed maps see p. 19 above.

[7] For references to the works of G. Nicolas on the rural Hausa of the Niger Republic see Hill (1972).

much the largest ethnic group group (some would denote them a mere linguistic group) in tropical Africa; their number is probably nearer to 30 than 20 million, but there has never been a reliable Nigerian population census,[8] and definitional difficulties attend the distinction between the Hausa and the non-pastoral Fulani.[9] Very staunch supporters of Islam,[10] especially since the holy war (*jihad*) of 1804, the Hausa were for long organised in emirates owing a common allegiance to the Caliph (Sultan) of Sokoto, but nowadays the powers of the emirs have waned following the establishment of state governments. The British conquest of Northern Nigeria, including Hausaland, was not completed until 1903, the short period of fifty-seven years of colonialism having ended in 1960 when Nigeria (in which Northern Nigeria had been incorporated in 1914) became an independent country; since 1967 Nigeria has been a federation of states (originally 12 states now 19); democratically elected federal and state governments, under an elaborate and long-debated new constitution, took over from the former military government of this oil-rich country in 1979.[11] Although the famous walled cities of Hausaland are many centuries old, and although the urban population has increased greatly in recent decades, the great bulk of the population, at least in Katsina and Kano Emirates, is still rural[12] in the double sense that it lives dispersedly on the farmland or in small villages and depends almost entirely on cultivation and associated rural activities for its livelihood: oil cannot have changed this.

Pre-colonial Mysore, which was ultimately incorporated in the much larger modern state of Karnataka,[13] had also been under Muslim rule – indeed it had represented the greatest military threat faced by the British in south India until their conquest of 1799. A British Commission administered the princely state, which (like Hyderabad) was not part of British India, from 1831 to 1881 when power was restored to a Maharaja. The great majority of the inhabitants of Karnataka, recorded as numbering 29.3 million in 1971, are Hindus – though the census of that year recorded 16% of the population of Bangalore city as being Muslims, 8% as Christians. The rapidly growing city of Bangalore, which is the state capital, had a population of about 1½ million in 1971, when it was the seventh largest Indian city. According to the census definition, about three-quarters of the Karnataka population is rural – defined (with some qualification) as living in settlements with populations of less than 5,000.

[8] See Hill (1972) and (1977). [9] See Appendix I(1).

[10] See *Nigerian Perspectives: An Historical Anthology* by T. Hodgkin, 2nd edn 1975.

[11] The first military coup of 1966 had been followed by the Biafran civil war of 1967–9.

[12] See Appendix XI(1). For a recent political and economic outline see *Nigeria since 1970* by A. Kirk-Greene and D. Rimmer, 1981.

[13] First inaugurated as Mysore in 1956, it was renamed Karnataka in 1973.

Anekal Taluk resembles several other polyglot areas in south India with mixed cultural traditions. The population is organised in numerous endogamous castes and sub-castes; up to four mother tongues (Telugu, Kannada, Tamil and Urdu) may persist in a single small village – more people speak Telugu than Kannada, the latter being the official language of Karnataka state.[14] As many as 21 castes[15] are represented in our six Anekal villages; members of the 6 Scheduled castes (Harijans) comprised nearly a half (47%) of all the 474 households there in 1978. War, famine, plague, climatic vagaries, inter-caste disputes . . . these were some of the factors which account for the mixed and recent character of much rural settlement.

POPULATION DENSITY

The population density in rural Hausaland is very variable:[16] the reasons for this are not always well understood, but sometimes have to do with such diverse factors as long-distance trade routes and the height of the water table. At one extreme there are vast tracts of quite lightly populated country, some of which are proving attractive to stranger-cultivators from certain more densely populated Hausa localities; on the other hand, there are some half-dozen densely populated rural zones of which much the largest and most remarkable is a locality of dispersed settlement, the so-called Kano Close Settled Zone,[17] where rural densities vary between (say) 600 and 1,500 per sq. mile – the highest densities occurring in the inner ring of the zone, near Kano city, which includes Dorayi.

In 1971 only one of the eleven Taluks[18] in Bangalore District had a higher population density than Anekal, which was c. 620 per sq. mile, much less than half the crude density at Dorayi. However, rough calculations relating to *cultivated* acres per head of the *resident* population showed a smaller discrepancy between Dorayi (0.4 acres) and the six Anekal villages (0.7 acres) than was indicated by the crude density figures. (A roughly comparable figure for Batagarawa was 0.9 acres of manured farmland per head – bush farms being omitted.)

[14] The few Indian vernacular words in this book are nearly all Kannada.

[15] See Appendix I(2).

[16] Marked variations in population density within fairly small regions are characteristic of rural West Africa. If Nigeria now has a population approaching 100 million – it is much the most populous and densely populated country in tropical Africa, as well as the richest, this being solely because of its oil exports – then its population density of c. 300 per sq. mile would be of the order of half that of India.

[17] The name given to it by the geographer M. J. Mortimore – see Mortimore (1967) or (1968) and Hill (1977).

[18] If a District, like Bangalore District, is thought of as corresponding to a county, then a Taluk is a kind of sub-county for which there is no English equivalent.

POPULATION GROWTH

Such anomalously high population densities in the Kano Close Settled Zone are not so much due to unusually high rates of natural growth, either today or in the past, as to high rates of immigration from *less* densely populated rural localities in former times, both of farm slaves who had been captured elsewhere and of free men who were attracted by the special opportunities of craftwork and long-distance trading there until the arrival, in force, of the urban-based lorry after the second world war.[19]

While there has also been much internal migration within south-eastern Karnataka and nearby Tamil Nadu, I doubt if its general direction is known, for it is even truer in south India than in West Africa that twentieth century migration is all too often falsely equated with increasing urbanisation. There are good reasons, connected with West African ethnic distinctiveness and lack of caste, why the concept of the 'stranger' should have been much more widely studied there than in south India.[20]

Reliable demographic statistics being altogether lacking for rural northern Nigeria, we can do no more than presume that population growth rates there are much lower than in Karnataka, if only because all reports suggest that infant mortality rates are still very high indeed, perhaps as high as 30–40% for children under four years.[21] The Anekal villagers, like most rural south Indians outside the State of Kerala, are little interested in modern contraceptive methods,[22] which are not available to the rural Hausa. For technical reasons (see p. 202) we know the growth rates for only three of our six Anekal villages during 1891 to 1971: these seem to be much in line with those for Anekal Taluk where population densities, after allowing for boundary changes, rose by 115% between 1891 and 1971 and by 15% between 1961 and 1971.

In the past both regions have been subject to appalling famines resulting from drought; and both are still subject to severe crop shortages caused by inadequate rains. More than a third of the human population of Anekal Taluk, and an even higher proportion of cattle, may have died in the

[19] See Hill (1977). (The West African railway network remains exceedingly ill-developed compared with that of south India.)

[20] There is, therefore, no south Indian counterpart of Fortes' discussion of categories of rural stranger in Ch. 13 in *Studies in African Social Anthropology*, ed. M. Fortes and S. Patterson, 1975.

[21] This is probably mainly because the incidence of malaria in West Africa is as high as ever, for that disease is often a contributory, if not a main cause of infant deaths. In south India, where the post-war campaign to control malaria was remarkably successful, infant mortality rates are in places lower than in parts of Europe half a century ago.

[22] On this subject see *Family Web* by Sarah Hobson, 1978, which is a well-observed, intimate, description of life in a single household in rural Karnataka.

terrible famine of 1876–8.[23] In Hausaland much the worst famine within living memory was in 1914.[24] Fortunately, given modern transport developments, such disasters could never recur in these localities.

THE SPATIAL DISTRIBUTION OF THE RURAL POPULATION

South-eastern Karnataka resembles most of peninsular India, other than parts of the state of Kerala, in that the bulk of the rural population lives in compact villages or hamlets, surrounded by farmland. In Anekal Taluk, which is presumably not exceptional in the Indian context, the size-distribution of these villages is unknown since there are numerous hamlets, some quite sizeable, which are not listed in the population census, but misleadingly swell the population of a neighbouring older settlement which may even be smaller.[25] However, since recorded village population figures always tend to be inflated we can at least be sure that most of them are quite small – perhaps in the range of some 200 to 400.

There are two distinct modes of rural settlement in Kano and Katsina Emirates. Although official demographic material is generally unilluminating, given the good coverage of large-scale aerial photography concerned with land use, and other relevant material such as maps, we can be sure that the bulk of the rural population in those two emirates lives dispersedly on its farmland, particularly in the Kano Close Settled Zone. In some localities topographical features are lacking to the extent that the dispersal might suggest that the inhabitants had landed by parachute from the skies;[26] in others, geological features, such as long bands of uncultivable rocky outcrops, create bizarre residential patterns.

Under the alternative Hausa mode the rural population lives in small nucleated villages such as Batagarawa, which were formerly mostly walled or stockaded. In densely populated old localities of dispersed settlement, like Dorayi, many farming households are apt to have lost the ownership, over the years, of the farmland which surrounds their habitation, their various farm-plots then being nearly as widely dispersed as those owned by the inhabitants of nucleated villages. (Although dispersed settlement is common in many other regions of West Africa, we 'cannot yet claim to be fully clear as to why some West African populations are addicted to a dispersed settlement pattern, whilst others have opted for life in large compact villages'.[27])

[23] See Appendix XII(4). [24] See Hill (1972), pp. 284–5 (*malali*).
[25] See Chapter X, pp. 202–3, for discussion of this astonishingly neglected subject.
[26] See plates showing aerial photographs in Hill (1972) and Fig. 5, p. 74, in Hill (1977).
[27] See 'Stateless Societies in the History of West Africa' by Robin Horton, in Ajayi and Crowder (eds.), Vol. I, 1971, p. 97.

MIGRATION

Finally, it is necessary to add some notes on migration to this brief summary relating to the rural population. Rates of outward migration of men, from all 8 localities, were rather low despite the proximity of the great cities. From neither Dorayi nor the Anekal villages is there any migration at all to less densely populated localities in search of more or better farmland – as there is from Batagarawa: I shall later offer an explanation for this.[28] As for inward migration, the capacity of some localities in both regions to continue to absorb strangers is quite notable, given the high population densities.

MARRIAGE

The Hausa communities are basically polygynous, in that most men aspire, sooner or later, to have more than one wife;[29] the Karnataka communities are basically monogamous, though there is a low incidence of polygyny among lower castes. Hausa polygyny is associated, as in West Africa generally, with very high divorce and remarriage rates; in the Anekal villages, divorce, which is usually informal separation,[30] is rather rare and widow remarriage occurs among the lower castes only. Caste or sub-caste endogamy is absolute in the Anekal villages, as it is not in Bangalore city, and nearly all marriages, many of which involve close kin in other villages, are parentally arranged; in rural Hausaland quite high proportions of marriages are probably not arranged since so many of them are not the woman's first marriage and since 'kin-marriages' have become increasingly rare – much more so than in Anekal. In both regions wives remove to their husband's house, which is often his parental home, on marriage; the socio-geographical network resulting from the high propensity of women in both regions to marry outside their natal community is wider for the Anekal villages than for the two Hausa localities.[31] Notes on the systems of marriage payments in the two regions are provided in Appendix I(4).

In both regions everyone who is not physically or mentally handicapped gets married at least once in their youth; the age of first marriage of girls in Dorayi has recently *fallen* greatly and is much lower than in Anekal, where it is rising;[32] in both regions there is considerable variation in the age of first marriage of men, which may be delayed until the late twenties.

[28] See p. 197.

[29] Polygyny is made possible by the higher average age of men than of women on first marriage, not by any necessary imbalance of the sexes.

[30] Marriage under the Marriage Act is very rare indeed in the villages.

[31] See Appendix X(1).

[32] On this matter there is some vague awareness in the villages of legislative attempts to impose a minimum age of marriage.

FARMING HOUSEHOLDS AND THE POSITION OF WOMEN

Matters pertaining to 'farming organisation' are not discussed in this chapter. However, it is necessary to mention that in both regions the great proportion of the rural population lives in 'farming households', which are partly or mainly dependent on the land for their livelihood, whether as cultivators on their own account or as labourers. Most members of such households, in both regions, are either direct descendants of the household head or their wives.

During the past thirty years or so the wives of rural Katsina and Kano Emirates have become *increasingly* secluded in their homesteads, which are usually walled compounds open to the sky. This new practice of full Muslim seclusion, in the open countryside, where women are no longer a feature of the landscape,[33] not even veiled, may be unique in the world. Most sadly, the townsmen, whom the male villagers are emulating by enforcing seclusion, are usually unaware of the change. Although the secluded women do little, if any, farming,[34] they are apt to be very active house-traders, the houses being linked by children.

VILLAGE AUTHORITIES

When the British conquered northern Hausaland they found that there were three levels of political authority under the Emir, which still exist today – the District Head (*hakimi*), the Village Head (sometimes known as *dagaci*) and the Hamlet Head (*mai unguwa*). The District Heads, of whom there were very few in Kano Emirate, for example, were mostly aristocrats who lived in the capital city, many of them being kinsmen of the Emir;[35] holding aloof from their people, most of them had little detailed influence in their areas – they never, for example, had any connection with the allocation of farmland. In Kano Emirate the numerous appointed Village Heads were nearly all relatively insignificant men (as shown, for example, by the fact that no land pertained to their offices), unless their village was large and nucleated – as it usually was not. As for the humble Hamlet Heads, they were the only real representatives of their people, being 'elected' from below. The Village Head was effectively responsible for

[33] While it may be that most free women did little farming in the years before farm-slavery ended around 1925–30, at least they were able to move around the village.

[34] Except, inexplicably, in some anomalous villages. Such relatively free communities are not to be confused with those of the non-Muslim Hausa, known as the Maguzawa, who may number several hundred thousand.

[35] See *Religion and Political Culture in Kano* by J. N. Paden, 1973; Hill (1977); and *The Kano Civil War and British Over-Rule 1882–1940* by A. M. Fika, 1978.

1 Hausa women walking to a Muslim naming ceremony, being released from purdah for the occasion

2 Hausa men after attending a Muslim naming ceremony

collecting the 'community tax' (*haraji*) which was introduced by the British as a kind of head tax[36] on adult males only, though it varied slightly with the 'wealth' of the taxpayer.

Since the recent legal abolition in Karnataka of the hereditary village officers,[37] the functions of the headman (*patel*) and the accountant (*shanbhog*) have been taken over by the chairman of the elected Village Panchayat,[38] which is commonly based on a grouping of 3 to 5 villages (together with their associated hamlets), who is assisted by the Panchayat Village Secretary, an official who is responsible for all the land revenue statistics and associated tax collection, and who is ill-paid and overworked. Not surprisingly – considering what little support the Secretary ordinarily receives from the elected Panchayat, whose members are so apathetic that, in Anekal Taluk at least, they seldom manage to achieve a quorum – the quality of the village land records is deteriorating fast[39], but real rates of land revenue on dry land are now so much lower than in 1891, when revenue settlement was first introduced in Anekal Taluk, that no one seems to mind about this.

The 50 Village Panchayats of Anekal Taluk are grouped into 4 Hoblies, whose officials are mainly concerned with tax inspection. The principal Taluk officer is the appointed Tahsildar (formerly often known as the Amildar), who is assisted by an elected Taluk Development Board and numerous officials.

There are no village courts in either region and no caste institutions, or caste elders, in rural Karnataka.

CLIMATE AND CROPS

Although all matters of farming organisation are left for later chapters, perhaps I cannot postpone a brief mention of climate and crops. Both regions are on plateaux, northern Hausaland at c. 1,500 ft and south-eastern Karnataka at c. 3,000 ft – and consequently a little cold at some seasons. (Hausaland is flatter and lacks the marvellous outcrops of gneiss which add such charm to the rolling Karnataka landscape.) Both climates are rather dry with average annual rainfalls not much exceeding 30 in

[36] Which in Kano Emirate replaced numerous other taxes, including taxes on crops – see Appendix XII(3).

[37] These officers included the hereditary village servants (*thotis*) who, being indispensable, have successfully resisted abolition – see Appendix XV(1). The Mysore Village Offices Abolition Act, 1961, did not take full effect, so far as the two major village offices were concerned, until about 1970.

[38] See Appendix III(1).

[39] See Appendix II(1).

3 A high caste woman harvesting *ragi*, which is the crop in the foreground

(c. 75 cm) in Anekal and 20 in (c. 50 cm) in northern Hausaland. In both regions cultivators are greatly troubled by the erratic monthly distribution of the rains[40] and, as I have said, by fairly frequent droughts, most recently in northern Hausaland in 1972–4. Although there are two annual monsoons in Karnataka and only a single short rainy season in Hausaland, the two regions are alike in cultivating single annual crops of basic grains on dry land – these being mainly *ragi* (a very short-stalked low-yielding, fine-grained millet – *Eleusine coracana* or finger millet) in south-eastern Karnataka, and both the tall bulrush millet (*gero*, *Pennisetum*) and the even taller guinea corn (*dawa*, sorghum) in northern Hausaland. In both regions there are, as we shall learn, many subsidiary crops, much the most

40 I began to understand why everyone gave me a different description of the Karnataka climate when I found that in the ten years 1967 to 1976 the wettest months in Anekal Taluk were May (once), June (once), August (twice), September and October (each thrice).

important being groundnuts[41] (peanuts, *Arachis hypogaea*) in Hausaland, the production of which is very low in Anekal.

About a tenth of all the farmland cultivated by members of the six Anekal villages is irrigated by reservoirs (always known as tanks) on which paddy (rice) is cultivated – sugar cane is grown elsewhere in Anekal Taluk. As it happened that there was very little marshland[42] (*fadama*) in Batagarawa or Dorayi, and no rivers, the only significant irrigated crop was onions, grown on small channelled plots, watered from shallow wells, in part of Dorayi only. The Anekal villagers owned about 65 irrigation wells, mainly used for growing a variety of vegetables.

FARM TOOLS, TRANSPORT AND LIVESTOCK

We know from the works of Francis Buchanan[43] (in south India) and Hugh Clapperton[44] (in Hausaland) that ordinary farm tools and cultivating equipment in both regions, with the exception of the metal plough which is a twentieth century innovation, have remained basically unchanged for at least 150 years, still being made by local blacksmiths, carpenters and other craftsmen. Hausa cultivators depend almost entirely on a range of hoes designed for different operations; while the range of tools is much wider in Karnataka, for it includes such equipment as seed drills and harrows, the larger types are still made of wood and bamboo, no metal tool being as large as the common Hausa ridging hoe, the *galma*, which Clapperton[45] told us was 'used in all the heavy work instead of a spade'.

There are still no wheels,[46] other than bicycles, on the West African farmland, and the heavy loads, including crops and manure, which in Karnataka are mainly carried by two-wheeled wooden carts, drawn by a

[41] Which were, until very recently, an important export crop – indeed the only one of any significance produced in northern Nigeria. (There is a large rural consumption of groundnut oil.)

[42] Low-lying land which is subject to flooding or water-logging during the wet season and which is economically important in some Hausa localities.

[43] *A Journey from Madras through the Countries of Mysore, Canara and Malabar* by Francis Buchanan, 3 vols., 1807. The author of this magnificently detailed work had heeded Wellesley's instructions in 1800 that 'the first great and essential object of your attention should be the Agriculture of the Country' (p. viii).

[44] Clapperton's works include *Journal of a Second Expedition into the Interior of Africa*, 1829, reprinted 1966.

[45] *Ibid.*, 1966, p. 221.

[46] The entire lack of wheels, including potters' wheels, is not really understood by historians, especially considering the importance of the trans-Saharan trade in gold, slaves and other commodities over many centuries. But see 'Wheeled Transport in Pre-colonial West Africa' by R. Law, *Africa*, 3, 1980.

4 The Hausa 'hand plough' (*galma*) in motion

pair of cattle, are mainly head-loaded by women and children in the southern forest zone and borne by donkeys in the savannah; as most Hausa households *do* own donkeys and as most Karnataka households *do not* own carts, the ordinary villager's control over transport is much more limited in Karnataka than in Hausaland. (Large numbers of bicycles were owned by the Dorayi and Anekal villagers – who owned hardly any motor scooters and no cars, lorries or tractors.)

Before the recent introduction of the metal plough in parts of savannah West Africa, West Africans had never harnessed animals to work for them except for carrying men or loads; and owing to endemic animal trypanosomiasis[47] in the forest zone, where the tsetse fly flourishes, cattle rearing is generally impossible, so that humans remain entirely unaided by animal power. In south India cows and bullocks are multi-purpose animals, employed not only in tilling the land and in operating irrigation equipment but also in threshing most of the grain – work which is done by hand in savannah West Africa.

While nearly every Anekal household aspires to own cattle, though

[47] See *West Africa* by W. B. Morgan and J. C. Pugh, 1969, pp. 206–8.

many are too impoverished to do so, in Katsina and Kano Emirates this is not so, most of the cattle being owned by Fulani pastoralists.[48]

In former times the extensive system of Hausa long-distance trade[49] (*fatauci*) was mainly based on the donkey caravan. Lugard, the first High Commissioner of Northern Nigeria, referred to a wonderful caravan road:

> I have seen nothing like it in Africa. The track is often 50 feet wide, and one meets ceaseless caravans of laden donkeys, men, women and live stock along its whole length. I must have passed many thousands in the 250 miles we traversed to Kano.[50]

Such donkeys were not owned by specialist transporters, as were the pack-oxen of south India in the pre-railway age, but by ordinary village cultivators, many of whom were also traders on their own account.[51] In contemporary Hausaland many millions of donkeys are still used for transporting all manner of loads.

THE VILLAGE ECONOMIES

In both regions all the main food crops are grown both for household consumption and for sale, and any attempt to distinguish 'subsistence' and 'cash' crops (or subsistence and cash farmers) begs the very questions with which we are primarily concerned.

Putting the matter absurdly briefly, the rural communities, as such, should be thought of as assemblages of households, surrounded by cultivated farmland, which mainly connect to the outside world by means of 'exporting' certain types of farm produce which enables them to pay for the 'import' of a great variety of essential consumer goods, building materials and so forth, which they cannot make for themselves.

In Karnataka the secular tendency for rural craft goods to be ousted by factory made wares had largely worked itself through by the end of the last century; and in the Anekal villages only tiny proportions of those households which belong to the specialist artisan or service castes are actually mainly dependent on the traditional occupation. In rural Hausaland, where various types of men's and women's craftwork continue to flourish, while others have languished or died, there are no craft guilds and no restrictions on entry to any occupation.

[48] See Appendix I(1).

[49] See Hill (1972), pp. 243–5, for a summarised list of historical sources. See, also, Appendix XII(1) below.

[50] 'Northern Nigeria' by F. D. Lugard, *The Geographical Journal*, 1904, p. 22.

[51] Trading continues to be a natural activity, involving many people in rural Hausaland, as it has never been in rural Karnataka. See Appendix XII(1).

VILLAGE AMENITIES

A sketch-plan of Batagarawa[52] in 1967 shows the public amenities in a Hausa village which was markedly superior to most villages owing to being the seat of that high, and rare, dignitary – a District Head. Most notable was the primary school, a quite outstandingly excellent and spaciously built establishment;[53] then, there was a fairly large, recently built, Friday mosque (one of the few cement buildings in the village) – as well as 10 privately owned small mosques, mere rooms in houses; third, there were 5 concrete-lined, drinking-water wells, with walled tops, which provided superior water to the ordinary house well; fourth, was the District Scribe's office, with its associated small library; fifth, was an inferior slaughter slab for butchers; sixth, was a privately owned, mechanically operated grinding mill, where produce could be ground for a fee; and seventh, was a privately owned, tiny shop – most selling being done by women in their houses, or by men sitting in the street. There were no postal services, electricity supplies, dispensary, bus services nearer than Katsina city, or public latrines; no attempt had been made to fill several ugly, odorous, insanitary, space-wasting ponds, from which earth had been extracted; and the only male public official ever to be seen at work was a resident sanitary inspector whose main occupation was farming.

Members of the ruling class (the *sarauta*) lived in superior, spacious, mud-built houses[54] – no corrugated iron sheets, except on the mosque, had yet disfigured this charming village. The quality and size of the houses occupied by other people varied greatly according to their means and the sizes of their households: all were essentially unroofed yards or compounds, surrounded by walls or impervious fences or hedges, in which all necessary living structures were set, and where most household activities, including cooking, occurred; all were provided with separate sleeping huts for each wife and with granaries and pit latrines.

No public amenities were to be found at Dorayi which, as an arbitrarily demarcated locality of dispersed settlement, even lacked any kind of 'central place' – unless a position where a few butchers displayed their fly-ridden meat be considered such. There was no primary school[55] (though, as in Batagarawa, there were many privately run Koranic classes), no public

[52] See Hill (1972), Fig. 4, p. 11 which relates to the nucleated village (*gari*) only.

[53] Founded as early as 1946, it was renowned for its high standards, many of its pupils having proceeded to higher education. (In 1964 less than 10% of all boys of school age in Katsina Province were at primary school.)

[54] See Hill (1972), Fig. 5.

[55] There was actually a school just north of the area, but only 2 or 3 boys from my research area attended it.

5 and 6 Two styles of rural Hausa 'mud' architecture

mosque, no shop, no concrete-lined public well, no public offices of any description, and the only grinding mill was out of order. In short, the inhabitants received nothing in return for the taxes imposed on them. Their houses, which were all mud-built, mainly by their occupants, lay dispersedly on the farmland, many of the smaller habitations, in particular, being architecturally delightful.

Turning to the Anekal villages,[56] while every village and hamlet, however small, has its electricity supply, this benefits few of the inhabitants, hardly any of whom can afford to connect or wire their houses, only 5 of whom owned electric pump sets – the only type of electric equipment in use there: however, the street lighting, when it had not been disconnected owing to failure to pay the bill, was certainly appreciated. There was, also, a postal service. The primary school buildings were small, dark and cramped (except in one case), consisting of a single room;[57] most of the Hindu temples were dilapidated and little used. There were no public (or private) latrines; and the drinking-water wells were insufficient, particularly as higher caste people illegally insisted that Harijans should only use wells within their own residential sections. While there were no dispensaries, a considerable number of minor health officials, mainly women, frequented the villages, travelling about by day; however, very few people could afford to go to hospital owing to the high 'fees' which were invariably demanded.

The quality of housing was very variable indeed, ranging from immense cement block houses with huge glassed verandahs and separate cattle sheds[58] (but no separate bedrooms or latrines, though there were a few bathrooms) to the worst of the squalid, dark, tiny, one-roomed habitations in the Harijan sections – most of which are nowadays tiled not thatched. The most deplorable aspect of these villages is the extreme overcrowding in the old Harijan sections – for Harijans, though no longer 'untouchables', must still, of course, be residentially segregated – though in some villages a serious effort has been made by government to assist Harijans to build tiny new tiled houses on the outskirts of villages. Some of the non-Harijan streets, also, are very dirty, as well as congested, for there is a strong reluctance to enlarge the built-up village site, as population increases, by encroaching on surrounding farmland. There are no outdoor granaries, which so embellish the landscape in Hausaland.

For those who enjoy the light of the day, and the stars of the night sky, as

[56] See Appendix I(5) for a sketch-map of Bukkasagara village.

[57] In Hullahalli there was, exceptionally, an excellent nursery school run by a young Brahmin woman teacher.

[58] Most cattle in the Anekal villages are kept inside dwelling houses, however small. See Appendix IV(4).

7 The chairman of a Village Panchayat outside his house

well as a certain minimum of privacy while sleeping, Hausa habitations are, in principle, superior. But such a conclusion does not befit the introductory chapter of a book which is mainly concerned to demolish the concept of averages which, in the words of Lenin,[59] 'obscure the differentiation, and are therefore purely fictitious'.

APPENDIX I(1)

The Fulani

A high proportion of the cattle in many sections of the West African savannah is owned by the Fulani, a distinctive pastoral people, with straight hair and pale skins, who, originating further north, have peacefully proliferated over the centuries throughout a vast area extending eastwards through the savannah for some 3,000 miles. Many of these people are still specialist transhumant pastoralists, tending to move northwards during the rains and southwards in the dry season; others have become sedentary or semi-sedentary cultivators.

So great has been the admixture of Hausa and Fulani people over the centuries, especially since the Jihad of 1804 which established the present Fulani dynasties of Hausaland based on the Caliph at Sokoto, that some contemporary writers prefer

[59] *Collected Works*, vol. 3, by V. I. Lenin, p. 103.

to denote the general run of inhabitants of Hausaland[60] as 'Hausa–Fulani' rather than Hausa, although it is well known that the great majority of those who, rightly or wrongly, claim Fulani descent do not speak the Fulani language. Unfortunately, official demographic material is of little use, both because census enumerators have never received any official instructions[61] regarding the distinction, if any, between the two groups; and because respondents have a tendency to claim Fulani origin merely because of the prestige it is supposed to bestow.

Many of the cattle-owning Fulani pastoralists enjoy a symbiotic relationship with Hausa cultivators, providing them with sour milk and manure (dung) in exchange for grain and other produce. The proportion of northern Nigerian cattle which is owned by pastoralists (most of whom are Fulani) is very high, but inestimable.

An idea of the extent of the very large and learned literature on these extraordinary people may be gained from *Organisation sociale des Peul*[62] by Marguerite Dupire, 1970, which also provides a map of the geographical distribution of Fulani speakers from Gambia to Cameroun.

APPENDIX I(2)

Caste

In this brief Appendix I am in no wise discussing the 'phenomenon' of caste in Hindu India, but merely presenting, as straightforwardly and plainly as I can, a few 'facts' about caste in rural areas for the benefit of readers with little or no knowledge of south India.

1. Caste is usually defined as a system of social ranking in which the population is divided into corporate groups, defined on the basis of descent, occupational specialisation and geographical origin, and ranked hierarchically, according to criteria of ritual purity and pollution. Each caste or *jati*[63] has a set of common customs governing marriage, eating, etc. and a myth of caste origin; all are endogamous.

2. The two quite separate schemes of caste ranking, which are *varna* and *jati*, are not to be confused. Under the *varna* scheme, which is an idealised formulation of the organisation of Indian society, the four *varnas* (Brahmins, Ksatriyas, Vaisyas, Sudras) actually provide us with only the roughest set of status categories – a theoretical framework into which ethnographers, as well as Indians themselves, have sought to fit the practical operating *jati* divisions which are seen to exist.

[60] For a map of Hausaland see Fig. 1 in Hill (1972).

[61] See Hill (1972), pp. 248 and 266.

[62] Of all the many different names by which the Fulani are known the French favour Peul.

[63] Many castes are divided into endogamous sub-castes, which are also known as *jati*. See the straightforward textbook *Caste in Contemporary India* by Pauline Kolenda, 1978, p. 10, where many other meanings of *jati* are listed.

Harijans are literally 'non-*varna*' – outside the scheme according to the classic formulation.

3. As any respectable statistical reference book is apt to indicate,[64] many caste names in any state have numerous alternative spellings and variants. Because this was so, because fashions changed so rapidly, because the very act of enquiring about caste produced new caste names and categories,[65] and for numerous other excellent reasons, the attempt to classify the population by caste in the decennial Indian population censuses was abandoned after 1941.

4. For the student of economic inequality much the most significant characteristic of caste is that the members of some of them are apt to be much richer than the members of others – a matter which is closely bound up with endogamy, former occupational specialisation and concepts of hierarchy. (See (8) below.)

5. While most village people, and particularly most women, have a good general idea of which castes are higher or lower than their own, the principal criterion involving pollution-contagion, it would be a mistake to imagine that lurking underground, if only one knew how to expose it, is a model 'caste hierarchy' which would be bound to find general acceptance in any community. How could this be when, as Kolenda has put it, 'pollution-contagion is not the only basis for caste ranking in a locality',[66] and when the lists of castes represented in neighbouring villages are so diverse?

6. This inability to agree on a detailed model hierarchy applies even to the question of 'untouchability' – or to whatever acceptable euphemism one employs in its place. Embarrassed officials are, therefore, obliged to declare that the Bhovi, for example, are Scheduled (i.e. Harijans) in certain Karnataka Districts, and not in others, a 'fact' which is then enshrined under Article 341 of the Constitution of India. (' "Scheduled Caste" is a bit of legal jargon developed by the British, as was the theory behind it. The term was first adopted in 1935, when the lowest-ranking Hindu castes were listed in a "schedule" appended to the Government of India Act for purposes of statutory safeguards and other benefits.')[67]

7. Nowadays few castes of any size are occupational groups; but some castes have a lien on particular occupations and ritual tasks which their members may exercise if they wish. (In the Anekal villages most members of traditional 'artisan and service castes' do not follow the caste occupation.)

8. If the situation in the six Anekal villages is any guide, there is apt to be a small number (say, one or two) dominant castes in a Karnataka village – taking account of numbers, wealth (particularly land ownership), political power, ritual status and so forth.

[64] For instance, Vol. II, *Population and Education Particulars* of the *Report of the Karnataka Backward Classes Commission*, Government of Karnataka, 1975 (The Havanur Report).

[65] According to C. J. Baker, the number of caste names in the census rose from 3,208 in 1871 to some 25,000 in 1891 – 'the caste categories were essentially invented inside the Census office'. *South India*, ed. C. J. Baker *et al.*, 1975, p. 224.

[66] Kolenda, 1978, p. 79.

[67] 'Scheduled Caste Politics' by Lelah Dushkin in *The Untouchables in Contemporary India*, ed. J. M. Mahar, 1972, p. 166.

	Hullahalli	Bukkasagara	Mahantalingapura	Nanjapura	Vabasandra	Srirampura	Total
1. Reddy	23 (22%)	12	–	34 (39%)	1	11 (22%)	80 (17%)
2. Kuruba	2	19 (18%)	1	16	19 (45%)	–	57 (12%)
3. Gowda	7	–	44 (51%)	–	–	–	51 (11%)
4. Brahmin	2	1	–	2	3	–	8
5. Valmiki	–	8	–	–	–	8	8
6. Viswakarma	–	4	2	–	–	1	7
7. Satani	–	4	1	–	–	–	5
8. Golla	–	3	2	–	–	–	5
9. Agasa	3	1	–	1	–	–	5
10. Six other Non-Scheduled	5	6	1	1	–	–	13
Total 1 to 10 Non-Scheduled	42 (41%)	58 (56%)	51 (59%)	54 (62%)	22 (52%)	12 (24%)	239 (50%)
11. Adikarnataka	54 (52%)	27 (26%)	5	30 (34%)	17 (40%)	1	134 (28%)
12. Adidravida	–	15	3	–	–	–	18
13. Pichiguntala	–	–	–	–	–	38 (75%)	38
14. Bhovi	–	2	20 (23%)	–	3	–	25
15. Korama	6	2	–	–	–	–	8
16. Jangala	–	–	–	3	–	–	3
Total 11 to 16 Scheduled	60 (58%)	46 (44%)	28 (32%)	33 (38%)	20 (48%)	39 (76%)	226 (48%)
Total 1 to 16 (Hindus)	102 (99%)	104 (100%)	79 (91%)	87 (100%)	42 (100%)	51 (100%)	465 (98%)
17. Muslim	1	–	8 (9%)	–	–	–	9 (2%)
GRAND TOTAL	103 (100%)	104 (100%)	87 (100%)	87 (100%)	42 (100%)	51 (100%)	474 (100%)
Total number of castes in village	11	16	10	7	3	4	22

N.B. Percentages are given for the two largest castes in each village only.

9. It is sometimes stated that each villager belongs to an exogamous named patrilineal clan – a *gotra*; but informants were very vague about this, to the point that brothers might claim membership of different *gotra*.
10. I draw the following two citations on the Brahmin (Brahman) caste from *Encyclopaedia Britannica*, 1970 edition: 'The most heterogeneous collection of minute and independent subdivisions that ever bore a common designation' – see CASTE. 'Brahmans represent the only caste group whose status is constant throughout India and recognition of their supreme ritual status is one of the marked features of Hindu unity' – see BRAHMANS.

APPENDIX I(3)

Castes in the Anekal villages

Notes on Table I(1)

Some of the 'named groups' which I denote 'castes' in Table I(1) are divided into sub-castes, others are not; a few of these groups may not be castes, in the usual sense, at all. I can only say that household classification by caste presented little practical difficulty in the villages.
1. There was a total of 22 castes (regarding the Muslims as such) in the six villages, of which 6 were Scheduled.
2. The number of castes in any one village varied between 16 in Bukkasagara and 3 in Vabasandra.
3. Exactly half of all the households were members of Non-Scheduled castes; 48% of households were Scheduled and 2% were Muslims.
4. The proportion of Scheduled caste households was everywhere high; the lowest figure was at Mahantalingapura (32%), the highest at Hullahalli (58%) and Srirampura (75% – an anomalous hamlet).
5. The Adikarnataka (formerly Holeya) were the largest caste in the six villages taken together, comprising nearly a third (28%) of all households; the next largest were the three dominant castes (none dominant in all villages), the Reddy (17%), Kuruba (12%) and Gowda (11%).
6. The Adikarnataka were the largest caste in two villages (Hullahalli and Bukkasagara), the Gowda in one (Mahantalingapura), the Reddy in one (Nanjapura), the Kuruba in one (Vabasandra) and the Pichiguntala in one (Srirampura).
7. Only one caste, the Adikarnataka, was represented in all the villages; as many as 18 of the total of 22 castes were represented in no more than three of the villages.

Very brief notes on the individual castes in the Anekal villages

1. *Reddy.* Commonly known, like the Gowda, as Vokkaliga (Okkaliga), official statistics fail to distinguish these two castes. ('As a caste category the

Vokkaligas originated in the nineteenth century censuses of South India',[68] denoting grain cultivators.) In Anekal Taluk the Reddy are a high caste of Telugu-speaking agriculturists. In the 1891 population census it was recorded that 61% of all *patels* (headmen) in Bangalore District were Vokkaliga – presumably mainly Reddy. (The number of Vokkaligas in the State population is exceeded only by the number of Lingayats.)

2. *Kuruba.* Traditionally shepherds and blanket weavers, they still occasionally pursue these occupations in the Anekal villages.

3. *Gowda* – see *Reddy*, who are a higher caste.

4. *Brahmin.* There were no Brahmin priests in the Anekal villages, most of the Brahmin householders being ex-*shanbhogs* (accountants) who continued to cultivate the land that had been officially allocated to them.

5. *Valmiki.* Also known as *Beda*, they were traditionally supposed to be hunters, though usually farmers.

6. *Viswakarma.* Known by a great variety of names, they were traditionally blacksmiths, goldsmiths, carpenters, etc., as some of them still are today.

7. *Satani.* Often known as Vaishnava, they are priests.[69]

8. *Golla.* Traditionally cow-keepers and rearers – but in some areas shepherds.

9. *Agasa.* Village washermen, one of the few castes which still concentrates almost entirely on its traditional occupation.

10. The six other Non-Scheduled Hindu castes in the Anekal villages were:

(i) *Bhajantri* (4 households), often known as *Nayinda* and by numerous other names; traditional barbers, though not for Harijans.

(ii) *Thigala* (3). Strongly concentrated in Bangalore District, they are specialist gardeners.

(iii) *Thogata.* (2). Often known as *Neygi*, they were traditionally weavers.

(iv) *Bestha* (2). Traditional occupation fishing.

(v) *Lingayat* (1). Originally a sect rather than a caste, they incorporated converts from a wide occupational range.[70]

(vi) *Balajiga* (*Banajiga*) (1). Traders and farmers.

Scheduled Castes

11. *Adikarnataka* (AK). Formerly often known as Holeya.[71] The hereditary village

68 'Caste Associations in South Asia: a comparative analysis' by D. Arnold *et al.*, *The Indian Economic & Social History Review*, 1976, p. 360. 'The six largest sections into which the Vokkaligas were said to be sub-divided, had similarities in their rituals, sectional legends and social status but they generally inhabited different areas of Mysore. Where an overlap occurred, the sections never intermarried, interdined only rarely and viewed one another as separate *jatis* pursuing similar occupations. The Vokkaliga category was a highly artificial entity.' *Ibid.*, p. 361.

69 Buchanan, 1807, Vol. I, p. 323, regarded them as 'the remains of a very extensive priesthood'.

70 Starting as a challenge to casteism, their numerous converts included agriculturists, merchants, priests, washermen, barbers, oil-pressers, tailors, goldsmiths, etc. They are now the largest 'caste' in Karnataka.

71 Buchanan called them *Whallias* or *Whalliaru*. See Buchanan, 1807, Vol. I, p. 313.

servants (*thotis*) belong to this basic, indigenous, formerly non-landowning caste, which is much discussed in this book. The various sub-castes are either Kannada or Telugu speaking.

12. *Adidravida* (AD). Formerly known as *Madiga*. The lowest caste in the Anekal villages, they are far less numerous than the AKs who consequently have to perform many of their customary menial tasks, such as the removal of the carcasses of animals. They were traditionally leather-workers and sandal-makers.

13. *Pichiguntala*. A rare caste, found in few Karnataka villages.

14. *Bhovi*. (*Vodda*). While many of them still follow the traditional occupations of earth-digging and stone-work, they are nowadays reluctant to move about constantly in search of work, but prefer to settle down as full or part time farmers.

15. *Korama*. Traditionally nomadic grain traders and basket-makers,[72] they are now commonly farmers and basket-makers. Like the Bhovi they are a Scheduled caste in certain Karnataka Districts only.

16. *Jangala*. No information.

APPENDIX I(4)

Brief notes on marriage expenses

In Hausaland the system of marriage payments and ceremonies involves a very complex nexus of payments and counter-payments by the parents of both parties as well as by the bridegroom personally – who will hope to be assisted by his relatives, particularly by his father. (See Hill (1972), pp. 293 *et seq.*) Also, the heavy expenses connected with the Muslim naming ceremony for the first child of the union are an integral part of the system. The actual expenses incurred vary greatly according to the means of the parties concerned; even so, impoverished bridegrooms, particularly those who are fatherless, may find great difficulty in raising the sum required if the bride has not been married before – they may even have to sell land. Divorce is so common that most Hausa women contract two or more marriages during the course of their lives; their second and subsequent marriages involve much less ceremony and expense than their first marriage.

In Karnataka the basic marriage expenses, which are always known as 'dowry', are incurred by the bride's parents, the main beneficiaries usually being the bridegroom's parents, rather than the bridal pair. Rich parents disburse large sums and rich bridegrooms with special qualifications, such as university degrees, are very demanding; poor Harijans often have much difficulty in meeting the minimum required. If a bride's father is dead, her brothers or other relatives will assume responsibility.

In principle, Karnataka families assume permanent responsibility for incoming brides; thus if a husband dies, the widow, with her children, will normally remain

[72] See *ibid.*, p. 249. Thurston in *Castes and Tribes of Southern India*, Vol. III, 1909, p. 438, regards this caste as permeating the entire length of the Indian peninsula.

with her affines and not return to her natal kin – as in Hausaland. This important distinction partly explains why so many houses in the Anekal villages are headed by widows (see p. 112 below), there being none such in Dorayi.

APPENDIX I(5)

Village lay-out

As I have already published a village plan for Batagarawa[73] and a map showing the distribution of homesteads on the farmland at Dorayi,[74] I here provide a village plan for one of the Anekal villages (Bukkasagara) only.

The congested Anekal villages have few streets, many houses being approached by alleyways. Bukkasagara has one main street, where the primary school, the main shop, the smithy and several temples are situated, and another street at right angles to it, which is the Harijan quarter. As in the other Anekal villages, the edge of the

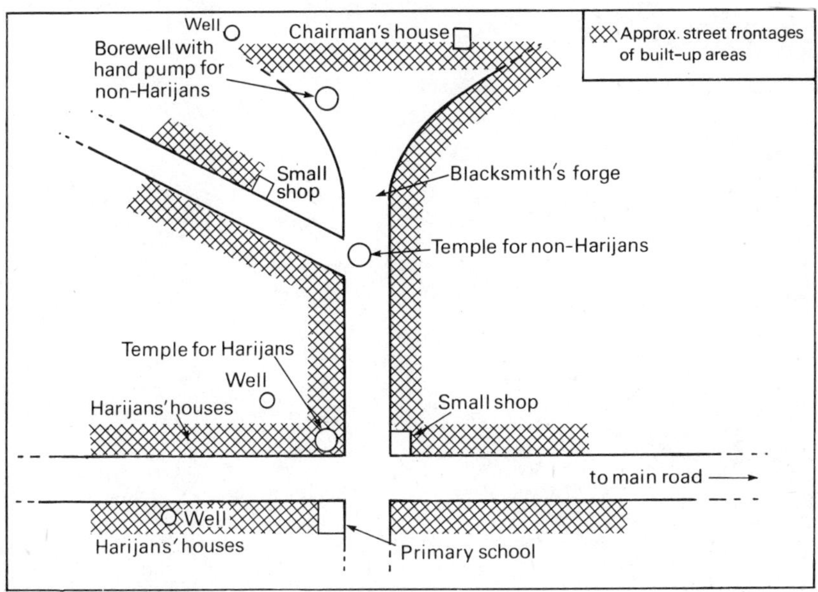

Fig. I(3) Sketch plan of Bukkasagara village. 'Harijans' relates to AKs and ADs only, members of other Scheduled castes not being residentially segregated. A number of the Harijans' houses are quite close to those occupied by non-Harijans.

[73] Hill (1972), Fig. 4. [74] Hill (1977), Fig. 5.

Harijan quarter immediately adjoins the main village – there is no residential gap between the communities.

While the houses of the different caste members in the main village are mixed together, so that there is not, e.g., a 'Reddy section', the strong tendency for close relatives to live near each other produces small 'caste clusters'.

The Adikarnataka, who consider themselves superior to the Adidravida, reserve one of the two wells for themselves in the Harijan's quarter. The well with a hand pump near the Chairman's house is reserved for non-Harijans – this strictly illegal practice occurs in all the villages.

In the Anekal villages generally, the only Scheduled castes which are residentially segregated are the AKs and the ADs – the erstwhile 'untouchables'. In villages, such as Mahantalingapura, where the AK and AD population is small, there is no separate Harijan quarter.

The Harijan section has become so congested at Hullahalli that ten new box-like houses have been built with government assistance; unfortunately, they are nearly half a mile away, on an exposed windy site, and are not at all popular.

CHAPTER II

A Dry Grain Agrarian Mode

As already emphasised in the Introduction, there is a crying need for the systematic categorisation of broad types of rural under-development in the contemporary, tropical, third world – for a respectable typology of agrarian systems. The main purpose of this book is to identify one of these types in terms both of the conditions necessary for its existence and the main consequences which flow from them.

My approach is necessarily experimental. My idea is to test the hypothesis that a system, which I denote a *dry grain mode*, has recently come into existence in two very densely populated (and populous) tropical regions where unirrigated grains (millets and sorghums) are the basic crop and where certain other conditions are satisfied. As this hypothetical dry grain mode in no wise resembles a mode of production in any neo-marxian sense, I have been strongly urged to employ less provocative terminology. But, after prolonged thought and discussion, I can find no alternative set of words which will convey the idea that my formulation is intended as a model with potential application to similarly situated rural economies in other tropical regions, not only in northern Hausaland and south-eastern Karnataka.

I cannot sufficiently emphasise that this particular *dry grain mode* is certain to be one of several such – but not one of many, for our aim must be large-scale classification.[1] Naturally I cannot postulate the existence of *the* dry grain tropical mode when such basic parameters as population density and land tenure conditions vary so enormously; I hope that no one will

[1] It is astonishing that so little emphasis should be placed in the economic literature on the urgent need to classify agrarian systems in the tropical third world into a number of types (modes) which, I would venture to suggest, should be nearer twenty in number than one thousand. K. N. Raj has claimed (see E. A. G. Robinson, 1970, p. 31) that heterogeneity is pervasive although economists of all kinds are indifferent to this: 'the major constraint on development is the heterogeneity of socio-economic structures in the developing countries as a whole'. Roxborough asserts that the construction of a typology of agrarian systems is an urgent task and points out that if the notion of a plurality of such systems were accepted 'the Byzantine debates about the correct definition of a "peasant" would become irrelevant'. *Theories of Underdevelopment* by I. Roxborough, 1979, p. 95.

suppose that I am attempting anything so preposterous – which is not, of course, the same thing as saying that certain of the characteristics identifying this dry grain mode are not common to others, for it is the whole set of characteristics (or conditions) which determines the whole.

In compiling the list of necessary conditions for the existence of this contemporary dry grain mode, I have tried to formulate a logically articulated set, not an arbitrarily selected bundle – although I am only too well aware that it is often difficult to distinguish cause and effect. Before discussing this important question further, I present my list. No particular significance attaches, I think, to the order in which the conditions are listed.

Necessary conditions for the existence of this dry grain mode

(1) *The population is so dense that nearly all of the available farmland is necessarily manured and cultivated every year* – and densities are increasing fast.
(2) *The bulk of the farmland is used for cultivating basic food grains* (which in Hausaland and Karnataka are millets and sorghums) *without irrigation.*
(3) *The farmland is effectively owned by individuals or households – being inherited by sons* on, or before, their father's death.
(4) *Cultivation is undertaken by household members with or without the help of agricultural labourers.*
(5) *Cultivators have for long been accustomed to buy and sell farmland for cash.*
(6) However, land scarcity and rising prices have *recently led to a much reduced incidence of land-selling.*
(7) *Grain yields per acre are very low on any standard*, two of many reasons for this being the reliance on scarce organic manure and the fact that a single annual grain crop is usually taken from the land.
(8) *Most farm tools and equipment*, which are of 'traditional design', *are made by local blacksmiths and carpenters.*

To this list I add the following, which relates to Hausaland and Karnataka, but might have to be expressed somewhat differently in other regions where this dry grain mode applied.
(9) In a sense which will later be defined, there has been *a long-term withdrawal* (which is not a large-scale migration) *from the countryside.*

Perhaps the most deplorable aspects of our dry grain mode are high incidences of profound poverty and *socio-economic stagnation* – an expression with many levels of meaning, as will be seen. Our set of 'necessary conditions' has a certain logical coherence in that it represents a system of increasing stagnation with no saving graces. I take a very small number of examples of what I mean. Because populations are so dense and increasing so fast, there is increased landlessness coupled with a decreased demand for agricultural labour – the largest holdings constantly diminishing in size. Because married sons have no rights over land, other than those gained through inheritance, and because land has become prohibitively expensive and difficult to find, the sons of poor fathers (and this applies to most Harijan sons) are trapped in their poverty. Because basic grains take up so much of the land and have such a low yield (and, also, because of inflation) the village communities are obliged to 'export' more and more grain which they badly need to eat themselves, in order to pay for essential 'imports'.

The choice of characteristics identifying any particular agrarian mode must involve experience, judgment and (above all) the testing of hypotheses. Although the process is likely to involve some degree of appeal to common historical circumstances (such as that land has *for long* been saleable), our particular example shows that societies which are highly disparate culturally (the one Muslim and casteless, the other Hindu and caste-ridden) may yet have similar (or convergent) agrarian systems today – even though the systems were considerably divergent until quite recently. Many agrarian systems are obviously non-comparable. Thus, there could be no possible point in comparing the agrarian system of a matrilineal society (such as the Ashanti of mid-Ghana) where farmland passes to a single heir in the female line on the owner's death, with that of a patrilineal society (such as the Tallensi of northern Ghana) where property is subject to division between sons. Nor, turning to an agronomic matter, could any meaningful agrarian mode bracket systems dependent on the production of root crops (yams, cassava, etc.) or plantains, which are storable only for short periods, with those reliant on readily storable grains.

As emphasised in that fascinating work *Green Revolution?*,[2] most Indian socio-economic research 'is done in relatively developed areas with high levels of infrastructural provision',[3] there being, for instance, a dearth of research information relating to dry areas in Tamil Nadu. Resolved to avoid 'delta bias',[4] twelve villages in inland north Arcot in Tamil Nadu

[2] Subtitled *Technology and Change in Rice-growing Areas of Tamil Nadu and Sri Lanka*, and published in 1977, it is written by thirteen workers 'qualified in economics, geography, hydrology, sociology, statistics and the study of administration of development' (p. xi), and edited by B.H. Farmer; it is one of the few successful inter-disciplinary works of this type and scope ever brought to completion.

[3] *Ibid.*, p. 32. 'It has been fairly widely accepted that we can only speak of "pockets" of Green Revolution . . .'

[4] Research is slanted 'towards Indian deltaic areas, which, for all their teeming populations and huge rice production, have particular environmental and other features such that their conditions . . . cannot necessarily be extrapolated to the non-deltaic areas which cover almost the whole of Sri Lanka and much of the interior of South India, with its insecurity and poverty'. *Ibid.*, p. 2.

were selected for study by the authors of *Green Revolution?* In terms of their ownership of electric pump sets and/or proportions of farmland which are high-yielding tank-irrigated paddy lands, these villages are 'highly developed' compared with the Anekal villages studied here, and they also have, in all save one case, much higher ratios of 'cropped acreage' per head of population. I am, therefore, glad to have gone one step further in studying communities with unfavourable environments, especially as they are representative of such huge total populations in both Karnataka and Hausaland, and because the Indian agronomic literature, until recently, has

> tended to ignore reliance on other than the major cereals, although the various millets, together with sorghum, occupy slightly more than a quarter of the total area of India's planted fields.[5]

But how can I justify my temerity in basing a hypothetical dry grain mode on conditions in eight small rural communities only – for it is obvious enough that those who oppose the idea of large-scale classification of agrarian systems may even insist that each community is unique, or that any idea of a 'representative village' is intellectually unsound? In reply to such doubts I can only say that one's detailed fieldwork in chosen villages is conducted within a wider framework of experience gained from visiting many other villages in the general neighbourhood and from reading numerous publications and archival material including (essentially) historical sources – all of which enables one to gain a general impression of what 'typicality' implies. Although I do not myself care for the concept of 'a representative village', I yet think that it is permissible to regard particular communities, on the basis of all that one knows, as 'not notably atypical' – except, perhaps, in certain respects to which one can draw attention. Even though each of our eight communities is evidently atypical in certain respects,[6] yet each of them has many features which, one's judgment tells

[5] 'Indian Civilization and the Tropical Savanna Environment' by D. E. Sopher, in D. R. Harris (ed.), 1980, p. 190. Sopher notes (p. 189) that the steady, continuous use of dry land, as under our dry grain mode 'offers one of the most difficult agronomic problems in the humid tropics'.

[6] Batagarawa is the seat of a District Head; Dorayi is exceptionally over-populated; members of the Adikarnataka caste make up half of the population of Hullahalli; Bukkasagara and Mahantalingapura have a large uncultivated hinterland; Nanjapura is exceptionally impoverished; only 3 castes are represented in Vabasandra; and Srirampura (which is the most atypical of all) is mainly inhabited by immigrant members of a rare Harijan caste who own unusually little land. (It should be added that the general analysis in this book takes account of conditions in other localities, as the List of References shows. The large number of references to Hill (1972) is accounted for by the fact that that book includes an alphabetical 'Commentary' of 134 pages which largely consists of references to other authors' work on rural Hausaland.)

one, would be found in hundreds of other villages. Such a statement will not satisfy the sceptics who doubt whether detailed fieldwork is ever more than an end in itself; but it is the best I can offer in the space available.

In this summary chapter I try to capture the attention of readers by drawing attention in a condensed way to many of the common features of the contemporary agrarian systems of northern Hausaland (as represented by Batagarawa and Dorayi) and of south-eastern Karnataka (as represented by the six Anekal villages). It contains little which will not be repeated and expanded elsewhere. In the later chapters I reverse usual procedures by dealing first with the contemporary convergence of the systems in the two regions, before turning to discuss, in Chapters XII to XVI, the divergent systems that existed until recently, as well as the historical processes of urban withdrawal from, and neglect of, the countryside, which are in large part responsible for the present abject stagnation there.

FARM-PLOTS AND FARM-HOLDINGS

There are large tracts in both regions where cultivable farmland is a scarce factor in the simple sense that if additional reasonably accessible land[7] were available the total acreage under cultivation would increase. In both regions most farm-*holdings* (a holding being the total area cultivated by an individual or household) consist of a set (a 'portfolio') of separate farm-plots, many of them no larger than an acre or so, a fair proportion even smaller, which are often fairly widely scattered. So far as I know, in West African and south Indian vernaculars there are usually no words for farm-holding, the so-called *farm* (from which *farmer* or cultivator derives) being the farm-plot; so when cultivators need to refer to their whole portfolio they can do no more than pluralise the word for plot or field. This simple deficiency has had, as we shall see, momentous consequences in the literature on economic under-development, in which plot and holding are frequently and disastrously confused, 'farm' usually going undefined. In Hausaland, more often than in Karnataka, single-plot holdings which surround the farmstead may exist in sparsely populated, recently settled zones; but such a Eurocentric notion of 'farm' is generally inapplicable to our dry grain mode.

Most holdings in most localities consist of several farm-plots simply because the separate plots were originally cultivated or acquired over a period, maybe in response to the growth of a farmer's family. When a

[7] In both regions there is a strong preference for cultivating land within about a couple of miles of the homestead.

8 A Hausa farm-plot after harvest showing the henna boundary and guinea corn stalks both stacked and laid out to dry

cultivator decides to acquire more farmland it commonly happens that his neighbours have already started to farm the land adjacent to his existing plot(s), so that he has to move elsewhere. As time goes by, and as farm-holdings are roughly (necessarily roughly) divided between the sons on death, as they are in both regions, as well as being broken up by other processes such as selling, it is obvious that the total number of farm-plots tends to increase. Whether the number of plots per holding will also tend to increase will depend on various demographic and other factors, including the reluctance of cultivators to divide plots smaller (say) than half an acre.[8]

In Anekal Taluk, which is presumably not atypical, the village land records are so out-of-date and inaccurate[9] that I cannot offer any statistical tables relating to plot size. In one of the villages, Nanjapura, it is certainly likely that a half (probably more) of the unirrigated (dry) farm-plots owned by resident villagers are smaller than 2 acres and at least three-

[8] It is mistaken to assume that cultivators are unaware of the dangers of 'fragmentation' – an emotive word which is best avoided. Thus, in Batagarawa I found that farm-plots under one acre were seldom divided on death, the brothers usually distributing entire small plots between themselves. See Hill (1972), pp. 184–5.

[9] See Appendix II(1).

quarters may be under 5 acres.[10] Most plots over 5 acres either consist of marginal land, or are remnants of former large hereditary estates, or belong to men who were brotherless and inherited all their father's land. In Nanjapura the recorded number of dry farm-plots per holding varied between eleven and one.

The comparable statistics relating to Batagarawa and Dorayi in Hausaland are more reliable, as I was able to map the farm-plots using aerial photographs. In Batagarawa about three-fifths of all plots were less than 2 acres, the corresponding proportion for densely populated Dorayi being at least as high as nine-tenths – and this despite the omission of many tiny plots smaller (say) than quarter of an acre which could not be mapped. In both Hausa areas about a half of all farm-holdings consisted of two or three plots.

The 'dispersal of farm-plots' is so fundamental a feature of this agrarian mode that it could no more be changed by administrative fiat than could the inheritance system. Particularly in Karnataka, where the absurd, and ignored, Prevention of Fragmentation Act, 1966, seeks to prevent the partitioning of plots of less than 3 acres on death,[11] those who invent such unrealistic legislation are unaware of the inevitable powerlessness of minor officials for whom villagers feel little respect. Moreover, there is surprisingly little evidence that, *given existing technology*, yields per acre would be increased by consolidating plots. The simple metal ploughs in both regions are easily operable on small plots – indeed, in the Anekal villages several ploughs are often operated simultaneously on such plots.

THE SIZES OF FARM-HOLDINGS

I take it as axiomatic that *laissez-faire* rural economies, where most inter-household transactions and services involve cash,[12] and where land resembles a saleable commodity, are necessarily innately inegalitarian: such rural economies invariably operate in a way which tends to favour richer households at the expense of poorer.[13] Admittedly the financial power and

[10] See Appendix III(2) for some additional statistics on plot size in Nanjapura. One of the few research workers to provide reliable material on plot size was H. H. Mann. In a village near Poona he found that 23% of all plots were between one and two acres – more than half of all plots being smaller than this. *Land and Labour in a Deccan village* by H. H. Mann, 1917, p. 48.

[11] Which should pass, by lottery if necessary, to one son. There are several formulae in the Act, this being the one which applies where the local rainfall averages between 25 and 35 inches annually!

[12] While it is true that agricultural labourers in the Anekal villages often demand, or prefer, payment in grain, not cash, there are good reasons for regarding the two forms of payment as equivalent in this context.

[13] See Hill (1972), Chapter X.

status of richer villagers is apt to be enhanced by their dominant role in financial dealings with the outside world; but it is usually *because* of their high local status, which derives largely from their wealth, that these men succeed in representing their communities in the wider credit-granting world – not *vice versa.* As land is much the most valuable type of property under our dry grain mode, it follows that it will necessarily be distributed very unevenly between villagers, unless governments intervene.

This the governments have not done. It *is* true that in Hausaland the colonial government was partly instrumental in suppressing farm-slavery (which it was powerless to prohibit) so that after about 1930 there was no class of person which (like the slave class) was denied access to land – and it does happen that a side effect of the suppression of slavery was a reduction in the proportion, and size, of large farm-holdings. It *is* true that in Karnataka the abolition of large hereditary estates owned by prominent outsiders was ultimately successfully achieved[14] following legislation in 1954. But the subsequent Karnataka Land Reform legislation, which was designed to reduce inequality within village communities, was a separate operation – one which had no bite in Anekal Taluk mainly because of the very small number of village cultivators whose holdings were above the permitted 'ceilings' and also because of the possibility of evasion by division of farmland between kin.[15] Finally, it *is* true that administrative efforts have been made under Karnataka Land Grant Rules to allot small plots, on favourable terms, to Harijans, most of whom, with the exception of the village servants (*thotis*), were probably landless at the time of Indian Independence. But, owing to poverty, such plots, which often consist of rather infertile, erstwhile grazing land, were often not claimed or retained or even offered, so that, as has also been recorded elsewhere in Karnataka by Epstein,[16] most Harijans still own little land. In 1978 the 30 Harijan households in Nanjapura together owned about as much land (recorded as 37 acres) as the richest individual there (recorded as 44 acres).

One convenient way of assessing the inequality of land-holding is to rank farmers according to the size of their holding and to compute the proportion of farmland owned by the 'top 5%', 'top 15%' and so on. I found that inequality was about equally pronounced in Batagarawa and Dorayi in that in both places the 'top 5%' owned about 20% of the farmland, the 'top 15%' about 45%. But, the proportion of farmers who owned less than one acre was far higher in densely populated Dorayi (about one-third) than in Batagarawa (about 12%) – the corresponding

[14] See Chapter XIV. [15] See Appendix II(2).

[16] See *South India: Yesterday, Today and Tomorrow: Mysore Villages revisited* by T. Scarlett Epstein, 1973.

proportions for those owning 10 acres or more having been about 2% (Dorayi) and 15% (Batagarawa).[17]

In the Anekal villages land ownership remains to such a degree a function of caste that statistical tables which omit this variable have little meaning. Again taking Nanjapura as an example, we find that 9 out of 10 of the largest land-owning households are all high caste (6 Reddy, 2 Kuruba and one Brahmin), the interesting anomalous exception being a very low caste man whose educated son had entered one of the professions: representing 13% of all male-headed Nanjapura households, they owned some 46% of the male-owned farmland (excluding land owned by outsiders) – the corresponding proportion owned by the 'top 5%' being about 27%. Considering the degree of estimation in these figures I merely conclude that inequality is more or less equally pronounced in Nanjapura and the two Hausa localities.[18]

It is much more interesting to note that the following generalisations apply to the villages in both regions. *First*, the largest holdings of resident villagers are about the same size in both regions – say 30 to 40 acres; I think that nowadays the limit is often set by the number of agricultural labourers who may be supervised by a farmer and his dependants. *Second*, very small proportions of farmers now cultivate more than (say) 25 acres. *Third*, there is a strong tendency for high proportions of cultivators to farm less than (say) 4 to 5 dry acres – an area which a household with two able-bodied workers may be able to manage without assistance. *Fourth*, there is always a considerable proportion of farmers whose crop production is altogether insufficient for their household needs, so that they and/or their dependants have to supplement their household income, for instance by working as daily-paid labourers for others. *Fifth*, there is invariably a fair degree of landlessness – this condition is nearly always deplorable for, in both regions, there are few householders who are not aspirant farmers. *Sixth*, there is a fairly close correlation, as we shall see, between the size of farm-holding and the living standard of the household.

THE RENTING OF FARMLAND

In both regions the proportion of farmland that is rented is nowadays very low. In fact in the Hausa localities there is not, and never has been, any 'renting' in the usual sense of that word; the casual system of temporary

[17] See Hill (1977), p. 122.

[18] As there is considerable variation between localities within any region, it is, of course, absurd to press these comparisons at all far. (For data on land-holding in eleven Hausa localities see Hill (1972), p. 238.)

'land-borrowing' (*aro*), which commonly involves close kin, is essentially a means by which richer cultivators assist poorer men by lending them odd plots for one season,[19] usually in return for an unspecified small quantity of grain after harvest. In the Anekal villages, where renting is technically illegal under Land Reform, most present-day 'landlords' are probably impoverished men or widows who are financially incapable of farming effectively, for few, if any, richer cultivators own more land than they could conveniently farm themselves with the help of labourers.

In south-eastern Karnataka the rent is either fixed in advance in grain or cash (*guttige*) or is a share, usually a somewhat nominal half (*vara*), of the crop yield. But, contrary to general belief, *vara* is seldom share-cropping, which strictly involves landlords in providing inputs, such as plough animals, which are additional to the land itself; I judge that share-cropping proper is as rare today as, archival material suggests, it was at the end of last century. It is very rare indeed in Hausaland.

THE SALE OF FARMLAND

In both regions the outright sale of dry farmland for cash has been common practice, in densely populated localities, for more than a century;[20] yet the colonial myth, which was especially strong in Hausaland,[21] that 'the communal ownership of land', whatever that expression might have meant, had necessarily prevented alienation, is still far from dead – and not only because it had originally appeared to justify governments in claiming all the land for themselves. Of course these matters will be properly discussed in later chapters: meanwhile I need to emphasise that the recent rapid rise in the price of farmland in the Anekal villages and in Dorayi (information is lacking on Hausaland generally)[22] has tended to put a brake on selling. Especially in the Anekal villages, where the price of dry farmland is almost preposterously high in relation to the very low yield of the basic crop *ragi*,[23] land owners are very well aware that land, like house property and jewellery, is a valuable hedge against inflation. It is no wonder that, in both regions, the frequent loss of farmland following mortgaging causes so much distress.

[19] See Hill (1977), pp. 131–2.

[20] In Hausaland this applied only to annually cultivated manured farmland – see Hill (1972), pp. 240–1.

[21] While the myths disseminated by Lugard were sincere reflections of his own misapprehensions, they were yet ideologically necessary. See Hill (1977).

[22] Where prices were very low indeed in most areas until recently – see Hill (1972), pp. 239–40.

[23] See Appendix VII(1).

INHERITANCE OF FARMLAND

In both regions the transmission of farmland to sons, either on the death of the father or when the sons start cultivating separately, is far more common than selling. I found that in Anekal Taluk the actual division between sons is as rough and ready as in Hausaland.[24] In both regions the laws which decree that daughters, as well as sons, should inherit a share of their father's property – in Hausaland daughters should receive half as much as sons – are largely ignored, especially in relation to farmland. In both regions, accidents of inheritance (one household having a single son, another four) often account for the changing fortunes of particular families. The dissolution of the largest holdings through division between sons is particularly apt to occur in polygynous Hausaland where it was found that rich landholders tend to have more wives,[25] and hence more sons, than other men.

THE FARMING HOUSEHOLD

In both regions the basic productive unit is the farming household, not the individual cultivator, the various household members, other than women in Hausaland, being jointly concerned to cultivate the family land. In both regions the subordinate members of the household work, rather strictly, under the authority of the household head, who is always a man in Hausaland and sometimes a widow in Karnataka. Although in strict legal principle the head of a Karnataka joint household – which is here conventionally defined as including two or more married sons – is the mere manager of the jointly (i.e. corporately) owned property, including farmland; and although there is no corresponding concept of joint ownership in Hausaland – yet for various practical reasons, including the high-handedness of many Karnataka household heads, such extended family units as include married sons in the two regions are apt to operate rather similarly if considered as mere 'farming units'.

In both regions the basic core of most farming households is a conjugal group, with or without married sons, which daughters usually abandon on marriage; only very low proportions of household members are unrelated to the household head whether by blood, marriage or adoption. In both regions, middle-aged and elderly men are seldom sonless, this being partly

[24] In Hausaland there is much misunderstanding about this as educated Muslims usually assume that the courts are always concerned with the division – as seldom happens unless there is a dispute.

[25] See, for instance, the three tables on pp. 114–15 in Hill (1977). Whereas 79% of rich men had 2, 3 or 4 wives, the corresponding figure for poor men was 22%.

due to polygyny and adoption in Hausaland and to 'adoption' of sons and sons-in-law (*iltam*) in Karnataka; but Batagarawa differs from both Dorayi and the Anekal villages in that a fair proportion of married sons who work (in *gandu*) on their father's farms reside in separate houses or house-sections.

In both regions farming households, which vary considerably in size,[26] resemble living organisms of constantly changing composition; they may continue in existence indefinitely, some members of the *n*th generation of male descendants occupying the house originally built by their founding ancestor and/or farming his original land – or they may die out altogether. As for the fascinating question of how the potentially, or actually, conflicting interests of fathers and married sons are resolved, it seems that each region can tell us something about the other. In both regions fair proportions of married sons manage to achieve an amicable separation from their father, who gives them his blessing as well as farmland for their own use – but Dorayi is an extraordinary exception, for there the only escape from life-long co-residence with the father is permanent migration, maybe to an unknown destination. In both regions sensible fathers know how to grant concessions to their sons, and their daughters-in-law, to persuade them to remain; and fathers are very seldom abandoned by all their sons. It is likely that the conflicting interests of fathers and sons lead to more unpleasantness and misery in Karnataka than in Hausaland generally, if only because Hausa fathers usually allow, or even encourage, their dependent married sons to do some farming on their own account, as never happens in Karnataka. But even so, the general point I am trying to make here is that, considered as a farming unit, the Karnataka household is subject to the same kinds of strains, represents the same kind of compromise, as similar households elsewhere in the world: it is not nearly so 'special' as Indianists often suppose – though, as we shall see, male household heads are apt to be notably authoritarian.

In both regions 'the incidence of jointness' refers to the actual number of joint households relative to the potential number – a simple statistical calculation that is often overlooked, especially by those who casually deplore the decline of the joint household. Owing to the youthfulness of many households heads or (which may be an aspect of the same point) to the high proportion of fathers who die before their sons marry, in both regions the potential number of joint households is a fairly small proportion of all households – less than a quarter in Dorayi. In neither region is there any evidence of a decline in 'the incidence of jointness' for two-generational

[26] Partly owing to polygyny, the proportion of large households is greater in Hausaland than in Anekal. See Table V(2), p. 111 below.

households, which is very high in the two Hausa localities as well as among the richer households in the Anekal villages. However, in both regions, fraternal extended families, headed by an elder brother, are fast disappearing; and special circumstances, such as the early death of the father, usually account for such cases as survive for any length of time.

In both regions married sons who hive off, forming separate farming and cooking units, often remain close, both physically and psychologically, to their parents. In the Anekal villages they may be allotted a separately partitioned section of their parental home, which usually has its own front door; in Hausaland it is fairly common for separated sons to be allotted a section of their father's compound, which is approached by the common entrance hut.

In the Anekal villages any member of a farming household over (say) twelve years old may be called upon to work on the family farmland, though school children are usually exempted. The contribution of female members may be nearly as great as that of males, for although they never operate ploughs and other equipment hauled by cattle, they are responsible for much of the transplanting, weeding and harvesting, as well as the grazing of cattle. In Hausaland, as we have seen, most wives are prevented by Muslim seclusion from working on the land – a highly anomalous situation in world terms, in relation to this or any other agrarian system, especially as it affects poor and rich households alike, but one which is much relieved by women's important activities as house-traders, food processors (for sale) and craftworkers.

Under our dry grain mode individual farming households are seldom isolates. In particular they are related by agricultural labouring, for in 1925 the Russian author A. V. Chayanov was more than a century behind the times, as the work of Francis Buchanan shows, when he included India in the long list of countries which were 'unacquainted with the categories of wage-labour and wages'.[27] Chayanov's models have acquired far too much universality in the past decade partly owing to M. Sahlins' analysis of the 'domestic mode of production' in his influential *Stone Age Economics*,[28] which is such that it 'anticipates no social or material relations between households except that they are alike'.[29] It is extraordinary that he should include the sophisticated Nupe of northern Nigeria,[30] who as near

27 See 'Chayanov and the Theory of Peasantry as a Specific Type of Economy' by B. Kerblay in Shanin, 1971, p. 152.

28 First published in the United States in 1972 and Britain in 1974, it leans heavily on Chayanov.

29 *Ibid.*, p. 95.

30 When the first Europeans arrived at their town of Raba, on the river Niger, in the nineteenth century, the Nupe were so strongly linked with the outside world that their

neighbours of the Hausa have much in common with them, in a book on 'stone age economics'. But he is right in stating that 'a fair percentage of domestic groups persistently fail to produce their own livelihood, although organized to do so'.[31]

FARM-LABOURING

In Hausaland and Anekal Taluk, as we shall see, there has long been no tendency for production 'to be geared to the family's customary requirements':[32] some households produce far too much for their needs, some far too little – given the unforecastable effects of the wildly variable weather on the size of the harvest any correspondence between production and requirements in any particular year is necessarily fortuitous. In both regions, considerable proportions of farming households, even a few of the most impoverished, employ daily-paid farm labourers at times; in both regions, the working members of most of the poorest farming households and of many with medium holdings, do some labouring for others; and in both regions, a fair proportion of households is mainly dependent on daily farm-labouring for their livelihood.

Wage rates are extremely low in both regions. In Dorayi in 1971 the usual rate for a day labourer for a long morning's work of about six hours was the equivalent of about 30p together with food served on the farm, the rate for evening work having been about 15p; but these rates represented a sudden rise consequent upon the advancing inflation (which since then has hit West African rural communities far more severely than their south Indian counterparts). Thus, in Batagarawa in 1968 the rate for a long morning had been no more than about 12p to 15p. In the Anekal villages in 1978 daily wages for men were commonly Rs 4 (with some variation), for women about Rs 3 (but varying with the type of work), plus meals on the farm as in Hausaland; these rates were the equivalent of about 29p and 21p – or a slightly greater value of grain (*ragi*), if that were the medium of payment.

In both regions labourers are seldom hired for more than a few days at a time – the casualness of employment, and the poor bargaining power of labourers being explained by a substantial surplus of labour at almost all times. In Batagarawa and Dorayi I saw hardly any evidence for the shortage of labour which is so often supposed to occur at certain stages of the farming season: in particular, there was no rush to recruit labour at the beginning of the rainy season, for the farmland had been prepared in

markets were 'full of precious goods from Hausa, Bornu and North Africa'. *A Black Byzantium* by S. F. Nadel, 1942, p. 85.

31 Sahlins, 1974, p. 69. 32 *Ibid.*, p. 77.

advance and the sowing of seed grain was mostly done, quite quickly, without hired labour. In the Anekal villages, also, spasmodic employment seemed to be the lot of nearly all labourers, at nearly all times.[33] Were this not so, there would be a much more pronounced tendency for particular labourers to work fairly regularly for certain employers. As it is, farm labourers are very commonly recruited the evening before they are required, for work which usually lasts for only one to three days. In both regions the work of labourers, other than ploughmen, is invariably supervised, the employer and/or his dependants often working too; so as to finish the work quickly and to lighten the task of supervision, large groups of labourers are sometimes employed.[34] It is obvious that employers are not to be blamed for the unfortunate system of casual day-labouring in both regions, reflecting as it does the financial inability of nearly all cultivators to offer regular work owing to the peculiar vagaries and pronounced seasonality of the tropical climates as well as the small size of most farm-holdings.

For the same reason, few present-day Anekal cultivators would be able to afford to maintain full-time adult 'bonded labourers' – regular farm servants, who receive all their daily requirements from their employers to whom they are indebted – and it is not owing to its illegality[35] that, as we shall see, adult bonded labouring is not a regular feature of our late twentieth century dry grain mode in south India.

The erstwhile systems of communal labour on privately owned farmland are unimportant under our drain grain mode; while they persist in some localities to some small extent, they are nowadays always voluntary. Known as *gayya*[36] in Hausaland, the system usually involves groups of young men in working on farmland for less than the prevailing wage, for reasons of obligation, friendship, pity, enjoyment, and so forth. While in the Anekal villages households may occasionally render mutual assistance on their farmland,[37] most help involving friends and relations is quite informal.

[33] Thus, at the height of the *ragi* harvesting season in October 1977, one Hullahalli farmer had no difficulty in recruiting 18 labourers for one day's work; he had gone round the houses the day before, offering only Rs 3 with a meal.

[34] An interesting system, known as *oppanda* in the Anekal villages, involved the payment of a lump sum to one man who may then recruit and pay as many labourers as he chooses to undertake certain specified work, which is usually harvesting. (Epstein in *Economic Development and Social Change in South Asia*, 1962, reported on a women's work group known as *gumpu*, but this was not known in the Anekal villages where *oppanda* involved both men and women.)

[35] First declared 'illegal' under Mrs Gandhi's Twenty Points Programme, legislation followed later in 1975.

[36] See Hill (1977), p. 251.

[37] Known as *muyi* (or *muyi kelasa*) – a word of many meanings.

9 Seven Hausa labourers under supervision

NON-FARMING HOUSEHOLDS

In both regions the great majority of householders are either largely (or partly) dependent on farming on their own account for their livelihood or are *aspirant farmers* – i.e. financially disabled landless, or near landless, men who (themselves and their dependants) are reluctantly obliged to pick up a living in the interstices of the rural economy, by working as farm and general labourers and/or by grazing cattle, collecting firewood for sale, and so forth. It is partly because, in both regions, most farm labourers are drawn from households which are not landless that, as we shall see,[38] the category 'landless labourer' is virtually useless for our purposes. But is there a small category of 'non-farming households' whose members never aspire to work for themselves on the land?

In general in rural Hausaland I think that such a category is lacking. Virtually everyone there aspires to be a cultivator. Prestigious religious teachers, well-known blacksmiths and important produce traders, are so far from being exceptions to this rule, that the higher their status in their non-farming work the more ambitious and successful they are apt to be as cultivators – and a man's status is closely related to his scale of farming. Farming and non-farming activities are regarded as complementary until

[38] See, also, p. 57 above.

some time in middle age when 'retirement into farming' becomes the ideal. As for the householders who own little or no farmland, hardly any of them, with the exception of a few drummers and other musicians, have a specialised occupation which is so time-demanding and remunerative that they would abandon farming had they any choice in the matter.

The general situation in old-established Anekal villages is surprisingly similar: high status is correlated with success as a cultivator, and land-hungry men find few good opportunities in non-farming work. As we know – Appendix I(3) – most working members of the households of the traditional service and artisan castes are mainly engaged in agriculture – and such households anyway comprise only 4% of the total.[39] Most non-farming households are anomalous, small and poor – as in Hullahalli, for instance, where half of them are headed by recent migrants.

OTHER ASPECTS OF INEQUALITY

The fundamental basis of economic inequality under our dry grain mode is the very uneven distribution of farmland, the total value of which far exceeds that of any other property. What other important types of property are also unevenly distributed? For the Anekal villages I have already emphasised the very great variations in the size and quality of houses, a few very rich people inhabiting grand residences, most Harijans living in great squalour; but, in general, housing conditions there do not reliably reflect household living standards, and many reasonably well off people enjoy little living or sleeping space and endure the close proximity of cattle. The only other important forms of property which are likely to be ill-distributed there are gold ornaments and jewellery, which I cannot value,[40] and irrigation wells, which are hard to value as so many of them are out of order.[41] In Hausaland, where houses are almost 'valueless' in the sense that they are never sold (although occasionally rented), the most valuable form of property is probably granary stocks[42] – which are very unevenly distributed since richer farmers are apt to store so much produce for sale when prices have risen.

[39] Excluding the Korama basket-makers, whose main occupation has long been farming, the traditional service and artisan castes – see Table I (1) – may be regarded as the Viswakarma, the Satani, the Agasa and the Bhajantri, only 21 households in all.

[40] I strongly hold that in surveys of this extensive kind it is impossible to obtain reliable estimates of such property or of cash hoards; and in the Anekal villages I would have found it impertinent to touch on the subject.

[41] See Appendix VI(4), p. 140 below.

[42] See Hill (1972), Table V6, p. 78, on the ownership of granaries by household heads; as some granaries are very much larger than others, this table under-estimates the degree of inequality of granary stocks.

Under our dry grain mode there is so much pressure to convert common grazing ground into arable land that the ownership of livestock is much less unequal than formerly. In the Anekal villages, where few richer households find it worth their while to maintain large herds of cattle, but where poor households attach importance to cattle ownership, as a self-reproducing store of value, the members of the three poorest Scheduled castes (the AKs, the ADs and the Pichiguntalas) actually owned as many as 0.9 cows per household against 1.7 for other castes – though the ownership of the more valuable, and much less numerous bullocks, was less equally distributed.

Statistics relating to the distribution of cattle ownership in Hausaland by cultivators, whether Fulani or Hausa, are very poor. It is even doubtful whether any proper estimates of total ownership, including that by pastoralists, have ever been made.[43] I estimated that the few Hausa cattle owners in Batagarawa owned between one and two hundred animals,[44] including 36 plough oxen; there were no cattle owners or ploughs in Dorayi.

Other animals (goats, pigs, donkeys and fowls) represented a rather unimportant store of wealth in the Anekal villages, so I postpone examination of its household distribution. In Hausaland, on the other hand, almost every household, however poor, aspires to own at least one transport donkey and several goats, and considering the low value of these animals, it was usually a mark of terrible impoverishment not to do so – for they do not necessarily require any food other than grass, dung may be sold as manure, and donkeys may be hired out. Since few households have any need for more than about four donkeys, the distribution of the total stock of these animals is not very uneven: what is significant is that in Dorayi over two-thirds of the poorest group of households owned no donkey. As for goats, it was interesting that in Batagarawa, where they are an important store of value for poor people, especially women, ownership by richer and poorer households was nearly equal. On the other hand, the ownership of the more valuable sheep, and especially rams, was concentrated in richer households.

Given the great simplicity of most farm tools and equipment in each of the regions,[45] the value of this form of agrarian capital is remarkably low and, as implements are often borrowed, little significance attaches to the

[43] According to *Rural Planning in a Savanna Region* by J. G. T. van Raaij, 1974, p. 97, in Katsina Province the official cattle population figures, based on the cattle tax, needed to be stepped up by 50% – and since then the tax has been abolished.

[44] In West Africa cattle owners often place animals in the charge of Fulani pastoralists, which makes the estimation of herd-size very difficult. See Hill (1970).

[45] See Appendix II(3).

distribution of such capital between households except in the case of metal ploughs. In northern Hausaland, where there are no wooden ploughs, the ownership of metal ploughs is apt to be heavily concentrated with rich cultivators; this is not because, as is so persistently and erroneously supposed,[46] they are the only farmers whose scale of production is large enough to justify plough ownership (for plough owners are often mainly interested in the profits of plough-hiring), but because of the high value of the trained plough oxen.

As for transport equipment, much importance attaches to the ownership of farm carts in Anekal Taluk (as we know, there are none in Hausaland), for they are seldom hired out – though they may be borrowed by close kin such as separated sons. It was impossible to value the estimated stock of 123 carts in the six villages, many of which were broken or old. (There were 3 superior carts with pneumatic tyres, said to have been worth some £200 each, against some £85, or less, for a common cart.)

THE MEASUREMENT OF INEQUALITY

It is my strong conviction that the relative living standards of farming households[47] under our dry grain mode cannot, and should not, be measured in terms of estimates (they must *be* estimates) of annual household income – which are so commonly, indeed almost invariably, attempted by those undertaking conventional surveys in both rural and urban India. Among the many reasons for the impossibility of obtaining reliable estimates from even the most willing of householders the most basic is that they have no occasion to think in such terms.[48] ('To the extent that cultures differ, ideas of what is "wealth" will also differ; all such theories find their sole justification in their own systems of values, and cannot appeal to any "economic facts of life".'[49]) Under our dry grain mode it is possible that people of very varying living standards tend to conceptualise their economic situation in terms of generalised assets and liabilities and generalised (maybe seasonal) ebbs and flows; not only is there no *answer*, such as a taxman would demand in the West, but householders (other than the poorest) usually have no idea of whether they are *net* creditors or debtors[50] – in which connection it must be remembered

[46] See Hill (1972), pp. 307–9. See also n. 15, Ch. XVI.

[47] I henceforth employ 'farming household' to refer to all households which derive their basic livelihood from the land, whether from farming and/or labouring and allied activities.

[48] See Appendix VI(1) for more discussion.

[49] *Societal Accounting* by T. Gambling, 1974, p. 106.

[50] I would go so far as to insist that all surveys of rural indebtedness in third world countries which are based on asking people about their debts are necessarily deeply suspect.

that, as in the West, the biggest gross debtors tend to be the richest people. So in assessing relative living standards one's methodology must follow prevailing village concepts.[51]

My first realisation that ordinary intelligent members of village communities are well able to assess, and to discuss, comparative household living standards came in Batagarawa, in 1967, when I found that carefully selected village assistants were largely agreed in classifications of village households and that my own subsequent assessments, based on a much later analysis of land ownership and other salient variables, gave similar results.[52] In Dorayi and in the Anekal villages I adopted similar, though not identical, methods which are discussed in Appendix VI(1). Here I am merely attempting a preliminary justification, partly in terms of its results, of my research methods.

In both Batagarawa and Anekal Taluk most farming households were classified in one of four 'wealth' groups: 'rich' (on village standards),[53] middle, poor and very poor – in Dorayi the classification was into three groups only. (Very crudely, rich households may be regarded as those which would not only be well able to withstand temporary calamity, such as the total failure of local harvests owing to drought, but would be able to render assistance to others less fortunate; as for poor (and very poor) households, they are those which invariably suffer severe deprivation when times are 'normal'.) While, on the one hand, I am certainly not claiming that my notion of 'rich' necessarily showed much correspondence as between the two continents;[54] on the other hand, 'poor' and 'very poor' are, indeed, similar concepts – in both continents very poor households own 'hardly anything', apart from the torn and bedraggled clothing[55] they stand up (and sleep) in, their mean and squalid houses, and a few mats, blankets, cooking and water storage pots and vessels, grinding stones,

51 It is worth noting that no one attaches any significance to household self-sufficiency in grain – though they often pretend otherwise. Particularly in the Anekal villages, the usual objections under our dry grain mode to distinguishing 'subsistence' from 'cash' crops are given added irony by the fact of grain (*ragi*) being so near an approach to cash, for instance in the payment of labourers.

52 I was particularly impressed to find such a close association between my assistants' household classification and the size-distribution of farm-holdings, considering that their knowledge of relative areas was wholly 'intuitive' – non-numerical. See Hill (1972), pp. 75–6.

53 Although my usage of 'rich' has caused much ribaldry, I can unfortunately think of no simple alternative.

54 Since rich Anekal households own most of the irrigated paddy land, this might be thought to be the main explanation for the apparently greater 'prosperity' of many of them, compared with their Hausa counterparts who own no irrigated land; but I must emphasise that I attach no significance to such crude inter-continental statistical comparisons.

55 Someone in Batagarawa once defined very poor households as those entirely dependent on gifts of cast-off clothing.

simple lamps, bowls, elementary farm tools, and maybe a few small livestock.[56] The Western world may have some notion of the extent of dire rural poverty, but they have little comprehension of its depth.

THE STATISTICS OF INEQUALITY

I now deal very briefly with some of the statistical findings regarding the 'rich' and 'poor' groups. In Batagarawa, which is far more representative of northern Hausaland generally than overcrowded Dorayi, about 10% of all classified households were regarded as rich: these households owned, on average, 19.5 acres of manured land (against 4.2 acres and 2.8 acres for the two poorest groups), only two of them owning less than 5 acres. In the Anekal villages the proportion of rich households was 22% – the proportion varying between 57% for the richest caste (the Reddy), 26% for other Non-Scheduled castes and 3% for the most numerous Scheduled caste, the AKs.

As for the 'poor' and 'very poor' households, these accounted for about two-thirds of all households in Batagarawa; 71% of the 'poor' and 90% of the 'very poor' households owned less than 5 acres of manured farmland – about a third of them cultivating no 'bush' (unmanured) land. In the Anekal villages 37% and 15% of all households (a total of 52%) were 'poor' or 'very poor' – uninteresting averages, since the respective (total) percentages for the Reddy caste, for other Non-Scheduled castes and for the AKs were 16%, 36% and 86%. As many as 72% of all the 'very poor' households were AKs.

My main premisses, which I shall be at pains to justify in later chapters, are that a rather small proportion of households enjoys any reasonable degree of economic security; that high proportions of impoverished households are an inevitable characteristic of such systems; that in the Anekal villages, caste (which is associated with land ownership) is the main determinant of living standards; and that the free availability of some uncultivated land within a reasonable distance of the village, as at Batagarawa,[57] is no guarantee that a high proportion of farmers will have the financial strength to cultivate effectively.

The overlapping concepts of 'too poor to farm' or 'no time to farm', are generally applicable to our dry grain mode, where land hunger is not the only problem facing cultivators. A Batagarawa householder who has an

[56] Many richer households own little, if any, moveable household property such as furniture. See Hill (1972), p. 69.

[57] See Hill (1972), pp. 213–14. It is relevant to note that the richest households actually cultivate more of this unmanured land per household than other people.

empty granary at the beginning of the farming season may well have to earn his living every day by means of sundry paid occupations, including farm-labouring, so that he can spare no time to cultivate on his own account. As for the concept of 'too poor to farm', this has particular application to those Anekal householders who do not own, and cannot borrow, plough animals and other equipment – although, in both regions, there are many other circumstances in which it applies, such as when manure is lacking.

In both regions fairly high proportions of rich householders were the sons of large farmers; on the other hand, owing to the division of farmland on inheritance, many of the sons of such farmers are not rich – a fact which, as I constantly reiterate, has particular reference to polygynous rural Hausaland where richer men tend to have more wives and hence more (inheriting) sons than poorer men.

The chance that a poor man will escape from the poverty of his forebears is becoming increasingly small in both regions as the price of farmland rises. Some statistics relating to the sons of retired fathers in Dorayi show that of the 23 impoverished sons of retired fathers, as many as 17 had fathers in similar plight.[58]

However, in both regions there is some tendency for younger men whose poverty is not 'absolute'[59] to suffer less as they grow older. This is suggested by the following statistics relating age to wealth. In both Dorayi and Anekal no more than about a tenth of householders under 40 to 45 years old were rich, against about a quarter of older men. Provided a certain threshold of 'impossible poverty' is passed, there is some chance that household standards may improve as the family working force grows and the chances of forming a joint household increases – and, particularly in Hausaland, as a man builds up his reputation in some specialised occupation such as trading.

DIVERSIFICATION AND INTENSIFICATION

Finally, I revert to my assertion (for it is little more at this stage) that uneven land ownership is the fundamental basis of inegalitarianism. But I do so for the purpose of emphasising that this is not mainly because of the

[58] See Hill (1977), pp. 142–3. (A 'retired father' is one who has stopped farming and divided his land between his sons who maintain him.)

[59] 'Absolute poverty' might be generally thought of as applying to a man who has no particular reputation, no power to borrow, no particular friends or relations who will help him – in short no power of manoeuvre. See 'Rural Poverty Unperceived: Problems and Remedies' by R. Chambers, *World Development*, 1981, for reasons why rural poverty (and 'absolute poverty' in particular) is 'systematically underperceived or misperceived' by those who are not its victims.

superior productive capacity, in terms of dry grains, of the larger farmer, but rather for indirect reasons, including the superior borrowing power of those who can offer large farm-holdings to a bank as security for loans.

Under our dry grain mode richer men cannot hope to continue to prosper without intensifying and diversifying their farming and non-farming activities. In both regions the yields of basic grains are so low[60] that agricultural intensification by means of cultivating (maybe interplanting) other more lucrative crops is the aim of all richer farmers, who also seek to diversify their non-farming interests. Less wealthy men, also, must devise some means of escaping from their reliance on low-yielding dry grains and unrewarding farm-labouring – for it is only by running very fast forward that they will be enabled to stay in the same place.

Details of the types of occupation open to rich and poor respectively are given on pp. 143 *et seq.* below and are not repeated here. As a substitute I now provide notes on a rich Batagarawa household, which brings out the importance for both men and women of non-farming activities, and also on two desperately poor Anekal households, most of whose young sons have been obliged to become temporary bonded labourers (*sambalagaras*).

Alhaji Mai Goro[a] of Batagarawa lives in a fine, large mud-built compound, with a vaulted entrance hall, which is the home of 25 people, including 2 sons and 2 brother's sons each with their own living sections. His 3 wives are all prominent house-traders, the senior wife selling cooked meals, kola nuts, sour milk, incense, roasted groundnuts, *kulikuli* (groundnut cake), groundnut oil,[b] various tasty snacks, locust bean seeds – which she buys and stores for a seasonal price rise – and spun cotton thread. Each of his wives is a member of several rotating credit associations[c] (*adashi*). He owns a metal plough[d] and a groundnut decorticator[e] and he is a cattle owner[f] who grows much tobacco[g] on heavily manured farmland. He and his 2 married sons-in-*gandu* (who are both prominent farmers, having bought much of their farmland) are on the short list of those who sell groundnuts at all seasons. He himself employs few farm labourers, having a large family labour force, but one of his sons-in-*gandu* is a notable employer, mainly in the evening. He buys kola nuts in large packages which contain at least 2,000 nuts, and probably meets much of the village demand for nuts for ceremonial purposes.

Notes

a His title 'Alhaji' indicates that he has made the pilgrimage (nowadays by air) to Mecca; his nickname 'Mai Goro' derives from his importance as a local trader in kola nuts (*goro*), which are grown only in far-away southern forest country, although much the most important item in numerous Hausa ceremonies and gift exchanges and being widely consumed as a stimulant.

60 However, I challenge the conventional view of an inverse relationship between scale of farming and yield in Chapter VIII, so far as this dry grain mode is concerned.

b Village women laboriously make much groundnut oil for sale from nuts which they buy from their husbands and other men.
c See p. 217 below.
d He is one of only 13 Batagarawa farmers who owns a plough.
e These simple hand-operated machines may be used to shell as much as 1½ tons of nuts daily; like ploughs, they are constantly hired out by their owners.
f Only about 6 Batagarawa men owned significant numbers of cattle, which were put out for rearing to specialised pastoralists.
g A 'rich man's crop' which is grown by only about 10 Batagarawa farmers – see Hill (1972), p. 326.

Sixty-seven years old, and too decrepit to work as a labourer, this landless Adikarnataka man lives with his wife, one married son and another son aged 18 who is a local *sambalagara*[a] (temporarily bonded labourer), in a windowless one room hut, thatched with rotten sugar cane leaves, which is too small for them all to lie down in at night, the overflow reclining under a small outside canopy. Of his four other sons, two are married and have taken refuge with their wives' parents in other villages, the two youngest boys being *sambalagaras* living with their employers elsewhere. His wife, his married son, and his daughter-in-law all work as daily-paid labourers – when work can be found. They own practically nothing save two calves, but have been lent a cow; somehow, the mother of the house (a proud, eager and spontaneous woman) contrived to look unusually smart and well dressed.

Note
a See Appendix XIII(1).

A younger brother of the foregoing, who lives in an adjoining hovel, and is also landless, four of his sons (two of them sons of his deceased first wife) are *sambalagaras* in other villages. The other occupants of the single room are his second wife, her widowed sister together with her adult daughter, and one young son. They own virtually nothing except for two sheep and a hen.

Since many important characteristics of our dry grain mode have received little or no attention in this chapter; since historical aspects have been virtually ignored; and since all the subjects discussed in it will be examined afresh in later chapters – my summarised conclusions on this agrarian mode are postponed until Chapter XVII is reached. I should also add that while I have concentrated on describing the internal structure of these rural communities, almost as though they were isolated from the rest of the world, the matter of 'external relations' receives much attention in later chapters.

APPENDIX II(1)

Defects in the Karnataka village land records

This discussion of some of the main defects in contemporary village land records in Karnataka is based on the belief that the unreliability of the statistics of land-holding is not the fault of the new generation of officials, the Panchayat Secretaries, who succeeded the deposed hereditary accountants (*shanbhogs*) some ten years ago, but derives mainly from factors which are beyond their control. The Secretaries are expected to collect far too much detailed information from far too many people, many of whom have good reason to be quietly unco-operative; and they inherited defective records from their predecessors, who also had their problems, though their burden of work was usually considerably smaller, one Secretary having often succeeded several *shanbhogs*.

In referring to the 'unreliability of the land records', we must distinguish between the basic information relating to each registered (numbered) farm-plot, and the manner in which this information is processed when preparing statistical tables, such as those relating to the size-distribution of farm-holdings. I deal first with the basic information.

For each registered plot there is a large printed form, in the Kannada language, known as *pahani*, on which a mass of information is (or ought to be) recorded. This information includes:[61] the name of the cultivator (who may or may not be the owner), the area (in acres and *guntas* – a *gunta* being a fortieth of an acre), the land revenue chargeable, the general type of cultivation (distinguishing the area of dry, tank-irrigated and 'garden' land – the latter usually being irrigated from a well), other categories of land (such as waste, uncultivable, grazing) and means of acquisition of the plot by the present cultivator if bought or rented.

When a registered plot is divided into two or more portions (on inheritance, sale, etc.), each portion continues to bear the original number with a sub-section number: thus, if plot 68 has been divided into six portions, six separate registration papers will relate to plots 68/1 to 68/6 respectively. Needless to say, plot size varies very greatly from 2 *gunta* upwards – the great majority of tank-irrigated plots being smaller than an acre.

I now list some of the defects in this basic material.

1. *Name of cultivator*

(a) There are numerous reasons why the named cultivator of the plot may not be the actual cultivator, most of which have to do with the failure of the original owner or his heir to get the name altered. Many plots are registered in the names of deceased fathers, a few in the names of deceased grandfathers; and it is unusual for a father who allots a plot to a son who has separated from him to change the

[61] While the whole list of types of information is very much longer, much of it is inapplicable to the Anekal villages.

registration. As most renting is illegal under Land Reform, rented land is usually, though not invariably, registered in the name of the owner – an unimportant point, as the incidence of renting is now very low. Mortgaged land, also, may be registered in the name of the mortgagor who has no cultivating rights.

(b) In most cases the cultivator is identified as (say) 'Muniappa son of Thimappa', which is necessary as so many men bear the same name; in some cases, however, the cultivator's name is simply recorded as 'Muniappa' – making it difficult to establish his identity, especially if he is an outsider.

(c) Plots are often registered in the name of one cultivator, for instance the eldest of three brothers, although actually cultivated by several men; as joint cultivation, except by fathers and sons, never occurs, such a plot is, in fact, several plots.

(d) Plots are sometimes registered in more than one name – for instance, if portions of a plot are sold to three men, each of their names will be recorded; unfortunately, in such cases, the respective acreages are never stated.

2. *Inaccurate acreages*

Especially when large areas, such as former grazing grounds, are divided among many cultivators, the acreage allotted to each is apt to be rounded, clearly being notional.

3. *Farm put to several uses*

If, as is common, part of a plot is wooded, the area is seldom recorded. Nor is such information always kept up to date.

The sizes of farm-holdings

Given these defects in the basic material, the difficulty in compiling reasonably reliable *estimates* of the size-distribution of farm-holdings will be evident enough, especially if an endeavour is made to include such cultivators as separated sons in whose names little land is officially registered. Panchayat Secretaries maintain old-style registers known as *khata*, which are used for revenue collection; unfortunately these registers, which ought to list the numbers of all the plots cultivated by each taxpayer, are not kept up-to-date[62] and have to be amended by reference to the *pahani* mentioned above, before they can be used as the basis of statistics of farm-holdings, as in my work.

It was also necessary to supplement this statistical material by numerous enquiries of cultivators – a job which is not made any easier by the fact that few cultivators know the survey numbers of their plots. This means that when a Panchayat Secretary is officially asked to prepare statistical tables relating to farm-holdings, he will have no alternative but to 'cook the figures' in the way he thinks best. There is a mystery here. I have never seen any such official figures which

[62] As a result the Secretary, maybe assisted by the Panchayat Chairman, 'negotiates' the tax due with each taxpayer.

distinguish the holdings of villagers and outsiders, even though size-distribution by caste is sometimes shown.[63]

Unregistered land
Unfortunately in such areas as Mahantalingapura, where there is some uncultivated land, there are two categories of privately cultivated farmland, known as *darkhast* and *karabu*, for which no acreages are available in the village records. *Darkhast* is officially allocated to landless people who pay little tax; *karabu*, on the other hand, is spontaneously 'appropriated' by the cultivator – it is usually, though not always, of rather poor quality.

APPENDIX II(2)
Karnataka Land Reform legislation

There are, perhaps, three main reasons why the literature on the effects of the Indian Land Reform legislation of the 1960s is very weak. First, the legislation, which is a matter for individual states, is very lengthy[64] and complex; second, the generally poor condition of the village land records would make it very difficult to ascertain the effects, even had there been no evasion; and third, is the difficulty of arriving at any estimate of the extent and nature of evasion, much of it (such as the ousting of tenants) having been in anticipation of the long expected commencement of the legislation.

However, in Anekal Taluk the Karnataka Land Reforms Act of 1961 (as subsequently amended), which did not come into effect until 1965, has lacked significance since the 'ceiling', provisions, relating to the maximum size of holding, did not lead to the compulsory breaking up of a single large holding.[65] Under Chapter IV of the Act, the ceiling for a family of less than six members is 10 acres of prime tank-irrigated land or 54 acres of dry land;[66] for every additional family member the ceiling is increased by 2 acres of prime tank-irrigated land or 10.8 acres of dry land – the absolute maxima being 20 and 108 acres respectively.

No doubt there were some large land-holders in Anekal Taluk who divided their land among their relatives in order to evade the ceiling, but if the example of the six villages is a reliable guide, as I think it is, the number would have been very small –

63 As in the series of *Village Survey Monographs* published by the census authorities following the 1961 population census; whether the land-holdings of outsiders are included is never stated.

64 Including the Land Reform Rules the Karnataka Act runs to 208 printed pages.

65 Information kindly provided by the Special Tahsildar of Anekal Taluk in July 1978. (The matter of the break-up of the *jodidar*'s estates is, of course, quite distinct.)

66 This is a summary. There are, in fact, four separate categories of land, of which these two are the most and the least valuable. The complicated formula involves counting each category as the equivalent of a certain number of units, the ceiling being the aggregate of units for each category.

for in those villages no evasion would have been necessary, all holdings being well below the ceiling. So far as dry land was concerned, this was no accident, for (as we know) holdings above 40 acres, or so, are necessarily very rare under our dry grain mode.

Although tenancy has been prohibited under the Act since 1974 this, also, is a matter of little significance, since the scarcity of farmland is such that larger land-holders have long lacked the incentive to rent out land – the only landlords of any importance having been the former *jodidars*. As for the small land-holders who, for one reason or another (usually involving poverty or decrepitude) decide to rent out their land, they are able to ignore the legislation with impunity – which is just as well.

APPENDIX II(3)

Simple technology

Given the small size of most farm-plots, and the small proportion of large farm-holdings of over (say) 20 acres, it is for agronomists to judge whether improved farm tools and other cultivating equipment, of a type (unlike tractors) which an ordinary farmer with (say) 5 to 15 acres could afford, would be likely to increase the yield of basic grains per acre in either region. On the supposition (it can be no more) that this is likely to be so, I have tentatively included 'simple technology' in the list of variables on p. 50 above, which is associated with the existence of our dry grain mode.

Two possibilities need to be distinguished: that with improved equipment, increased yields might result either from decreased labour inputs or from improved cultivation systems (labour requirements being unchanged). Given the high incidence of under-employment under our dry grain mode, the first possibility is of little interest; it is the second possibility which concerns us and which, unfortunately, must be left to the technical experts.

Cultivating equipment exclusive of ploughs

The evidence is that in both regions ordinary farm tools remain basically unchanged since they were described by Buchanan[67] and Clapperton[68] at the beginning of last century. The Hausa relied, and still rely, on a range of hoes; the cultivators of south-east Karnataka, on the other hand, had a much wider range of locally made

[67] On returning from the field in 1978 it was fascinating to find that the tools shown in Plates II, IV and X, for example, in Vol. I of Buchanan (1807) were identical with those used in the Anekal villages today.

[68] See Ch. XVI, p. 277, below on the large hoe, the *galma*, which was described by Clapperton, 1829. A list of Hausa farm-tools is given in Hill (1972), p. 242.

10 Several metal ploughs inside a Karnataka house

implements, including harrows and seed drills[69] which were hauled by cattle and hand tools such as picks and reaping hooks (sickles).

Ploughs

Colonial Departments of Agriculture were responsible for introducing metal ploughs in both regions in this century, though metal-tipped wooden ploughs were already in use in parts of south India. In both regions progress was slow in the early stages,[70] especially in Hausaland, where cultivators had hitherto owned no suitable plough oxen, and where there was little response until after 1945.[71] In the Anekal

[69] At the beginning of the last century British observers were delighted by the seed drills, weeding ploughs, etc. they saw – which are of similar design today. 'They have a variety of implements for husbandry purposes, some of which have only been introduced into England in the course of our recent improvements.' From a report on Indian agriculture, dated about 1820, cited in *Indian Science and Technology in the Eighteenth Century* by Dharampal, 1971, p. 185.

[70] In the 1920s official reports were full of complaints about the lack of response. Slater noted that there was only one metal plough in use in a village in Kolar District (Mysore) – *Some South Indian Villages*, ed. G. Slater, 1918, p. 105. In Mysore in 1935 there were recorded as being only 23,000 iron ploughs against 822,000 wooden ploughs. (*Report on the 4th Census of Livestock and Agricultural Implements*, Delhi, 1936.) See J. A. Voelcker, *Report on the Improvement of Indian Agriculture*, London, 1893, pp. 217 *et seq.*, for a sympathetic account of the resistance to metal ploughs expressed by ordinary farmers.

[71] See Ch. XVI, n. 15, below.

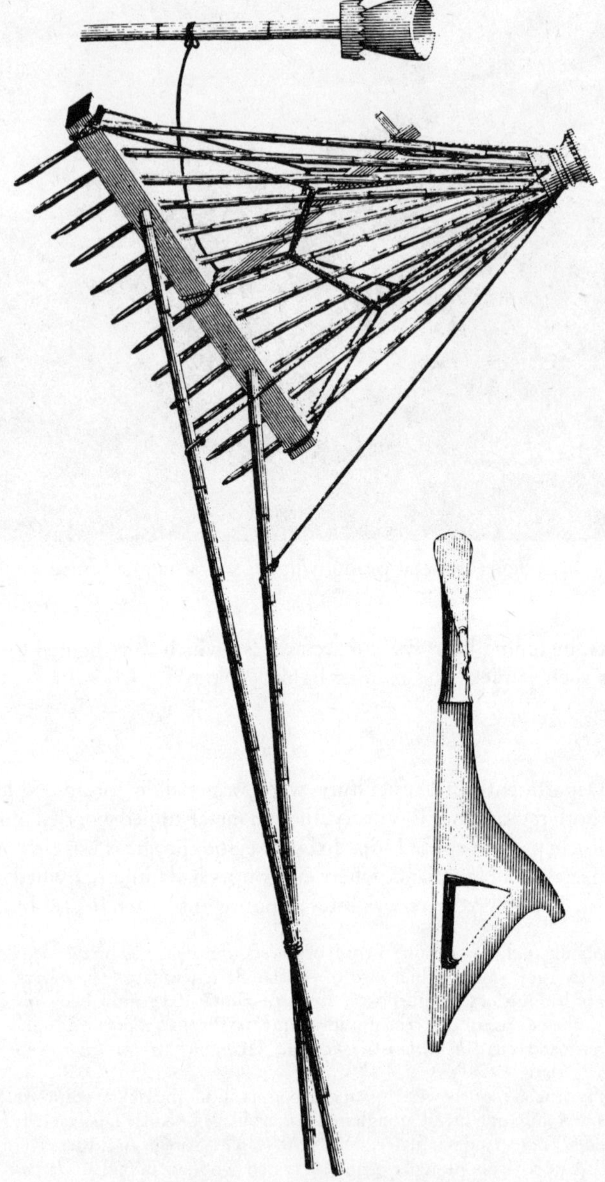

Fig. II(1) Seed drill and small hoe.
Source: F. Buchanan, *A Journey from Madras through the Countries of Mysore, Canara and Malabar* (1807), Vol. I, Plate XI.

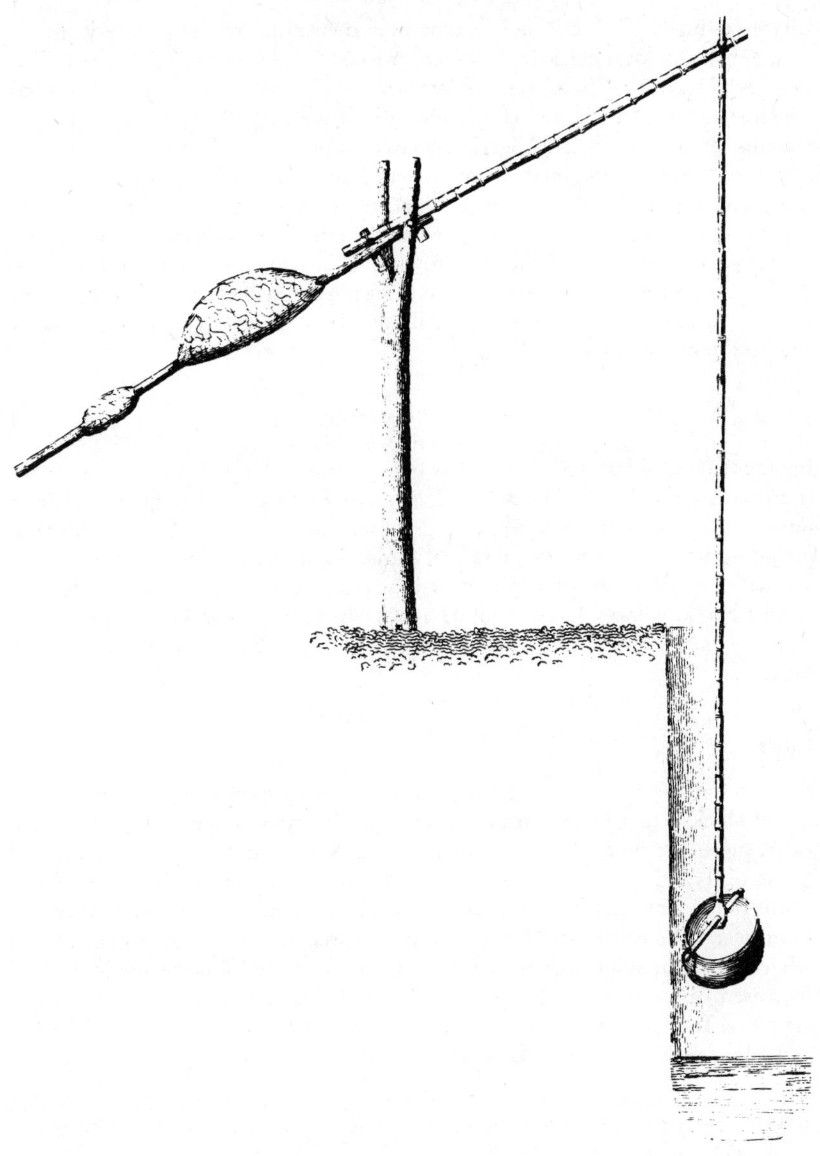

Fig. II(2) Simple manual water-lifting device of a type still found in both continents. Source: Buchanan (1807), Vol. I, Plate X.

villages virtually all Reddy households now own metal ploughs of very simple design made by local blacksmiths, which are considered superior to the primitive wooden plough (see Ch. XVI, p. 277) – which still has a number of special uses and which is also used by those who cannot afford the metal plough. Since ploughs manufactured in northern Nigeria replaced imported implements, statistics of ownership, which vary greatly from place to place,[72] have been lacking. While one of the greatest advantages of plough ownership derives from the speed with which the land may be prepared for sowing when the rains start, owners may be equally interested in the profits from hiring-out.[73] Plough design apart, it must be presumed that the efficiency of ploughing in south India is much reduced by the poor quality of many of the plough animals, especially the cows, owned by poorer cultivators and by the general lack of yokes.

Threshing

In Hausaland grain is hand-threshed by beating, much of it by women; as this work is most laborious and time wasting, all household produced grain is stored unthreshed in specially built outdoor granaries. In south India all types of grain, including paddy, are threshed on special yards, established by richer farmers, which are made by sealing farmland with cow dung after harvest; and threshed grain only is stored in the villages. Until about the 1920s when stone rollers (*gundu*), pulled by a pair of cattle, were introduced for threshing, the grain was usually trodden by cattle.

Carts

Considering the nature of the terrain and the exceedingly poor road network, it is not at all clear that Hausa farmers would benefit from the introduction of farm carts, given the ubiquity of the transport donkey, which links both farms and homesteads and villages and lorry routes. Any idea that the wooden farm carts of south India, with their two high spoked wheels, are 'traditional' is mistaken, for until nearly the end of last century country carts, at least in Mysore, had small wheels made of solid slabs of wood. (See Charlesworth[74] on the significance of increased cart ownership by richer farmers in Maharashtra at the end of last century.) The Hausa transport donkey has many advantages over the south Indian cart so far as village trading is concerned.

[72] There were 15 ploughs (and 36 plough oxen) in Batagarawa in 1968 and none in Dorayi in 1972. See Hill (1972), p. 308, on the importance of plough ownership in the Niger Republic.

[73] See Chap. XVI, n. 15 below.

[74] 'Rich Peasants and Poor Peasants in late Nineteenth-Century Maharashtra' by N. Charlesworth, in Dewey and Hopkins (eds.), 1978, pp. 102 and 105.

CHAPTER III

The Village Farmland

The vast literature on individual Indian villages is seldom much concerned with the concept of the village farmland. Are nucleated villages usually embedded in a tract of arable land, with visible or well-known boundaries, which pertains to that particular village, perhaps because most (if not all) of the farmland there is owned by resident villagers? If that were so (which it is *not* in Anekal Taluk), would it tend to follow that resident villagers cultivate little farmland outside their 'village area'? I think that such questions cannot, in general, be answered because they are seldom asked.

The process of domesticating or taming the land under our dry grain mode commonly enhances its topography. Much of the great dry, flat plateau of northern Hausaland would be topographically featureless had not human beings or households, usually as members of wider communities, introduced useful trees and crops and erected appropriate domestic architecture. At Batagarawa it was amazing to witness, in the space of a few months, the conversion by the members of the village of an apparent desert, with its dry soils swirling in the wind, into a great tropical garden, carpeted with groundnuts, the sorghum (guinea corn) standing up to 15 or 20 ft. While undulating south-eastern Karnataka is scenically far more varied and attractive, with its hills, standing rocks, temples, tanks and streams, the tracts of arable land are as visually uniform and depressing as rural Hausaland when unclothed with vegetation.

In both regions the arable dry tracts are commonly devoid of natural boundaries. In south-eastern Karnataka, where farmland has been taxed for centuries, the British found an administrative need to carve up the territory of the various Taluks into Village Areas (revenue areas),[1] each nowadays bearing the name of the principal settlement within it – several such areas comprising the land of a modern Village Panchayat.[2] But, as a

[1] The Survey Settlement of Anekal Taluk was not completed until 1891.
[2] See Appendix III(1).

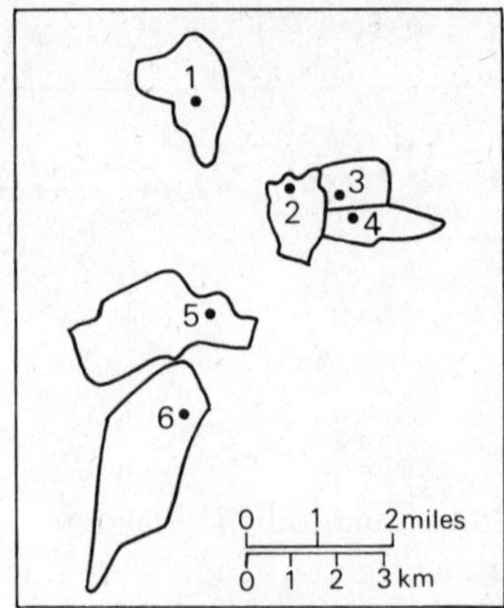

Fig. III(1) Sketch-map of the 'village areas' of (1) Hullahalli, (2) Nanjapura, (3) Vabasandra, (4) Kyalasanahalli (within which Srirampura is situated), (5) Bukkasagara and (6) Mahantalingapura. The location of the principal village giving its name to each area is shown, but it will be remembered (p. 28) that there are also other settlements within most areas. See, also, Fig. III(2). Source: *Census Handbook* for Bangalore District, 1971.

glance at the Taluk maps showing Village boundaries[3] at once reveals, the resultant mosaic pattern derives from surveyors, who love straight lines, rather than from the cultivating practices of the local inhabitants or the natural topography – thus, boundaries often run through the middle of irrigation tanks.

In Hausa localities of dispersed settlement the concept of 'village area' has little meaning in relation to farmland and refers primarily to the general area in which the habitations are located. While each household belongs to a named Village Area,[4] under the authority of an appointed Village Head, the boundaries of these administrative areas are to such a degree vague or indeterminate that their very existence is doubtful:[5] as one Dorayi farmer put it, it is the general direction of the boundaries, rather than their actual location on the ground, which is known. This makes good sense, for the right to cultivate or to buy farmland is unrelated to the 'Village' of

[3] In the case of Bangalore District these are only available, so far as I know, in the *District Census Handbooks*, Census of India, 1971. (Of course, there are maps for each Village Area, showing plot boundaries, and survey registration numbers; but these are very roughly drawn, unprinted, very out-of-date and difficult to obtain. See Appendix III(2).)

[4] For the sake of clarity, I capitalise 'Village', 'Hamlet' etc., when referring to administrative units.

[5] This is reflected in the lack of maps. See Hill (1977), p. 77, for reference to a District map which failed to record the existence of a Village which had come into existence at least thirty years before the map was issued.

residence – and there is no tax on farmland. While it happens that at Dorayi the demarcation lines which one could readily sketch around groups of habitations belonging to any particular Village Area[6] did not interpenetrate, this may not everywhere be so. While each household is likewise assigned to a Hamlet,[7] the boundaries of Hamlet lands are even more faintly conceptualised than those of Villages, though the habitations often form quite distinct clusters.

In terms of population the administrative Hamlet of Batagarawa consisted of a congested nucleated settlement, a *gari*,[8] together with 26 dispersed houses, most of which lay within about a half and one mile of the *gari* in the zone of manured farmland (*karakara*) which surrounded it.[9] There, as at Dorayi, the administrative boundaries were rather vaguely conceptualised and the right to cultivate bush (unmanured) farmland in any locality was unrelated to the Hamlet or Village of residence. But Batagarawa was quite unlike Dorayi in that virtually all the farmland in the manured zone was owned by Batagarawa residents, who were prohibited by the village authorities from selling such land to non-residents and who, until quite recently, had had to hand over their farms to the District Head, to dispose of as he wished, if they migrated.[10] So if a stranger wished to acquire *karakara* at Batagarawa he had first to get permission, which was usually readily granted, to take up residence there.

Whereas Dorayi cultivators might well happen to be unclear as to the location of each of their farm-plots in terms of Village Area, this is, of course, not true in the Anekal villages where each registered farm-plot is included in the list of one Village Area. (These lists were not amalgamated when villages were grouped in Panchayats in the 1960s.) Even so, the boundaries of the Village Areas are not known to the inhabitants in detail – in other words, the position of the lines joining the four boundary pillars

6 See Hill (1977), Fig. 5, which was drawn with the help of the aerial photograph.

7 But to such a degree does the concept of 'Hamlet' depend on a person, not on the land, that if a popular Hamlet Head dies no successor may be appointed, so that the Hamlet effectively ceases to exist for the time being.

8 In his semantic study of the extraordinary Hausa word *gari*, D. Dalby has provided 203 examples of its usage, ranging from its basic meaning of village or town with its surrounding lands to any part or aspect of a settlement and its community, including centre of habitation, human population, local weather and sky. See Hill (1977), Appendix I(2), '"*Gari*" and the concept of settlement'.

9 For a sketch-map of the manured zone showing farm boundaries and dispersed homesteads see Hill (1972), Fig. 6.

10 Despite having made fairly widespread enquiries on this matter in Kano, Katsina and Kazaure Emirates, I cannot say how general such prohibitions are, or were, except that they would not have existed in localities of dispersed settlement; also, pilgrims who went overland to Mecca in former times could always retain their land, however long their absence.

(which are supposed to exist) are not generally known except to those who own plots near the boundary.[11] But Anekal resembles Dorayi in that resident villagers are free to sell their plots in their village to whomsoever they wish, with the result, as we shall see, that large proportions of plots in all the Village Areas are owned by non-residents.

Under our dry grain mode farmers have a particularly strong preference for cultivating land within a radius of two or three miles of their habitations – were this not so, an even larger proportion of the farmland in the Village Areas would be cultivated by non-residents.[12] Among the numerous reasons for this (aside from the obvious wish under any system to save time in walking to the various fields for cultivation purposes) are: the need for regular inspection of crops on scattered plots; the great labour of transporting grain to the village or homestead for threshing and storage; the burden of transporting manure in the opposite direction; and the need for constant supervision of daily-paid farm labourers, who require food on the farm. In the Anekal villages where there are no pack animals, and where most farm-plots are inaccessible to farm carts, these arguments have even more cogency than in Hausaland; besides, as Buchanan implied long ago, the custom of living in congested settlements, rather than dispersedly, increases the average distance between habitation and farm-plot within a village area.

> A great impediment to good cultivation arises from a practice very common in India, of all the farmers living in towns and villages. The fields that are distant from the houses cannot receive manure, and of course produce little . . . . No one will give more than a fourth of the valuation for lands that are distant from his village.[13]

Owing to the abolition of the large hereditary estates in Karnataka; to the replacement of farm-slaves by daily-paid farm labourers in Hausaland; as well as, presumably,[14] to the declining yields per acre under our dry grain mode – for these and other reasons urban dwellers have become less interested in cultivating village land than formerly, a matter which will be discussed in Chapter XII on 'the withdrawal from the countryside'. So while it is true that a large proportion of the farmland in each of the Anekal Village Areas is owned and cultivated by non-residents, most of them are

[11] This is customary, for according to Rice's edition of the *Mysore Gazetteer*, Vol. I, 1897, p. 692, no permanent boundary marks had ever been erected prior to the Revenue Survey of the late nineteenth century.

[12] As population densities increase and land gets scarcer, the objections to farming further away from home presumably diminish.

[13] Buchanan, 1807, Vol. III, p. 427.

[14] This presumption is in turn based on the presumptions of declining cattle populations and manure supplies.

not townsmen but inhabitants of nearby villages within a radius of (say) five miles. The general evidence for both regions would seem to be that, under our dry grain mode, low proportions of village farmland are owned by urban-dwellers except possibly in attractive localities which are very close to large towns or cities – and even then the farmland has to be readily accessible by motor vehicle.

For four Anekal Village Areas[15] it was possible to estimate the proportion of the farmland which was owned by outsiders: the figures ranged between 22% and 53%. The details for Nanjapura showed that the owners of the 51 plots which were registered in the names of outsiders lived in at least ten different nearby villages and that few, if any, of them were resident in Bangalore. Owing to vagueness about boundaries, it was impossible to make similar estimates for Dorayi – where the 'interpenetration of Village Areas' was certainly very high.

Before examining some of the implications of this interpenetration,[16] I must consider some of its causes – though to a large degree there is no need to look for special causes considering that the nearest farmland to a particular homestead quite often happens to be in a different Village Area. First, is the fact that Village Areas sometimes have very odd shapes, it being nothing unusual, at least in Anekal Taluk, for the main settlement to be quite near the boundary of the village land – see Appendix III(2) for an example. Second, the inhabitants of nearby villages often know each other very well, many of them being linked by marriage, so that there is nothing odd about selling a farm to someone from another village. Third, men sometimes migrate to a nearby village on marriage to live near their wife's parents, particularly in Anekal Taluk where sonless men commonly invite their daughter's husbands to live with them as substitute sons (*iltam*); such migrants may retain, or later inherit, farmland in their natal area. Fourth, are the consequences of differential rates of population change resulting from migration or special hardship; in former times many Anekal Village Areas became wholly depopulated, all the farmland being, in due course, taken up by outsiders.[17] Fifth, in both regions land is sometimes inherited by daughters, usually because they are brotherless; when they migrate on

15 Reliable estimates could not be made for Mahantalingapura and Srirampura.

16 It is a matter which has been ignored by nearly all writers, exceptions being Mencher (see n. 18 below) and Chambers and Harriss who noted (in Farmer (ed.), 1977, p. 303) that in two North Arcot villages outsiders owned no less than 54% of the land.

17 I have found no reference to uninhabited villages (*becharkh*) in publications other than census reports where, decade after decade, they are solemnly included in the lists of villages, although no statistics other than the areas of different categories of land are shown against them. In Anekal Taluk, where 23 of the 223 listed villages are uninhabited, accounting for 4% of the rural land, I think that most, if not all, of them lost their population as long ago as the great famine of 1876–8.

marriage they may retain their farmland, possibly leaving it in the care of relatives. Sixth, rich Anekal cultivators may hope that no one will notice that their total holding is above the ceiling imposed by Land Reform if their plots are included in more than one register.[18] Finally, it is worth noting that when groups of migrants establish new hamlets on a site in any Village Area, their population will inflate that of the named village in that area in the population census, even though much of the land they cultivate may be in another Village Area.

For all these and other reasons, there is apt to be a lack of correspondence between the village, considered as a residential unit, and the village land which is presumed to surround it: putting the matter another way, it is fallacious to suppose that villages as corporate units own neatly demarcated tracts of arable land.[19] Under our dry grain mode the incidence of farm-selling (often to outsiders) was apt, until fairly recently, to be so high that nucleated villages should be seen as residential clusters of farming households which, in diagrammatic terms, own decreasing proportions of the farmland in each successive concentric ring of farmland as one moves away from the village site – such a diagram being centred on the individual habitation in localities of dispersed settlement. I think this is a matter of great significance both because it does so much to demolish the conventional, sentimental, traditional notion of the semi-autonomous, if not self-sufficient, village community, neatly tucked into its land, and because, as we shall see, it invalidates so many statistical calculations which implicitly relate villagers and 'their land'. (It, also, incidentally, greatly complicates the task of field workers, as well as reducing the reliability of their findings; it is even necessary to omit cultivators whose farmland lies mainly outside their village from tables showing the size-distribution of farm-holdings.[20])

The failure to give any proper thought to the concept of 'village land' in south India lies behind the extraordinary refusal to list 'new' hamlets separately in the population census unless (in Bangalore District at least), they have populations of 500 or more[21] – a refusal which has had momentous statistical consequences. In this discussion of the ownership of village land by outsiders, it would have been logical, in some cases, to regard the hamlet-dwellers as the equivalent of outsiders. The land owned

[18] For an excellent discussion of this whole question see *Agriculture and Social Structure in Tamil Nadu* by Joan P. Mencher, 1978, pp. 97 *et seq*.

[19] It is true that at Batagarawa the villagers owned nearly all the manured farmland around the village as they were prohibited from selling it to outsiders without permission; but I think that it was an atypical village owing to being the seat of that rare dignitary, a District Head.

[20] For obvious reasons, this was a particularly serious problem at Dorayi, but it also caused considerable difficulty in certain of the Anekal villages.

[21] See p. 202 below for discussion of this important question.

by the Bhovi inhabitants of the hamlet of Chattekerepalya,[22] which is situated within the Hullahalli Village Area, is still the separate block which was allotted to them by the former *jodidar* over half a century ago. The Bhovi arrived as strangers and in a sense they are strangers still.

The idea that compact villages are primarily residential clusters of farming households dotted about in a sea of arable and grazing land, allows one to lay stress on the political, social, religious and economic interdependence of villages; it also enables one to see that the principles of residential nucleation and dispersal are not so different as is commonly supposed. The common nineteenth century belief in the economic autarchy and political autonomy of the Indian village[23] unconsciously postulated the existence of village boundaries with functions which they did not possess.

APPENDIX III(1)

Village Panchayats

The Karnataka Village Panchayats and Local Boards Act, 1959, which was concerned to give effect to the process of democratic decentralisation ('Panchayat Raj'), which had been envisaged by Article 40 of the Indian constitution, was much more successful than any previous legislative attempt to devolve a whole range of functions onto village councils. (Earlier attempts had included the Mysore Local Boards and Village Panchayats Regulation VI of 1918 under which Village Panchayats had been set up in 16 Anekal villages; and the Mysore Village Panchayat Regulation, 1926, which was passed with the object, among others, of placing village self-government on a statutory basis.)

Under the 1959 Act the population of a Panchayat, which ordinarily consisted of groups of revenue villages, was to lie between 1,500 and 10,000. They were to be run by groups of members elected by the entire adult population (not less than 11 or more than 19 members, with prescribed numbers of seats for members of Scheduled castes and women), one of whom was elected chairman by the members themselves. The Panchayats had both obligatory and discretionary functions, the list of the former being very lengthy and including matters, such as the construction of public latrines, which are invariably neglected, as well as general concerns such as 'the promotion and development of economic conditions with reference to agriculture'. The long list of descretionary functions included 'establishment and maintenance of markets', implementation of schemes for 'village and cottage' industries and the welfare of Harijans. The annual government grant was fixed at 30% of the land

22 See Appendix X(3).

23 See 'The Indian Village: Myth and Reality' by M. N. Srinivas in *Studies in Social Anthropology*, ed. J. M. Beattie *et al.*, 1975, p. 47.

revenue collection of the village, based on the average collection over a period of five years.

Following the abolition of hereditary village officers, the duties of the former *shanbhogs* were assumed by the appointed secretary of the Village Panchayat, who was responsible for all record keeping relating to land revenue (a formidable task considering that the work, which is complicated enough, had usually previously been done by several *shanbhogs*), as well as for revenue collection, in which task he is assisted by the chairman – who, in many cases, was a former hereditary *patel* of one of the villages. The only elected member who appears to have much status owing to his position is the chairman, who is constantly personally blamed, both publicly and privately, for 'all the things that don't happen in the village'. But the elections are taken seriously, and are very orderly, as I witnessed for myself on 8 July 1978, when they were at last held after many years of postponement.

So far as my limited experience went, the apathy of the Village Panchayats was summed up by the fact that they could seldom summon a quorum:[24] statutorily obliged to meet at least once monthly, they actually met most infrequently – the common reply to 'When did you last meet?' being 'I can't remember'. So almost everything seems to depend on the personality and efficiency of the chairman and the ability of the secretary to handle his arduous duties. In 1978, when secretaries had no official offices or houses (in that year it was proposed that small houses should be built), their working conditions were usually well nigh intolerable, seated as they were in tiny rented rooms, surrounded by a sea of paper.

Whether the setting up of these organisations has done much to enhance inter-village co-operation and to promote development it is too early to say – most of the secretaries were not appointed until about 1970 and they are constantly moved from one village to another. But the fact that one chairman has usually replaced three, four or five village headmen (*patels*) seems to have created a gap in leadership, especially when the villages are not close together.

APPENDIX III(2)
Maps of village farmland

As I have already published maps of the farmland showing farm boundaries for Batagarawa and Dorayi – Hill (1972), Fig. 6, and Hill (1977), Fig. 6 – as well as aerial photographs for Batagarawa on which many details, including farm boundaries, habitations, trees, animals, etc. can be seen, I am not reproducing this material here, but provide only a rough sketch relating to the farmland of Nanjapura in 1923.

[24] *Report on the Administration of the Village Panchayats for the Year 1928–29* (Karnataka State Archives) made the same complaint about the working of the 1926 Act. The inability of the Village Panchayats to spend more than a small part of their income was there attributed 'partly to poverty'. 'For various reasons the spirit of self reliance is now largely dormant and the low condition is largely responsible.' (p. 8).

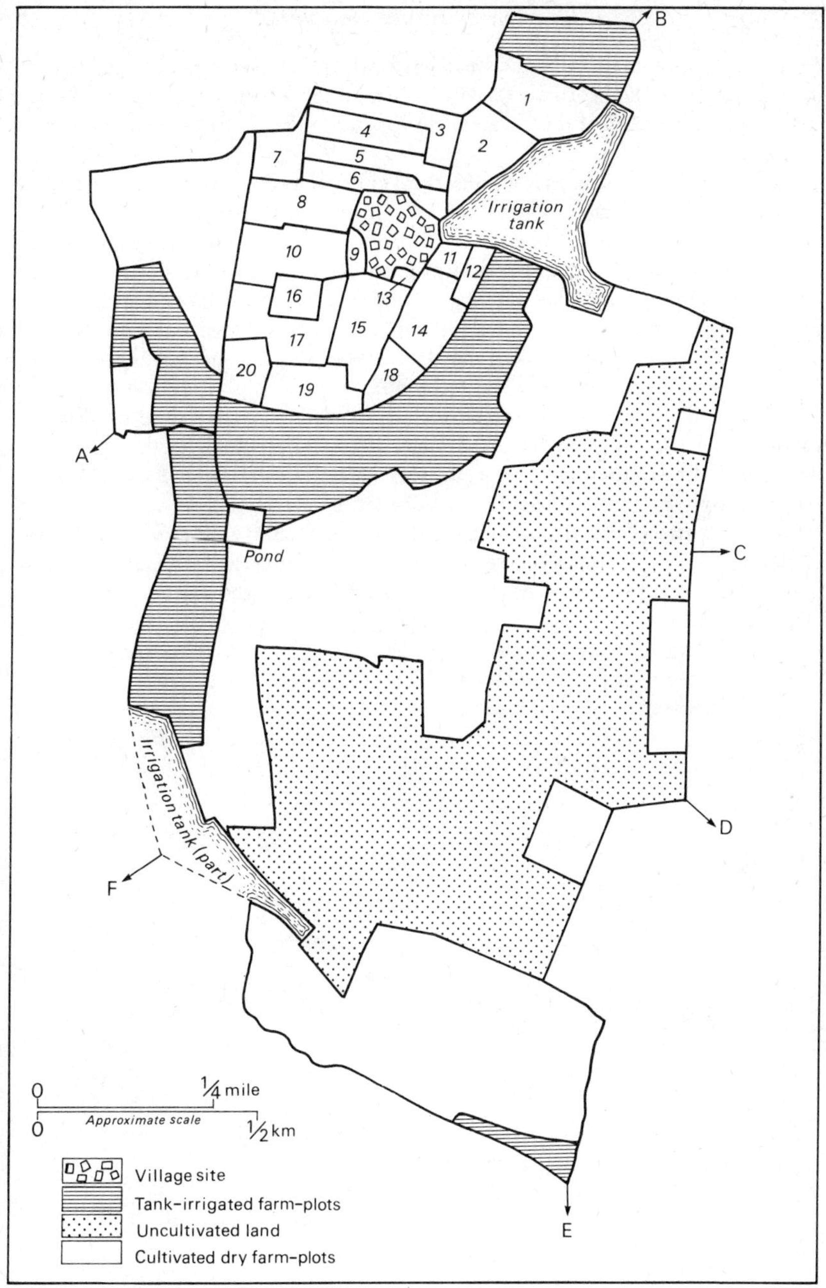

Fig. III(2) Sketch-map of Nanjapura village land, 1923.
N.B. To simplify the map, farm boundaries are shown only for 20 dry farms round the village site. The Nanjapura village land shares a common boundary with Hulimangala between arrows A and B, the boundaries with five other village areas also being indicated with arrows.

Although the original Nanjapura map from which the sketch is taken (it is very roughly drawn and not printed) is dated 1940, I think it had not been revised since 1923 – probably most of the village maps for Bangalore District are likewise very out of date.

As the sketch shows, in 1923 about a third of the Nanjapura village area consisted of an uncultivated tract, which was presumably partly used for grazing; the remainder was divided into about 120 farm-plots. According to the village records in 1978 there were 252 registered farm-plots of which 48 were portions of the original grazing ground; but for reasons discussed in Appendix II(1) the actual number of plots was bound to have been far larger. The 1978 records indicated that 75 of the plots shown on the 1923 map had not been divided meanwhile – another figure which is bound to be much too low.

It seems likely that the figures in the 1971 census report relating to different categories of land must be based on material contemporary with the 1923 map. Thus, according to the 1971 census, the total area of the village land was 566 acres, of which only 254 acres was cultivated dry farmland, as much as 153 acres being 'cultivable waste' (defined as uncultivated for more than five successive years); but according to the detailed village records in 1978 the total area of cultivated dry land was as large as 476 acres – of which, incidentally, 118 acres was cultivated by outsiders.

From the sketch map it will be noted that the Nanjapura village site (the built-up area) is very near the boundary with Hulimangala, being situated near a tank. (Much of Nanjapura's tank-irrigated land is fed from a tank in another village area.) The Nanjapura village land, which has an unnatural ragged shape, shares common boundaries with a total of six villages.

CHAPTER IV

The Farming Household: (1) Joint Households

Owing to the difficulty, in both regions, of distinguishing 'farm-labouring households' from households which are mainly dependent on farming their own land; and owing, as we have seen, to the very low proportions of 'non-farming households' whose members never work on the land – it seems practicable to regard the latter type of household as anomalous to the degree that in most contexts we can effectively regard the entire population as organised in 'farming households', the working members of which all contribute to the household income. On the one hand farming households (or households as I shall often call them) are seen as the basic productive unit; on the other hand it is necessary to emphasise the high degree of economic interplay between them, especially owing to the importance of farm-labouring. It follows that economic inequality, which is one of the most inherent features of our dry grain mode, has to be conceptualised and assessed in terms of households (not individuals) – households which come in many shapes and sizes and have many varying characteristics.

As we have seen in Chapter II, the basic kin structure of farming households in the two regions is remarkably similar. Since very low proportions of household members are unrelated to the household head, whether by blood, marriage or adoption, I shall not clutter these pages with a detailed analysis of the kin structure of all the households,[1] but shall rather plunge into a discussion of the most central organisational issue determining the size, strength and viability of individual households, namely the degree to which fathers (or widowed mothers in Anekal[2]) are successful in retaining the services of their married sons.

Under our dry grain mode, which applies only to localities where population density is so high that most reasonably accessible farmland is under regular cultivation, we may take it as axiomatic that *married sons*

[1] But see Table V(3), p. 113 for a summary analysis for the Anekal villages of houses headed by men and women respectively.

[2] Few Hausa households are headed by women – see p. 112 below.

usually find considerable difficulty in establishing independent, viable households which are mainly dependent on farming their own land, unless they receive some help from their father – or in Anekal Taluk from their widowed mother. On the other hand, we may take it as axiomatic, on general grounds,[3] that *fathers prefer family labour to hired labour*, so that they are usually anxious to retain the services of their married sons,[4] especially as the heads of large extended households are apt to be well respected by the village community. It follows that fathers who are in the prime of life are capable of exerting more power over their sons than *vice versa*, a situation which will become reversed if they survive until their dotage. Nor are the heads of impoverished households, which cultivate little or no land, necessarily any exception to this rule, for such fathers often value the greater security provided by larger family labour forces, as they increase the chance that at least one member will be employed on any particular day.

The degree to which fathers actually exert their superior power against the wishes of their sons, obviously depends on numerous factors, including mutual love and respect or hatred and fear, overcrowding of the parental home, the attitudes of women (which are often crucial), the feasibility of dividing the farmland, the risk of driving sons to migrate, and so forth. In short, every father of a married son, and every married son of a surviving father, is likely sooner or later to be faced with the need to calculate and compromise – there being, as we shall see, no standard solution or expectations,[5] as in Western industrial society where each newly married couple is regarded as 'entitled to' its own habitation.

As Dorayi is a peculiar case, I shall start by comparing the position of married sons in Batagarawa and the Anekal villages. Some very simple statistics make a clear point, which is that in both regions the majority of resident married sons[6] are not economically detached from their fathers. In Batagarawa only 10 (14%) of the 69 resident married sons had left *gandu* and were farming on their own account – and they were the sons of only six

[3] Fathers would never stoop to calculate (if they could) the relative costs of family and hired labour, for the preference for the former derives, especially in the Anekal villages, from its superior exploitability and instant availability, as well as from its greater reliability, so that it requires no supervision.

[4] Though in the Anekal villages, where many of the houses are so small and where everyone is apt to sleep in the same room, fathers may urge sons with large families to remove. (See Hobson, 1978, p. 117, for the sexual implications of such lack of privacy.) See Appendix IV(4).

[5] Except in Dorayi where, as we shall see, married sons almost always live with their fathers.

[6] A resident married son is, of course, a man whose father, as well as himself, is resident in the village.

fathers; in the Anekal villages only 67 (29%) of the total of 229 resident married sons had separated from their fathers or widowed mothers.

In both regions relatively very few parents had been abandoned by all their resident married sons. Only 2 out of 43 fathers (of resident married sons) were in this plight in Batagarawa; the corresponding figures for fathers and widowed mothers in the Anekal villages having been 16 (11%) of a total of 148 parents[7] – as many as 7 of whom had resident unmarried sons who would be expected to remain at home after marriage.

As for the extent to which married sons leave the village in order to escape from their parental home, this is obviously rather hard to assess,[8] especially in Anekal Taluk where fathers sometimes urge their sons to remove in the hope that, sooner or later, they will benefit from financial remittances. But even there only about 61 married sons (21% of the total) had migrated compared with 229 who remained at home. In Batagarawa it was clear that most of the young men who migrated came from poorer households which gave them little hope for the future.

In overcrowded Dorayi where, paradoxically, fathers cling to their married sons as though they were life rafts, only 4 of the 211 resident married sons had separated from their fathers and only about 20 married sons had migrated – none of them in order to take up farming in less densely populated localities.[9] However, about two-fifths of the resident married sons had fathers who had retired from farming – some of them prematurely, since the promise of retirement before old age had set in was often a sop offered to sons to dissuade them from migrating.

As already noted, in both regions the death of a surviving parent commonly results in the separation of any co-resident married brothers. In Batagarawa the number of actual fraternal *gandaye* (sing. *gandu*) was only 7 – representing but 19% of the potential number;[10] in the Anekal villages the corresponding proportion was 24% – 15 cases out of a potential total of 62.

BIG HOUSES

I now digress by referring to one of the most astonishing features of the densely populated inner ring of the Kano Close Settled Zone, which has been the development, during this century, of exceedingly large houses or compounds, inhabited by a number of separate households, nearly all of the male members of which are paternal kinsmen, who are descended in

[7] Resident sons-in-law are here regarded as the equivalent of sons.

[8] See Chapter X. [9] See p. 197.

[10] The potential number is, of course, the number of sets of resident, parentless, married brothers.

many instances from one man.[11] The growth of these big houses, which may be the home of 200 people or more,[12] and which are extraordinary in world terms, is a direct response to the persistent and intensifying pressure of population on the farmland as well as to that connected factor, which has just been discussed, the exceptional life-time cohesion of fathers and married sons. As it was not always possible to ascertain how many separate households there were in a very big house,[13] I dealt with the size-distribution of big houses in Dorayi in terms of the numbers of married men who dwelt there; over a third (38%) of the total Dorayi population lived in the 24 big houses inhabited by seven or more married men and their dependants, the largest of which was the home of 22 married men, or 106 people. (In Batagarawa, by contrast, no house was inhabited by more than five married men.)

These big houses are not mere conglomerations of paternally related kinsmen and their wives and other dependants. Like other houses (*gida*) they have a single household head (*mai gida*), and most of them have a single entrance. Some big houses include a network of mud-walled paths leading to architecturally distinct 'sections' (households), the whole having the air of a tiny compact village[14] (*gari*); at the other extreme the unpartitioned compound erroneously appears to consist of a wholly haphazard conglomeration of huts, granaries, open working-places, shade trees and so forth.

Big houses are very stable domestic organisations which tend to expand fast,[15] particularly as separate sections never hive off intact. As they grow the house site increases in size, encroaching on the surrounding farmland, so that they are seldom, if ever,[16] found in nucleated villages, which are usually far too congested. One of the functions of big houses is to provide 'nodes on the economic landscape' in localities of dispersed settlement where social centres are otherwise singularly lacking. One big house, the home of 71 people, resembled a species of market-place, serving both outsiders and residents – the latter being able to buy nearly all their food requirements from their co-resident kin.

[11] There were some anomalous cases, such as the big house some of whose members were descended from a deceased slave owner, others from three of his slaves.

[12] The biggest house I visited, which was just outside Dorayi, was inhabited by at least 41 married men.

[13] See Hill (1977), p. 187. (As it was impossible to base the analysis of economic inequality in anomalous Dorayi on households, the married man together with any dependent married sons was the basic unit – fraternal *gandaye* were exceptionally rare there.)

[14] See a detailed diagram, based on a large-scale aerial photograph, of such a very large house in Hill (1977), Fig. 7.

[15] The rate of migration from big houses is lower than from other houses.

[16] On the geographical distribution of big houses see Hill (1977), Appendix XII(2).

The big houses are a bizarre expression of the possible consequences, in localities of dispersed settlement under our dry grain mode, of anomalously high and increasing population densities: they are an interesting indication of what can happen in extreme circumstances, but not of what is generally in the least likely to happen.

JOINT HOUSEHOLDS AS FARMING UNITS

I come now to the nub of this chapter which is a comparison of the Hausa institution of *gandu* and the Karnataka joint household, both of them being essentially regarded, for present limited purposes, as productive organisations or farming units. Under our dry grain mode, where (as we have seen) the interests of fathers and married sons are liable not to coincide, and where fathers are apt, until they are old, to have more power over sons than *vice versa*, the means by, and extent to which, the parties achieve some kind of *modus vivendi* is clearly of the highest interest.

The literature on the Indian joint family (or household) is so voluminous, and *The Household Dimension of the Family in India*[17] by A. M. Shah provides such an excellent and capacious critical review of the main Indian field studies,[18] that there is certainly no need to attempt another overview here. However, it is necessary to start by noting the distinction between 'the principles of jointness', which operate at all times, and the manner and extent to which these principles take expression in the actual existence of joint households – which is our concern here. (The principles of jointness regulate the distribution of jointly owned property both to the so-called co-parceners, who are all males, and to those whom S. J. Tambiah[19] has denoted 'the fringe of female members composed of incoming wives and daughters of the house', all of whom have rights of maintenance, the incoming wives even as widows and the daughters until marriage.)

The literature on *gandu* in Hausaland is comparatively very slight.[20] However, it has an interesting degree of historical depth since the contemporary version of *gandu*, at least in Batagarawa, is very similar to

[17] Subtitled *A Field Study in a Gujarat Village and a Review of other Studies*, 1974.

[18] Later sources include *Caste and Kinship in Kangra* by J. P. Parry, 1979 and Sarah Hobson, 1978.

[19] 'Dowry and Bridewealth and the Property Rights of Women in South Asia', in *Bridewealth and Dowry* by J. Goody and S. J. Tambiah, 1973, p. 78.

[20] It is very briefly reviewed in Hill (1972), pp. 249–50, which includes references to G. Nicolas's writings on *gandu* among the Hausa of the Niger Republic; the first significant treatment of *gandu* in Nigerian Hausaland is in *The Economy of Hausa Communities of Zaria* by M. G. Smith, 1955.

that which regulated the labour of privately owned farm slaves, the elements of which are well understood,[21] partly because farm-slavery ended so recently that it is still remembered by older people. The terminology remains unchanged: the erstwhile farm slaves worked in *gandu* on their owner's *gandu* farms, alongside their owner's sons, and were granted plots (*gayauna*) which they could cultivate in their spare time, on their own account, as are the sons-in-*gandu* today. In Kano Emirate the farm slaves even resembled the sons in having the right to demand their freedom.[22]

The two main conclusions of this discussion are now anticipated, since they may whet the appetite of readers. They are, first, that the two-generational Indian joint household, *considered merely as a farming organisation*, is not nearly so peculiar as Indianists often suppose; and second that there is no evidence from the Anekal villages that the compromise which its actual existence reflects is less acceptable than in former times – indeed, for demographic and other reasons, it is possible that 'the incidence of jointness' is actually on the increase.

There are two common statistical definitions of the two-generational Indian joint household:[23] in the one case it includes at least *one* married son, in the other at least *two*. Considering that the second of these generations would never be applied to *gandu*,[24] it might be thought better, for comparative purposes, to reject it in Karnataka – were it not that Karnataka villagers and urban-dwellers alike strongly prefer it and were it not, also, that Anekal parents are seldom abandoned by all their married sons.[25] So I follow local preference by adopting the 'two son' definition.

At first sight, the important differences between the joint households in the two regions are so marked as to negate any attempt to emphasise the resemblances between important institutions in the two regions – resemblances which justify the concept of a dry grain mode. First, the Anekal joint household, unlike its Hausa counterpart, is legally a joint property-owning group. Second, the subordinate members of the Anekal households, unlike their Hausa counterparts, enjoy very little, if any, economic autonomy, and are generally subjugated to a much greater degree. And, third, which is an associated matter, Hausa sons, not only fathers, have

[21] See Chapter XIII below.

[22] More precisely, they had the right to demand that they be temporarily released to earn the necessary ransom money for their total freedom.

[23] For the time being, 'joint household' excludes fraternal joint households.

[24] The Hausa word *gandu*, as used in villages, has many varieties and levels of meaning and might well refer to any kin group cultivating the same land. See Hill (1972), p. 38.

[25] As we are concerned with compromise, there would be no point in studying a situation which gave sons hardly any power of choice.

recognised rights, as well as obligations, in relation to their farming work, as the Anekal sons have not.

But if we examine these salient differences in relation to each other, we can see that the bundles of rights and obligations[26] (or lack thereof) in the two regions are all attempts to deal with the same inescapable dilemma: how to maintain family property intact over the generations, while giving the younger generation of men (not so much women) a fair deal. Of course this dilemma is apt to exist in all societies, but it has particular significance under our dry grain mode owing both to the scarcity of farmland and to the fact that young men acquire no automatic rights over land from a lineage or community, as so commonly in West African societies,[27] so that they have to be launched by their fathers.

If, for the sake of comparison, *gandu* be regarded as a voluntary institution, the Karnataka joint household as involving compulsory elements, we can begin to understand the nature of the compromises involved – for the reason that both represent ideal principles, which are partly ignored, partly followed.

In fact sons in the Anekal villages very seldom take their fathers to court in order to obtain their legal share of the household property, even if, as often happens, they sell farmland or cattle without consultation and semi-secretly incur massive debts which are then 'joint debts'. And, *in fact*, profligate Batagarawa fathers, who recklessly sell inherited farmland against the wishes of their sons, are apt to be despised, even restrained by fellow villagers.

Then, take the question of the degree of economic autonomy accorded to Hausa sons, who are by no means invariably at their father's beck and call. The point here is that fathers accept the principle that the voluntary work undertaken on the *gandu* by their sons should not be full-time – for the *gandu* is not their property. Anekal sons, on the other hand, must devote themselves entirely to the welfare of the household.

As for the complicated collection of rights and obligations which links fathers and sons in *gandu*, these follow the principle that the system is not voluntary in detail so long as father and son agree to remain together – in other words there are customary rules to be observed provided the parties do not separate, as they are perfectly entitled to do. The Anekal fathers and sons, on the other hand, have no list of rights and obligations: the father as the manager of the jointly owned property is entitled to give orders, on the supposition that he alone knows what is best for all concerned.

These questions will be pursued further. Meanwhile I examine the

[26] For particulars see Appendix IV(1).
[27] See my chapter on the West African farming household in J. R. Goody (ed.), 1975.

prevalence of joint households. As we have seen, the great majority of married sons in both regions are economically subordinate to their fathers. But as only 25% of all heads of farming households in Batagarawa had such resident sons, the corresponding proportion for the Anekal villages being 31%, it follows that joint households necessarily represent but a small proportion of all households. In fact, had joint households been similarly defined, as including *one* or more married sons,[28] in both regions, those proportions would have been 24% (Batagarawa) and 27% (Anekal); applying the more conventional definition to the Anekal villages, the proportion falls to 7%.

Setting aside, for the time being, the question of migration,[29] the proportions of potential joint households depend on a number of demographic factors, including the ages of men and women on first marriage, and the expectation of life of parents. In both regions, but more especially in the Anekal villages where life expectancies have risen very rapidly in recent decades, it may be that both of these variables have operated so as to increase the proportions of potential joint households since (say) 1900. As for 'the incidence of jointness' (the proportion of potential joint households which are actual joint households), this is very high in both regions.[30] Adopting the 'one or more married son' definition in both regions, the incidence would have been 95% in Batagarawa and 88% in the Anekal villages. Applying the 'two-son definition' to the Anekal villages the incidence of jointness was 56% for all households and 89% for the richest group of households – much higher proportions than some might expect.[31] Under our dry grain mode high proportions of household heads achieve their ambition (if such they have) of retaining the services of their married sons.

Considered as economic organisations, severely impoverished joint households, which do exist in both regions, are necessarily anarchic: the daily struggle for existence knows no rules, everyone is apt to fend for him or her self and to neglect the interests of others – in Batagarawa it was not

[28] Even then the definitions would have remained dissimilar since widowed mothers with married sons are never household heads in Hausaland.

[29] In the Anekal villages the total number of joint households would have risen from 33 to 53 had no son broken a joint household by migrating – on the unrealistic supposition that none of these sons would have set up their own households in their natal village.

[30] Perhaps it is here necessary to reiterate that the shorthand expression 'both regions' usually means 'in the particular localities in both regions'. Thus, 'the incidence of jointness' may vary considerably as between densely populated localities within a region.

[31] These findings are entirely at variance with those of Beals who stated that in a Mysore village he named Namhalli it had 'become almost customary' by 1953 for families to divide as soon as the children reached maturity'. 'Interplay Among Factors of Change in a Mysore Village' by A. R. Beals, in Marriott (ed.), 1969, p. 92.

uncommon for households to be 'too poor to cook', each adult member being dependent on buying cooked food from other households. But such households have their ups as well as their downs and, like shipwrecked mariners on a life raft, sometimes benefit from being a group. So while impoverished joint households have a lower survival expectancy than richer households, some actually manage to survive. But these survivors, who may even be landless, are an anomalous class, the archetypal joint household being primarily engaged in cultivating the family land.

THE FLEXIBILITY OF *GANDU*

Some particulars of the rights and obligations of fathers and sons-in-*gandu* are given in Appendix IV(1), and the special case of Dorayi is dealt with in Appendix IV(2). Taking richer households as my examples, I here examine the possible efficacy of *gandu* in dealing with the inescapable dilemma of the erosion of family property over time under our dry grain mode.

A father's attitude to his sons-in-*gandu* in many ways resembles that of the erstwhile slave owner to his slaves. While he should do his best to provide all the food required by a son and his dependants for the main evening meal during the farming season, he is not obliged to provide any food during the dry season, when a son may have to fend for himself, if he has insufficient food in his own granary.[32] It is the father's hope that his son, like the slaves before him, will earn sufficient during the free time, which is invariably granted, to enable him to meet a considerable part of his household requirements. Not only that, but the hope is that the son will, in due course, acquire farmland for himself, additional to the plot which his father is obliged to allot him. Ideally, the enterprising son flourishes sufficiently, under the umbrella of security provided by his rich father's *gandu*, to become one of the more prosperous farmers in the community in his own right – in which case, he will also be bound to have a lucrative non-farming occupation. Thus, as in the following case, the total area of farmland available to all household members increases as a result of the sons' efforts and the father is assured of a comfortable retirement.

The most respected, if not the richest, farmer in Batagarawa, who has nine family workers, still genuinely retains the services of his two eldest sons who work on the *gandu* farms along with everyone else – there is no need for paid labourers. These sons had become quite prosperous. One of them has bought over 15 acres of

[32] Although the ancient precautionary right of closing the *gandu* granary is falling into desuetude, many fathers are far less liberal over grain supplies in the dry season than at other times. As many as 46 of the total of 59 sons-in-*gandu* in Batagarawa owned their own granaries: the 96 granaries they owned were nearly a fifth (17%) of all the village granaries.

farmland; lives in a separate house bought for him by his father; and, with the aid of many donkeys, buys some 50 tons of groundnuts annually on behalf of a rich man in Katsina city; he formerly employed day-labourers on his farms, but is now assisted by his working sons. One of his three wives is a very prominent house-trader, who also runs a savings group (*adashi*). His brother, who lives in a separate section of his house, only owns about 4 acres of farmland (on which he employs labourers), but he is a very well-known trader in hides and skins, who finds time to travel for this business even during the farming season, and is also a 'table-trader', in the street, well known for selling bread baked in the city. Between them the two brothers own as many as eleven private granaries.

It is evident enough that both fathers and sons may benefit from the *gandu* relationship. The same is, of course, true of joint households in the Anekal villages.

Because of a dispute a Bhovi man left Bangalore and settled in Mahantalingapura. Now dead, his surviving widow has 3 married sons, 4 married grandsons and 15 unmarried descendants resident in the village in three households, two of which are rich joint households, the third being headed by a son with young children. The working male members of both of the joint households are all of them active both as cultivators and as rock agents, stone traders or stone cutters at the nearby quarry[33] – fathers and sons being associated in their work there. While the extent of their farmland, which had been mainly bought from the proceeds of quarry work, could not be precisely ascertained, the heads of the two joint households were among the more prominent farmers.

His father died when he was very young and he (a Reddy man) built up his position by cattle trading, buying in markets and reselling in villages, and was thus able to buy more land. Much helped by his two married sons, he is able to spare the services of another son whom he hires out with his plough for Rs 20 daily – he has 4 bullocks and 3 cows. Preferring large groups of labourers, he hired as many as 18 for a single day's harvesting. He owns an irrigation well and a brightly painted cart with pneumatic tyres. He is most unusual in sending one of his sons to buy manurial refuse in Bangalore, which is cheap, but the transport by cart takes a whole day.

THE SEPARATION OF SONS

As we have seen, a much higher proportion of Anekal than of Batagarawa sons had separated from their fathers and established their own households in the village – in fact (despite the high incidence of jointness) nearly a third of Anekal married sons were in this position. In those congested villages the joint household is often seen as a device for facilitating the later separation of sons. For the first few years after the elder sons marry they remain with their father, whose position is apt to improve with their help;

[33] See Appendix VII(6).

and then at some stage a one-by-one separation starts, usually reasonably amicably, especially as the prospects that the joint household will remain intact as the younger sons grow up are usually good in such cases – and younger sons are more often those who remain permanently with their father. In the Anekal villages prosperous joint households are seldom dramatically dismantled. If a father is still working (as he usually is not) when the final division between all the sons occurs, he may (notionally) retain the same area of farmland as he allots to each of his sons.[34]

Considering how commanding and tyrannous some fathers are, the sons and daughters-in-law sometimes being treated little better than servants, why is there so little open revolt? The main explanation probably lies in the economic weakness of those sons who want to abandon their parent against his wishes. Unlike the Hausa sons, they have been unable to build up their economic strength while under their father's command and, as already noted, they seldom contemplate court action[35] if they receive less than their fair share of the land on their departure.[36] Then, their efficiency is anyway likely to be impaired by the lack of such capital as plough animals, which they may be obliged to borrow from their reluctant fathers at times convenient to him; also, their housing conditions may be very poor. Finally, there are few opportunities of pursuing lucrative non-farming occupations, of which they are likely to have had little previous experience. For these and other reasons, sons who defy their fathers are apt to suffer a fall in living standards for which their increased freedom is insufficient compensation.

In all but the most prosperous households, the willingness of parents to part with their sons becomes greater as the number of grandchildren increases and as the sons' restiveness grows with age. Whereas over three-quarters (77%) of potential joint households headed by a parent in his/her fifties[37] were actual joint households, the corresponding proportions for parents in their sixties and seventies were 62% and 38%.

FRATERNAL JOINT HOUSEHOLDS

In Batagarawa it has not been common within living memory for brothers to regard the life phase of fraternal *gandu* as more than temporary: after

[34] Or he may retain nothing, relying on maintenance from his sons – which, it was said, should consist either of food or an annual allotment of grains, but not both.

[35] Significantly, villagers do not contemplate the joint family in legal terms, such as are employed in legislation, but use vernacular expressions only, such as 'we are all living together', 'we are living separately'.

[36] It was probably more owing to the reluctance of fathers to register formal division, than to actual errors in the land records, that it was often very difficult to estimate the size of the farm-holding of a separated son. See Appendix II(1).

[37] Ages are necessarily estimated – see Appendix VI(1).

sampling the experience, and fending off the shock of their father's death, it is usually not long before they mutually agree to part, usually all simultaneously;[38] in Hausaland generally, fraternal *gandaye* probably usually result from a father's early death. In Batagarawa 2 of the 7 cases were blacksmith's households, this being the only craft which involves relatives in working together; there was also one fraternal-*cum*-paternal *gandu* – the only case in either region.

In the Anekal villages, where the general incidence of fraternal joint households was much the same as in Batagarawa, the incidences for both the richest caste (Reddy) and the lowest, well represented, caste (the Adikarnataka) were very low: individual rich Reddy men usually strongly object to farming with their brothers, and fraternal joint households stand little chance of survival unless they are fairly prosperous – as few AK households are. It was interesting that each of the 15 actual fraternal joint households was wholly intact, not a single brother having broken away; evidently, the departure of one brother tends to destabilise the group.

In general, then, under our dry grain mode, fraternal joint households are temporary or anomalous farming organisations: fatherless men cannot tolerate fraternal domination, and fathers increasingly anticipate this by dividing the farmland before they have retired.[39] This is true even in Dorayi where brothers never farm jointly although they are nearly always co-resident[40] – astonishingly, only 18 of the 298 fatherless men who had brothers living in Dorayi were resident in separate houses. In Dorayi the obligation of fathers to retire and to divide their farmland had become so formalised that the number of married sons who had retired fathers (86) actually exceeded the number of such sons who were in *gandu* (75).

THE DEVELOPMENTAL CYCLE

Readers may be surprised by my failure to mention the conventional three-phase model of the developmental cycle which is such that each head of a farming household is a member of a domestic group which 'comes into

[38] See Appendix IV(3) for an example.

[39] Owing to the inadequacies of the land records and the differing views that are expressed, it is hard to say whether, in the Anekal villages, there are any standard ideas on how the property generally *ought* to be shared – see n. 34 above. One man said that if a father had 4 sons (2 of them married) his property ought to be divided into six parts, one each for the father and each son and one to meet the marriage expenses of the unmarried sons. He then completely contradicted himself in terms of the division of house property and the expectations of unmarried sons. Owing to the 'lumpiness' of much property, it is certain that the division is often quite unequal.

[40] It must be remembered that in Dorayi residence in the same house (*gida*) may or may not imply residence in the same house section.

being, grows and expands, and finally dissolves'.[41] My reason for this is that the conventional second stage of the cycle, the stage 'of dispersion or fission' which 'begins with the marriage of the oldest child and continues until all the children are married',[42] is hardly appropriate, as we can now see, to our dry grain mode.[43] Not only do fathers endeavour, with a good degree of success, to cling onto 'enough of their sons', but even the stage of formal retirement from farming does not usually signify a decline in the father's fortunes, not only because all his sons have an obligation to support him but because some of them nearly always continue to live in his house.

Regarded as a social security system, the 'joint household principle' actually tends to operate in a way which supports old men and women in their dotage as well as younger men, who are both landless and burdened with dependent children, in their prime. But the whole of this discussion on the archetypal joint household relates, as I earlier said, to the organisation of richer households which cultivate enough farmland to occupy their members. Although, in both regions, fair numbers of impoverished joint households actually exist, their members are necessarily so preoccupied with the struggle for existence that each household tends to be a law unto itself. The neglect of impoverished households in this chapter will be properly repaired in Chapters V and VI.

APPENDIX IV(1)

Gandu *in Hausaland*: *The reciprocal rights and obligations of fathers and sons*

I here briefly summarise the mutually interacting rights and obligations which reciprocally link fathers and sons-in-*gandu* in Batagarawa,[44] as representing rural Hausaland; Dorayi, being a special case, is dealt with in Appendix IV(2). I start by dealing with rights. First, the father has the right to insist that his son should work on the *gandu* farms, without cash payment, for up to about five hours in the morning; the son, for his part, has the right to refuse to work during the non-farming season (when he may take up any work in any place), is entitled to at least one regular off-day per week during the farming season, and expects payment for any evening work on the *gandu* farms. Second, the father has the right to any

[41] See *Social Structure: Studies presented to A. R. Radcliffe-Brown*, ed. M. Fortes, 1949, p. 60.

[42] See the introduction by M. Fortes to *The Developmental Cycle in Domestic Groups*, ed. J. R. Goody, 1958, pp. 4–5.

[43] See Hill (1972), pp. 166–7, for details of a model life cycle for a prosperous Batagarawa household.

[44] For further particulars see Hill (1972), pp. 43–5.

earnings which the son gets from working in the morning on the farms of others. Third, the father may dismiss his son from *gandu*, though not without good reason; while the son has a right to leave *gandu* against his father's wishes, he will not then expect to receive a portion of farmland.

Turning to the father's obligations, the main one is to provide his son with grain and/or cooked food during the farming season. While he is not obliged to give his son any portion of the *gandu* groundnut crop, he should give him 'something extra' to finance the purchase of clothing and other needs. Third, the father should allot a portion of manured farmland (*gayauna*) to a son who requires it for his own use, and should allow him to dispose of the crop as he wishes; the son, as we know, may also buy farmland for himself.[45] Fourth, the father should provide his son with adequate housing, maybe in a separate house. Fifth, the father should do his best to meet his son's marriage expenses, especially for his first marriage, and to contribute to the cost of the Muslim naming ceremonies of any children. Sixth, the father should allow his son to use the *gandu* tools, including any ox-plough, on his private farms. Seventh, if the father becomes unable to work through age or illness he should delegate authority either to his eldest son or to all his sons – if the latter, each son will be partly responsible for the father's daily maintenance.

APPENDIX IV(2)

Gandu *in Dorayi*

As constantly stressed in this book, many aspects of the socio-economic organisation of farming in Dorayi are anomalous, peculiar and even bizarre, in terms of our dry grain mode – none more so than the relationship between fathers and married sons. Dorayi may be seen as providing us with a model of what *can* happen when rural communities are near the end of their tether, owing to the persistent and intensifying pressure of population on the land over a long period, in conditions of unchanging simple technologies and low-yielding crops. It is an interesting case not because it indicates future trends (for conditions in Dorayi are so peculiar for historical reasons that they are unlikely to be replicated elsewhere), but because in some respects it is a consistent mirror image of the norm.

We have seen that, in general, *gandu* is best regarded as a voluntary relationship, which ought to benefit both fathers and married sons alike; but this is not so in Dorayi where sons have few options other than to hold on until their fathers either die or retire from farming. Not only are Dorayi sons necessarily debarred by their

[45] About three-fifths of all sons-in-*gandu* owned manured farmland. The total area they owned was about 142 acres (13% of the total) about a third of which may have been bought by themselves; two-thirds of the son's holdings were between one and 3 acres; three sons had holdings of between 8 and 15 acres, one of them being the remarkable case of a son whose manured acreage was three times that of his father, although he was genuinely in *gandu*. About nine sons employed significant numbers of farm labourers.

poverty and subordination (and by the high price of farmland) from setting up as local farmers in their own right, but such is their parent's wrath if they threaten migration that only those who are prepared to sever all links with their home community contemplate removal (see Chapter X) – most migration in fact being triggered by the father's death.

As *gandu* in Dorayi is not a voluntary relationship, it follows that fathers have no need to sustain it by encouraging the 'private enterprise' of their sons – on the contrary, they rather seek to bind them to themselves. No father, however much farmland he may possess, follows the normal practice of allotting his son a private plot. Then, fathers expect their sons to hand over a large part of their independent earnings, not only those from farm-labouring; only the daughters-in-law retain their traditional economic independence – as they must, since they are likewise independent of their husbands. Again, fathers do not give their sons the option of residing in their own house or of receiving grain, rather than cooked meals, as the reward for their work. In fact, the only formal way in which fathers encourage their sons to remain with them is, as we have seen, by promising earlier retirement than in former times.

As there is much household poverty in Dorayi, and as relatively few impoverished men are able to be active *gandu* heads, it seemed that about a fifth of all married sons were not effectively in *gandu* although resident in their father's houses; most of these men had poor fathers – about a half of them commuted daily to Kano city where they earned regular, though very small wages in humble types of work, for they lacked the influence to obtain factory jobs.

APPENDIX IV(3)

The break-up of a fraternal gandu

Three Batagarawa half-brothers, each with different mothers, lived for a long time in fraternal *gandu*, their father having died before any of them had married – another half-brother had migrated. Three of the brothers combined together to assist the fourth (a Koranic scholar or *malam*) to meet his marriage expenses – his marriage having been delayed owing to prolonged Koranic studies which had prevented him from farming. This *malam* left his teacher and proceeded to build a house, where he could receive students, on a farm; the other two brothers thereat decided to separate, building a strong wall between two sections of their father's house, retaining a single entrance from the street. Each brother having retained the plot earlier allotted to him by his father, the bulk of the *gandu* farmland was divided in the presence of witnesses – but the trees, which were ill-distributed on the land, were considered as joint property which 'represented the unity of the family'. They had large numbers of livestock, including (exceptionally) about 10 horses (kept in various villages), more than 10 cows and as many donkeys, and countless goats, sheep and fowls. The villagers sold the horses and the Fulani sold the cattle (which they were herding), the proceeds being divided between the brothers, who bought farmland with the money. The other livestock, and the farm tools, were shared out, not sold.

APPENDIX IV(4)

House division in the Anekal villages

Very often when an Anekal father and his son(s) agree to separate there is no alternative but to divide the existing family house, often to the great inconvenience of all concerned since house sites are already very small and there is usually little possibility of taking up adjoining vacant land. Kitchens tend to become darker than ever; the cattle stalls are even more oppressive in their proximity; and it may become difficult for everyone to find the space to lie down prone at night. But still the process continues and the following diagrams[46] illustrate the kinds of solutions adopted – as well as the degree of overcrowding, most of the rooms being very small. The only requirement is that each house section should have its own entrance, preferably giving onto the outside world – often *via* the cattle stalls.

1. *Paternal separation*

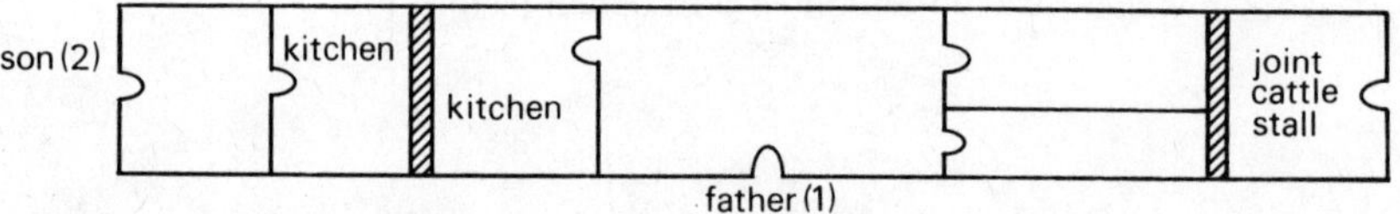

A. *Kuruba caste.* A father with 2 married sons lives in section (1), his eldest married son in section (2). Seventeen people live in the four rooms.

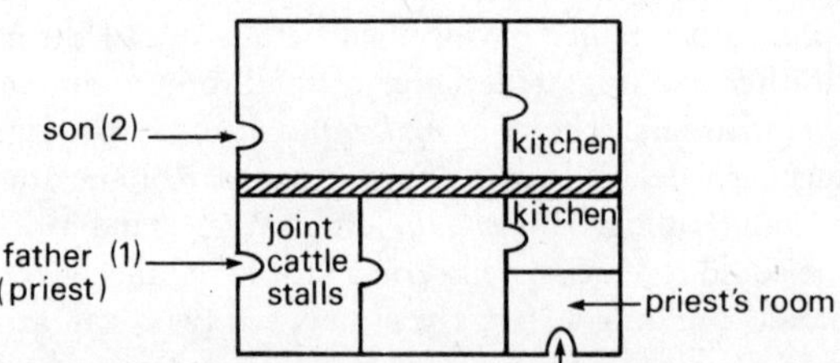

B. *Satani caste.* Two married sons are in the priest's section which is approached through the cattle stalls – the priest himself having his own private room. A third son lives in section (2). Twelve people live in the two main rooms.

46. All the walls partitioning the separate rooms are shown, as well as the doors. Nothing is drawn to scale.

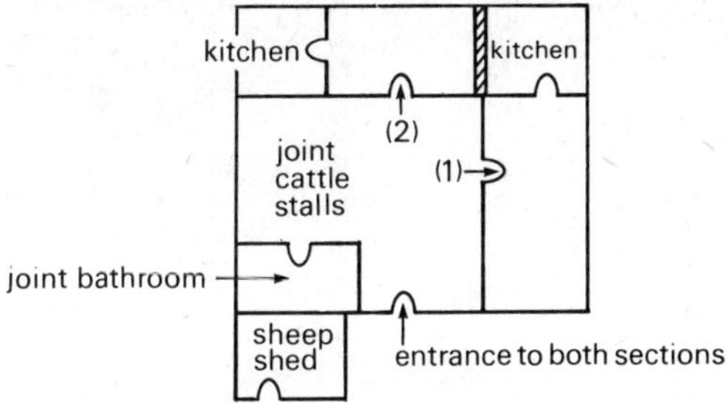

C. *Golla caste.* An old and decrepit father supported by one married son (another son is a paraplegic) lives in section (1); two other married sons with three children live in the 'one room/one kitchen' section (2).

II. *Paternal cum fraternal separation*

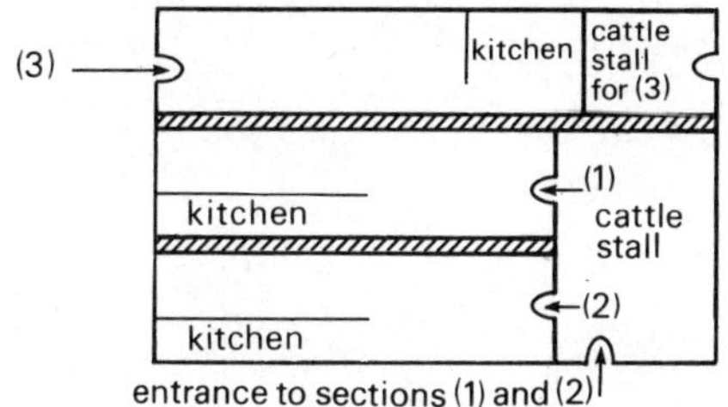

D. *Gowda caste.* A father with one married son is in section (1); his brother with 7 children is in section (2); and another married son is in section (3). A total of 19 people in three rooms.

III. *Fraternal separation*

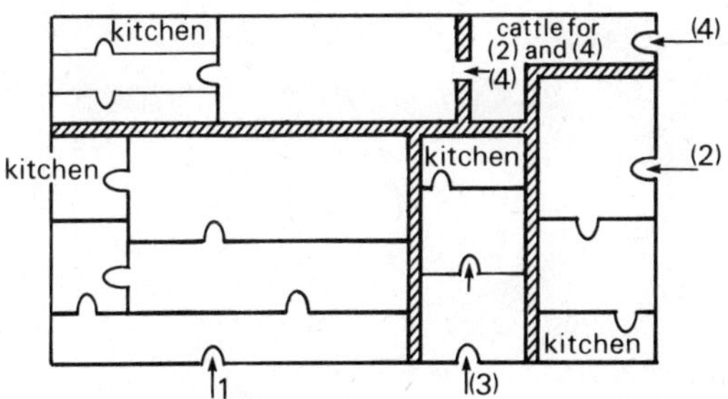

E. *Reddy caste.* Four brothers built the house long after their father's death – he had died when they were young. Brothers (1) and (3) have a separate cattle shed. The populations of the 4 sections total 28, including a 'hundred year old' grandmother of the brothers.

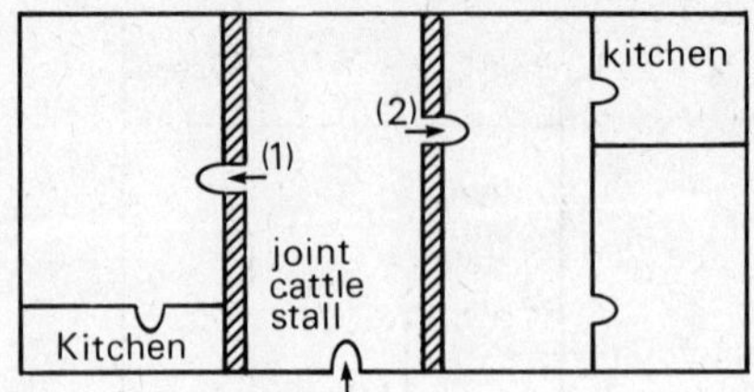

F. *Korama caste.* Each section is occupied by a brother. The house had been divided like this before the father died, one son having already separated.

CHAPTER V

The Farming Household: (2) Miscellaneous Aspects

The main purpose of this brief chapter on miscellaneous aspects of farming households is to provide background material needed for the discussion in subsequent chapters of our central theme of economic inequality.

THE SIZE OF THE HOUSEHOLDS

Since, as we know, the majority of households in both Batagarawa[1] and the Anekal villages are basically nuclear, essentially consisting of parents and children only, it comes as no surprise to find that in both regions the great majority of non-joint households have between (say) 4 and 10 members – 74% in Batagarawa and 76% in the Anekal villages, as Table V(1) shows. The proportions of such households with one or two members only is little more than 10% in both regions, the proportions with more than 10 members being negligible.

As Table V(2) shows, as many as 85% (Batagarawa) and 88% (Anekal) of the members of non-joint households live in households with between 4 and 10 members.

As for joint households, Table V(1) shows that more of them are large in Batagarawa than in the Anekal villages – the respective proportions with 16 or more members being 34% and 19%, the average sizes being 11.7 and 10.7 persons. Even had it been possible to define joint households identically in both regions, the Batagarawa joint households would have been larger than those in Anekal owing to Hausa polygyny, for the heads of the former households had more wives, and hence more children, than the average householder. It is partly for this reason that the proportion of the population living in joint households was as high as 61% in Batagarawa, compared with only 19% in the Anekal villages.

[1] There was difficulty with the Dorayi statistics; see Chapter IV, n. 13.

Table V(1). *Size of farming households: number of households of each size*

Number in household	Joint households				Other households				Total			
	Batagarawa		Anekal villages		Batagarawa		Anekal villages		Batagarawa		Anekal villages	
	No.	%	No.	%	No.	%	No.	%	No.	%	No.	%
1	–		–		5	4	14	3	5	3	14	3
2	–		–		10	8	39	9	10	6	39	8
3	–		–		15	12	46	11	15	9	46	10
4	2	4	–		10	8	76	18	12	7	76	16
5	2	4	–		21	17	81	19	23	13	81	17
6–10	20	42	25	52	60	49	167	39	80	47	192	41
11–15	14	29	19	40	1	1	3	1	15	9	22	5
16–20	8	17	4	8	1	1	–		9	5	4	1
21–30	2	4	–	–	–		–		2	1	–	
TOTAL	48	100%	48	100%	123	100%	426	100%	171	100%	474	100%

Notes:

1. It happens that there were 48 joint households (including fraternal households) in both Batagarawa and the Anekal villages.
2. Joint households are defined in Chapter IV.
3. All sons-in-*gandu* in Batagarawa are regarded as belonging to their father's joint household.
4. The statistics for Batagarawa are drawn from Hill (1972), Table II.4, p. 33.

Table V(2). *Size of farming households: percentage of total population in households of each size*

Number in household	Joint households		Other households		Total	
	Batagarawa	Anekal villages	Batagarawa	Anekal villages	Batagarawa	Anekal villages
1	–	–	1	1	neg.	1
2	–	–	3	4	2	3
3	–	–	7	6	4	5
4	1	–	6	14	4	11
5	2	–	16	19	9	15
6–10	32	27	63	55	49	52
11–15	31	54	2	1	15	10
16–20	25	19	3	–	13	3
21–30	9	–	–	–	4	–
	100%	100%	100%	100%	100%	100%
Average household size	11.7	10.7	5.4	5.1	7.2	5.7
Proportion of population	61%	19%	39%	81%	100%	100%

See Notes on Table V(1).

HOUSEHOLD COMPOSITION

In both regions the very great majority of household members are either direct descendants, wives or daughters-in-law of the household head – if he be a man. But an important point of distinction between the regions is the position of widowed mothers. In Batagarawa and Dorayi no farming households were formally headed by women (which is not to say that a middle-aged widow might not happen to be the most generally influential and respected household member), for middle-aged or elderly widows (or divorcees) usually took refuge with their married sons as dependent household members.[2] In the Anekal villages, on the other hand, about a fifth of all farming households were headed by widows,[3] many of whom were the dominant household decision-takers whether or not a married son were living with them; as proportionately more women than men household heads were in charge of large two-generational joint households, nearly a quarter of the whole population actually lived in these women's households. From this it follows that the role of women in agriculture in the Anekal villages is even greater than mere concentration on the relative volume of male and female labour might suggest.

Table V(3), which shows the relation of household members to household heads in the Anekal villages,[4] brings out the differences in the composition of male-headed and female-headed households; it shows, in particular, that far more women than men household heads have married sons residing with them.

THE HOUSEHOLD DIVISION OF LABOUR

In Anekal Taluk, and probably in south India generally (except where there are many Brahmin farming households), the participation of women and girls in agriculture is nearly as great as men's[5] – and, as we have just

[2] In Batagarawa – see Hill (1972), p. 33 – as many as 9% of all dependent adult women were widowed or divorced mothers of male household heads; in Dorayi – see Hill (1977), p. 89 – the percentage was nearly as high.

[3] If a widow were aged or decrepit I did not regard her as the household head if she had a resident married son. While the proportion of women's households was roughly equal for Harijans and others, it was lower for the two richest castes – Reddy (10%) and Kuruba (14%).

[4] Corresponding figures for Batagarawa are given in Hill (1972), Tables II.2 and II.3.

[5] See reference on p. 19 above to the findings of the (All India) *Rural Labour Enquiry 1963–5*; on this basis the ratio of women to men labourers in Mysore state was nearly the highest in India. Women members of 'agricultural labour households' in Mysore were recorded (p. 125) as working 192 days per year in agricultural labour and 11 days in 'non agricultural occupations'.

Table V(3). *Anekal villages. Relationship of household members to household head*

Relationship to household head	Households headed by men (Hullahalli and Bukkasagara only)	Households headed by women (All villages)
	percentages	
Self	17	19
Sons–married	5	12
–unmarried	24	13
Daughters–married	1	2
–unmarried	20	7
Daughters-in-law	5	12
Unmarried grandchildren	8	30
Sons-in-law	1	1
Wives	16	–
Other	3	4
	100%	100%
Proportion of females	50%	58%

Notes:
1. The statistics for male-headed households relate to two villages only, as this seemed to be a sufficiently large and representative sample.
2. For the definition of households headed by women see n.3 above.

seen, they are often in charge of farming operations, especially those involving labourers. It is true that in Anekal Taluk females never plough, drive carts or undertake any other operation, including well-irrigation, which involves controlling draught cattle; but for some types of work, notably transplantation, their labour is preferred – and not only because their wages, as day-labourers, are usually about two-thirds or three-quarters of those of men.

Unfortunately the importance of women's participation is little appreciated, partly because the occupational statistics in the south Indian population censuses appear to grossly under-estimate the participation of women[6] – and in a most inconsistent manner; but also because of the belief disseminated by anthropologists, most recently by J. R. Goody, that women's agricultural role is far less important in plough than in hoe economies.[7] But all those with first hand acquaintance of village life in south India appreciate the significance, indeed the indispensability of female labour. Thus, J. Harriss states that 'the most labour-intensive operations in paddy cultivation (transplanting, weeding and harvesting) are carried out mainly by women'[8] and Mencher insists that the importance of women's roles has been under-estimated.[9] Epstein[10] even goes so far as to say that in Dalena, where there was no wet land, women were responsible for all cultivation except ploughing, thus releasing the men for work on irrigated farmland elsewhere.

In the Anekal villages it was impossible to judge whether women participated to a greater degree in family labour than in wage labour. If the husbands of women belonging to the three dominant castes, Reddy, Kuruba and Gowda, were sometimes reluctant, for reasons of status, to allow them to work as paid labourers (although the men were prepared to work themselves),[11] this might be the case; and there is also the fact that owing to their domestic and child-rearing duties a fair proportion of women at any time may not be free to work as full-time labourers, although they may render some help on family fields or in grazing animals. However this may be, at least 30% to 40% of day labourers are likely to be women – this being nothing new, as Francis Buchanan made clear in 1807.

In Batagarawa and Dorayi, where all wives are secluded during the hours of daylight, women's role in agriculture is negligible, though they and their children occasionally go out grubbing for groundnuts lost in the soil after harvest and pick cowpeas and other vegetables. While this represents the general situation in Muslim Hausaland, sceptics can sometimes mention the case of a rare anomalous village where women are not only free to wander about the village but actually undertake regular cultivation. I came upon one myself in Kazaure Emirate.

In south India all economically active members of the farming house-

[6] See p. 19 above.

[7] See 'Inheritance and women's labour in Africa' by J. Goody *et al.*, *Africa*, 1973.

[8] In Farmer (ed.), 1977, pp. 227–8.

[9] Mencher, 1978. [10] Epstein, 1962.

[11] Relatively high-caste men are even prepared to work as labourers on Harijans' farms – though they sit separately when eating. As for women, I think that attitudes must have changed since 1948 when M. N. Srinivas observed (*The Remembered Village*, 1976, p. 137) that higher-caste women did not participate in agriculture.

hold work on the farmland under the authority of the male or female household head: like the fathers and sons-in-*gandu* in Hausaland, they are apt to form a unified production group.[12] This being so, there is nothing very interesting to report about the sexual division of tasks (other than those involving draught animals), few of which are beyond the strength of women. Even if women's labour be preferred for any particular task, such as transplanting, men will perform it if necessary. Also, despite the common separation of the sexes in other places and contexts,[13] men and women commonly work together in agriculture and on the threshing yards; as groups of workers perform more happily and efficiently than lonely individuals, social barriers fall and men and women of all castes, whether Scheduled or non-Scheduled, family or hired, freely associate on the fields and the threshing yards.

Srinivas has provided a useful summary of the numerous tasks ancillary to actual cultivation which are the duty of Karnataka women:[14] these include carrying food to the group working on the family land, fetching water (often an onerous task), collecting cow dung for manure, sweeping the cattle stalls and carrying the sweepings in a basket to the domestic manure heap, grazing and caring for animals, and cleaning and grinding grain. Although they often carry firewood, women are not to the same degree rural porters as in many regions of southern West Africa where they, and their children, are virtually the sole 'beasts of burden', there being no carts or donkeys.

HOUSEHOLD UNDER-EMPLOYMENT

The remainder of this chapter is devoted to the terrible scourge of 'household under-employment' which affects a high proportion of all households under our dry grain mode. I shall concentrate on agricultural work, other occupations being dealt with in Chapter VII.

In both regions agriculture is a very seasonal activity, which necessarily leaves much time for other occupations. In Hausaland, where guinea corn is apt to be harvested in about November, nearly two months after the cessation of the rains, the non-farming season, when men-in-*gandu* may

[12] This is probably a standard feature of our dry grain mode, though it is by no means usual in many West African societies with varying types of agrarian systems, where wives are no more apt to work under their husband's authority when cultivating the crops than when doing the cooking.

[13] Sharma emphasises the significance of 'mixed sex work parties' in agriculture in a society where there were limitations on the degree to which men and women associated socially. 'Segregation and its Consequences in India' by Ursula Sharma in Caplan *et al.* (eds.), 1978.

[14] Srinivas, 1976, pp. 138 *et seq.*

travel to seek their fortunes if they wish, lasts for roughly half the year;[15] and in south-eastern Karnataka, where the two monsoons are apt to follow hard upon each other, the arable land is dead and desolate for the first half of the calendar year or so, even for a couple of months after the south-west monsoon has started, the precise period depending upon the vagaries of the weather. But, fortunately, following an interval after harvest, the *ragi* threshing yards present grand scenes of activity and sociability as late as February, for that grain, unlike paddy, requires drying in stacks for several months.

As for employment in agriculture during the rains, in both regions it is only the richest households which provide more or less regular work for all their members throughout the period; the various operations (ploughing, sowing, weeding and the rest) do not succeed each other with rhythmic regularity and most households find that work is spasmodic, proceeding by fits and starts. For that reason, and also because no one expects, or is expected, to work a seven-day week on the land,[16] artisans, traders, priests, Koranic teachers, building labourers and others do not have to abandon their 'occupation' during the farming season but can interpose it between bouts of farm work – albeit at lower levels of intensity than in the off-season.

Under our dry grain mode it is dubious whether we should postulate the inevitability of serious 'labour bottlenecks' at certain points in the farming season, for instance when sowing or weeding.[17] Of course such shortages are commonly postulated by textbook writers who cannot tolerate the idea of perpetual disequilibrium at almost all times during the farming season. But the evidence does not support their presuppositions, especially in the Anekal villages where I observed with surprise that the cool of the morning was often wasted by starting work very late – say 10 a.m., as in city offices.

Under our dry grain mode it is reasonable to assume that during the farming season priority is given to agricultural work, both because that is the general ethos (shared up to a point by both rich and poor alike) and

[15] Cultivators are enormously worried and inconvenienced by the fact that the planting rains may fall as early as April or as late as mid-June – in the latter case the farming season is bound to be short. Seed germination may be hastened by the practice of sowing in advance of the rain (*binne*).

[16] In Hausaland, as we have seen, men-in-*gandu*, like the former farm slaves, are entitled to one or two regular off-days in the week – and other household heads would never expect their subordinates to work every day. In the Anekal villages the tradition that plough cattle should be rested on Mondays was not always observed; otherwise there appeared to be no particular regularities, though there were a great many holidays and other festivities.

[17] Much qualitative observation supports this view. See Hill (1972), p. 259, for some reasons for doubting the general belief that labour shortage at the time of grain sowing accounts for the late planting, and hence low yields, of groundnuts in Hausaland.

because certain operations need to be performed with little prior notice, for instance after a heavy storm. It is, therefore, interesting to attempt a crude assessment of the incidence of potential under-employment in terms of the ratio of household workers to household land, taking account of hired labourers.

Of course, under-employment particularly afflicts poorer households. If the richest of all households be omitted, there is little variation in the average size of richer and poorer households though much variation in the average areas they cultivate. In both regions the evidence is that the volume of wage-employment offered to agricultural workers is quite insufficient to compensate for the low land/man ratio of the poorer households.

I deal first with the case of Batagarawa, for which the best statistics were collected.[18] In that village the average household size for the middle, poor and poorest groups of farmers was 7.6, 6.1 and 6.1 persons.[19] The average acreage of manured farmland cultivated and/or owned by households in each of these groups was 8.4, 4.2 and 2.8 – giving a crude[20] land/man ratio of 1.1, 0.69 and 0.46 respectively.

But to what extent should the land/working man ratio for the poorer households be reduced to take account of employment as day labourers? Table V(4) shows that as only about 17% (23 out of 139) of the work force of the 'poor and poorest households' could hope to be employed as labourers on any day, these households had nearly twice as much family labour per acre available for their own farming (3.4 acres per worker) as the richest households (6.4 acres per worker) – and the latter may themselves have suffered from some under-employment. Taking the family labour force as a whole, the table shows that only 11% (27 out of 247) of the workers available on any day were employed as labourers – against a figure as high as 17% for the poor and poorest households. (According to an enquiry made by D. W. Norman in three Zaria villages in Hausaland, hired labour varied between 6% and 29% of total farm-labour during the year ending March 1967.)[21]

In the Anekal villages the incidence of under-employment resulting from the inadequate demand for day labourers may well be greater than in Batagarawa; more labour is available from the poorest households both because women as well as men seek work and because there is a higher

[18] See Hill (1972), Chapter VIII. This excellent material on farm-labouring was collected for me by Alhaji Sabi'u Nuhu in 1968 after I had left the village.

[19] *Ibid.*, Table IV.1, p. 61.

[20] There having been found to be little variation between groups in the proportions of children and working men, this crude ratio is a sufficient indicator.

[21] See 'Labour Inputs of Farmers' by D. W. Norman, *The Nigerian Journal of Economic and Social Studies*, 1969, I, Table 4.

Table V(4). *Batagarawa. The transfer of farm labour between richer and poorer households*

Groups of households	Estimated daily employment (nos.): Day labourers employed (1)	Estimated daily employment (nos.): Day labourers provided for employment (2)	Family workers available: *Gross* (3)	Family workers available: *Net* (4) (3)−(2)	Family & employed workers (nos.) (5) (4)+(1)	Acreages of manured farmland: *Total* (6)	Acreages of manured farmland: *per worker* (7) (6)−(5)
Rich	10	1	43	42	52	331	6.4
Middle	7	3	65	62	69	378	5.5
Poor & poorest	2	23	139	116	118	401	3.4
	19	27	247	220	239	1,110	4.6
Men-in-*gandu*[(a)]	5	..	..	..	..	..	..
'Ruling class'[(b)]	3	–	..	..	..	..	..
TOTAL	27	27	247	220	239		

Notes:
(i) The table is based on the arbitrary assumption of a five-day working week.
(ii) The table is drawn from p. 120 of Hill (1972), where the basis of estimation is discussed.
(iii) Estimates are exclusive of labourers drawn from outside Batagarawa.
(iv) The estimates in col.(2) relate to a survey covering employment offered by 40 farmers over a period of 12 weeks.
(*a*) The estimate relates to the private farms of these men.
(*b*) Most of the farmland of the ruling class was situated outside the Batagarawa Village Area: apart from labourers from Batagarawa and elsewhere they employed regular 'farm servants' (*barori*).

incidence of landlessness. Another consideration is the low labour requirements for *ragi* cultivation – though this would be partly compensated for by the high labour intensiveness of paddy. One of the particular difficulties in these villages is that many of the richest households, who might be thought to be among the largest employers of labour, have sufficient (male and female) family workers to be able to dispense with hired labourers except on rare occasions.[22] In Hullahalli and Nanjapura the average area per family worker for the richest households was only 3.2 acres. Although these rich households own much more than their fair share of the farmland – in those villages a third of the households owned about two-thirds of the farmland – few of them are large employers of labour. If, on average, a

[22] Thus about a quarter of all the richest households in Hullahalli and Nanjapura had 5 or more family workers available – counting boys and girls under eighteen years as the equivalent of 'half-workers'.

quarter of the labour force of the two poorest groups worked on the farms of the richest cultivators on any day (an unrealistically high proportion), the poor households would still be left on average with only one acre per working member – much too little to occupy them for a reasonable proportion of their time.

These are the basic reasons why, under our dry grain mode, there is so much under-employment in agriculture and why the labour market is in a chronic state of disequilibrium – many people spending a large part of their time vainly searching for work. The miserably low wage rates[23] consequently bear no relationship to 'minimum needs' – an intentionally vague statement both because household needs vary so greatly with such factors as the ratio of earners to non-earners in a household, and because there is a sense in which wages are so low that there is not even any point in considering how low they are, especially as work is so spasmodic.

[23] See p. 62 above.

CHAPTER VI

The Essence of Inequality: Land Ownership

One of the most paradoxical recent developments affecting farmland under our dry grain mode is that its price has suddenly risen so high in relation to the yield of basic crops, especially in the Anekal villages, that it is becoming increasingly regarded, by both rich and poor alike, as the safest of all hedges against inflation – almost as an heirloom which should be sold only in the direst emergency or owing to a complete change in circumstances, such as migration. Consequently, the market in land, having once been so active,[1] has now become sluggish and erratic, perhaps mainly involving reluctant or furtive sellers who are in dire extremity or those concerned to cheat their relatives.

But because the market is so sluggish; because prices are rising so fast; because farmland varies so greatly in location and quality and hence in intrinsic value; and because impoverished sellers usually receive low prices, having poor bargaining power owing to being in a hurry – for these and other reasons it is very difficult to indicate realistic price ranges for land. I shall only record that in 1977–8 in the Anekal villages Rs 3,000 per acre (say £200) was the kind of price that was mentioned for dry land and that Rs 10,000 per acre (say £700) might have been a reasonable valuation for high-quality tank-irrigated land.[2] Using these values, the Anekal villagers

[1] Especially in Hausaland, where in early colonial days most farm-plots in densely populated areas were apt to have been sold at one time or another – see Hill (1972), p. 240. But land-selling was by no means uncommon in Mysore at the end of last century.

[2] To a West Africanist the literature on land-selling in south India seems remarkably weak, especially as transactions have long involved much documentation. Few recent writers have discussed the subject with any precision: most have been content with generalisations like those of A. Béteille in *Caste, Class and Power*, 1965. But Epstein has emphasised the great increase in land values resulting from canal irrigation – she put the price before irrigation at Rs 100 per acre (1962, p. 4) and later stated that partly as a result of purchases by urban speculators wet land prices increased by about 330% between 1958 and 1971 (1973); she also noted the reluctance of local farmers to sell land. Harriss (in Farmer (ed.), 1977, p. 129) stated that the price of dry land in Randam, in North Arcot, had risen from Rs 100 per acre in 1960 to about Rs 3,000 in the early 1970s. Srinivas (1976, p. 108) claimed that the price of dry land in Rampura in 1948 was as high as Rs 1,000 per acre, wet land having fetched Rs 3,000–4,000 – or more where it was especially well situated.

would have been the owners of farmland worth more than £½ million[3] – a very high valuation, as we shall later see, in relation to the annual yield of the land.

Six years earlier, in 1971–2, high prices were having the same dampening effect on the land market in Dorayi, where local farmers were feeling bewildered by the rapid rise in prices.[4] At that time the official rate of compensation for land which was compulsorily acquired for road-building in that area was £60 an acre. Whether this was a realistic price for transactions involving local residents I was unable to ascertain, despite much enquiry,[5] but it is certain that the rich strangers who bought roadside land at much higher prices were not the only 'land speculators'.

This imperfect sluggish market in land, prices being so high in relation to yields, is one of the most important features of our late twentieth century dry grain mode. It partly explains both the well-known fact that the living standards of individual households are considerably determined by accidents of inheritance – young householders, in particular, hardly ever being in a position to buy land; as well as the little known fact that the *richest householders can seldom buy sufficient land to compensate for the erosion in holding size resulting from increasing population density and division on inheritance*. It explains why most Harijans are so anxious to hold on to such land as they possess, even when poverty prevents their cultivating it for themselves. The pattern of land ownership has become more inflexible than at any time within living memory.

The market in farmland is commonly furtive, involving reluctant, miserable, bashful sellers – as well as the forced sales which so often result from mortgaging. It is easy to imagine a hidden market in gold trinkets, but can a market in farmland really involve so much secrecy if every villager always knows who owns each plot? Rather suprisingly, the reply to this question, at least in the Anekal villages, is that many people are vague about the actual ownership of many of the smaller plots: in other words, if a man is seen working on a particular field, it may not be generally known, for example, whether he is a hired labourer, a mortgagor who is permitted to remain on his land, the son of an absentee owner or an owner-cultivator. (Such genuine ignorance enhanced the difficulty of checking ownership statements.)

3 This sum is based on the ownership of 170 acres of wet land and 1,641 acres of dry land – figures which are certainly under-estimates.

4 See Hill (1977), p. 128.

5 One of my particular assistants, a man of no special status in the village, was a prominent 'land broker', facilitating negotiations between the parties. Yet even with his help, which was entirely frank, there were many reasons, including the sale of unmeasured plot-portions, why reliable prices per acre could not be ascertained. See Hill (1977), p. 134.

MORTGAGING

It is possible that in both regions a great proportion of all land transfers, other than those involving fathers and sons, results from the failure of mortgagors to redeem their land.[6] In the Anekal villages enquiries were greatly hampered by the local creditors' professed, if not actual, belief that the private mortgaging of farmland had recently been made illegal, as it had not been, and my guarded enquiries of creditors had therefore to be made in the past tense.[7] Several Harijans related, in heart-broken fashion, how their mortgaged farms had been 'seized' by their creditors, who always seemed to be local men; but none of them produced any written agreements or could relate in any coherent way what they thought the original terms had been. The idea that documents might safeguard their position was quite alien to such people – not necessarily, I think, because of the frequency with which they are falsified by inflating the sum borrowed. As for Batagarawa, I had no idea of the extent of land mortgaging (*jingina*) there, until it ultimately proved possible to make secret enquiries through third parties, when it was found that as many as 16 of a total of 39 transactions in land had originally involved mortgaging.[8]

THE GENERAL SIGNIFICANCE OF LAND OWNERSHIP

Research has revealed that high status in the rural communities, in both regions, is achieved by no one who disdains or neglects farming as a way of life. Ownership of a reasonable acreage of well-cultivated farmland is an absolute necessity for every man of substance in the community, whatever his other occupations may be – this partly reflecting the high esteem in which heads of prosperous joint households are held in both regions.

The importance of land ownership to middle-aged men is analogous to, and connected with, their craving for sons: both land and sons are necessary components of a comfortable and contented middle age, and a man with 'plenty of sons' ought to provide them with 'plenty of land'. It is the common aspiration of men in both regions 'to retire into farming' in their middle or later years – whatever their former occupations may have been. In Hausaland, as in West Africa generally, few rurally-based 'business enterprises', other than the cultivation of farmland, stand much

[6] See Srinivas, 1976, p. 112.

[7] While the most common system probably involves the forfeiting of the farm failing repayment by a certain date, one creditor spoke of a system such that the creditor's use of the mortgaged farm for a certain period automatically extinguished the debt.

[8] See Hill (1972), p. 273.

chance of surviving the retirement or death of their founders; the sons of successful Hausa traders in farm produce seldom take over from their fathers, and traders' 'goodwill' is never saleable. So families hope to derive a sense of being 'perpetual corporate property-owning groups' (spurious though this idea is) by means of their ownership of farmland – and, in a few cases, in the Anekal villages, by the ownership of a substantial house. Cattle are constantly sold and sometimes die; jewellery and gold trinkets are hidden and pawned and may be stolen; clothing wears out – but land should be there in perpetuity for all to see, and is also certain to rise in value.

In the Anekal villages nowadays few householders take much interest in the possibilities of being 'modern farmers' – owning electric pump sets, superior irrigation wells and tractors,[9] and applying chemical fertilisers to appropriate 'high-yielding varieties'. But insofar as a man wishes to make a move in this direction, he stands no chance whatsoever of raising the funds required unless he can offer sufficient security mainly in the form of land to the banks and other official agencies who alone can help him – though, as we shall see, they usually fail to respond to his applications.[10]

Every householder, however prosperous, feels bound to produce significant quantities of basic grains. So anachronistic is the attitude to grain production, in both regions, that the richer the householder the greater the necessity that everyone in the village should suppose that he is pulling his weight by producing (and retaining) sufficient grain to provide for his own full sustenance as well as for his farm-labourers who may prefer payment in grain. (Indeed, if 'subsistence' must be admitted to our vocabulary, the richest cultivators are the only real subsistence farmers.) This is a matter of great significance, as we shall see, since only those with considerable holdings are able to continue to produce large quantities of grain while diversifying their agricultural output.

From this very brief summary of the reasons why richer householders covet land beyond any other form of property, we can understand that 'effective landlessness'[11] amounts almost to a condition of economic disenfranchisement in the village. So heavily are the dice weighted against landless men in their day-to-day life in the village that, as we shall see,[12]

[9] Although no farmer in the six Anekal villages owned a tractor, there were a few to be seen in the general neighbourhood. (In Dorayi in 1972 many farmers did not know what a plough looked like – though they, too, had seen tractors.)

[10] See Chapter XII.

[11] In this book I often employ 'landlessness' to include those who own up to (say) a couple of acres, both because these small holdings are apt to be of very poor quality and because their owners often fail to cultivate them.

[12] Chapter IX.

they stand hardly any chance of 'economic emergence' unless, as occasionally happens, they succeed in establishing satisfactory contact with the wider world – contact which need not involve daily commuting or any other *urban* connection.

Throughout this book I emphasise the close correlation between the scale of a man's farming and the lucrativeness of his non-farming occupation. While it is true that the profits of either form of activity may happen to nourish the other, it is also a fact that the starting point is land ownership. 'Without land you can travel nowhere.'

THE CLOSE RELATIONSHIP BETWEEN 'WEALTH' AND SIZE OF HOLDING

The closeness of the relationship between a household's standard of living (which for convenience I refer to as its 'wealth'[13]) and the size of its farm-holding, is revealed by Table VI(1) – which also shows that there were more large holdings in Batagarawa than in the Anekal villages. For Batagarawa we see that: whereas over a half (53%) of the rich men had holdings of 20 acres or more, hardly any other farmers had such large acreages; whereas nearly a half (47%) of the very poor men had holdings under 2 acres or were landless, there were no rich men in this position; and that whereas hardly any of the rich households had holdings under 5 acres, the proportions for the other three wealth groups were 27%, 63% and 88%.

Turning to the Anekal figures, we see that only 10% of rich households had holdings of 20 acres or more (cf. 53% in Batagarawa) and that nearly all (92%) of the poorest farmers were 'virtually landless' – cultivating 2 acres or less. Nearly all (96%) of the rich Anekal farmers had holdings of 5 acres or more, against 32%, 2% and nil for the other three wealth groups.

In which area is inequality more pronounced? Paying regard to the size of the largest holdings of the richest farmers, then the contrast between rich and poor is greater in Batagarawa; but concentrating on the proportion of virtually landless farmers, inequality is a far worse problem in the Anekal villages. Such a pair of conclusions was predictable given the higher population density in the Anekal villages.

[13] The methods by which households in the three research areas were classified by wealth (and by the age of the householder) are outlined in Appendix VI(1). In Appendix VI(2) I deal with the methods of estimating the size of individual farm-holdings, using aerial photographs in Hausaland and the official revenue survey records in the Anekal villages. Such great difficulties were encountered, especially in the Anekal villages, that the estimates are not nearly as reliable as I would wish – even though many hundreds of hours were devoted to the work.

Table VI(1). *Estimates of the size-distribution of farm-holdings in relation to wealth*

Acreage range	Rich		Middle		Poor		Very poor		Total	
	Bata.	Anekal	Bata.	Anekal	Bata.	Anekal	Bata.	Anekal	Bata.	Anekal
	(% of households)									
Nil	–	–	–	–	6	7	10	41	5 } 23	10 } 36
under 2.0	–	[2]	7	13	19	42	37	51	18 }	26 }
2.0 to 4.9	[6]	[2]	20	54	38	50	41	8	31	30
5.0 to 9.9	12	41	42	30	32	[2]	12	–	28	19
10.0 to 19.9	29	45	27	[2]	4	–	–	–	12	12
20 and over	53	10	[4]	–	–	–	–	–	6	3
TOTAL	100%	100%	100%	100%	100%	100%	100%	100%	100%	100%
Number of households	17	51	45	46	68	60	41	37	171	194

Notes:

Batagarawa

(1) Acreages relate only to manured farmland in the Batagarawa Hamlet Area.
(2) The figures are derived from Table V.4 on p. 76 of Hill (1972).
(3) Sons-in-*gandu* who live in separate houses from their father are regarded as belonging to their father's household – see p. 104 above.
(4) Land farmed by sons-in-*gandu* on their own account is included in household holdings; however, Table V.3 of Hill (1972) provides similar figures excluding these holdings.

Anekal villages

(1) The figures relate only to Hullahalli, Nanjapura and Vabasandra, for they are probably more reliable than those prepared for the other three villages.
(2) A few households had to be omitted owing to the impossibility of making reliable estimates – because, for example, much of the household's land lay in another village area for which the records were not available.
(3) Households, headed by women (see p. 112 above) are excluded.

WEALTH AND CASTE

The statistics in Tables VI(2a) and VI(2b), which should be read in conjuction with Table VI(3), bring out the very strong relationship between size of holding and caste in the Anekal villages by contrasting the situation of members of the richest caste (Reddy) with the poorest (Adikarnataka[14]) for two villages in which these two castes comprise some 75% of the population. Whereas nearly two-thirds (62%) of the Reddy households had holdings of 5 acres or more, only 6% of the AKs were thus situated; whereas 54% of the AK households were virtually landless,[15] only 11% of the Reddy were so ill-endowed. It is true that membership of the Reddy caste is no guarantee of prosperity, especially for sons who have recently separated from their fathers – Table VI(3) shows that 17% of all Reddy householders were classified as poor; but to be an AK means that there is hardly any chance of owning sufficient land to occupy one's family workforce properly. However, the condition of virtual landlessness is by no means confined to the lowest caste, for – see Table VI(2a) – as many as 42% of the households of 'other castes' were in this plight.[16] Only one of the 69 (classified) AK householders was rich (Table VI(3)), compared with over a half of the 54 (classified) Reddy householders.

DOMINANT CASTES

Srinivas's concept of the dominant caste in a village[17] has been subject to a good deal of unjust criticism, especially from Dumont,[18] who has rejected his definition altogether, partly because population size is one of Srinivas's criteria. But, following Parry,[19] one may reinstate the idea, provided that two castes, not necessarily one only, may sometimes be characterised as having 'decisive dominance' in a village. Taking account of wealth (including land ownership), numbers (except in one case), political power, ritual status and educational standards, there is no shadow of doubt as to which are the dominant caste(s) in each of the six Anekal villages;[20] the

[14] The poorest of all the castes, the Adidravidas, was not represented in these villages.
[15] The proportion for Nanjapura, taken separately, was even higher.
[16] Most of the virtually landless members of this very mixed collection of castes were: recent migrants; members of Scheduled castes other than the AK: sons who had recently left their fathers; or members of a very few craft or service castes (most notably the Agasa, the washermen) who take little interest in farming.
[17] See, for instance, 'The Dominant Caste in Rampura' by M. N. Srinivas, *American Anthropologist*, 1959.
[18] Dumont, 1970, p. 162.
[19] Parry, 1979, p. 57.
[20] See Appendix VI(3) for further discussion and statistical tables. See, also, *Peasant Society in Konku* by Brenda E. F. Beck, 1972, pp. 15–16, for an interesting discussion of the criteria of dominance – none of which is the size of the group.

Estimates of the size-distribution of farm-holdings in relation to caste: Hullahalli and Nanjapura

Table VI(2a)

Acreage range	Reddy		Adikarnataka		Other castes		All castes	
	(% of households)							
Nil	4	11	21	54	21	42	15	36
Under 2.0	7		33		21		21	
2.0 to 4.9	26		40		29		33	
5.0 to 9.9	31		6		17		17	
10.0 to 19.9	28	31	–		7		11	13
20 and over	3		–		5		2	
TOTAL	100%		100%		100%		100%	

Table VI(2b)

Acreage range	Reddy	Adikarnataka	Other castes	All castes
Nil and under 2.0	10	61	29	100%
2 to 4.9	27	51	22	100%
5 to 9.9	62	14	24	100%
10.0 and over	78	–	22	100%
TOTAL	34	41	25	100%
Numbers of households classified	57	70	42	169

Notes:
(1) Households headed by women (see p. 112 above) are excluded.
(2) A few other households had to be omitted owing to lack of reliable figures.

short list of such castes includes only the Reddy, the Gowda and the Kuruba, one or two of which are dominant in each village.[21]

Table VI(4) shows that as many as 82% of all the households classified as rich in the six villages belong to these dominant castes, which comprise

[21] For the names of the dominant caste in each village see Table VI(6), p. 137. The Reddy, the Kuruba and the Gowda are either the sole or more dominant of two castes in 4, 3 and 2 villages respectively.

Table VI(3). *Wealth in relation to caste: Hullahalli and Nanjapura*

Wealth classification	Reddy	Adikarnataka	Other castes	All castes
		(% of households)		
Rich	57	1	22	25
Middle	26	13	38	23
Poor	17	48	35	34
Very poor	–	38	5	17
	100%	100%	100%	100%
Numbers of households classified	54	69	40	163

Note:
With the possible exception of the Kuruba (17 households), no castes other than the Reddy and the Adikarnataka were sufficiently well represented in the villages for their separate classification in this table to have been statistically significant.

Table VI(4). *Wealth in relation to caste: dominant and Scheduled castes, six Anekal villages*

Wealth classification	Dominant castes	Scheduled castes	Other castes	Total
		(% of households)		
Rich	82	8	10	100%
Middle	56	30	14	100%
Poor	24	67	9	100%
Very poor	12	79	9	100%
Numbers of households classified	167	180	40	387
%	43%	47%	10%	100%

Note:
One or two castes are regarded as 'dominant' in each village. For the names of these castes see Table VI(6) in Appendix VI(3), where there is also a table showing wealth in relation to caste for each village.

43% of all classified households. However, membership of these castes is no guarantee of economic security, especially in some of the villages, for as Table VI(7), p. 138, shows, the proportion of dominant caste households which were classified as poor or very poor, was as high as 43% and 29% in Mahantalingapura and Nanjapura respectively – compared with only 7% in Hullahalli and nil in Vabasandra. As Table VI(4) shows, as many as 24% and 12% of all households in the two poorest wealth groups were members of the dominant castes, compared with 67% and 79% for all Scheduled caste households.

Rough estimates indicate that the proportions of land owned by members of the dominant castes in Hullahalli (Reddy and Gowda), Bukkasagara (Reddy and Kuruba) and Mahantalingapura (Gowda) were 64%, 44% and 59% respectively – the figures for the proportions of dominant caste households in each of these villages being 29%, 30% and 50%. (See, also, Table VI(5).) The question of the ownership of tank-irrigated land by dominant castes is dealt with in Appendix VI(4).

CHANGING TRENDS IN LAND OWNERSHIP

When village land markets were active, as they are not under our dry grain mode today, there was necessarily a strong tendency for individual richer households to add to their holdings by purchase from poorer households: more and more of the farmland necessarily became concentrated in the ownership of richer people *as a group*.[22] This is not to say that individual richer households necessarily tended to own more farmland as time went by, for this depended on numerous demographic and other factors, including differential birth rates and rates of outward migration. But in recent years, as the pace of land-selling has lessened, few households have been able to maintain the size of their holdings.

Material collected in both Batagarawa and Dorayi shows the process of redistribution at work in former times. In both these localities I went so far as to try to ascertain the 'provenance' of each mapped plot – whether inherited, bought, cleared from bush, etc., by the present owner. Although I now doubt whether the interest of the results justified the enormous labour involved,[23] the statistics do at least show that in former times richer farmers had bought much more of their farmland than poorer men. In

[22] Or so one would suppose. But in 'Landownership and Inequality in Madras Presidency: 1853–4 to 1946–7', *Indian Economic & Social History Review*, July–Sept. 1975, Dharma Kumar concluded (p. 261) that in that area there were no clear trends indicating that land ownership had 'become increasingly concentrated' during that period.

[23] See Hill (1972), Notes on Table IV.3, pp. 64–5, and Hill (1977), pp. 136–7.

Table VI(5). *Estimated land ownership by caste: six Anekal villages (% of land owned by resident villagers)*

(a) The stronger, or the sole dominant caste	52	
(b) The weaker dominant caste–if any	10	
(c) Dominant castes–total		62
Other mainly non-immigrant castes:		
(d) Adikarnataka and Adidravida		15
(e) Valmiki in Bukkasagara		3
(f) Brahmin		5
Castes which are mainly recent immigrants:		
(g) Bhovi in Mahantalingapura		4
(h) Pichiguntala in Srirampura		3
(j) Other		9
(k) Owned by resident villagers		100%

Notes:
(a) The figures vary between 64% for the Kuruba at Vabasandra and 27% for the Reddy at Bukkasagara.
(b) The figures vary between 26% for the Kuruba at Bukkasagara and 10% for the Gowda at Hullahalli.
(c) The figures vary between 73% for Nanjapura and 40% for Srirampura.
(d) Only low proportions of the households belonging to these Harijan castes are recent immigrants.
(g) Although many of the Bhovi were originally attracted by work at the nearby quarry they are nowadays also interested in cultivation.
(h) The Pichiguntalas, who are Harijans, own more land in Srirampura than the dominant Reddy who are not numerous.
(j) A mixed group of castes, none of which owns much land, some native to the villages others not.
(k) Excluding land owned by 'outsiders'; however, land owned by Nanjapura farmers in the Vabasandra Village Area and *vice versa* is included.

Dorayi rich men were recorded as having earlier bought at least 44% of their farmland, against 12% for the middle group and a negligible proportion for impoverished men; and a remarkably close relationship was found between the size of the farm-holding and the proportion which had been bought, the figure rising steadily from 7% for holdings of under an acre, to 36% for those between 5.0 and 7.5 acres and 41% for the largest holdings. In Batagarawa it was estimated[24] that the proportion of farmland which had been bought by heads of farming households fell from 27% for rich farmers to 25%, 6% and 3% for middle, poor and very poor farmers; very painstaking work also established that most farm-sellers had been poorer farmers.[25]

Now that the land market has become so sluggish that even the most impoverished landowners prefer to rent out rather than to sell their land, the tendency for richer households as a group to gain land from the poorest households will become much reduced – and the average holdings of richer farmers will diminish more rapidly. But the incidence of virtual landlessness will simultaneously increase, as has already happened in Dorayi, if only because of the impossibility of dividing very small holdings between several sons.[26] As already noted, chance factors of inheritance, such as having no brother, will assume more importance than ever;[27] and it will become more and more evident that individual richer households must intensify their production if they are not to fall into the common rut.

In the Anekal villages during the past few decades richer households have accumulated land by encroaching on the communal grazing ground (*gomal*) as well as by purchase – a process which has now gone so far that little grazing land remains in most villages. Other households have encroached also, including Harijans (who have received official allocations of marginal land) and newcomers. Although the compilation of Table VI(5) has involved much estimation,[28] it is a fact that members of 'immigrant castes' now own about a tenth of all the farmland. The table shows (a matter which will be discussed elsewhere) that the principal Harijan castes (the AKs and ADs), who formerly owned very little land have improved their position slightly, mainly as a result of the departure of the *jodidar* from Hullahalli.

The map of the farmland and the land revenue statistics for Nanjapura village show that the encroachment on grazing grounds, by both villagers and outsiders, has been particularly pronounced there since the most up-to-date farm map was drawn in 1923 – see Appendix III(2). If the census figures for Nanjapura are reliable it seems certain that the Reddy and

24 See Hill (1972), Table IV.2, p. 62.

25 See *ibid.*, pp. 88–91.

26 In Dorayi, where very tiny plots of a tenth of an acre (or so) are common, men have begun to see the absurdity of such an attempt at achieving fairness between brothers, and one brother may inherit all his father's farmland, maybe financially compensating the others.

27 See Hill (1977), pp. 152 *et seq.*

28 However, it is somewhat more reliable than tables relating to ownership by individual households which often involve estimating the actual division of land registered in the names of dead fathers or fathers with separated sons.

Kuruba populations there have at least doubled[29] between 1921 and 1971; but as land ownership by other castes is certain to have been very small in 1921, as it is today, and as there was no local *jodidar* whose lands have been distributed, acreages per head could only have been maintained by much larger encroachments on grazing land than are likely to have occurred. So in that particular village[30] it is likely that average acreages per household for the Reddy and Kuruba populations have fallen – while the parlous position of the Harijans has hardly improved.

The discussion in this chapter has been very generalised and broadly statistical, and the constant references to the inflexibilities resulting from the stultification of the land market may have suggested that the circumstances of individual households are nowadays almost entirely determined by accidents of inheritance and family size – which would indeed be an exaggeration, except so far as the great majority of Harijans are concerned. There has been no mention, for example, of such a subject as the collapse of rich *gandu* organisations in disarray on the father's death[31] – to the hiatus which is apt to occur, especially in Hausaland, on the death of the head of a joint household; or of the tendency for wealth to increase with the age of the household head. These and many other matters relevant to economic inequality will be discussed in the chapters which follow.

APPENDIX VI(1)

The methods of classifying households by 'wealth' and age

In Chapter II (pp. 67–9) I touched on the methods I adopted for classifying farming households in the two regions in accordance with their standard of living, and I also argued that conventional classifications based on estimates of annual income must be eschewed mainly because rural people would not conceptualise their living standards in terms of a single figure, even were it to be ascertainable with a reasonable degree of accuracy – as it never is. Although the methods I have

[29] Nanjapura has no associated hamlets to complicate the census statistics, so that the population of that nucleated village may actually have risen by some 110% (from 230 to 483) between 1921 and 1971. There are reasons to think that the ratio of the Reddy to the total population has increased somewhat in the past few decades.

[30] In demographic terms Nanjapura may be a reasonably typical Anekal village. Its crude population density was some 480 per sq. mile in 1971, against 550 for rural Anekal Taluk; and the proportion of Harijans in its population in 1971, according to the census, was 37% against 29% for rural Anekal Taluk.

[31] See Hill (1972), p. 184.

adopted have many limitations, I know of no superior procedures open to research workers who lack a very large staff of assistants whose task is to measure the actual income (and possibly also the expenditure) of individual households over a whole year – for given the pronounced seasonality of rural economic life no shorter period would do. Furthermore, even if funds had been available I would not myself have employed armies of fieldworkers because their very presence would have been bound to have distorted the rural economies; because supervision would necessarily have been inadequate; because their team spirit, however well meant, would have induced a conformity of attitude which would have imposed itself to some degree on the villagers themselves, who might have altered their behaviour; and, finally, because the friendliness that develops between field assistants and indigenes necessarily results in collusive work. It is because of the importance, for this kind of research, of classifying all (or the great proportion) of the farming households, rather than a sample,[32] that any classification based on actual income would necessitate the employment of so many educated field assistants.

In this context the expression 'household standard of living' cannot be at all rigorously defined: I, therefore, attempt no definition whatsoever. But the commonsense concept of economic inequality, which is inherent in the knowledge that some people are 'much better off' than others, is far from arbitrary, especially in the villages themselves where, as we shall see, there is a surprising degree of consensus as to who, roughly speaking, is richer than whom – and where the other main elements of social differentiation, viz. power, status and caste (in India), are separately distinguished in people's minds. People can compare the magnitudes of things which they cannot measure statistically.

For the sake of linguistic convenience and also to emphasise the inevitability of inconsistency, I often refer to the grouping of households in accordance with their standard of living as a 'wealth classification'. Unsatisfactory though the use of the positive word 'wealth' is in relation to communities where so many households are poor beyond the imagination of most 'urban rich', and where 'wealth' in the sense of 'capital' can seldom be evaluated, its employment involves an implicit rejection of any short-run 'income approach'[33] and also allows us to take account of such an unevaluable form of 'property' as a well-educated son. More objectionable, perhaps, is my employment of 'rich' to denote the group with the highest living standards; all I can do about this is to follow the Hausa villagers who constantly declared that 'rich', implies 'rich on village standards'.

I have already outlined (p. 68 above) my first tentative approach to the problem of 'wealth classification' in Batagarawa, using the subjective judgments of depend-

[32] Among the many objections to sampling in research of this type are: first, that any method of stratifying the sample in advance presupposes that the salient variables are already known – as is unlikely; second, that uniquely interesting households may happen to be omitted; and that there are apt to be unexpected advantages from the possibility of relating everybody to everybody else. (Partly owing to the emergence of 'new variables' in the course of the work, most samples prove to be far too small to be statistically significant.)

[33] Mainly owing to climatic vagaries, under our dry grain mode there is much variation in harvest size, and thus of income, from year to year.

able local assistants. Using the resultant classification as a guide, numerous simple calculations were later made for the households in each 'economic group' (as the wealth groups were then called) relating to such economic indicators as acreage of manured farmland per head, means of acquisition of farmland, ownership of granaries and livestock, *all* of which seemed to show not only that the average rich household was better off than the average middle household (and so on), but that the range of variation within economic groups, for most of the economic indicators, was remarkably small compared with the range of variation for the whole population.

From the village assistants we also learnt of certain salient indicators of well-being or poverty, which they would discuss when making their final assessments.[34] I cite the following 'marks of poverty' from a much longer list:[35]

'Having no manured farmland, he is just like somebody in a river, trying to catch the weeds.'

'He is always earning daily money for food and finds no time for cultivation.'

'He sold standing crops before harvest.'

'No food is cooked in his house.'

'The *gandu* is not serious.'

'He begs for second-hand clothes from his friends.'

'He sold all his compound sweepings as manure.'

'He is never given *bashi* or even *ramce* except by fools or strangers.'[36]

Experience in Batagarawa and elsewhere showed that ordinary members of the farming community were such excellent judges of household inequality because a man's 'wealth' is one of his inherent attributes, like his name, his height, his relative age, his physical strength – or his caste,[37] or sub-caste, in the Anekal villages. While an ignorant observer may search all the time for uniformities, *the insider's view constantly emphasises heterogeneity.*

In Dorayi much reliance was again placed on the wealth assessments made by village assistants;[38] but this would not have been appropriate in the Anekal villages partly owing to the prejudices and ignorance associated with caste differentiation. For the Anekal villages our classification was based on everything relevant that I, and my two regular non-village assistants, had recorded about each household,

[34] Each man made his original assessment independently; they then later discussed any cases of disagreement.

[35] See Hill (1972), pp. 148–9.

[36] A condition of 'too poor to borrow', *ramce* being a shorter-term loan than *bashi.*

[37] In village life it is as though a person's caste or sub-caste were as 'obvious' as (say) his skin-colour – which, of course, it is not; urban university students, on the other hand, make a point of asking no questions, so that they may well be ignorant of a close friend's caste.

[38] The work was peculiarly difficult in Dorayi, where it was necessary to classify the numerous sons of retired fathers separately, although they were resident with their fathers.

including acreages of wet and dry farmland, employment of (or as) farm labourers, ownership of equipment and livestock, non-farming occupations and housing; however, 8% of all households, most of which were certainly fairly poor, proved to be unclassifiable owing to insufficient information,[39] and all households headed by women which included no married man, such as a married son, were omitted – they amounted to 10% of all households.

Finally, readers should be warned that these wealth classifications should not be used to compare living standards or relative degrees of inequality in Batagarawa, Dorayi and the Anekal Villages. *They are mere statistical tools facilitating the analysis of the causes and consequences of inequality within each of the rural communities.*

The ages of household heads

In work of this kind it is essential to ascertain the ages of household heads, a task which proved almost as difficult in the Anekal villages as in Hausaland. Ordinary adult villagers in both regions do not regard their numerical age in years as of much significance and when asked to guess their ages, or those of others, are often wildly inaccurate. In both regions, also, one was hampered by a lack of interest in key dates to which people might relate salient events in their own past lives. In Dorayi the difficulties of age assessment were so great that I was obliged to ask my local assistants to classify each married man in one of our indigenous age-*cum*-status groups,[40] roughly corresponding to young, young middle-aged, middle-aged and old – (say) over 60 to 65. In the Anekal villages where we endeavoured to ascertain the age of every member of each household, this additional information was a check on the age of the household head; although our final classification had to be in ten-year age bands, 20+, 30+, and so forth, it was certainly more reliable than the estimates for Hausaland.

APPENDIX VI(2)
The estimation of the size of farm-holdings

In Hausaland, where there were no official farm maps, the farm-plots were elaborately mapped using aerial photographs which had been kindly lent by Survey Departments.[41] Although the farm boundaries, which were mostly low grass ridges in Batagarawa and henna hedges at Dorayi, were clearly visible on the photographs,[42] which had fortunately been taken during the dry season, it was, of course,

39 Examples of those who had to be omitted were certain new arrivals, households which depended mainly on work at a local quarry or brick factory and farmers whose land lay wholly or mainly outside the village area.

40 See Hill (1977), pp. 110–11.

41 For further details see Hill (1972), pp. 63–5, and Hill (1977), pp. 136–7.

42 See Plates 33 to 35 in Hill (1972).

necessary to walk around each farm discussing ownership details with a well-informed companion, and also noting, for example, cases of 'false boundaries' (resulting, for example, from reluctance to uproot valuable henna bushes when two plots were combined) or 'non-existent boundaries' – e.g. cases when fathers had failed to mark off land given to sons. After the farms had been mapped by my assistant on tracing paper, I spent a great many days in my house or office inviting my local assistants to check the ownership of the plots, since I found that they could stroll through the farmland in their imaginations, 'personalising' each tile in the elaborate mosaic of farm-plots, and that their senses of direction, in terms of the points of the compass, were fairly accurate; I also asked them to say how each farm-owner had acquired his plot, whether by inheritance, purchase, etc. Although there were some special problems relating, for instance, to the ownership of farmland by women,[43] to plots allotted by fathers to sons, and to plots which had been temporarily lent out (*aro*), the results were fairly reliable, as numerous checks showed. The main difficulty resulted from the ownership of land outside the range of the aerial photograph; this was a particularly serious problem in an area of dispersed settlement like Dorayi, and some farmers whose plots appeared to lie mainly outside the mapped area had to be omitted from the statistics of farm-holdings.

The land revenue records in the Anekal villages provided a much worse basis for compiling statistics of land-holdings than the Hausa aerial photographs, as will already have become obvious to readers of Appendix II(1). There is also the difficulty arising from the fairly strong propensity, especially in some villages, to own land outside the village area. As in Hausaland, it was necessary to omit some land owners from our statistical tables owing to defective information. Although I hope that I have done sufficient to warn readers that the word 'estimate' is even something of a euphemism in relation to my statistics of farm-holdings, yet at the same time I have to emphasise that my figures are far more reliable than they would have been had I relied merely on informants' own statements of their acreages. While Anekal farmers, unlike Hausa men, often speak in terms of acres[44] (though never in terms of *guntas*, the official measure of a fortieth of an acre), they do not *think* in terms of this obsolete colonial measure – thus, they lack the art of glancing at a field and estimating its acreage with any reliability.

APPENDIX VI(3)

Wealth in relation to caste: dominant and Scheduled castes

Table VI(6), which is derived from Table I(1) above, shows that the very great majority of all households in the six Anekal villages belong either to a dominant

[43] In Hausaland no one, not even the parties themselves, may know whether the ownership of a wife's plot has in fact passed to her husband.

[44] Although India has adopted the metric system for most purposes, it is not surprising that there is no interest in replacing acres by hectares in the land records.

Table VI(6). *Classification of households by caste*

Village	Dominant castes	Scheduled (percentages)	Other	Total
Hullahalli	29	58	13	100
Bukkasagara	29	44	27	100
Mahantalingapura	51	32	17	100
Nanjapura	57	38	5	100
Vabasandra	45	48	7	100
Srirampura	22	76	2	100
All villages	39	48	13	100%

Note:
The dominant castes were: Hullahalli (Reddy and Gowda); Bukkasagara (Kuruba and Reddy); Nanjapura (Reddy and Kuruba); Vabasandra (Kuruba); and Srirampura (Reddy).

caste (39%) or to a Scheduled caste (48%), and that only in Bukkasagara do more than a fifth of all households belong to other castes.

Turning to Table VI(7) the following points may be noted:
(*a*) In two of the villages very few or none of the households of the dominant castes are impoverished (poor or very poor) – Hullahalli (7%), Vabasandra (nil); by contrast, in the other four villages quite high proportions of dominant caste households are impoverished – Mahantalingapura (43%), Nanjapura (29%–47% for the Kuruba, 21 % for the Reddy), Bukkasagara (25%–41% for the Kuruba, nil for the Reddy), Srirampura (27%).
(*b*) In all the villages save Mahantalingapura, the great majority of Scheduled caste households are impoverished; however, Mahantalingapura is exceptional because some four-fifths of classified Scheduled caste households belong to the Bhovi caste – see p. 42.
(*c*) There is little variation between the villages in the proportion of households which are rich or middle. (But Srirampura has an exceptionally low proportion of rich households, owing to lack of farmland and many immigrants.)
(*d*) Other castes (neither dominant nor Scheduled) as a group, have a notably even distribution between the wealth groups, but this is of little interest since the group is very mixed, the relatively rich Brahmins (4 out of 6 classified households being rich) being included with, for example, the impoverished Satani (4 out of 5 of whom are impoverished).

Table VI(7). *Caste and 'wealth'*

Village	Rich	Middle	Poor	Very poor	Total
	(% in each wealth group)				
1. *Dominant castes*					
Hullahalli	64	29	7	–	100
Bukkasagara	50	25	18	7	100
Mahantalingapura	23	34	34	9	100
Nanjapura	35	35	25	4	100
Vabasandra	53	47	–	–	100
Srirampura	27	45	27	–	100
2. *Scheduled castes*					
Hullahalli	2	19	46	33	100
Bukkasagara	3	13	63	21	100
Nanjapura	3	7	55	34	100
Vabasandra	6	6	31	56	100
Total 4 villages	3	13	51	33	100
Mahantalingapura	12	44	44	–	100
Srirampura	3	21	70	6	100
Total 6 villages	4	17	54	25	100
3. *Other castes*					
All villages	20	35	32	13	100
1–3. *All castes*					
Hullahalli	26	22	33	20	100
Bukkasagara	21	24	39	16	100
Mahantalingapura	17	38	38	7	100
Nanjapura	25	25	36	15	100
Vabasandra	31	28	17	25	100
Srirampura	9	27	60	4	100
All villages	22	26	37	15	100%

Note:
For the names of the dominant castes in each village see the note to Table VI(6).

APPENDIX VI(4)

The unequal distribution of tank-irrigated paddy land

The distribution of paddy land by caste is hardly more favourable to the dominant castes than that of dry land. As Table VI(8) shows, about two-thirds (68% and 69%) of the paddy land is owned by the dominant castes in three villages[45] – the corresponding proportions for dry land being 64% and 70%. However, the Adikarnatakas own proportionately somewhat less of the wet than of the dry land – in Hullahalli they own 16% of the wet and 22% of the dry land, the respective figures for the other two villages being 8% and 11%. In Hullahalli some of the ex-*jodidar*'s wet land was obtained by AKs, and 12% of all wet land there is owned by

Table VI(8). *Ownership of tank-irrigated land by caste*[(a)]*: three Anekal villages*

Caste	Nanjapura and Vabasandra		Hullahalli		Nanjapura and Vabasandra		Hullahalli	
	% of wet land				% of households which own no wet land			
Reddy		54	Reddy	64	Reddy	38	Reddy	22
Kuruba		14	Gowda	5	Kuruba	57	Gowda	–
Total dominant castes		68		69		48		17
Brahmin		16		3		40[(b)]		–
Adikarnataka								
Thotis		8		4		79		54
Other		–		12				
Other		8		11		87		68
All castes		100%		100%		60%		42%

Notes:

(*a*) The ownership of land by outsiders is omitted; they owned about 57 of the total of 182 acres.

(*b*) The figure would be 20% were it not that one ex-*shanbhog*'s land is all situated at his former village.

(*c*) Households headed by women are omitted.

[45] Two of the villages (Bukkasagara and Srirampura) have no tank-irrigated land, though the former has a little rain-fed paddy land, and the statistics relating to such land in Mahantalingapura are defective.

AKs other than those who are *thotis* (village servants) – who retain their *inamti* (officially allocated) land; in Nanjapura and Vabasandra, on the other hand, the only AKs who own wet land are *thotis*. Most of the wet land owned by the few Brahmin households (they own as much as 16% of the total in Nanjapura and Vabasandra) is also *inamti* land.

However, wet land is more unevenly distributed than dry land if account be taken of the households which own none of it. The table shows that 60% of Nanjapura and Vabasandra households lack wet land, the proportion being as high as 48% for the dominant castes; again, Hullahalli is seen to be a somewhat different case since only 17% of all dominant caste households have no wet land.

In Nanjapura and Vabasandra some 20% of the holdings of resident villagers are under ½ acre, only 16% being over 3 acres. At least a quarter of all plots (probably more) are under ¼ acre, the proportion under one acre being at least 90%; the largest plot is about 2.6 acres.

A note on the ownership of irrigation wells

The wide-diametered, stone-lined, shallow irrigation wells, which are mainly used for growing unusual crops such as vegetables, are extremely unevenly distributed among cultivators. Since many of the wells have fallen into desuetude, or are seldom used; and since householders who are close kin often share wells (as they share no other form of property) – there would be no point in presenting elaborate statistics of the proportions of householders of various castes who are well-owners. The important and plain fact is that some four-fifths of all the 50 to 60 wells in working order are owned by members of the three dominant castes (Reddy, Gowda and Kuruba) and that only three AKs are well-owners or have a well under construction.

Only 5 of the wells are operated by electric pump-sets, all of them owned by 4 members of the Kuruba caste in Vabasandra. Most of the remainder are operated by cattle; but wells equipped only with hand-operated pulleys are not unusual. Nowadays new wells, which probably cost at least £2,000, are always largely financed by bank loans.

CHAPTER VII

The Diversity of Economic Activity

> When the peasantry combine agricultural and industrial occupations on a large scale, a combination of the two systems of classification is necessary . . . . The methods of summarising peasant household returns are not such a narrowly specific and second-rate problem as one might imagine at first sight.[1] Lenin

The contemporary conviction that rural inequality *necessarily* derives from the outside urban world is partly based on a failure to appreciate the diversity of rural economic activity. A 'peasant household' is presumed to be basically dependent on patiently cultivating the soil, with hoe or with plough, households being inherently similar, except for the matters of wealth, size and farm-labouring. Even though some 'peasant households' might be classified as rich, some as middle, some as poor, this differentiation is regarded as a mere matter of degree – as though all were members of the same animal species, some happening to be bigger and more powerful than others.

Orthodox radical ideas on this matter have slipped into vast over-simplification since Lenin inveighed so strongly against the misuse of averages,[2] ironically observing that all 'false ideas' about the differentiation of the peasantry would be 'eliminated once and for all' by the regular and exclusive use of average data on peasant farming.[3] And who are the contemporary writers who accept that rural domestic industry is the 'normal supplement'[4] of 'peasant production' – to the degree that it, rather than land, might happen to provide the basis of any system of rural differentiation?

LACK OF SELF-SUFFICIENCY IN GRAIN

Under our dry grain mode a great proportion of households are obliged to follow non-farming occupations, their grain production being altogether insufficient for household needs and farm-labouring being a highly

[1] 1899, *Collected Works*, Vol. III, p. 105. [2] Citation on p. 40 above.
[3] *Collected Works*, Vol. III, p. 171.
[4] *Capital*, Vol. III, Book III, by K. Marx (Progress Publishers, Moscow, 1971), p. 807.

seasonal occupation, which cannot even be relied on to provide regular employment during the farming season owing to the spasmodic nature of the demand for labour. Precise estimates cannot (of course) be made, but I think it likely that at least two-thirds of Hullahalli households would find it impossible to produce sufficient grain for their own consumption, even if none of the smaller producers sold grain after threshing to meet their debts and essential expenditure – as many of them do. In Appendix VII(1), on the low yields of millets and sorghum under our dry grain mode, I suggest that average yields per acre of *ragi* in south-eastern Karnataka are unlikely to exceed 400 lb per acre. If that is so, then household self-sufficiency demands that households should have *at least* one acre per head of population under *ragi*[5] – which, for the sake of simplicity, I regard as equivalent to 1.3 acres per head of weighted population,[6] children under 16 being regarded as 'half-adults'.

In computing the figures of 'acreage' per head of weighted population in Table VII(1) I have arbitrarily regarded one acre of irrigated paddy land as equivalent to 4 acres of dry land, to allow for the higher yield of the former type of land. The table shows that 69% of all Hullahalli households cultivated no more than 1.4 'acres' per head of weighted population – the proportion varying between 24% for Reddy households and 98% for AK households. It is therefore likely that *a majority of households failed to achieve self-sufficiency in grain*, even if no other crop were cultivated and no grain were sold – the number of self-sufficient AK households being negligible. (About a half (51%) of all AK households are seen to cultivate less than half an 'acre' per head of weighted population, very few[7] if any, Reddy households being in this position.) If bush farms be excluded, the statistics for Batagarawa show a similar distribution to those for Hullahalli; since many of the poorest Batagarawa households cultivated no bush land, the proportion of households which were obliged to buy grain was clearly very high there – perhaps of the order of a half of all households if grain yields were somewhat higher than in Hullahalli.

In this chapter on the various types of diversification practised by farmers with varying living standards, I have several aims. First, I am attacking the old-style colonial idea, which is still surprisingly influential, that village communities of our type are essentially aggregates of arable farmers and

[5] See p. 212 below for a discussion of grain requirements.

[6] About a half of the population of Hullahalli consists of children under 16 years. (All these estimates are deliberately rough to convey that we are necessarily concerned with orders of magnitude only.)

[7] The few households that were possibly in this position had to be omitted from the table as reliable estimates were lacking.

Table VII(1). *Estimated 'acreage' per head of 'weighted population'*

'Acreage' per head	Hullahalli All households		Hullahalli Reddy households		Hullahalli Adikarnataka households		Batagarawa All households	
	% of households							
over 5	6		19		–		9	
2.0 to 4.9	12		43		–		7	
1.9 to 1.5	12		14		[2]		16	
1.4 to 1.0	17		14		23		21	
0.9 to 0.5	18	69	[10]	24	23	98	27	68
0.4 and less	34		–		51		20	
	100%		100%		100%		100%	
Total number of households included	88		21		43		162	

Notes:

(1) In computing 'acreages' for individual households one acre of irrigated paddy land has been counted as the equivalent of 4 acres of dry land.

(2) Hullahalli households headed by women are excluded.

(3) Households for which reliable estimates of acreages were unavailable were omitted.

(4) In computing the 'weighted population' of each household children under sixteen were counted as 'half-adults'.

(5) The households which owned 0.4 acres or less may be regarded as 'effectively landless' since many of those with tiny acreages do not cultivate.

agricultural labourers, together with a few specialised artisans, washermen and so forth. Second, I shall provide evidence of the close relationship, especially in Hausaland, between household living standards and the types of non-farming occupation followed by men. And third, I shall emphasise the significance of livestock ownership, especially in the Anekal villages. Detailed particulars of a number of households will illustrate these and other matters.

DIVERSIFICATION IN BATAGARAWA

In rural Hausaland it is a general rule, to which the extreme case of Dorayi is a partial exception, that every able-bodied man and woman, with the exception of very young wives and some young unmarried men, has at least one occupation (*sana'a*),[8] which they invariably pursue on their own account, independently of their spouses, maybe at any time or during the long dry season only. In the case of men, though not, as we shall see, in the case of women, the more lucrative types of occupation are followed by members of richer households which are successful cultivators, since no one neglects his farming the better to pursue his occupation.

Considering the 62 household heads in the two richer wealth groups in Batagarawa, about a third of them were traders, of whom over a third were *'yan kwarami*[9] who buy grains, groundnuts and other farm produce in nearby markets, and elsewhere, for immediate retail sale, mainly in Batagarawa itself; other traders included sellers of sweet potatoes, kola nuts, cattle, small livestock and tobacco, as well as 5 shopkeepers or 'tablesellers' – who sell from small tables out of doors. About a fifth of all the richer household heads were craftsmen, including blacksmiths, builders, tailors and dyers; another fifth having been Koranic teachers and/or serious students. Only one of the 62 richer men had no occupation, he being decrepit.

The occupations of the 41 poorest householders provided a miserable contrast. Only 2 of them were traders and only 5 were craftsmen, including 2 builder's assistants. As many as 13 of them were engaged in collecting and/or manufacturing 'free goods' – such as firewood, other materials (such as grass for thatching) which might be freely collected, or manufactures therefrom, such as mats, thatches, ropes, fences, etc. Other occupations included general labouring (mainly earth carrying), drumming, barbering, butchering and the repair and decoration of calabashes (dried gourds used as receptacles). None of the 41 men, however old and decrepit, was without an occupation of some sort. I have already given particulars of the multifarious activities of the members of the household of Alhaji Mai Goro;[10] I now provide particulars for two other Batagarawa households, one rich, the other poor.

This elderly man was formerly, for many years, a long-distance trader, who used to

[8] *Sana'a* and 'occupation' are proper synonyms inasmuch as unpaid non-farming activities which take time and are systematically pursued, such as Koranic studies or *sarauta* (government), are included in the Hausa concept, along with skilled craftwork, long-distance trading, gambling and thieving, as a way of life. Indeed, Hausa speakers often use 'occupation' in place of *sana'a*.

[9] Ambitious younger men, who are able to borrow enough to finance their first purchase of a sack of grain for quick resale locally and who immediately buy more grain with the proceeds, often use this occupation as a pump-primer. Their economic role is an important one – see Hill (1972).

[10] See p. 71 above.

walk, with his loaded donkeys, as far as Ibadan, some 500 miles away; he was also a trader within Katsina Emirate, buying such produce as groundnuts, cowpeas and sugar cane at markets and villages and selling it in urban markets and elsewhere. Nowadays he buys farm produce mainly from householders in surrounding villages, who receive a commission for storing it for him in their granaries until he decides to resell, at a profit, at various markets or from his house. His wife, who has women assistants, makes large quantities of groundnut oil for sale from nuts which she buys from her husband and others. He is well known for lending grain before harvest and groundnut seed – for lending 7s worth of seed at planting time he would expect a return of 12s worth of groundnuts at harvest. His only resident married son, who is in *gandu* with him, is an active trader in fowls, which he buys locally and resells at about double the price in Lagos (some 600 miles away), maybe travelling to Lagos by lorry, with about 80 fowls in baskets, about five times during the dry season.

His father had sold all his farms except for a fragment which he had given directly to his grandson. Himself a farm-seller, he owns no manured farmland and hardly cultivates his bush farm. Little food is cooked in his house. He maintains himself mainly by firewood collection. His married son, who is in *gandu* only in the sense that he has not formally departed, recently succeeded in reclaiming a farm which, it was said, his father had sold to spite him – acting out the sins of his forefathers in so doing; being a serious farmer on his own account, and also a farm labourer and earth collector for builders, he (unlike his father) would seem to be emerging from his plight.

DIVERSIFICATION IN DORAYI

Dorayi is a somewhat different case both because of its high population density, which means that there are few 'free goods' to collect, and because of its closeness to Kano city where a fair number of richer men work as traders. The most directly lucrative occupation open to richer men in Dorayi is trading in farm produce, this involving the purchase of grains, groundnuts, locust beans, rice, cowpeas, etc. in less densely populated rural areas, mainly for resale from their own houses usually when seasonal prices had risen. Nearly two-thirds of all rich men are traders of one kind or another and/or Koranic teachers or students – the only other occupations of any significance being wood cutting[11] and tailoring. So limited are the opportunities in this anomalous place that the majority of richer men were not nearly as fully occupied as they would wish – there were, for example, only about ten traders whose operations were wholly unrestricted by local limitations of demand and supply.[12]

[11] See p. 159 below.

[12] See Hill (1977), p. 103. For the relationship between wealth and main non-farming occupation see Hill (1977), pp. 119–21 and p. 154.

Unlike richer men, few poor men benefited from the closeness of Kano city. At least three-quarters of all poor men were obliged to rely entirely on such occupations as general labouring, earth digging, paid transportation of many types of load (including manure from Kano, farm produce, firewood, etc) and the making of 'cornstalk beds' – flat, brittle mats made of guinea corn stalk, bound together with string, which are mainly sold in Kano city.[13] The short list of other occupations included well-digging, building, thatching, trading, wood cutting, barbering, clothes washing and drumming.

The general thesis that farming and non-farming occupations flourish in conjunction is well borne out by Dorayi: there are so few prosperous farmers (only 2% of all farm-holdings were over 10 acres) that hardly anybody possessed sufficient financial scope to allow him to branch out effectively in other directions. The following rich man was much admired in Dorayi.

The owner of at least 15 acres, this middle-aged man has prospered as a farmer and also as a produce trader – so that he is locally described as being 'just like a *madugu*', an old-style leader of a trading caravan. He buys produce in Katsina and Bauchi Emirates, and also in nearby markets, and undertakes much storage for a price rise; he sells both locally, from his house, and in the city. Unlike other Dorayi produce buyers he has several business associates. He is particularly noted for buying great quantities of locust beans, and three of his four wives make and sell locust bean cakes from beans which they buy from him. He grants loans, at high interest, to wage-earners in the city and is a local creditor.

But considering that about a third of the Dorayi population lives in big houses, including 7 or more married men and their dependants, we must not overlook all the economic activities that go on inside their walls – and close kinship, it must be remembered, never stands in the way of commercial dealings. Since women are among the most active members of this house, the following case notes may serve as an introduction to the economic role of women in Hausaland which has so far been neglected in this chapter.

As already noted, in localities of dispersed settlement, where nodes on the economic landscape are apt to be singularly lacking, a really big house, such as the following, is a species of market-place serving outsiders as well as its own members.

The members of this Dorayi house, which is the home of 14 married men and 71 people, can buy virtually all their requirements of foodstuffs, except meat, inside

[13] Owing to the paucity of opportunities many richer men, also, engaged in this humble, unskilled, ill-paid, craftwork. See Hill (1977), pp. 170 and 178.

the house, which also attracts many ambulant traders, selling cloth, clothing, shoes and sundry items for personal use. Two or three rich men in the house buy and resell all the grain that is required by its members, additional to their 'own production'; at least 8 wives make groundnut oil and cake[a] for sale and others make locust bean cakes;[b] numerous cooked snacks[c] are on sale; groundnuts, vegetables, palm oil, kerosene, kola nuts (in quantity), cigarettes, sugar, salt, natron,[d] etc. are usually available. A grinding mill for grains and other produce has been installed, women household members paying the same fees for its use as other people. One room in the house is reserved as a mosque.

Notes

a The cake (*kulikuli*) is the nourishing and tasty residue from the hand expression of groundnut oil.

b After elaborate processing, including fermentation, these beans are made by women into blackish cakes, which are an almost essential ingredient of many dishes.

c In Hausaland, unlike south India, rural women often buy cooked food, including complete meals, from each other.

d Natron (*kanwa*), which is sometimes misleadingly known as potash, is a naturally occurring substance, which replaces or supplements salt, and has many other uses; it still enters very extensively into long-distance trade in Nigeria. See Hill (1972), p. 301.

HAUSA WOMEN TRADERS

There are few West African regions where women are not the main retailers of foodstuffs for local consumption – and in some regions, especially in the south, they are also responsible for most of the food wholesaling; as traders, women operate entirely independently of their husbands and demand a reward for any selling they do on his behalf. By no means deterred by purdah, the house-bound women of Hausaland find full outlet for their independent enterprise as traders and as processors of many types of saleable foodstuffs, some of which, like locust bean cakes, still enter extensively into rurally-organised long-distance trade. When women were able to move about freely (and it must always be remembered that full rural seclusion is a very recent development), they often engaged in the purchase and storage of farm produce for sale at a seasonal price rise. (One reason why Hausa village women are traders when, by and large, Anekal village women are not,[14] is that produce trading generally is a rurally-based activity in the one region, but not in the other.[15]) Also, whereas Hausa husbands favour the economic enterprise of their wives as enhancing their

14 Women sometimes wander about the villages selling vegetables; and they are also, perhaps, the main vendors of farm produce at the very small market-places in Anekal Taluk (*shandies*), of which there are so very few. (I am grateful to Dr Susan Bayly for pointing out that women in specialist non-cultivating castes in Tamil Nadu are often heavily involved in trade.)

15 See Appendix XII(1).

economic independence and so reducing their burdensomeness, Anekal husbands often feel threatened by the implications of their wives' economic enterprise – if any.

In the case of Hausa women there is no close association between the standard of living of their household and the lucrativeness of their 'occupation': it is not uncommon for a notably impoverished farmer to have a wife who is a prominent house-trader, and not all of the wives of rich men prosper as traders. Any woman, however poor, can enter this work since the raw foodstuffs, such as grains and groundnuts, may be paid for after the processing and selling has been completed. In Batagarawa[16] about two-thirds of all women were engaged in house-trading on their own account, some of whom also sold grain and other produce on behalf of their husbands who were traders (*'yan kwarami*) – though men were usually the sellers of grain they had produced on their own farms. With the exception of meat and fresh vegetables, most of the normal day-to-day requirements of the villagers, including such manufactures as matches and kerosene, were met by these house-bound women traders, who also sold large quantities of snacks and other processed foods. The support given by husbands to this enterprise is shown by their willingness to assist in procuring supplies of manufactured goods which their wives would pay for and resell.

The hidden 'honeycomb market' of Batagarawa, the cells of which were linked by children, was a true substitute for an open market-place, in terms both of the range of goods on offer and its competitiveness – on any day the standard price of grain was known to everybody, as it would be in an open market. It is not surprising that many attempts to establish an open market-place in Batagarawa had failed.

In Dorayi, also, most day-to-day requirements were bought from secluded women traders.[17] Although there, as elsewhere, each woman trades on her own behalf, independently of her co-wives, there is some tendency for all the women living in big houses to specialise in producing a certain product, such as groundnut oil, since they enjoy co-operating in some of the heavy work of pounding and grinding: thus, as many as 19 of the 21 wives in one big house were apt to make groundnut oil for sale.

DIVERSIFICATION IN THE ANEKAL VILLAGES

Diversification in the Anekal villages is more directly related to agriculture, including the rearing of livestock, than in Hausaland, though few new annual crops of any significance have been introduced during this cen-

[16] See Hill (1972), pp. 268–9. [17] See Hill (1977), p. 178.

tury.[18] The main reasons for this include: the much greater importance of draught cattle, coupled with the lack of specialised pastoralists corresponding to the Fulani in Hausaland; the high demand for milk, which makes it economic to maintain enormous water buffaloes as mere milk producers;[19] the meagre opportunities of pursuing non-farming occupations, particularly trading; and the rapid expansion of the area of casuarina plantations.[20]

Table VII(2), which distinguishes between the non-farming occupations of members of the main Harijan castes and other castes, shows that only 5% of all male household heads in five[21] Anekal villages are traders and that only 8% are craftworkers or artisans – the comparable figures for Batagarawa being 26% (traders including butchers) and 13% (craftsmen). About half of the traders are village shopkeepers: their scale of operation in terms of turnover, range of stock and credit-granting is generally very small indeed – some of them even being impoverished strangers. In these villages there are no counterparts of either the rural produce traders of Hausaland who buy crops such as groundnuts and locust beans in large quantities, often in other localities, for the purpose of storage for a price rise, or of the *'yan kwarami* who buy elsewhere for immediate resale locally. Most Anekal village traders (apart from a few cattle traders or brokers and some shopkeepers) are fairly humble people, like the sole trader in *ragi* straw (a Harijan who does not even own a cart) or the Harijan trader in waste diesel oil for farm carts.

Although much the most important occupation of Harijans connects with the cutting of casuarina woods, except in the village of Srirampura this work is rather irregular; other occupations include hereditary and other crafts (6%) and village servants (*thotis*) – 5%. As many as 68% of all non-Harijan household heads (compared with 48% of Harijans) were recorded as having 'no occupation'[22] – but see note (1) on the table.

Rich men aim primarily at agricultural diversification as the following notes on six such men[23] (three of them brothers) indeed show. Thus, (A) aspires to be a modern tractor-owning farmer growing a great variety of crops; (B) owes his prosperity to his work as a casuarina contractor;

[18] This is probably true of much of India. Thus, Kessinger reported that in a certain north Indian village no new crops were introduced during 1848–1968. *Vilyatpur 1848–1968* by T. G. Kessinger, 1974, p. 103.

[19] See Appendix VII(3).

[20] See pp. 159–60 below and, also, Appendix VII(5).

[21] The statistics for Vabasandra were omitted, being incomplete.

[22] It is unfortunate that it was impossible to compile reliable figures of numbers of milk traders, since this can be an important source of income.

[23] To conceal identities, all the men's names are false and villages are omitted.

Table VII(2). *The non-farming occupations*[1] *of male household heads in the Anekal villages*[2]

	All castes other than main Harijan castes No.	%	Main Harijan castes[3] No.	%	Total No.	%
(a) Traders–shopkeepers	9	7	–	2	9	5
–others	8		3		11	
(b) Craftworkers–'hereditary'	18	8	4	6	22	8
–other	3		7		10	
(c) Stone-workers–rock agents	14	7	1	3	15	5
–rock-cutters	1		3		4	
–other	2		–		2	
(d) Casuarina–wood contractors	4	4	10	30	14	15
–wood-cutters	6		42		48	
(e) Priests	6	2	–	–	6	1
(f) Village servants–*thotis*	–	–	9	5	9	2
(g) Other	9	4	12	7	21	5
Total of above	80	32	91	52	171	40
(h) 'No occupation'	172	68	83	48	255	60
GRAND TOTAL	252	100%	174	100%	426	100%

Notes:

(1) Among the occupations which are excluded are casual labouring, milk trading, firewood collection and the cutting of incense sticks, since many people happen to do this work occasionally or spasmodically; the small number of men who commute to Bangalore for factory work is omitted since work appeared to be very irregular. If the household head is either retired or a woman the occupation included is that of his/her eldest married son. If a man has more than one occupation the most important only is included.

(2) The village of Vabasandra is excluded

(3) The main Harijan castes are here regarded as the Adikarnataka, the Adidravida and the Pichiguntala – the Bhovi, though Scheduled, are omitted, see p. 42.

Types of occupation

(a) While only 2 cattle traders and 2 sheep traders are included many men occasionally buy or sell animals on behalf of others.

(b) 'Hereditary' type craftsmen are regarded as washermen (5), barbers (3), blacksmiths (3), blanket weavers (2) and basket makers (9); of the 10 other craftsmen only 7 were recorded as being carpenters or masons – a figure which is probably too low.

(c) All in Mahantalingapura – see Appendix VII(6).

(d) See p. 159 below for the distinction between wood contractors and cutters.

(g) 'Other occupations' include 5 lorry drivers, loaders, etc. A brick factory near Bukkasagara provides some employment for women and children in that village, but little regular work for men.

(h) See note (1) above.

(C) made his fortune through milk production and trading; and the wider activities of the three brothers (D) include large-scale livestock ownership, the production of crops irrigated from wells and credit-granting.

(A) The late father of Krishnappa was one of the three enterprising and successful sons of a very important farmer, a Kuruba who had died about 1945, leaving large savings in the form of silver coin; four of his surviving sons and grandsons are rich. Krishnappa himself, who is about 40 years old, is extremely ambitious as a farmer and has bought much land outside his village area, possibly bringing his total holding to over 30 acres. He owns 2 of the 5 electric pump sets[a] in the six Anekal villages, keeping at least 4 acres under irrigation and growing transplanted *ragi*, paddy, beans, peas, other vegetables and sugar cane; he also has several acres of tank-irrigated farmland. He owns about 5 cows and 2 bullocks, and claims that he once had 'about 100 sheep and goats', and some buffaloes, all of which he had sold following the distribution of grazing ground to cultivators. He provided much documentary evidence of his failure, despite large-scale bribery, to get a loan for Rs 40,000 for a tractor. With three younger, unmarried brothers to assist him, he lives in a spacious modern house which had been built by his late father.

Note

a He had probably received bank loans for the purchase of both of these pump sets and for the construction of one of his stone-lined wells, said to be 60 ft in circumference.

(B) One of the very few rich Adikarnataka men in the Anekal villages, his prosperity is probably mainly due to his work as a contractor for the cutting of casuarina trees,[a] which enabled him to buy a farm of about 4 acres, which was partly planted with casuarina. His elder brother is an impoverished farmer, another brother a trader in Bangalore. He owns an irrigation well. He relies on day-labourers, all his children being young. He is an elected member of the Village Panchayat.

Note

a Originally a wood cutter, he presumably evolved into a contractor (see p. 159) with the help of private credit.

(C) A prominent elderly Reddy man, whose father had been an outsider who had married here, he claimed that his present prosperity had mainly derived from milk-trading by bicycle to Bangalore over a period of some thirty years and that he had once owned some twenty to thirty female buffaloes.[a] However this may have been,[b] he had been enabled to buy large acreages, for he and his two married sons, who live separately, probably own nearly 40 acres of dry land and over 6 acres of tank-irrigated paddy land.[c] (When first encountered he was sitting under a tree supervising the making of bricks[d] from tank silt for a house which his educated son was to build in Bangalore.) Although his separated sons[e] give him some help with his farming, he has no household labour force proper, except for a boy *sambalagara*[f] – the other occupants of his large house being his widowed daughter-in-law and granddaughter. He owns a well and a farm cart and has a large acreage of casuarina woods.

Notes

a Owing to the shortage of grazing he no longer owns buffaloes.
b He had probably been a secret money-lender, for he had formerly been very litigious.
c It was, unfortunately, impossible to ascertain the division of this farmland, which consisted of some 20 plots, between himself and his sons, possibly because it had only been temporarily effected, the actual responsibility for particular plots varying from year to year.
d The bricks, which were formed with a wooden mould, were fired in a ramshackle 'kiln' using casuarina and other logs as fuel. Men and women day-labourers, of various castes, were employed, together with a foreman.
e The separation appeared to have been entirely amicable, each son having received a separate house worth more than Rs 2,000.
f Before the Emergency he had employed 3 such boys, all of them on a temporary basis; the fathers had invariably demanded loans which were automatically liquidated by labour.

(D) The father of three rich elderly Reddy brothers, who had died when they were young, had been an outsider who had been 'adopted' (*iltam*) by his sonless father-in-law on marriage. The two eldest brothers are now heads of paternal joint households, the youngest having (as yet) but one married son. Each of them employs a boy *sambalagara*; each has bought land, their inherited land being altogether insufficient; each owns much equipment, including a farm cart; and each owns a considerable number and variety of animals – the second brother who is a well-known milk-seller, claimed that he owned 10 cows, 2 bullocks, 5 buffaloes and 40 goats. None of the brothers has any special non-farming occupation, but two of them are well-known creditors, whose debtors include outsiders. The brothers all grow vegetables and other crops on land irrigated by three wells which they share. A son of one of the brothers cycles twice daily to Bangalore, a total distance of over 50 miles, to sell milk carried in tiny churns; another son works in Bangalore returning home at weekends.[a] Another brother owns two houses in the village for letting and a plantation of coconut palms.[b] The youngest brother had been assisted to buy land by his rich father-in-law from another village; in 1978 he had a large field of hybrid maize.

Notes

a Few other Anekal villagers do this.
b Few Anekal villagers own such plantations perhaps partly because coconut, unlike casuarina seedlings, require watering for some years after transplantation.

CROP DIVERSIFICATION IN HAUSALAND

Insofar as historians are correct in postulating the inevitability of 'cash crop revolutions',[24] this occurred long ago in Kano Emirate for instance, as shown by the existence of a pre-colonial farm tax, *kudin shuka*, which was levied on plots which had been planted with non-grain crops such as sweet potatoes, groundnuts, cocoyams, sugar cane, cassava and yams – tax rates, in the local currency which was cowry shells, varying with crop and locality.[25] Even the 'groundnut revolution'[26] (which the textbooks always used to tell us was associated with the completion of the railway line to Kano city shortly before the 1914 war) is now seen to have been something of a mirage – for, initially at least, overseas exports must have been largely at the expense of rural consumption of groundnut oil most of which was produced by women for sale to other households. In Kano and Katsina Emirates no new field crops of significance, other than cotton for overseas export in the more southerly localities (which are outside our geographical scope), have been introduced this century, though there has been considerable experimentation with new seed varieties made available officially. However, in many localities, including Dorayi, a virtually treeless landscape has been transformed within living memory into 'farmland parkland' by the planting of useful trees, including mangoes and guavas.

In northern Hausaland the general rule is that remunerative special crops like tobacco,[27] sweet potatoes and cassava,[28] are grown only by richer farmers, poorer men lacking the necessary finance and being reluctant to reduce their grain output. While poorer farmers may cultivate some groundnuts, the high cost of seed severely restricts their acreages.[29] As for the much coveted type of marshland, known as *fadama*, on which rice and

[24] Iliffe probably reflects prevailing orthodoxy in his discussion of the origins of rural capitalism when he states that 'peasantisation', which he associates with production for 'larger economic systems which include non-peasants', is a 'once-for-all transformation' – *A Modern History of Tanganyika* by J. Iliffe, 1979, p. 273. This is one of my reasons for disliking the term 'cash crop revolution' since those who once produced for a wide market may revert to producing for local consumption – as is happening on a vast scale in impoverished Ghana today. Also, regarding these 'revolutions' in terms of land tenure, it was very interesting to see how land which had been bought for cash by individual migrant cocoa farmers in Ghana invariably evolved into family land after the owner's death – see Hill (1963).

[25] See Hill (1977), pp. 50–1. (The basic tax on grain land was separate.)

[26] See *Nigerian Groundnut Exports: Origins and Early Development* by J. S. Hogendorn, 1978.

[27] The native tobacco used to enter widely into long-distance trade. See Hill (1970), Chapter 6.

[28] Whereas in the forest zone cassava is one of the most common crops, in the savannah, where different low-yielding varieties are cultivated, it is eaten boiled as a kind of delicacy, being grown on a small scale in carefully hedged or fenced plots, mainly by richer men who can afford the time and labour involved. Contrary to general belief, it is not a new crop in the savannah – see Hill (1972), pp. 216–17.

[29] See Hill (1972), p. 257.

vegetables may be grown, possibly even in the dry season, this is concentrated in the ownership of richer farmers.

One of the most interesting pre-colonial Hausa 'export crops', apart from tobacco, was onions, which were probably mainly grown on irrigated river-side plots. A recent response to the intensifying pressure of population on the land at Dorayi has been the development of onion-growing on specially manured plots, irrigated by small wells, from which millet has already been harvested. As the elaborate preparation of the plots requires much work – the tiny squares of cultivation being watered by a network of leats – only rich farmers cultivate significant acreages, though many other men in one section of Dorayi obtain a useful supplement to their income from diminutive plots.[30]

THE SIGNIFICANCE OF LIVESTOCK OWNERSHIP IN HAUSALAND

Although donkeys are the local camels of Hausaland, their importance has been neglected in the West African literature, which often regards head-loading by women and children as the only real alternative to road, rail and water transport. In Hausaland, where secluded women are not available to act as beasts of burden, farmers' productivity would be much reduced were donkey transport unavailable. For transporting produce from, and manure to, farms, and for evacuating produce from the vast roadless areas, the donkey will remain indispensable for many decades to come. These small sturdy animals can manage loads of 200 lb and upward – about half that of a camel and double that of a man.

Transport donkeys, which are all males, were fairly cheap animals in Batagarawa in 1967 – perhaps worth some £3 to £5; as they cost virtually nothing to maintain, and provide valuable manure, and as men are often able to hire themselves out as transporters together with their donkeys, the extreme poverty of the poorest households is indicated by the fact that hardly any of them owned donkeys. As large fleets of donkeys are no longer required for long-distance trading, few households had occasion to own more than 3 of these beasts.

Since most cattle, as we know, are owned by Fulani pastoralists, and since the number of plough oxen in most villages is presumably fairly small, owing to widespread hiring, cattle populations are small relative to those in Indian villages. As for sheep and goat ownership, not only are all

[30] See Hill (1977), pp. 101–2, 135–6. Considering the cheapness of the wells, I was surprised that this type of intensification was so rare in the Kano Close Settled Zone, where the water table is apt to be very high.

official statistics highly suspect, but great difficulties arise when one attempts to collect meaningful figures for oneself, partly because men envy women owners[31] and also because sheep vary so greatly in size and quality – a large ram destined for ceremonial slaughter being nearly as valuable as a cow. However, there are nowadays few large herds in our densely populated localities, presumably mainly because of the nuisance of collecting forage during the farming season when free grazing is communally prohibited, so that these animals are seldom an important store of value for richer households. Indeed, in Batagarawa the general rule that richer households 'owned more of everything' was broken only by women's ownership of goats – women in the poorest of all households apparently owning more goats per head than those in the richest households. Sheep and goat droppings are an indispensable form of organic manure in densely populated localities where cattle ownership is low, but as the local market in such droppings is always active, the poorest people being landless or subject to the constant temptation of selling manure, richer farmers do not need to own these animals themselves to be assured of manure supplies.

THE SIGNIFICANCE OF LIVESTOCK OWNERSHIP IN THE ANEKAL VILLAGES

As noted in Appendix VII(2), much recent discussion of cattle ownership in Indian villages has little relevance to the Anekal villages since it is based on the two inapplicable assumptions that nearly all draught animals are bullocks and that surplus cows, many of them aging, are never sold.[32] In the Anekal villages only about a third of households which cultivate their own land own a pair of bullocks, and most plough animals are cows. And as cattle are an important store of value which must not be allowed to depreciate, cows are always sold before their decrepitude becomes evident, and no such beast as a 'surplus cow' exists – indeed, I think it likely that the market in cattle is so active that few animals are retained for more than a year or two, many being resold very soon after purchase.[33] However sacred cows may be, this does not stand in the way of their sale outside the village; maybe a fair proportion of owners would prefer not to sell their animals to butchers, but fortunately they can usually avert their minds from this

[31] In Batagarawa the *estimated* proportions of sheep and goats which were owned by women were 66% and 60% – see Hill (1972), p. 67.

[32] Most curiously, the statistics for Mysore derived from the official livestock censuses strongly belie this supposition. Thus, for the year 1947–8 the total number of cows over 3 years old which were owned neither for work nor breeding purposes was recorded as only 31,941 out of a total for all cows of this age of 1,686,256.

[33] This is not a new discovery: it was noted by Epstein, 1962, p. 238.

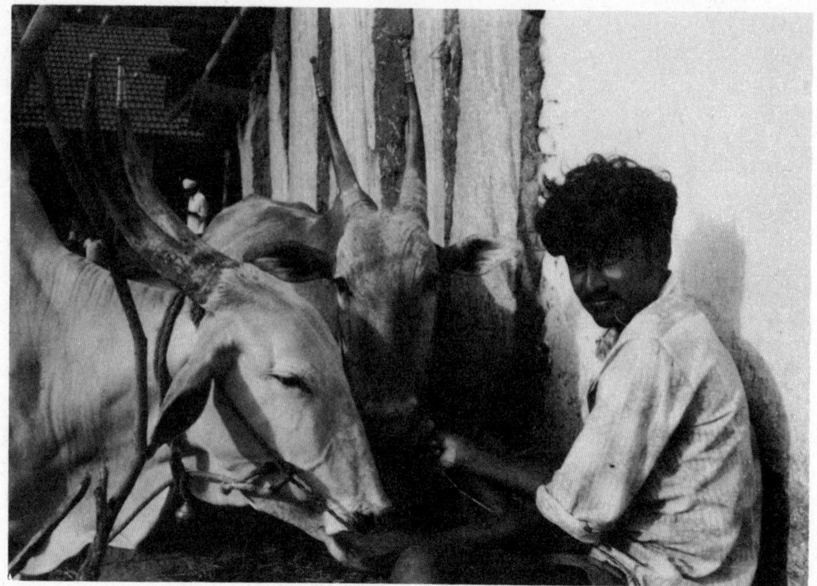

11 The hand feeding of cattle

possibility by selling to intermediary traders whose future intentions are unclear.[34]

Quite straightforward economic reasons account for the widespread use of cows (of which 670 were counted) for general draught purposes, including the pulling of carts. Bullocks are certainly superior draught animals,[35] as everyone knows, but cows (which are cheaper) also provide milk and calves. So, considerations of poverty apart, there may often be a positive economic preference for cows considered as a sensible investment which yields automatic increments (calves) and income (milk). Nearly all the bullocks are owned by richer households. The total number of bullocks recorded as owned by AK and AD households was only 14 in all the villages – 13 of them being in Hullahalli; nearly 200 bullocks were recorded as owned by households of other castes – about two-thirds of the owners of two or more bullocks being classified as rich.

[34] This is confirmed by Srinivas, 1976, pp. 133–4.

[35] In *An Introduction to Animal Husbandry in the Tropics* by G. Williamson and W. J. A. Payne, 1959, p. 239, it is stated that 'the dry cow gives quite satisfactory service in the plough; even a cow in milk may be used for moderate work for a few hours each day without greatly impairing her milk yield'.

The difficulties of collecting reliable statistics on cattle ownership are discussed in Appendix VII(2). Although my figures are bound to be somewhat inaccurate,[36] I think one may safely assert that the number of working cows (allowing for those disabled by the later stages of pregnancy) was of the order of two and a half to three times the number of working bullocks. I also think it likely that about a fifth of all households which cultivate their own land are obliged to borrow or hire one or two animals. It seems that about a third of all cultivating households own 2 draught animals; that another third owns 3 or 4 animals; and that the proportion owning 5 or more beasts is little more than a tenth.

Given the general reluctance to sell land, and the widespread eagerness to realise a profit from selling cattle, the significance of cattle ownership is out of all proportion to the total value of the stock, especially for poorer households for whom it commonly represents much the most important form of capital – other than land if they have any. Some two-fifths of all the AK and AD households which own cattle or look after them for others – see *palu* in Appendix VII(2) – cultivate no land for themselves; as only about a quarter of these households own a pair of animals, such as would enable their menfolk to hire themselves out as fully equipped ploughmen, whose wages would then be some four to five times that of an ordinary day-labourer, it seems clear that most of them primarily value their animals as a form of readily realisable capital with a strong growth tendency – as well as for their milk and dung. It makes good sense for a Harijan who has obtained a loan of Rs 500 in return for renting out his sole farm-plot for the planting of casuarina trees to invest the cash in a cow or calves.

Owing to the shortage of conveniently situated grazing and to the congestion in the villages where the animals are housed, there are probably very few herds of any size – though, for all one knows,[37] there may be some owners who board out several animals. According to our statistics, there were only 14 households, all of them 'very rich on village standards', which owned more than 7 cattle – the largest reported herd was 17; 15% of all the animals enumerated were in these herds. It is clear that there are few owners who retain animals surplus to their requirements of working cattle, except for the relatively small number of large-scale milk producers who sell their milk in Bangalore, and the above-mentioned landless Harijans – who may take their animals out to work on the land of others; accordingly, the 'middle' households in Hullahalli and Nanjapura

36 They are also spurious in that they were collected over a period of nearly a year and do not relate to a particular date.

37 All the information on the boarding out of cattle was provided by those who received them, the real owners preserving total reticence.

owned nearly as many cattle as the rich – an average of 2.7 per household against 3.3.

Since cattle always work in pairs, it is only to be expected that very high proportions of the richest non-Harijan householders own two or more animals – in Hullahalli and Nanjapura, for example, only one such man lacked a pair and he could use his father's animals. In grim contrast only 2 out of 30 Harijan households in Nanjapura owned a pair of cattle – though a half of all the Harijans in Hullahalli (who are somewhat better off, as we know) owned at least two animals.

The important matter of cart ownership may conveniently be inserted here. Considering the usefulness of carts; their fairly low price (less than £100); and the difficulty of borrowing them (except sometimes from brothers) – it is perhaps surprising that as many as a third of all rich households were cartless. Nearly a half of all 'middle' households owned carts, the proportions falling to 10% and nil for the lower groups. About a quarter of all householders were cart owners, the proportions varying between 50%, 41% and 41% for the three dominant castes (Reddy, Gowda and Kuruba) and 9% and 6% for the main Harijan castes (AKs and ADs).

The ownership of water buffaloes[38] is strongly concentrated in rich households. Of the total of 59 villagers who were recorded as owning these strange beasts, only 11 were poor, only 7 were AKs or ADs; since buffaloes are hardly ever used as draught animals in these areas, but are valued chiefly for their milk, it is the richer households which benefit mainly from milk trading, especially to Bangalore.

My statistics for sheep[39] ownership are even less reliable than those for cattle, informants being much given to rounding off the figures. Although it seems that continual profit-taking (buying and rapidly reselling) is nearly as common as with cattle, and although sheep are relatively cheap, poor people prefer cows as a store of value, presumably mainly because they can be put to work. Omitting Mahantalingapura, about four-fifths of all the recorded 534 sheep were apparently[40] owned by the two richest wealth groups; about a third of all households in these groups were owners, against 4% of the poorest households. While the Kuruba caste, who were traditionally shepherds and blanket weavers, own more sheep per household than any other caste, some 65% of them owned no sheep.

The Karnataka goat is a tall, slim, handsome animal, worth some Rs 250–350 in 1978 – nearly twice as much as a sheep. Apart from a few households who owned herds of (say) 10 or more goats, very few people

[38] See Appendix VII(3). [39] See Appendix VII(4) on sheep and goats.

[40] One uncertainty arises from the fact that sheep and goats, like cows, may be boarded out with poorer people on the *palu* system.

nowadays are interested in goat ownership; we counted a total of only 132 goats in five villages (excluding Mahantalingapura) of which 64 were in Bukkasagara.

CASUARINA PLANTATIONS

Casuarina plantations[41] provide the most interesting kind of economic diversification in the Anekal villages, for they are established on dry land most of which would otherwise be mainly planted with low-yielding *ragi*. According to all accounts the acreage under casuarina has increased greatly during the past few decades and it may be[42] that in several of the villages, notably Nanjapura and Hullahalli, a significant proportion of all dry land, even perhaps as much as a quarter, is under these trees.

Many landowners appreciate both the higher net yield per acre obtained from casuarina than from *ragi*,[43] as well as the element of compulsory saving entailed in waiting for a minimum of six years before the trees are ready for felling. Most of the wood is sold in Bangalore, primarily as fuel but also for building. Whether the plantations and the seedling nurseries create more employment over the years than the annual *ragi* crop it is impossible to say; but wood cutters are relatively well-paid men, and many of the villagers known as wood contractors, who arrange for the felling of the trees and sometimes buy the plantations outright before felling, are notably prosperous. The economy of one of the six villages, Srirampura, is greatly dependent on the casuarina, since most younger Pichiguntala men derive much of their income from wood contracting and/or cutting in other localities, to which they travel in groups.

Although the ownership of casuarina woods is heavily concentrated with richer men (at one village it was even possible that some 40% of the whole wooded area was owned by only three men, one from a nearby town), the possibility of letting out small plots for wood planting provides impoverished men with a reliable type of credit, since the lump sum granted to them at the outset is automatically liquidated by the landowner's share of the net value of the wood when it is sold, which is usually agreed as one half. As wood contractors, also, are commonly granted credit, mainly by rich village men, to finance their purchase of wood for felling, the casuarina tree provides many villagers with notable

41 See Appendix VII(5) for additional information.

42 Although the land revenue statistics purport to distinguish woods, the figures are out-of-date and many of the larger plots are only partly wooded.

43 One authority claims that casuarina 'is more remunerative than paddy' – see Mencher, 1978, p. 244; but much depends, of course, on the distance to the nearest urban market, which much affects the price received.

opportunities of countering the official attitude of disapproval towards private credit-granting in the countryside.

One influential man, who had about 13 acres of casuarina woods, claimed that (very exceptionally) he had largely switched away from grain owing to the lack of permanent labourers and shortage of organic manure; in other words, casuarina is less troublesome and more profitable than *ragi* – though villagers, with their fear of boastfulness, would never put it this way.

APPENDIX VII(1)

The low yields of millets and sorghums, with special reference to ragi

Under our dry grain mode the yields of millets and sorghums tend to be very low[44] (though variable) owing, among other reasons, to the chronic shortage of organic manure. As the probability is that the yields of the two staples in Hausaland, which are sorghum (guinea corn) and bulrush millet, are somewhat higher than that of finger millet (*ragi*) in south-eastern Karnataka, I here concentrate mainly on the latter for the general purpose of emphasising the remarkable inappropriateness of such low-yielding crops in conditions of very high population density.

The high incidence of crop mixtures[45] in northern Hausaland probably invalidates most official estimates of yield; but it is worth noting that sorghum, unlike bulrush millet, is said to be very responsive to organic manure, so that richer farmers are always likely to obtain higher than average yields. An FAO *Report*[46] of 1966 was so unimpressed by the potential yield of bulrush millet that it suggested (p. 178) that in the long run many millions of people should abandon northern Hausaland and resettle hundreds of miles to the south!

According to Purseglove,[47] Karnataka[48] is one of the principal regions of the world in which finger millet (*Eleusine coracana*) is the main staple, other regions being parts of Tamil Nadu and of East and Central Africa, notably Uganda.[49] It

[44] The same is apt to be true of other basic crops in India. 'With the exception of the new wheat varieties and above-average performance in other groups over limited areas, Indian yields are among the lowest . . . in the world.' *India: Population, Economy, Society* by R. H. Cassen, 1978, p. 266. For the low yields of Nigerian sorghums see 'Plant Density and Grain Yield of Nigerian Sorghums' by D. J. Andrews, *Savanna*, June 1976.

[45] See Appendix VIII(2).

[46] *Agricultural Development in Nigeria, 1965–1980* by the Food and Agricultural Organisation, 1966.

[47] *Tropical Crops: Monocotyledons 1* by J. W. Purseglove, 1972. See pp. 147–56 on *ragi.* This book also includes much information on bulrush millet and sorghum.

[48] The reference should have been to southern Karnataka since sorghum (*jowar*) is the basic grain in the north of the State.

[49] See *Agriculture in Uganda*, ed. J. D. Jameson, 1970, p. 145.

requires, according to Purseglove, a well-distributed rainfall with an absence of prolonged droughts, sorghum and bulrush millet being better suited to dryer areas. Its great merits are that it will store for very long periods (formerly, in Karnataka, in pits in the ground) and its high content of protein and various nutrients. Its great disadvantage in south-eastern Karnataka is that only one annual crop is usually taken[50] – also, its straw, which is a good fodder, is very short.

After examining numerous sources and listening to villagers, I judge that the yield of *ragi* in south-eastern Karnataka is unlikely to average more than about 400 lb per acre, and yields above (say) 600 lb are rare. However, if the seeds are grown in nurseries and the seedlings transplanted, considerably higher yields may be obtained on dry land – and *ragi* transplanted on wet[51] land (as it never is in the Anekal villages) is said to give enormous yields. Why so little *ragi* is transplanted on dry land by the Anekal villagers I cannot tell: inexplicably, most cultivators are content to sow the seed directly on the land around the end of June (the date depending on the weather), harvesting some five months later around November.

In 1977–8 the village price ranged between Rs 1.00 per kg immediately after threshing to about Rs 1.50 later in the season – certainly no higher. If we assume an average annual price of Rs 1.25 per kg, then the gross value of an ordinary acre of *ragi* would have been no more than about Rs 250 (assuming a yield of 200 kgs) – or (say) £20.[52] This sum omits the value of the straw which, short though it is, is by no means negligible, being considered a superior fodder to paddy straw.[53]

A curious and inconvenient feature of *ragi* is that the grain adheres so strongly to the husk that it cannot be properly threshed until it has been dried in stacks for some three months after harvest;[54] I found it hard to understand how the poorest people were supplied during this curious lull – but once threshing starts the economy is agog.

In Chapter IX below I argue[55] that the *ragi* which is 'exported' to the outside world from the Anekal villages (like the millet and sorghum 'exported' by densely populated Hausa localities) is not grain which is surplus to the requirements of these communities: it is sold because there is no other way of paying for essential 'imports', not because the people do not need it themselves.

50 This is not necessarily anything new; certainly, Buchanan and other nineteenth century writers constantly refer to single-cropping.

51 Sopher, in Harris, 1980, asserts, p. 191, that one-sixth of the area under *ragi* in India is irrigated.

52 Epstein concluded (1962, p. 47) that *ragi* was a remunerative crop – a conclusion which appears to be based on her erroneous supposition of a yield of 5.8 *pallas* (c. 1,100 lb) per acre, whereas in her later book (1973, p. 105) she stated that the yield *at the earlier date* had in fact been 2.4 *pallas*.

53 According to Epstein (1962, p. 50) about 20% of the value of *ragi* grown on dry land was fodder.

54 Buchanan was, therefore, probably wrong when he wrote: 'The farmers would always prefer thrashing it [*ragi*] out immediately after it is reaped; but the officers of revenue prevent them from taking it out of the stack until the balances of rent are paid, which sometimes takes up two or three months.' Vol. I, p. 286.

55 See pp. 212, *et seq.*

A very full and careful account of the cultivation of *ragi* in Mysore is provided by Wilks[56] (1810); such is the unchanging technology that it might have been written today. Then, as today, 'if the crop threatens to be too early or too luxuriant, it is fed down with sheep'.[57]

APPENDIX VII(2)

Cattle ownership in the Anekal villages

According to figures presented by K. N. Raj, in a very interesting article[58] analysing some issues concerning 'sacred cows' and 'surplus cattle', the number of mature cows per 100 male cattle in Mysore in 1956 was only 88, against an all-India ratio of 77; in only three states did the number of cows exceed the number of male animals, the highest ratio being 167 for Kerala. Considering the stress I have laid on the difficulty of collecting reliable statistics of household livestock ownership, readers may think that my conclusion that, in the Anekal villages, female working animals outnumbered males, by some three to one, is untrustworthy.

But, for the following reasons among others, such fears are unfounded. First, the pattern of distribution of bullocks among households made very good sense in terms of the presumption, which villagers constantly reiterated, that most poorer households cannot afford to buy bullocks.[59] Second, on numerous occasions we noted the relatively large number of cows used for ploughing. Third, the Anekal villages are unusually impoverished owing to the very high population density and poor irrigation facilities, and can afford to purchase fewer bullocks per household than the average community. Fourth, the working superiority of bullocks is much less marked in localities where little land is irrigated. Fifth, doubts about the reliability of our statistics, which were painstakingly checked in many cases, applies even more strongly to the official statistics.[60] Sixth, the good opportunities of selling milk in nearby Bangalore enhances the income from cows.

[56] *Historical Sketches of the South of India* by M. Wilks, Vol. I, 1810, p. 209 footnote. (Buchanan also provides much information.)

[57] *Ibid.*, p. 209.

[58] 'Investment in Livestock in Agrarian Economies: an analysis of some issues concerning "Sacred Cows" and "Surplus Cattle" ', *Indian Economic Review*, IV, 1, April 1969, p. 29. Other interesting publications concerned with the cultural ecology of India's sacred cattle are Harris (1966) and Heston (1971); but owing to the nature of their premisses they have little relevance here.

[59] It seemed likely that nearly all bullocks were bought and that male calves born in the villages are nearly always sold; although most cows, also, are bought there is some rearing from calf.

[60] Unless there is a cattle tax which is strictly enforced, official statistics of livestock ownership in third world tropical countries always seems to be serious under-estimates; it might be that in India, for all we know, under-enumeration particularly affects cows. It is surprising that there should be so little discussion about the reliability of the periodic cattle

In a survey of the kind we conducted in the Anekal villages it would have been quite impracticable to have inspected all the livestock owned,[61] so that we were necessarily dependent on householders' own statements. Here we were up against many obstacles, including lying, deliberate vagueness,[62] the difficulty of distinguishing heifers from cows, the duplication which is apt to arise when relatives share animals,[63] and the *palu* cow-borrowing system which may mean that both the borrower and the real owner list an animal; these difficulties were, to some extent, overcome by checking volunteered figures with impartial, trusted third parties, some of the more observant of whom claimed to recognise all the animals in the village.

I have seen no reference in the literature to the *palu*[64] cow-borrowing system which usually involves a rich man in boarding out a cow with a poor man who owns no cattle, sometimes as an act of charity. Whatever the incidence of *palu* may be (and I think it is rather low), it is certain that the demand for *palu* cows much exceeds the supply. The borrower usually receives the first calf, together with the milk and the dung, as his reward, and must return the cow to the owner before the birth of a second calf; alternatively, he may get a share of the proceeds if a cow and its calf are sold. If the first calf dies before the cow has been returned to its owner, the borrower may be entitled to a second calf. (A similar system applies to goats.)

Apart from *palu*, the various types of transaction involving village cattle include: informal exchange (any difference in value being made up in cash); informal purchase (involving no intermediary); sale or purchase through a village or travelling cattle trader; and buying or selling at weekly markets[65] or at the great annual cattle fairs,[66] which possibly mainly handle bullocks.

Finally, reference to an aspect of primitive technology may not be amiss. No shaped cattle yokes are in use – mere wooden poles rest on the working animals' necks, often causing sores. Head control is effected by a rope through a hole punched in the middle cartilage of the nose, close behind the muzzle.

censuses. Thus, K. N. Raj unquestioningly accepts the 'fact' that the bovine population of India has increased, with the human population, since 1921 (or so) – see 'India's Sacred Cattle: theories and empirical findings', *Economic & Political Weekly*, 13, 27 March 1971. The official reports on livestock censuses give little indication as to how the statistics are collected.

[61] Nor does inspection necessarily establish ownership. Two men each proudly paraded the same bull for our inspection – the only bull we heard of in the six villages, where most cows are artificially inseminated.

[62] Thus, an informant who had sold all his animals might include replacements he hoped to buy soon. See Hobson, 1978, p. 76, for a fascinating conversational attempt to unravel the meaning of 'about two buffaloes'. (The Anekal villagers, also, were apt to prefix 'about' to their figures.)

[63] If a father dies and his sons separate, there may be a considerable interval before the livestock are divided. If a son separates and is given an animal by his father, it may have to remain in his father's house if his own is too small.

[64] In this context *palu* is a shorthand expression – being Kannada for 'division'.

[65] The ordinary village market (*shandy*) is not large enough to handle cattle.

[66] *Jathre* – see Appendix XII(6).

APPENDIX VII(3)

Water buffaloes

In the Anekal villages, as in southern Karnataka generally,[67] the water buffalo is hardly ever used as a draught animal, as in many other regions, but is probably valued chiefly for its milk, although its hide may be manufactured into a type of heavy leather, its flesh is likely to be consumed (elsewhere) as meat and its droppings are used as manure. According to Williamson, the greatest advantage of the buffalo is its ability 'to subsist on the coarsest fodder';[68] however, although its milk production is apt to be greater than that of a cow and to be richer in butter fat (so that dilution with water is less easy to detect) it is 'not more economic than the cow as a milk producer when account is taken of her greater fodder consumption'.[69] The particular weakness of buffaloes, compared with cattle, is their greater susceptibility to certain diseases; in one of the Anekal villages it was said that most buffaloes had died of an epidemic some fifteen years ago. Being semi-aquatic in their natural habitat, they do not flourish unless they are able to wallow in pools, plastering themselves with mud.

In the Anekal villages, where virtually all adult buffaloes are milk producing females (young males being sold to butchers, as are older females before they become sterile), large herds are rarer than they were (say) fifty years ago, owing to the diminution of grazing grounds. Nowadays only about 12% of all households[70] own buffaloes, about half of them owning one animal only – only three households were recorded as owning 5 animals or more. As already noted, ownership is strongly concentrated in rich households: about a third of such households owned buffaloes, only 40% of the total stock being owned by all other households, including those headed by women. There was said to be much less speculative buying and selling of buffaloes than of cattle. If the average buffalo was worth about Rs 750, then the value of the 119 beasts recorded in our lists was some Rs 90,000 – say £6,500.

APPENDIX VII(4)

Sheep and goats in the Anekal villages

The neglect of small livestock (sheep and goats in particular) in the literature on south Indian rural economies is remarkable – virtually all attention being concen-

[67] See Srinivas, 1976, p. 131.

[68] Williamson *et al.*, 1959, p. 250.

[69] *Ibid.*, p. 257. These authors put average milk production in India as 150 to 160 gallons annually for buffaloes against 80 to 90 gallons for zebu cows.

[70] Our statistics are doubtless rather inaccurate for familiar reasons including false reporting, difficulty of defining calves and the *palu* system, which may lead to double reporting. But as

trated on cattle. Yet small livestock provide a generally meat-eating, but non-beef-eating, population with significant supplies of meat; also, goats provide milk, sheep provide wool (though in tiny quantities per head), and both animals are useful sources of manure.

In the Anekal villages there was general reluctance to discuss the ownership of small livestock by women, which is probably more common than either sex is prepared to admit, for it is generally opposed by husbands. (Everyone, on the other hand, agrees that most fowl are owned by women.) Certainly some women secretly acquire small livestock and put them out for rearing in other households; and it is worth noting that as many as a quarter of all households headed by women were recorded as owning sheep.

There has been a very great decline in the sheep and goat population in the Anekal villages within living memory; in the case of goats this may be related to the increased area of casuarina woods, since these animals are very destructive.

APPENDIX VII(5)

Casuarina plantations

R. H. Elliot, a coffee planter in Mysore, planted a row of casuarina trees (*Casuarina equisetifolia*, the swamp oak of Queensland where it probably originated) as early as 1859, and when he contemplated the trees some 34 years later,[71] standing about 150 ft high, with girths of over six feet at three feet above the ground, he stood astounded at his stupidity in not having planted them on a commercial scale. In Bangalore District serious planting by villagers probably started not long before 1877 when it was reported[72] that 'the wealthier ryots' had begun to lay down 'small plantations of casuarina and other trees', having found 'a ready and profitable sale of the wood and cuttings for firewood'.

As early as 1891 it was reported that in many Anekal villages casuarinas were 'being planted on occupied dry crop and rice lands',[73] and in 1897 B. Lewis Rice remarked that the numerous and extensive plantations, especially in Bangalore District, had 'visibly altered the landscape in some parts':

> As fuel it develops more heat in a given quantity than any other kind of local wood; in fact, for locomotive and domestic purposes it is found necessary to use inferior fuel with it, in order to moderate the intense heat, which would otherwise prove destructive to engines and utensils.[74]

the buffalo market is much less volatile than the cattle market, the ownership statistics may be more reliable than for cattle.

[71] *Gold, Sport and Coffee Planting in Mysore* by R. H. Elliot, 1894, p. 447.

[72] *Proceedings* of the Chief Commissioner of Mysore, 9 March 1877.

[73] A Report sanctioning the introduction of Survey Settlement in Anekal Taluk, *Proceedings* of the Government of Mysore, 13 April 1891.

[74] Rice, 1897, Vol. I, p. 169.

Nowadays the weary walker in Anekal Taluk is seldom far away from the refreshing shade provided by these feathery trees, which sing loudly in the wind.

No part of the tree is without its uses. Little girls go to the woods with rakes to collect pine needles as fuel; the twigs are used as kindling; branches of unfelled trees are cut for sale as firewood; and the roots, also, may be burnt. In 1977–8 the value of an acre of felled wood from a six-year-old plantation was put at around Rs 10,000 or more (say £700) – and many woods survive longer. The cost of planting an acre with saplings from a nursery was put at some Rs 200–300; but even this cost may be avoided as trees are often allowed to regrow from the old roots after felling.

According to Slater,[75] a seven-year-old plantation in the Madras area would have yielded about 35 tons an acre; and 'when the trees are cut down, and the roots removed, the land is greatly improved in fertility':

> Hence a plot of barren land planted with casuarina is a splendid savings bank for a ryot who can foresee a period of heavy expense in six or seven years' time.

APPENDIX VII(6)

The stone quarry at Balarbande

About a mile from Mahantalingapura there is a large quarry, known as Balarbande, where stone (gneiss) is extracted by local workers in exactly the manner described by Francis Buchanan. When slabs are to be extracted a small fire is made with kindling twigs. Then:

> A number of small square holes, about an inch and a half in diameter, and four inches deep, are cut in the line by which the stone is meant to be split. The work is performed by a small steel punch . . . which is driven in by a heavy iron mallet . . . . Blunt wedges of steel are then put in the holes, and each is struck upon in turn, until the stone splits [horizontally].[76]

By this means 'sheets' from a few inches to two feet in thickness may be readily extracted.

The quarry work affords a good deal of employment to two main groups of men in Mahantalingapura: the licensed rock agents who, in return for a fee, are permitted to extract and sell a certain tonnage of stone annually, and their workers the rock cutters. Like daily-paid farm labourers, the rock cutters usually work in small teams of (say) 4 to 7 men; they resemble farm labourers, also, in that their work is irregular. They are paid either daily or weekly (with advances) – different agents using different systems; the expert worker who knows where and how to light the fire receives higher wages than others – who are said to be unskilled men. It is probable that piece work is usual.

Most of the twenty (or so) rock agents at the quarry are members of the Bhovi caste or Muslims. As they could not be classified by wealth, and as a large

[75] Slater, 1918, p. 5. [76] Buchanan, 1807, Vol. I, p. 133.

proportion of them were migrants who had no interest in becoming farmers, they are effectively a group of industrial workers (the only one in the six villages) whose activities fall outside the scope of this book, although most of them live near the quarry or in Mahantalingapura.

CHAPTER VIII

Intensification

The fierce debate, which has been raging for some twenty years now, on 'size and productivity relations in Indian agriculture'[1] has, on the whole, been conducted in very primitive fashion, participants being mainly concerned with whether the relationship between farm size and yield is direct or inverse. There have been few who have suggested that the graph relating yield to size of farm-holding might be a curve rather than a straight line – and a curve, moreover, which might show an inverse relationship for one size range of farm-holding and a direct relationship for another. Rather has the debate been directed towards answering the over-simplified question: do poor farmers use their land more efficiently than large farmers? The general, though far from unanimous, conclusion over the past two decades has been in favour of the superior efficiency of the poor cultivator. The belief that poor farmers cultivate their farmland with more care, because they have little better to do, has taken a grip on the world.[2]

I begin by summarising my own attitude to this curiously emotive subject, *with special reference to this dry grain mode* – for my conclusions are not presumed to have general relevance to dry farming. My starting point is my conviction (which, as will be seen, is based on observation, commonsense, and the beliefs of villagers themselves) that the smallest dry grain cultivators, who (as we know) are also the poorest, obtain far lower yields per acre than the average; not only do such cultivators tend to lack resources, notably manure, for which labour is no substitute, but they are also hampered by numerous other factors such as the poor quality of their land (which is often marginal), and their inability to afford interplanting with more productive crops, such as groundnuts in Hausaland, which does

[1] This is how the debate is denoted by two of the key participants, Rudra and Sen, in a useful and sophisticated summary of the state of play up to 1980. 'Farm Size and Labour Use: analysis and policy' by A. Rudra and A. Sen, 1980.

[2] But see *Agrarian Structure and Productivity in Developing Countries* by R. A. Berry and W. R. Cline, 1979.

so much to enhance the yields of richer farmers.[3] Moreover, economically weak households which can hope to produce no more than a small proportion of their total grain requirements are apt to have very low morale as cultivating groups; the individual members, particularly the sons, do not seek to survive by means of working hard on the ill-manured farmland, but rather look round for something better to do. Maybe poor farmers have more reason to work hard than rich farmers; but they lack the ability to set themselves to work with any reasonable degree of efficiency. All this is very well known to villagers themselves. When walking through the farmland in their company they often point out the ill-cultivated plots owned by impoverished householders whose sons have stopped working for them, who have sold all their manurial droppings (if any) and who are obliged to neglect their weeding in order to earn daily wages in cash or kind. It is partly because of the sentimental belief that ownership of a couple of acres of miserably infertile land, such as is so often allocated to Harijans today, can transform the life of a formerly landless man, that the concept of 'too poor to farm with any efficiency' is seldom appreciated outside the villages.

My second conviction is that the graph linking yield and size of farm-holding is a curve, not a straight line, and that the shape of the curve, which may slope upwards as well as downwards for parts of its length, is bound to vary according to circumstances – from time to time and from place to place. Any concept of a straight line is a kind of caricature of the false notion of an amorphous peasantry.

My third conviction is that in south India the shape of the graph for irrigated paddy farming may well bear no resemblance to that for dry cultivation. Whereas a small household may be entirely supported by two acres of tank-irrigated paddy land, and may be able to afford to hire resources, such as a plough team, which it does not possess, two acres of dry land are altogether insufficient to establish a cultivator's economic viability – indeed it may be better to rent them out. So great is the labour intensity of tank-irrigated paddy farming, so high are the potential yields, and so standard the cultivating practices (which do not, of course, involve interplanting) that it would be *possible* that within the range of, say, one to ten acres, there was little variation of yield with size – whereas there would be no such possibility with dry farming.

My fourth conviction is that the unattractiveness of very small-scale farming, relative to farm-labouring or other types of work, is not only due

[3] See Appendix VIII(2). It is significant that manure receives hardly any mention in Berry *et al., ibid.*, and that it is wholly ignored in the theoretical chapter supporting the 'inverse relationship'.

to low yields, low morale and so forth, but also to the relatively low prices received by poor farmers owing to their particular need to sell grain immediately after harvest, when prices are lowest, in order to meet their urgent expenses and debts.[4] (Such an idea receives no attention in the textbooks since it is invariably presumed that grain that enters the market, however that is defined, is 'surplus' to growers' requirements.) It is all very well to refer, in the manner of many economists, to the relative cheapness of family labour compared with wage labour,[5] as providing an incentive to poor farmers to labour on their farms with especial intensity, but this is to overlook many factors which have already been discussed, as well as the superior efficiency of the large groups of farm workers, both family and hired, which are suitably employed only on the larger farm plots owned by larger farmers.[6]

Such, in outline, are some of my reasons for rejecting any idea that *under our dry grain mode* there might be a general inverse relationship, covering all acreage ranges, between size of holding and yield, and for doubting any belief in the superior efficiency of the smallest cultivators. What, then, is one to think of the numerous official Indian statistics (there are, of course, no corresponding statistics for northern Nigeria) which support such beliefs? I am afraid that some of them are suspect owing to the unqualified use of the ambiguous word 'farm', which may be either a plot or a holding. But even if farms are usually meant to be holdings, I am convinced that most of the statisticians who handle the aggregated figures after they have been collected in the field have little idea of the extreme difficulty of obtaining reliable, meaningful statistics of the size-distribution of farm-holdings.[7] And the difficulties of obtaining reliable figures of yields are so great that it is dubious whether large-scale surveys, which are not under the personal supervision of many expert agronomists with socio-

[4] This applies particularly to Hausaland where seasonal price fluctuations are much more pronounced than in south India and where more grain, that will ultimately be sold outside the village, is stored for long periods in village granaries. In Hausaland poor cultivators often borrow grain a few months before harvest in return for the repayment of twice the quantity after harvest – a perfectly 'fair' transaction, considering the huge price rise that is apt to have occurred in the interval.

[5] Considering that the alternative occupations for family labour are seldom known at all precisely and that the possible cost to richer householders of dissuading their sons from taking outside employment is never taken into account, this is a tricky supposition – though few potential family workers can hope to have outside work at all times.

[6] There is no reason to doubt the existence of a direct relationship between the size of farm-holdings and the average size of the plots of which they are composed. See, for example, Hill (1972), Table IV.2, line (15).

[7] See Appendix II(1). There is the special difficulty that many farmers own plots outside their Village Area. Also, little of the data relates to areas where our dry grain mode applies – and wet land is included.

economic training, or of suitably qualified statisticians, ever produce statistics which are relevant to this debate.

But as hardly any unofficial research workers in the socio-economic field in either West Africa or south India have ever had sufficient resources at their command to enable them to draw a 'size/yield graph' for dry grains which is based on a sufficient number of cases to be convincing,[8] does this mean, as many desk economists would presume, that we have nothing to contribute to this important subject? I think not. For there are relevant things that we can *say* about the expected behaviour of certain variables even if we cannot strictly *measure* their movements. I think, for instance, that we are able to form a rough judgment as to the proportion of farmland in a particular village which is cultivated by households which have 'too much land' in relation to their available labour, so that, for this reason alone, they lack the ability to farm as intensively as they might.

So I start by addressing myself to this question. From examination of statistics and other material relating to individual farming households I think that in all three research areas, in both continents, there are nowadays very few large land-holders who are in this position. The basic reason is that since the abolition of the slave estates in Hausaland, and of the *jodidars* who owned entire villages in south eastern Karnataka, there are very few holdings of 30 acres and none as large as 50 acres. Given the ample supplies of day labourers and the fact that no holdings are so large that the householder and his dependants are unable to supervise (as they must) the hired labour force that is required, and given also our proven association between land ownership and household 'wealth' – for all these and other reasons, we have no cause for supposing that any significant number of farmers is nowadays over-endowed with land in this sense. The widespread belief in such over-endowment probably stems from the supposition that estates of a hundred acres or more are still generally common and possibly also from a belief that the holdings of the richest farmers are still continuing to grow in size;[9] while such estates do still exist in some localities, and dangerous recent developments affecting the ownership of farmland by city-based farmers are reported from Kano,[10] our three research areas are not atypical of densely populated districts, where the collapse of the large estates together with the severe limitations

8 The most notable West African work is still *Economics of Agriculture in a Savannah Village* by Margaret Haswell, 1953, who dealt with millet production in the Gambia. See, also, *The Nature of Poverty* by the same author, 1975, which reports the results of a re-study of her original village in 1973–4.

9 Such orthodox pessimism takes little account of the importance of division of farmland on death in conditions of growing land shortage.

10 They are, of course, undocumented.

of the day-labouring system, have greatly reduced the maximum holding size – to the degree that in Anekal Taluk there were, as we know, no reported holdings above the land reform ceilings.[11]

Moreover, if a large landowner feels that he is over-endowed with farmland, perhaps because he is elderly and has insufficient dependants to manage the hired labour force efficiently on his behalf, it does not follow that he will in fact try to cultivate annual crops on all his land. In the Anekal villages his obvious course will be to plant casuarina trees, which will require little maintenance after the first year or two, and which grow so fast that they certainly do not represent an extensive type of cultivation. Then, a Dorayi farmer who finds himself 'long on land' in any particular year can derive much prestige by lending out plots (*aro*) to land-hungry men – but owing to polygyny, and the consequent tendency for rich men to have more sons than poor men, 'land surpluses' based on a shortage of sons are potentially much rarer than in monogamous Karnataka. As for Batagarawa, the *gandu* system there was so flourishing and the propensity to give away land to sons-in-*gandu* was so strong, that there were few farmers who had any need to lend farm-plots (*aro*) to anyone other than their close relatives.

So much for the large land-holders. But the interesting consideration is that it is not uncommon for small, and particularly very small, land-holders to be 'long on land' in the sense that they cannot farm their small holdings efficiently with their available resources and lack the finance to hire ploughs and labourers. In Anekal Taluk, as a consequence, the institution of 'landlordism', which has been weak throughout the past century or more, has now been stood on its head,[12] most of those who rent out land being widows and other small land-holders, who are quite right in thinking that the rent they would receive from a tenant is greater than the potential net returns from own-cultivation. In Batagarawa and Dorayi, where there are no renting systems, 'disabled cultivators', defined as those who were too poor to farm effectively, could either lend out their farm-plots, sell them, neglect them altogether, or farm them inefficiently – the latter possibility being more attractive than in Anekal Taluk where those who lack ploughs and plough animals have necessarily to hire or borrow them. As I constantly reiterate, the condition of being 'too poor to farm' (either at all or with any efficiency) was dreadfully common in Batagarawa.

I have left the most important question to the end. Is there any reason to think that within the range of (say) 5 to 25 acres there is likely to be any

[11] See Appendix II(2).

[12] I doubt whether this has much to do with the fact that renting is technically illegal under Land Reform.

marked relationship between size of holding and yield, given that all cultivators within this range use the same types of equipment, so that one of the particular reasons for expecting big cultivators to be more efficient does not apply?[13] My reply to this question is twofold. First, that as there are so many variables other than holding size which affect yield, no curve linking those two variables would be devoid of detailed kinks and bumps. Second, that 'financial power' and family solidarity (which leads to a high incidence of joint households) are sufficiently closely linked with size of holding for there to be a strong likelihood of a generally *direct* relationship between size and yield – provided the larger cultivators are not hampered by their inability to obtain adequate supplies of organic manure in the form of animal dung. The point about organic manure in this context is that although it is a saleable commodity, it is possible that a rather small proportion of total supplies actually enters the market – except at Dorayi, with its anomalous dependence on supplies bought in Kano city. Therefore, it is possible that the superior financial power of larger cultivators cannot take its usual expression in a situation where they resemble everyone else in suffering from the shrinkage of the grazing grounds – and where, for good or bad reasons, they usually lack interest in the application of chemical fertilisers to their basic grains. Manure being a strangely neglected matter in this context,[14] I consider it first, before turning to more general issues, with special reference to the Anekal villages.

A century ago large cultivators who could not rely on purchasing sufficient manure to maintain the fertility of their soil would always have been able to maintain large herds of cattle, maybe supplemented by other livestock, so that they would have been unaffected by any general manure shortage. Today, as we know, there are few large herds in the Anekal villages – indeed it seemed that there were no more than about 40 households which owned 5 or more cows and bullocks, though this figure may be an under-estimate if many more animals than one realised were lent out to others (*iltam*). If it is assumed[15] that the dry dung from one cow,

[13] Most writers on this subject seem to assume that nowadays every third world rural community includes, for example, some tractor owners – though there happened to be none in our three research areas. So far as the cultivation of dry grains was concerned, technology design was totally standardised in our areas – though richer farmers were, of course, apt to own better-quality equipment and draught animals.

[14] Since this debate started in earnest, economists have overlooked organic manure in almost Freudian fashion; but, Marx especially in Vol. III, Book III, of *Capital* is an exception, and Lenin (see Appendix XIII(1)) went further. As for the particular case of West Africa, it is still generally believed that the annual cultivation of manured farmland is extremely rare, if not anomalous; this belief is to such a degree an article of faith that evidence to the contrary from Hausaland is nearly always ignored.

[15] See Appendix VIII(1).

bullock or buffalo is sufficient for the manuring of only about 2 acres of arable farmland, then it may be very roughly estimated that some 70% of cultivators of 10 acres or more in Hullahalli and Nanjapura (in which villages acreages under casuarina woods were more readily estimable than elsewhere) probably produced insufficient manure for their own requirements, though much would have depended on their usage of other types of locally available manure, including tank silt, leaves, straw and other organic matter, some of it prepared in the large, deep, unsightly compost pits, full of earth and decaying rubbish, which mar the outskirts of so many villages. While poor people often sell dung from their own animals,[16] this being a strong reason for believing that many very small holdings are notably ill-manured, it is possible that a fair proportion of the largest cultivators would apply more manure if supplies were more readily procurable. If this be so, the existence of an inverse relationship between size of arable holding and yield cannot be wholly ruled out for holdings above (say) 10 to 15 acres – though considering the significance of other factors, which would be liable to operate conversely, this possibility is rather remote. (But this tentative conclusion must not be allowed to obscure the strong probability, which is further discussed in Appendix VIII(1), that a general shortage of organic manure is likely to harm the smallest cultivators most.)

It is unlikely that the largest land-holders in Batagarawa are ever short of manure considering that they are in a particularly strong position to attract visiting Fulani pastoralists to graze their cattle on their stubble after harvest – and considering, also, that there is a fairly active market in sheep and goat droppings, which impoverished cultivators are often obliged to sell.

Supplies of manure apart, I now seek to justify my contention that in the range of (say)[17] 5 to 25 acres the superior wealth and familial solidarity of the households with the larger holdings is likely to enhance their efficiency as farmers. Since I have already sufficiently demonstrated the strength of the relationship between size of holding and 'wealth', I shall henceforth refer to richer and poorer households, neglecting mention of holding size.

In the matter of labour, richer households have many advantages. Their family labour force is more disciplined, their joint households better organised; they can attract the best hired labourers, partly because they can provide them with more regular employment and larger work groups,[18]

[16] They may also laboriously collect it from the fields during the non-farming season – though most of it is dropped in the cattle stalls.

[17] Of course the appropriate range must vary from place to place; this particular range relates rather to the Anekal villages than to Batagarawa, where there are more large holdings.

[18] See Hill (1972), p. 115, on the strong preference for employing several labourers on the

but also because they can offer more 'perks'[19]; and they can time the various seasonal farming operations to their own best advantage, rather than having to wait on the convenience of others, like those who are dependent on hired ploughs. If a cultivator is rich or influential enough he may not even have to go to the trouble of recruiting his own day-labourers, but can make it worth someone else's while to do this time-wasting work for him.[20] Insofar as there is likely to be a direct relationship between *plot* size and yield – at least within the range of (say) a half to three acres – the richer farmers, with their larger average plot size, will be those who benefit. Finally, richer farmers are in a superior position to relate the scale of their arable farming to the varying size of their family labour force during their life cycle: they can take their own decisions rather than having them forced on them by others.

On the matter of crop diversity, I can do no more than record my field observation, which is in accordance with commonsense, that richer farmers are those particularly apt to produce financially rewarding special crops, such as groundnuts, tobacco (which requires heavy manuring), sweet potatoes, cassava,[21] onions, peppers, tomato and other vegetables, hemp, various tree fruit and seeds (notably mangoes and locust beans) in Hausaland; and a variety of pulses, hybrid maize, castor seed, sesame, numerous vegetables and tree crops, including mango and jackfruit, in the Anekal villages.[22] Poorer farmers have greater difficulty in financing the production of these crops; are less inclined to take the risks involved in their cultivation; and are more likely to feel obliged to devote the whole of their cultivated farmland to the production of basic grains. The same general considerations apply to interplanting or crop mixtures – unless, as sometimes in Hausaland, only the two basic grains, millet and guinea corn, are involved.

Finally, it is worth noting that richer cultivators are the very people who would not necessarily wish to push the scale of their cultivation beyond the point of decreasing returns – arising, say, from shortage of manure – mainly because of their superior opportunities of setting themselves to work in other ways. Whereas a Harijan with two acres of marginal land

same plot. The richest Batagarawa farmers tended to have much the largest work groups – the labourers themselves appreciate large groups.

19 Partly owing to a fairly common reluctance to pay more than the prevailing wage rate, other incentives, such as loans or gifts, may be offered by richer employers.

20 While no farmer, with the exception of one in an Anekal village, was rich enough to employ a full-time foreman during the farming season (in the manner of the ruling class in Batagarawa), some get part-time assistance of this type.

21 See p. 153n above. (This is not to deny that cassava is a poor man's crop under other agrarian systems.)

22 Elsewhere in Anekal Taluk the list would be longer, with mulberry, grapes, pumpkins, etc.

may decide to cultivate *ragi* because he suffers much under-employment as a hired labourer, a rich man faced with the opportunity of buying an additional plot, which does not particularly attract him, may rather decide to devote more time to his lucrative trading activities.

So, despite prevailing orthodoxy and a little uncertainty about manure supplies, there is good reason to insist that, within the range of holding size with which we are concerned, richer men are those best able to promote their own interests by intensifying and diversifying their dry land agricultural activities – just as they prosper by diversifying their non-farming activities. And there is certainly every reason to assume that under our dry grain mode the smallest cultivators are almost bound to be miserably inefficient – for reasons which are entirely beyond their control.

APPENDIX VIII(1)

Jottings on manure

The strange neglect of organic manure in the classical debate on the relationship between scale of production and yield has already been noted. An earnest search through the obvious sources has yielded little of interest except in the works of Marx and Lenin, which are certainly superior to any contemporary source in their treatment of manure – as well as another neglected, allied subject, namely the quality of draught, and other, animals.

Lenin was concerned to bolster up Marx's conclusion that large-scale producers had many advantages, as well as to pour scorn on 'bourgeois political economy'. His arguments are ingenious.

Lenin complains[23] that Ed. David in *Socialism and Agriculture* made his truism that 'manure is the soul of agriculture' the main basis of his defence of small-scale farming. But, he states, the argument is fallacious because David assumes that an equal number of cattle provides an equal quantity of manure – that cattle on big and small farms are of the same quality:

> Marxism asserts that the conditions under which cattle are kept . . . are *worse* in small-scale than in large-scale farming. Bourgeois political economy asserts the opposite.[24]

He approvingly[25] quotes the work of K. Klawki who argued that the yield of the great majority of cereals regularly and very considerably diminished with the reduction of farm size, the reasons for this including the inferior quality of the manure available to small farmers and their failure to 'plough their land deep enough, their horses being weak'.

[23] *The Agrarian Question and 'Critics of Marx'*, p. 148. Originally published 1905; citations from English edition of 1976.

[24] *Ibid.*, pp. 148–9. [25] *Ibid.*, p. 78.

Very relevant to our thesis is his remark that:

> Under the capitalist system the position of the small peasant in agriculture is *in every way analogous* to that of the handicraftsman in industry.[26]

In another work[27] he praises Kautsky for not providing an abstract formula in favour of large-scale production which ignored the enormous variety of agricultural relations. The superiority of large-scale production, he notes, applies only up to a certain limit. But in relation to agriculture as a whole:

> It is quite permissible to say that large-scale production is decidely superior to small-scale production.[28]

With a few notable exceptions[29] professional agronomists and field economists have shown a profound lack of interest in 'organic manure'[30] in northern Nigeria and south India during the past century, leaving the field open to amateur observers of the rural scene such as E. D. Morel[31] who visited Northern Nigeria in 1910–11, and who thought that European cultivators could learn much from the Hausa:

> Rotation of crops and green manuring are thoroughly understood, and I have frequently noticed in the neigbourhood of some village small heaps of ashes and dry animal manure deposited at intervals along the crest of cultivated ridges which the rains will presently wash into the waiting earth. In fact, every scrap of fertilizing substance is husbanded by this expert and industrious agricultural people.[32]

It is significant of official condescension that in 1913 P. H. Lamb, the recently appointed first Director of Agriculture[33] in Northern Nigeria, should have adopted an entirely contrary attitude, almost regarding Hausa cultivators as though they were newcomers to their own country, ignorantly destroying the natural fertility of the soil and profligately 'drawing upon the bounty of nature'.[34] Except for a short period between the wars,[35] professional agricultural scientists in northern Nigeria have been basically uninterested in this success of richer Hausa cultivators in extracting good crop yields from unpromising farmland, year after year, by lavish and appropriate manuring. They have, of course, concentrated on chemical fertilisers, ignoring indigenous supplies, which still make up the great bulk of total

26 *Ibid.*, p. 86. 27 See *Collected Works*, Vol. 4 by V. I. Lenin.

28 *Ibid.*, p. 119.

29 Including certain contributors to *Green Revolution?* ed. B. H. Farmer, 1977. The fullest and most interesting discussion is the chapter on manure in Voelcker, *op. cit.*, 1893, which is based on the supposition that the scientifically neglected subject of manure was of the highest importance to Indian agriculture.

30 This unsatisfactory term relates to local manures as distinct from chemical fertilisers – including, as it does, straw and leaves it seems superior to the more usual 'farmyard manure', especially as West African and south Indian farmers seldom have 'farmyards' in the European sense. See *Fertilizers and Manures* by A. Daniel Hall, 1st edn, 1909.

31 A fascinating and neglected political figure.

32 *Nigeria: Its Peoples and its Problems* by E. D. Morel, 1911, reprinted 1968, p. 115.

33 For all the hesitations on his appointment see Hill (1977), p. 30.

34 'Agriculture in Hausaland, Northern Nigeria', *Bulletin of the Imperial Institute*, XI, by P. H. Lamb, 1913.

35 See Hill (1972), p. 288, for references to the work of K.T. Hartley and M. Greenwood in the 1930s.

nutrients. This has been most unsatisfactory since indigenous methods of preparing, conserving and applying manure, though full of merit and ingenuity, are also apt to be thoroughly wasteful.[36]

Why has the matter of organic manure somehow failed to interest anyone outside the villages themselves – not even the redoubtable Myrdal?[37] It goes without saying that human excrement is an unmentionable type of manure in south India (where my observations suggest that it does little to enhance the fertility of the soil), but what kind of reticence has led to its neglect in Hausaland, where many men are expert in sealing their house latrines with earth for up to a year, when an inoffensive and pathologically harmless rich black earth, ready to spread on the fields, may be extracted?[38] Despite all the conventional complaint about the fact that a high proportion of the cattle of Hausaland are owned by Fulani pastoralists, there have been no proper studies of the extent to which these pastoralists are nowadays settled or semi-settled cultivators and little study of the symbiotic relationship between Hausa cultivators and Fulani pastoralists, grain being exchanged for dung. The only possible explanations for the general neglect of the study of organic manure is the respectability of scientific work on experimental farms at institutions and the lack of agronomic fieldwork designed to identify the salient variables determining the crop yields actually achieved by individual farmers.[39]

In both continents manuring is a very old practice. Francis Buchanan thought that farm carts[40] were used almost entirely for dung carrying. He realised that dung was a saleable commodity and noted that rubbish was sent out of towns to the farmland as it is from Kano city today:

> A good deal of attention is here paid to manuring the soil. Every farmer has a dunghill; which is prepared by digging a pit of sufficient extent; in this is collected the whole of the dung and litter of the cattle from the houses where they are kept, together with all the ashes and soil of the family. . . . The farmers who are within two miles of the city, send bullocks with sacks and procure from . . . the sweepers, the ashes, ordure and other soil of the town.[41]

In the case of Hausaland, our knowledge that land-selling is an ancient practice[42] is in itself sufficient evidence that manuring is likewise, for permanently cultivated manured farmland was the only category of saleable land.

> It is to be presumed that much of the extensive farmland within the walls of large Hausa cities (*birni*) has been permanently cultivated for centuries – that, over the course of time, there have been millions of Hausa farmers who have successively practised agronomic

36 In 1967 my heart was broken when I saw the neatly piled, finely prepared manure blowing away from the Batagarawa fields, as dust in the winds, in early June when we were all waiting for the belated planting-rains which did not fall until 14 June.

37 In *Asian Drama* by G. Myrdal, 1968, the references to manure are negligible. Also, Myrdal shows an uncritical acceptance of the belief in the inverse relationship between yield and scale of production, see p. 1254, in Vol. II.

38 See Hill (1972), p. 289, for a little detail and reference to one other writer on this subject.

39 The most amazingly crude aspect of the great debate on 'inverse yields' is the lack of interest in causality and the failure to appreciate the diversity of variables involved.

40 Buchanan, 1807, Vol. I, p. 121.

41 *Ibid.*, p. 122.

42 See Hill (1972), pp. 240–1.

systems, with no fallow, such that yields were not necessarily subject to progressive deterioration.[43]

In densely populated regions, such as northern Hausaland and south-eastern Karnataka, where little fertiliser is used, no discussion of crop yields, of economic inequality, or of worsening poverty, should ever omit mention of manure supplies and their distribution between farmers. This is especially true of south-eastern Karnataka where the number of cattle per acre of cultivated land is undoubtedly showing a marked secular decline. In Hausaland we do not know whether the population of sheep and goats, whose droppings are a vitally important type of manure, is keeping pace with the acreage of manured farmland.

Whether severely impoverished farmers will ever find it economical to apply chemical fertilisers to dry land will depend on government policy. But even if the quantity of fertilisers applied to dry grain increases greatly, organic manures are bound to retain their importance, for cultivators are surely correct when they claim that 'chemical fertilisers are much less effective alone than when used with organic manure'.[44]

It seems to have become conventional to assume that the properly conserved dung and urine from one head of cattle is sufficient to manure two acres of dry land – but given the great variations in the size and nutrition of cattle such averages are of little interest, especially as it is impossible to estimate the quantity 'wasted' as fuel, for sealing floors, threshing yards, etc. According to our count the total cattle and buffalo population of the six Anekal villages was a little short of one thousand; and the total area cultivated by villagers was of the order of 2,000 acres – including irrigated land with its higher manurial requirements. Given the unavoidable degree of wastage, such figures imply an absolute shortage, such as would necessarily harm the poorest cultivators most. Shortage of stalling space for cattle in these congested villages, as well as of natural fodder may be two of the reasons for the surprisingly small herds maintained by some of the largest farmers – as noted above, p. 174, about 70% of the largest cultivators in Hullahalli and Nanjapura were possibly obliged to buy dung from others.

APPENDIX VIII(2)

Interplanting or crop mixtures

If we define interplanting as involving the simultaneous cultivation of two or more crops on a farm-plot (so that it is to be logically distinguished from systems involving the successive cultivation of different crops in the farming year), then it is a very common system in both Hausaland and Karnataka – as in many other tropical regions. In the area of southern Hausaland where D. W. Norman undertook his rural surveys, he estimated[45] that only 17% of the cultivated acreage

[43] Hill (1972), p. 303.
[44] *Green Revolution?* ed. Farmer, 1977, p. 127.
[45] 'Crop Mixtures under Indigenous Conditions in the Northern part of Nigeria' in Ofori (1973), p. 132. (This interesting paper includes a bibliography.)

was under a sole crop, 42% and 24% respectively being under two-crop and three-crop mixtures – 26% being under the two-crop mixture of millet and guinea corn. While interplanting is common in the Anekal villages, observation suggests that in terms of the yields of subsidiary crops,[46] many of which are commonly planted, like *jowar* and castor seed, round the outside of the fields only, it is probably far less important than in Hausaland.

In both continents there are certain crops which are never or seldom grown in pure stands: these include cowpeas[47] and sweet potatoes in Hausaland and *jowar* and certain pulses[48] in Karnataka. But in Hausaland the main constituents of mixtures are millet, guinea corn, groundnuts and cotton all of which are fairly often grown as sole crops.

Needless to say, the practice of inter-cropping ought to be the despair of many official statisticians concerned with statistics of crop production and yield – though they usually display a cavalier disregard of it. According to D. W. Norman, agronomists and those concerned with agricultural extension commonly denigrate the practice, despite its continued popularity with the farmers, so that little 'co-ordinated research'[49] has been done. Yet Norman's own findings were spectacular: they showed that the yield per acre of crop mixtures was 62% higher than that of sole crops.[50] Norman concluded that this higher yield was partly due to the higher plant population density of mixtures and he, also, attempted some empirical verification of other statements made by farmers. Another writer on interplanting in northern Nigeria has noted that the practice enables the otherwise 'useless ridge' – i.e. the furrow between ridges – to be cultivated.[51]

However, this is not the place to review the numerous agronomic and other reasons why interplanting so often makes such good economic sense in both continents. My purpose is simply to suggest the likelihood, under our dry grain mode, that richer farmers benefit most from the intensification resulting from intelligent intercropping,[52] with its elaborate spatial arrangements, especially when it involves the agronomically valuable legumes, which the poorest farmers can ill afford to cultivate, if only because of the high cost of seed.

46 I think that in the Anekal villages, unlike Hausaland, it is possible to distinguish main and subsidiary crops in mixtures.

47 *Vigna unguiculata*. Sown after millet, this plant spreads over the whole field after the millet has been harvested.

48 See citation from Buchanan on p. 234 below. Buchanan, 1807, Vol. I, p. 100.

49 Norman, 1973, p. 130.

50 *Ibid*., p. 138.

51 Nadel, 1942, p. 210. ('Useless ridge' was the term used by the Nupe people themselves.)

52 It is true that Norman (1973), p. 139, found no correlation between size of 'farm' (I think he meant farm-holding) and the degree of interplanting; but he says nothing about the relative profitability of different types of interplanting which, with the smaller farmers, may usually have involved millet and guinea corn mixtures only. My own speculation seems justified by observation and commonsense, as well as by the wise remarks on mixed-cropping by Voelcker, *op. cit.*, 1893, pp. 233–4.

CHAPTER IX

Upward and Downward Mobility

Our preliminary discussion of changing trends in land ownership in Chapter VI, which dealt in terms of groups not individuals, showed that during this century different processes had been at work in Hausaland and the Anekal villages. Whereas in the Anekal villages the richer castes had not gained land at the expense of the Harijans (who had had hardly any land to lose), and may indeed have lost some to newcomers, in Hausaland the active working of the market had increasingly tended to concentrate land in the ownership of richer farmers, who had bought it from poorer men.

The recent stultification of the land market in both regions has scarcely affected the poor. In Hausaland they had already disposed of nearly all they possessed and have now become wary of selling the remainder; in the Anekal villages they usually manage to retain the little that they own unless forced into mortgaging it. Even so, the incidence of effective landlessness is bound to increase, if only because of the impossibility of dividing small holdings between several sons on death. As for the richer households as a group, there is no longer any appreciable tendency for them to gain land and, failing a large-scale exodus, average holdings are bound to diminish more rapidly. Only by diversifying and intensifying their various activities can members of this group hope to maintain their living standards.

INHERITANCE

As a preliminary to examining the changing fortunes of individual households, I now take a further look at the inheritance process which regulates the transmission of property between the generations during the father's lifetime as well as at his death. The general principle, under our dry grain mode, is that sons[1] should be treated alike – an absurdly idealistic idea, especially in polygynous Hausaland where an old man's last-born son may be half a century younger than his eldest half-brother. Equal

1. In neither of our regions do rural people consider that daughters ought to receive a share as a matter of right – which is why the legislation is inoperative.

treatment is impossible for a multitude of reasons many of which are bound up with such factors as: the gradual departure of sons from the joint household; the high rate of divorce in Hausaland; the granting of land outside inheritance to sons-in-*gandu*; the lack of proper provision for unmarried sons;[2] the physical impossibility of effecting a fair division of a large portfolio of farm-plots of very varying sizes and qualities; the chaos and disarray so commonly associated with death in Hausaland;[3] the need to provide for the widow . . . Unless the sons remain together for some considerable period following their father's death[4] (which, as we know, they are increasingly loath to do), the chances of equal division are usually remote.

THE INEQUALITY OF BROTHERS

In the case of Dorayi a good indication of the inequality of brothers is provided by the following statistics. There were altogether 20 sets of fatherless married brothers in Dorayi which included at least one brother who was classified as rich; but in only 7 of these 20 cases was there more than one rich brother in the set. Of the total of 51 married men included in these sets, 28 were classified as rich, 21 as 'middle' and 2 as poor.[5]

It was interesting to find that, using the same criterion, it was the equality of brothers which required emphasis in the particular case of the dominant castes in the Anekal villages. There were altogether 12 sets of fatherless brothers belonging to these castes which included at least one brother who was classified as rich; in as many as 8 of these 12 cases there was more than one rich brother in the set. Of the total of 42 men in these 12 sets, no fewer than 36 were classified as rich. Of course these figures tell us nothing about the transmission of wealth to sons by poorer members of the dominant castes, who are numerous in some villages,[6] as they relate to an unrepresentatively rich sample of households.

If we examine the condition of poor brothers we find no such contrast between Dorayi and the Anekal villages. In Dorayi there were altogether 13 sets of fatherless brothers which included at least one brother who was impoverished – the total number of men in these sets was 38, of whom as many as 31 were poor. In the Anekal villages, where there were 17 sets of

[2] There is a hole in the anthropological literature on this subject – see Hill (1977), p. 126.
[3] See Hill (1972), p. 184.
[4] In Karnataka the turning point is often the death of a widowed mother.
[5] These statistics may be compared with estimates – Hill (1977), p. 153 – of the proportion of rich Dorayi men who had had favourable inheritance situations: this proportion was about two-thirds for both rich fatherless men and rich sons with living retired fathers.
[6] See Table VI(4), and p. 191.

fatherless Harijan brothers, there was no set which did not include a man classified as poor or very poor: of the total of 37 men in these 17 sets, only one was classified as rich and 3 as 'middle', the remainder being poor (16) and very poor (17). One of the implications of these simple statistics is that penurious men in casteless Dorayi are almost as tightly locked in their inherited poverty as the Harijans in the Anekal villages. It is a condition of *individual impasse.*

INDIVIDUAL IMPASSE

If a young man happens to be poor then, as we have seen, a concatenation or conspiracy of circumstances necessarily works against him in the village, and there is much truth in the Hausa philosophy of *arziki*[7] which asserts that, however energetic or intelligent he may be, it is only if luck is on his side that he can fight back successfully. By what practical means can such men try to escape? I start by examining the circumstances of the few richer members of the AK and AD castes in the Anekal villages since most of them had had an exceptionally bad start in life.

Out of the total of 111 AK and 11 AD households (which were classified by wealth) only 15 and one, respectively, were classified as 'rich' or 'middle'. Apart from being somewhat older than the average, were these 16 men markedly unrepresentative in any other obvious demographic respect? Rather unexpectedly, they were found to have fewer resident brothers[8] than other Harijan householders; and the detailed evidence suggested that, desperately poor though most of their fathers had been, it had yet been advantageous, as so often with richer men, to have been his sole heir – as had actually been the case in 11 out of 16 cases, as Table IX(1) shows.

Exclusive of the 4 *thotis*, who are a somewhat different case, the table shows that half of the 12 richer householders owed their position to assistance rendered by richer absentee relatives or 'in-laws'. In some cases this assistance had enabled them to follow a rewarding occupation, such as trading or casuarina wood contracting, the profits sometimes being invested in farmland; in other cases it took the form of loans or gifts of animals. Considering that 3 of the remaining 6 men were a driver, a rock agent and a wood contractor, it is clear that almost the only road to betterment for a Harijan, who does not migrate,[9] involves help from, or

7 See Appendix IX(1).

8 Brothers who had migrated were excluded since their village property had usually passed permanently to their resident brothers.

9 The rate of outward migration is not only low, but in the particular case of the Harijans it usually involves joining wife's relatives. See Chapter X.

Table IX(1). *Richer Harijans*

Basis of 'prosperity'	Number of householders[(a)]
Thotis	4 (3)
Rich relatives elsewhere	3 (3)
Rich 'in-laws' elsewhere	3 (2)
Driver in Bangalore	1 (–)
Rock agent at local quarry	1 (–)
Casuarina wood contractor	1 (–)
Other	3 (2)
	16 (11)

Note:
(*a*) Brotherless men – see n. 8 on p. 183 – are shown in parenthesis.

direct economic contact with the outside world – contact which may sometimes be safely relinquished as the farmer's position in the rural community improves.

Certain important details have had to be omitted from the following summarised case histories of 'successful Harijans' to avoid revealing their identities.

Probably with the help of a brother, who is a trader in Bangalore, he managed to acquire some 4 acres of dry land formerly owned by the ousted *jodidar* and half an acre of paddy land. He has 6 children under 15 and lives in a tiled house in the Harijan's quarter which has 4 rooms. He has planted a casuarina wood. He has received official loans for constructing an irrigation well and for rearing pigs. His elder brother, who is a part-time road worker, remains very poor.

A young man, with a pleasant small house in the Harijan quarter, whose rich absentee father-in-law helped him to buy land and presented him with a pair of bullocks and a cow. As he is much respected, a rich Reddy villager most exceptionally allowed him to rent some excellent paddy land, for one season, in return for a third of the crop.

A village *thoti*, he planted a casuarina wood on part of his inherited land and is now far better off than his brother. He has 3 good cows, one bought (like part of his farmland) from the proceeds of selling wood; he has 15 sheep, reared by his household, and a cart, a bicycle and a radio. A late brother's son is a member of his joint household, which is quite viable.

He inherited no land, but helped by a sister who lives in Bangalore he borrowed money to establish himself as a trader in village farm produce, ultimately buying

$3\frac{1}{2}$ acres of farmland, including half an acre of paddy land. An educated son works in Bangalore. He has planted casuarina woods on much of his dry land.

The same conclusion regarding the vital importance of direct contact with the outside world applies to Dorayi. There, as in the Anekal villages, the victims of extreme indigenous poverty – poverty of a kind which necessarily exists under our dry grain mode – nearly always need to develop some direct relationship with the outside world, such as does not involve the mere sale of basic crops, before they can raise their living standards to anything like a decent level. Such links may be entirely personal, involving a relative or friend in town, city or wider countryside; or they may be entirely occupational, involving such jobs as lorry driving or wood contracting. Since impoverished men tend to have poor friends and relations and since their ability to secure rewarding jobs is circumscribed by their poverty, it is no wonder that so few Dorayi men escape from the vicious circle of village poverty without migrating.

But before the great rise in the price of land, which has occurred in Dorayi during the past twenty years or so,[10] a fair proportion of men who had inherited no land, since they were of slave descent, had succeeded in raising themselves to the general level of ordinary men of free descent – as would not have been possible today. A few had excelled themselves, as the following two examples show.

Alhaji Ibrahim was a well known Koranic teacher who in 1972 was still travelling annually to Hadejia to teach, being rewarded with sacks of grain which he brought home. Born about 1890, as a young man he had travelled widely in northern Nigeria with other men (all with their donkeys) buying grains and other farm produce for resale; he had also traded in kola nuts and sugar cane. At various times he had been a weaver, a thatcher, a well-digger, a house-builder, a messenger for the District Head and an earth-carrier with his donkeys. Like others he was emphatic that he was far too eccentric to be considered as endowed with *arziki* (see Appendix IX(1)), but in 1972 he lived happily and comfortably and hoped to go to Mecca.

The son of two well-remembered slaves, Malam Yusufu first followed his father by working in the lowly occupation of butcher. On his marriage he built a room in part of a dilapidated house and very very gradually established himself as a farmer, first cultivating borrowed (*aro*) land and finally managing to buy over 9 acres. The breakthrough occurred when he successfully cultivated several acres of irrigated onions. He purchases much grain, rice and locust beans in markets and elsewhere, storing the produce for a price rise and selling it from his house with the help of his two rich wives. He is a creditor.

Such cases were rare. In 1967 the ordinary moderately successful man of slave descent owned between one and three acres of manured farmland and

[10] See Hill (1977), p. 128.

followed some main occupation which was somewhat more rewarding than farm-labouring, porterage, donkey transport or the making of cornstalk beds – though he would have been unlikely to have spurned all these occupations. As in the Anekal villages, the relatively lucrative occupations were apt to be directly linked with the outside world – this even applied to well-known Koranic teachers, most of whose students were attracted from elsewhere.

As in the Anekal villages, firewood cutting was a rewarding occupation for young strong men – this was not due to the extreme closeness of Kano city which attracts firewood supplies from much more than fifty miles away. But as there are no privately owned firewood plantations in the farmed parkland of Dorayi, only isolated trees, groups of skilled fellers and wood cutters often travel to other areas in search of trees for sale, some of them being financed by rich men. Owners of suitable local trees may either arrange for the felling themselves or sell the standing tree[11] to someone else. In either event the work of cutting, splitting and bundling the wood, in bunches of standard size, is apt to be done by hired workers who are often rewarded with half the bundles they cut, for sale by themselves.[12]

Finally, I must re-emphasise that, especially in the Kano Close Settled Zone, where such a high proportion of the population lives dispersedly on the farmland, and where the road network is very poor indeed, the idea of *direct contact with the wider world as the only means of self-improvement for impoverished men* does not imply any need for urban linkage. A Hausa trader who travels fifty miles to buy groundnuts in a remote area where prices are low, for the purpose of reselling locally or in village markets, is as much linked with the wider world as anyone who happens to sell dried henna leaves in a city market.

The conclusion must be that unless the poorest men can somehow manage to get into direct contact with the wider world – like the enterprising travelling wood cutters, the Harijans of Srirampura – they are likely to become ever more sunk in their distress.[13]

WEALTH AND AGE

I now turn to the general question of the relationship, under our dry grain mode, between the ages of household heads and their wealth. The statistical

[11] See Hill (1977), pp. 168–9, on firewood cutting (*faskare*).

[12] This sale of most local supplies of firewood, much of it for 'export', is very hard on local residents, who may have to deprive themselves of grain to buy their requirements of firewood for cooking.

[13] As Batagarawa was in a transitional stage in 1967 in terms of the market in land, I have taken all my Hausa examples from Dorayi. But see Appendix IX(2) on poverty in Batagarawa.

evidence shows that, on the one hand, there is a strong tendency for the proportion of rich men to increase with the age of the householder, while on the other hand the incidence of poverty shows little age variation. Before considering possible explanations for these two 'rules', I turn to the evidence in Tables IX(2) and IX(3).

Table IX(2) shows that the tendency for the proportion of wealthy men to increase with age is particularly marked in Hausaland, for all age groups. In Dorayi, for example, the proportion of rich men rose from 4% for those under 40 years to 11%, 22% and 27% for the older age groups. In the Anekal villages, where the proportion of rich men in the whole population is much higher than in Hausaland, men under 40 years were notably poorer than the average – the statistics in col. (3), which cover all castes in the Anekal villages, in fact relate mainly to the dominant castes as they comprise 83% of all rich households. As for the Harijans in the Anekal villages, the figures in col. (4) show a striking relationship between wealth and age in terms of the proportion of the two richer wealth groups.

Table IX(3), which is concerned with the second rule, shows that in Hausaland, in particular, the incidence of poverty shows remarkably little variation with age – thus in Dorayi about a quarter of the married men in all age groups are impoverished. In the Anekal villages there is a slight tendency among the Harijans for the incidence of extreme poverty (col. 6) to decline with age. (The figures in col. (4) have little meaning as they relate to all castes.)

The first rule – that the proportion of rich men increases with age – is not difficult to explain in terms of such factors as: the weak financial position of the youngest householders; the familiar tendency for family labour forces to increase in size during a man's middle, or even his later, years; the absence of a declining final phase in the life cycle – few parents are abandoned by all their sons, many retaining the services of most of them; and the gradualness of the process of building up lucrative non-farming occupations, which are seldom inherited from a father, such as the buying and storage of farm produce for a price rise in Hausaland or wood contracting in the Anekal villages.

On the first of these matters our approach should involve the idea that, failing special circumstances, *poverty is the natural condition of younger household heads*,[14] many of whom lost their fathers when they were quite young, few of whom have yet had time to establish viable farming

[14] The proportion of all householders who were under 40 years was higher in Batagarawa (42%) than in the Anekal villages (26%). The main explanations were probably polygyny (which substantially increases the average age of fathers when their children are born and therefore leads to an increase in the proportion of fatherless young men) and the higher mortality rates of middle-aged men in Batagarawa.

Table IX(2). *Wealth in relation to age: proportion of rich men in each age group*

Age of household head	Batagarawa (1)	Dorayi (2)	Anekal villages (3)	Rich and 'middle' Harijans in Anekal villages (4)
Under 40 years	4	4	12	6
40 to 49 years	10	11	22	} 15
50 to 59 years	16	22	30	
60 and over	23	27	26	19
All ages	10	13	22	13

Notes:

(a) For difficulties of age estimation see Appendix VI(1). In the case of Dorayi the youngest age group would be better denoted 'under 35 years'.

(b) The Batagarawa figures, in col. (1), are drawn from Table V.7 on p. 79 of Hill (1972). It should be noted that the total number of rich households was only 17.

(c) The Dorayi figures, in col. (2), are drawn from Table VI.1 on p. 114 of Hill (1977). They relate to all married men, not only to household heads.

(d) As the number of rich Harijans was far too small for an analysis by age group, the statistics in col. (4) relate to 'middle' as well as rich AK and AD household heads. Owing to special difficulties of age estimation the two middle age groups are here amalgamated.

General note: No significance should be attached to the relative percentages of rich men in the three research areas, especially as col. (2) relates to all married men not household heads only.

Table IX(3). *Wealth in relation to age: proportion of poor men in each age group*

Age of household head	Batagarawa Poor (1)	Batagarawa Very poor (2)	Dorayi (3)	Anekal villages Poor and very poor (4)	Anekal villages Harijans Poor (5)	Anekal villages Harijans Very poor (6)
Under 40 years	46	23	28	71	53	41
40 to 49 years	31	25	28	45	} 48	37
50 to 59 years	36	} 26	22	47		
60 and over	36		27	39	50	31
All ages	39	24	27	50	50	37

Notes:

(a) See notes (a), (b) and (c) to Table IX(2).

(b) Cols. (5) and (6) relate to AK and AD men only.

(c) No significance should be attached to the relative percentages of poor and very poor men in the three areas.

households or to develop useful contacts with the outside world or with potential creditors.

In Batagarawa, where the early death of fathers was an especial cause of poverty, it seemed that the predicament of many young fatherless men partly resulted from the community's failure to modify certain conventional practices, notably those involving the payment of large marriage expenses, which had evolved at a time when domestic groups were larger than today. It was as though these young men were

> Victims of the community's unconscious belief in the continued existence of an obsolete patrilocal residence pattern . . . according to which young men could be assured of familial support.[15]

Having no relatives to help them, many of them were obliged to work to raise funds for their own marriage expenses.

In Hausaland younger household heads are so economically vulnerable that many of those with rich forebears do not prosper: thus in Dorayi only 8 out of 27 sons of rich retired fathers were themselves rich.[16] Nearly all the younger prosperous men had some lucrative non-farming occupation involving direct contact with the wider world. As many as 17 of the 23 sons of poor retired fathers were themselves poor, and none were rich. Certainly, *young married men never prosper unless they had rich forebears – and often fail to do so despite that favourable start in life.*

The situation in the Anekal villages was not dissimilar though members of the rich Reddy caste were a special case. Nearly all of the 9 Reddy householders under 40 years old who were classified as rich had had rich forebears;[17] on the other hand, none of the 8 such householders who were classified as poor had had a favourable start in life. While the number of cases is rather small for proper analysis, it does seem that the advantage of being the son of a rich Reddy nearly always compensates for the disability of being a young householder – it being impossible to say the same of any other group in either continent. There is no doubt that in the Anekal villages many younger non-Reddy men with dependent children who have decided to separate from their fathers do so in the full knowledge that they will be poorer for some time as a result since, as we saw in Chapter IV, they will have enjoyed little, if any, independent economic activity before the separation occurs.

As for our second rule, which is that the incidence of dire poverty varies little with age, it seems that the explanation must be that if a poor man does

15. Hill (1972), p. 168. 16. Hill (1977), p. 142.

17 In three cases the men had benefited from having been, for some time, in a fraternal joint household with their elder brothers.

Table IX(4). *Wealth and size of household workforce: number of workers per household*

Wealth classification	Batagarawa	Two Anekal villages: Reddy caste	Two Anekal villages: Harijans
	(1)	(2)	(3)
Rich	3.6	3.6	} 4.5
Middle	2.0	3.0	
Poor	1.8	2.0	3.2
All households	2.0	3.2	3.5

Notes:
(a) No significance should be attached to the relative figures for Batagarawa and the Anekal villages since there are no women workers in Batagarawa – see, also, notes (b) and (c).
(b) Col. (1). The figures are drawn from Table IV.1 on p. 61 of Hill (1972). As school attendance of older boys in Batagarawa was very high (much higher than in the Anekal villages) working youths were considered the equivalent of working men.
(c) Cols. (2) and (3). The statistics relate to Hullahalli and Nanjapura. Women workers are regarded as equivalent to men; but youths and girls under 18 were arbitrarily regarded as 'half-adults'. Col. (2) relates to the richest caste (the Reddy) and col. (3) to the poorest Harijans – the AKs.

not begin to emerge from the basic morass when he is between (say) 35 to 50 years old, that then there is little hope for him – though in Dorayi there were a few men who flourished for the first time in their late retirement owing to help received from enterprising married sons. Middle-aged impoverished fathers are those peculiarly apt, as we know, to lose the services of their married sons, which may be the main explanation for the relatively small number of workers per household in poor households which is revealed by Table IX(4). If a man has not developed a lucrative non-farming occupation by the time he is in his forties, then he is unlikely to do so – and this at the very time when he may have to face up to the need to raise marriage expenses for his sons (in Hausaland) or for his daughters (in Anekal). *There is a kind of economic threshold over which a man must pass in his middle years if he is not to remain forever impoverished.*

THE COLLAPSE OF RICH HOUSEHOLDS

The Hausa philosophy of *arziki*[18] lays much stress on the impermanence of wealth, on its non-transmitability and on the need to risk everything in the game of chance; it is no surprise when a rich man suddenly loses the whole of his fortune – though it may be that attitudes will gradually change following the recent rapid rise in land prices. In both Batagarawa and Dorayi there were many sad cases of failure – there were even some houses which were literally disintegrating round the heads of those who refused to follow their brothers by migrating. In this harsh economic climate, any chance misfortune such as a wife's death, or the departure of a son from *gandu*, might set off a train of events which leads to collapse – sometimes eventually to migration, as the only way of escaping from debt. Brief details of nine men who fell into poverty though they had formerly been much better off are provided in *Rural Hausa*[19] – I cite two of them here.

Now in his fifties, he was much better off until recently when he became greatly impoverished, partly (or so he complained) as a result of the marriage expenses of several daughters whose mother had died – he was also indebted to the co-operative society. Although his financial difficulties caused him to sell some farms, this hardly affected his plight, particularly as he has no working sons. He has now resorted to collecting firewood and working for builders, as well as to manure-spreading for payment during the dry season. He produced no millet in 1967. His present wife is an active trader; she largely maintains his household and holds him in contempt.

One of 3 sons of a well-known farmer, he has sold most of his manured farmland to meet many expenses including those connected with his second marriage and a naming ceremony, and now has the utmost difficulty in providing for his family of 8 dependants. One of his 2 wives assists in financing the household – he sold her a farm which is cultivated on her behalf. He sells firewood at all seasons and is a carpenter.

No similar philosophy exists among the dominant castes in the Anekal villages. Why should it considering that those castes are so well entrenched; that household heads possess so much more power of command than in Hausaland; and that it is so rare for well-established households to fall on really hard times? It is true that 42 dominant caste householders were classified as poor or very poor, but no more than about 7 of them were men who had come down in the world; of the remainder, as many as 12 were newcomers, 6 were sons (with living fathers) and no fewer than 8 were the sons of two fathers who had far too many sons to be able to provide for them all. In the Anekal villages there was no case of a formerly large joint

[18] See Appendix IX(1). [19] Hill (1972), pp. 143–4.

household which had collapsed owing to the sudden departure of all the sons. The individual richer households of the dominant castes were confident in their security, though losing land all the time owing to population increase; hence 'the equality of brothers' which I discussed above.

CONCLUSIONS

I now sum up some of the conclusions of this rather complex chapter. First, the inheritance systems do not, in general, work in a manner which ensures the equality of brothers, though the rich Reddy households of the Anekal villages provide an exception. But, in general, it will become increasingly true that no man can hope to prosper unless he had a rich father – though many of the sons of rich fathers will not prosper. Second, deeply impoverished men in both regions stand little chance of bettering themselves unless they establish some kind of direct economic contact with the outside world: the village economies operate in such a manner that no poor man, however intelligent or energetic he may be, can hope to emerge from the bottom of the pile without outside help. Third, I attempted some explanation of our two rules relating wealth and age: the one rule that asserts that men stand a much greater chance of prospering as they get older and the other which says that the incidence of extreme poverty hardly varies with age. Finally, I contrast Hausa fatalism regarding the collapse of rich households with the secure outlook of members of the dominant castes in the Anekal villages.

APPENDIX IX(1)

The Hausa concept of arziki

The Hausa concept of *arziki* represents a philosophical and fatalistic theory of classlessness in a milieu of inequality. With the double sense of prosperity and good fortune, the word seeks to represent life as a game of chance, which some men are much more likely to win than others – though they, too, may lose.

Arziki, or the lack thereof, is a personal attribute. It is a gift:

> which cannot be rationally explained in terms of inheritance, hard work, many sons, intelligence, religious piety or learning, relationships with rich or influential outsiders, political position – or by a conjunction of such circumstances or attributes. A man may appear to possess every advantage in life, but unless he happens to be endowed with *arziki* he cannot flourish.[20]

[20] Hill (1977). pp. 155–6.

And a man may suffer a withdrawal of *arziki*. As M. G. Smith has put it,[21] when the essential prerequisites of *arziki* operate together, *arziki* continues, but:

> when they cease to cohere, *arziki* withdraws, and left to his own individual resources, the formerly fortunate man rapidly loses the last traces of his fortune.[22]

Arziki also conveys a sense of hopelessness about the chances of preserving family wealth intact over the generations, for it is a non-transmittable attribute which cannot even be passed on to a favourite son.

APPENDIX IX(2)

Poverty in Batagarawa

The very low price of farmland in Batagarawa in 1967 did not reflect the degree to which good-quality land in the manured zone (*karakara*) was coveted by farmers – such farmland was, indeed, a scarce resource. But in the limited sense that land prices were low (or at least not high in relation to grain yield) and that some bush land[23] was available, Batagarawa was in a somewhat transitional state. Even though it was rapidly becoming increasingly difficult for potential land buyers to find willing sellers, it was yet true that men stood a greater chance of escaping from their inherited poverty than in Dorayi.

The case of Batagarawa is interesting because it shows that most of the main characteristics of our dry grain mode become evident before farmland becomes an absolutely scarce resource – the general and inescapable trend having already become abundantly clear to all concerned. It is also enlightening as showing that impoverished men may be unable to take advantage of the availability of bush land because they are 'too poor to farm' or because farm-labouring is more remunerative than their own hopelessly inefficient attempts at cultivation – thus, about a third of the members of the two poorest wealth groups cultivated no bush farm. So strong is the prevailing belief that land alone is a panacea, that the idea that it might require backing up with other resources before it is effectively cultivable can find no place in prevailing orthodoxy.

Batagarawa was also a transitional case in that its rural economy still boasted certain unexploited interstices or niches, so that impoverished men did not necessarily have to establish contact with the outside world in order to raise themselves. It was not beyond the bounds of possibility, though very difficult, for an ill-endowed man to emerge from penury by engaging simultaneously in several

21 Smith, 1955, p. 15. A longer excerpt from his excellent formulation is cited in Hill (1972), p. 185.

22 The low prices, though somewhat incomprehensible, were not atypical of Hausaland – see Hill (1972), pp. 239–40. No doubt they have risen steeply since 1967.

23 Land which could be freely cultivated by any member of the rural community. (Similar land was also available in two of the Anekal Village Areas – Bukkasagara and Mahantalingapura.)

occupations such as collecting firewood or other 'free goods' (for sale) or by making humble craft goods, such as ropes, thatches and mats, from local materials for local sale. Then, local house-building, invariably in mud, and carpentry, as well as local Koranic teaching, were among numerous other rewarded (if not rewarding) occupations.

The multifariousness of some men's activities was extraordinary. Although Mati Na'ida[24] was moderately prosperous and had never known penury, some of his activities were of a type which might have been pursued by anybody, however poor, so that I list them here.

Among the numerous non-farming occupations followed by Mati Na'ida during the course of his life were house-building, firewood collection, trading at various times in henna, okro, snuff, kola nuts, secondhand clothing, scent and other wares handled by village 'table-traders'. In 1967 he owned about a hundred pigeons which lived in a compartmentalised pigeon cote which he had built of mud; he sold some of the birds as meat and their droppings as manure for onion farming. He stored much produce, including groundnuts and cowpeas, for a price rise. His two wives sold much grain from his house on his behalf, in return for a commission. Apart from basic grains and groundnuts, his own crops included cassava (which he sold in plenty in Katsina city), rice, tomatoes and pepper – the latter planted after the rains had ended.

But as Mati Na'ida himself was the first to insist, there were many men who were unable to raise their living standards above a very low level, despite the existence of these various local opportunities. This is the fact which requires emphasis here – not the limited (though unquantifiable) degree of upward mobility which actually occurs.

[24] See Hill (1972), pp. xiii and 158.

CHAPTER X

Migration

It is the common lot of women, as we know, to migrate to a new community on marriage.[1] In Hausaland and the Anekal villages only a minority of men migrate at any stage of their life; and migration is usually permanent, perhaps mainly because migrants seldom retain rights over farmland which they could resume were they to return home.[2] In this chapter I look at the nature and incidence of male migration from each of the research areas, and I also touch on the neglected topic of inward migration to village communities.

There are many reasons why men migrate – and there are also some cogent factors which impede migration. Migration may be an act of defiance or desperation, as when a young Dorayi man disappears into the blue and is never seen again or when a debtor escapes the clutches of his creditor; it may be a long planned entry by a highly educated man into the urban professional world of doctors, lawyers and accountants; it may involve joining friends or relatives in city or countryside; it may be undertaken at the behest of a father or against his wishes; it may start as daily commuting; it may or may not involve wives and children; it may be seen as an adventure, a removal to the terrifying unknown city to seek one's fortune; it may be (as commonly in Batagarawa) a removal for farming to a sparsely populated locality; it may involve much suffering, and not only in the early stages . . . While the list could be continued indefinitely, and many men have mixed and confused motives, it is yet possible to describe the basic pattern of outward migration for each of our localities and to draw some general conclusions.

METHODOLOGY

The difficulty of estimating the incidence of outward migration from rural communities is much greater than is commonly realised, and there are few

[1] See Appendix X(1).
[2] See Hill (1972), pp. 101–2 and Hill (1977), p. 150.

good estimates for Hausaland and none, I think, for Karnataka. Laborious work is necessary since questions such as 'How many men have left this house?' are answered with the (polite) vagueness that they deserve. (In Dorayi, where the extremities of the situation so often demand extreme solutions, no father would admit that a son had departed, so that the information had to be obtained from others.) The only reliable method I know of is to study migration obliquely in the course of compiling household 'genealogies'[3] – a rather formal term for enquiries on household kin structure which have little time depth. If a man is asked whether any of his brothers has left he may forgetfully say 'no', but if, summing up the conversation, one says 'So you only have one brother?', he may remember better. Another difficulty involves time span; in my enquiries I endeavoured to list living migrants only, so that I might relate their number to the total now resident in the community. My intention was to list only those males who had migrated as youths or adults: so I omitted children who left with their mothers, students who are away (and will often return), boys who are adopted elsewhere, and young bonded labourers (*sambalagara*) from the Anekal villages whose employment is always temporary. Seasonal migration is not considered here.[4]

Special difficulties were encountered in each area. In Batagarawa the rate of outward migration was too high to be properly estimable; but reliable statistics of the whereabouts of 184 men who had formerly attended the primary school there were interesting – 79 of them had migrated (some with their fathers), 96 were still farming in their home areas (which included hamlets outside Batagarawa) and 9 had died.[5] Both in that village and in Dorayi my enquiries on the history of transactions in farmland incidentally yielded valuable material on migration. Two special difficulties in Dorayi were the above-mentioned reticence about absent sons and the 'vanished houses' – in this area of dispersed settlement, abandoned houses, which are never sold, rapidly return to the earth whence they came.

MIGRATION FOR FARMING

Whereas Batagarawa men commonly migrate to less densely populated localities, some distance away, where they may establish large farms

[3] The main objection to this method is that it omits migrants from households which no longer exist; for this, and other reasons, one's estimates of incidence are certain to be on the low side.

[4] It happens that the incidence of seasonal migration in our two Hausa localities was very low – it is very high in some parts of northern Hausaland.

[5] See Hill (1969). The figures suggest a misleadingly high rate of migration since they include students in higher education and the sons of the ruling class – virtually all of whom migrate.

around their houses, there is no such migration for farming from Dorayi although it is much more densely populated – and enquiries elsewhere in the Kano Close Settled Zone showed that Dorayi was not a special case. In Batagarawa it had been found that hardly any of the young ex-schoolboys had migrated for farming, but that the typical migrant was a moderately prosperous younger middle-aged man with working sons who accompanied him – that is, a man who could both afford to migrate[6] and who was supported by his kin in so doing. The reason there was no such migration from Dorayi was that so few men of the right age group had the necessary finance, and those who had usually lacked the incentive.[7] From the Anekal villages there was little deliberate migration for farming of the type that occurred in Batagarawa, although, as we shall see, there were indeed many men who happened to remove to other rural areas.

MIGRATION TO URBAN AREAS

Migration to towns and cities is not the automatic panacea that it is commonly supposed to be, as a little arithmetic shows. Since our three regions are (and will long remain) predominantly rural and since rural, like urban, populations have high rates of natural increase, an increase in an urban population of 50% within a ten-year period might reflect an outward annual flow from rural areas of some 1% only,[8] thus being compatible with rapidly rising populations in the hinterland.[9] Since our three research areas are all close to large cities, many more of their sons could be expected to drift to those cities than from remote areas. But in Batagarawa the general economic pull of the big city was weak, especially in its effect on younger men – thus few of the 184 ex-schoolboys were in the cities, although there was no regular daily commuting. Although two-fifths of all the migrants from Dorayi went to Kano city, most of them after their father's death, the general incidence of migration was so low that this meant that no more than about four men left for the city each year. About a half (55%) of all

6 Before the great inflation it is likely that migrants would have required some £100 to £200 to tide them over until their first crops had been harvested and to meet their transport, building and other costs.

7 See Hill (1977), p. 150. (This contrast ought to interest those who presume that the incidence of outward migration is apt to be directly related to population density.)

8 Thus if an urban population of one million rose to 1½ million in ten years, and if half of this increase were due to the arrival of strangers, the original rural population of (say) 4 million would have been depleted by only ¼ million – or less than 1% annually.

9 As a matter of fact the concept of hinterland, in this context, is very dubious in both Hausaland and Karnataka, many migrants to the cities coming from towns a long way away so that they do not speak the local language. (The predominant language in Bangalore is Tamil not Kannada.)

migrants from the Anekal villages went to Bangalore city, the proportion being lower for Harijans than for other castes.

MIGRATION FROM THE ANEKAL VILLAGES

The most interesting finding in the Anekal villages was that about half of the Harijans who migrated to destinations other than Bangalore city married women there. Whether this can strictly be regarded as 'migration on marriage', comparable to that for women, I cannot say since it is possible (though unlikely) that a fair proportion of the migrants did not know their future wives before they migrated. However, it is certain that a fair number of these men married women with no brothers (*iltam*); and that the marriage of kinswomen was common.

As for the incidence of migration from the Anekal villages, this varied considerably, but probably averaged about 20% – in the sense that about 20% of the adult male population was living elsewhere, a proportion which showed little variation with caste, but was possibly lowest for the dominant castes and for the richest households generally. Of the total of 115 recorded migrants, about two-thirds (77) were sons of living parent(s), though, as we know, few potential joint households were broken by migration; about a half of the migrants were Harijans (members of the Adikarnataka and Pichiguntala castes) compared with 33 members of the dominant castes.

Of the 38 members of non-Harijan castes who went to Bangalore city only 3 were in the professions; 6 were clerks or minor officials, 7 were in transport (lorry drivers, etc.) and 8 were manual workers – only 3 were traders. As for the 21 Harijans in Bangalore, there was only one professional man and 2 clerks among them, most of them doing labouring or similar work.

The general presumption is that non-economic factors determined the destinations of most migrants who went to rural areas, most of which were no more than about twenty miles away, none of them being far afield. About a third of them went to other localities in Anekal Taluk and about two-fifths to nearby southern Bangalore District, these rough proportions applying to Harijans and other castes alike.

MIGRATION FROM BATAGARAWA

Turning to the case of Batagarawa, most migration for farming was intended to be permanent, as shown by the frequency with which farmland was sold on departure – often to brothers, since convention demanded that they should have the offer of first refusal. Most of these migrants travelled some distance to localities where they could hope to cultivate more land very near to their house than was possible in an old-established farming area like Batagarawa, where the largest holdings were always composed of numerous scattered plots. However, it was noteworthy that outstandingly successful cultivators, and their sons, seldom migrated for farming: for those with money, the situation was always under control; there was no long-term, ineluctable, irreversible, tendency for yields to fall; there was no compulsion to remove.

As for the type of migration which involved young men in taking work as labourers, house servants, butchers, lorry mates, etc., this mainly appealed to the sons of impoverished farmers – the younger sons of richer farmers seldom migrated except for work in the 'educated sector'. The general pull of the big Hausa cities being weak, young men often sought work in small towns or villages. But very poor men never contemplated migration as a possible solution to their problems.[10]

Finally, I must stress that the circumstances of Batagarawa in 1967 were highly unusual within the general context of rural Hausaland owing to the excellence of its primary school, which had been founded as early as 1946. In 1967 less than 10% of the boys in Katsina Province were at primary school and Batagarawa was most unusual in sending so many of its youths, including members of the ruling family, to higher education – nearly all of whom later became members of the urban elite.

MIGRATION FROM DORAYI

Although the rate of outward migration from Dorayi was about equal to that from the Anekal villages (about one Dorayi man out of five being resident elsewhere), the locality was so desperately over-populated that I found myself constantly thinking in terms of 'the failure to migrate'.[11] That young men were deterred from migrating by the moral pressure applied by their fathers, and other kin, was shown both by the fairly strong tendency for two or more brothers to migrate simultaneously, or in quick succession, following their father's death – and by the high proportion of young migrants with living fathers who had vanished overnight from their parental home.[12] Also, the fact that the rate of migration from big houses was no more than about half that for the community as a whole indicated a preference for such a mode of residence.

10 See Hill (1972), pp. 98–9, for a summary of the findings on migration from Batagarawa.

11 I was a partial victim of the prevailing false belief that in West Africa the tendency to migrate is directly related to population density. See Hill (1977), Appendix IX(1).

12 This is a distinct category of migration in many Hausa localities – see Hill (1977), pp. 142–5.

Analysis of the destinations of Dorayi migrants showed that 41% of them went to Kano city, 24% vanished to unknown destinations, 7% removed to nearby countryside – and that at least a third sought fortunes outside Kano Emirate, mostly elsewhere in Hausaland. It seemed that most Dorayi migrants sought their individual fortunes with no intention of joining relatives or others who had preceded them.

By 1972 hardly any Dorayi boys had ever attended a primary school, and only one member of the educated elite (he a teacher) was identified. While the lot of some Dorayi migrants may improve in the longer run, the number who enjoyed real success as traders, contractors or transporters was diminutive and only 5 migrants had made the prestigious pilgrimage to Mecca compared with 10 pilgrims who had not migrated. (However, some migrants to Kano had the advantages of both worlds, since they continued to cultivate some (or all) of their Dorayi farmland, sometimes with the help of labourers.)

The situation would have been more readily comprehensible had a high proportion of those who 'failed to migrate' been successful in obtaining paid work in Kano city, to which they could have commuted. But as we have already seen, very few men from poorer households worked in the city, except for the small numbers employed as lowly gardeners and watchmen. Perhaps the refusal of fathers to permit their sons to migrate to the city during their lifetimes made it much more difficult for the older men to find work when they were free to leave. But the fact of the matter is that men who lack all qualifications, and who cannot afford to spend months or years searching for work, cannot usually hope to better themselves by the mere act of removing to the city.

MOVEMENT INTO THE VILLAGES

Our analysis of outward migration has shown that much of it is intra-rural, so that one would expect our research areas to be receiving areas for migrants – as indeed they are, though the rate of migration into over-crowded Dorayi is very low.

In Hausaland men who remove from one rural locality to another seldom become household heads unless they deliberately migrate as farmers taking up new land. In other cases the migrants are usually absorbed into existing households, most notably in the capacities of son-in-law or father's ex-wife's son.[13] So it is more difficult to study the incidence of inward than of outward migration and I here deal only with

[13] Thus in the big houses in Dorayi as many as 9% of the married men were related to the household head through women – Hill (1977), p. 184.

those newcomers who established themselves as household heads.

Although male migrants are made welcome in Batagarawa and may buy, or otherwise acquire farmland once they have been granted permission to live in the village, only 10 of the 171 household heads[14] were themselves immigrants and it seemed that there had been little permanent movement into Batagarawa during the past few decades.

Much the same was true of Dorayi where relatively few households were headed by newcomers or by men whose fathers had been strangers. However, there was a small number of men who, having originally arrived as butchers, Koranic students, imams (prayer leaders), barbers, etc., had later settled down and acquired small acreages. In earlier times, the Kano Close Settled Zone had drawn in many migrants from less densely populated localities who were attracted by the opportunities of craftwork and trading there and many farm slaves had also come in.[15] But in 1972 those days were long over, and although the ancient principle that 'strangers are always welcome' remained intact, few outsiders in fact sought entry to this overcrowded locality.

The situation was quite otherwise in the Anekal villages where about a fifth of all household heads were men who (themselves or their fathers) had removed from elsewhere. So significant is this recent inward migration that it is largely responsible for the elaborate multi-caste structure of these villages for, see Appendix X(2), the 'basic indigenous castes', who are the three dominant castes together with the Adikarnatakas, have lower immigration rates than other caste members. Quite a high proportion of migrants originally came to the Anekal villages as shopkeepers (4 out of 9 of whom are migrants), quarry workers or rock agents, barbers and craftworkers – most of whom later became farmers.

However the strangers are not a meaningful aggregate, not only because of the numerous castes and occupations involved but also because so much depends on whether they marry into the village, as more than half of them do. It was satisfactory to find one of our findings on outward migration confirmed: again, we find that members of the AK and AD castes hardly ever risk migration unless they intend to marry in the new area.[16] On the other hand, there were 11 strangers, belonging to 8 minority castes, none of whose members had migrated on marriage.[17]

[14] As already noted, the concept of household head in Batagarawa is such as includes a few men (among them a few immigrants) who farm independently while living in someone else's house. See Hill (1972), p. 97, on the male immigrants.

[15] See Chapter XIII.

[16] I estimate that at least a half of the strangers who married into the Anekal villages were married to close kin or had *iltam* relationships.

[17] See Appendix X(2).

NEW HAMLETS

The absorption of migrant men (often on marriage) by established communities is one mode of intra-rural migration in Anekal Taluk. A different mode involves the formation of new hamlets which are wholly composed of migrants who happen to settle on previously uncultivated land in a village area with which they have had no previous connection. While the first type of migration had been little studied in Karnataka, it comes as no surprise to find that it exists; but the existence of the second type is inconsistent with prevailing ideas which always seem to be based on the supposition that hamlets emanate from the village in whose administrative area they are situated rather than from further afield.[18] I touch on this matter here, before embarking on any historical discussion, as the existence of these hamlets makes nonsense of contemporary analyses of 'village size' based on the census statistics, for hamlets established since some early census year, earlier than 1901, always seem to be subsumed under the name of a village in the original list.[19]

On my first day's fieldwork in Anekal Taluk I found myself in Hullahalli, a village which had had a recorded population of 1,075 in 1971 according to the population census. To my astonishment I found that the actual population of the village in that year had been no more than about half of the official figure since two hamlets, which had been established by immigrant members of the Bhovi caste over half a century ago, had been enumerated with Hullahalli. One of these hamlets, Chattekerepalya,[20] was shown in the village records as having as many as 82 houses; situated over a mile from Hullahalli, it had been settled by immigrant landless Bhovi from Bangalore South Taluk who had been offered uncultivated land by the then *jodidar*. Chattekerepalya in no wise emanated from Hullahalli; indeed, there is no reason to believe that any member of the Bhovi caste has ever lived there within living memory.

On my subsequent walks in Anekal Taluk I visited many other similar hamlets, some of them basically inhabited by a single caste, others by

[18] This is the conclusion I draw from numerous conversations, although in my experience it is actually very rare for residents of a nucleated village to move out onto surrounding farmland, except for the occasional individual.

[19] The local administration is, of course, well aware of the existence of these hamlets, in which polling stations may be set up when there is an election; but even if they are larger than their false parent, from whom they are supposed to have emanated, they are ignored in the population census and therefore inevitably in statistical analyses based on it; however, in an Appendix to one of the census volumes for Bangalore District there is a list, showing the total population only, of all hamlets with populations of 500 and more – of which there was one in Anekal Taluk.

[20] See Appendix X(3), which also deals briefly with some other migrants' villages.

several castes. In most cases the farmland, nearly all of which was dry, had been allotted to the migrants by a *jodidar* – at Chattekerepalya he is said to have cleared the land of wood, which he then sold, before parcelling it out to individual migrants who paid land revenue in lieu of rent. But in the rocky and hilly hinterland of Mahantalingapura, which until recently was almost uninhabited, new settlements are still being formed by members of the Lambani and other castes. The only way to study the history of these settlements is to go there and ask the people – who invariably give one a good reception. If a Taluk which is so exceptionally densely populated as Anekal can be explored in this way, the opportunities elsewhere are likely to be greater.

APPENDIX X(1)

The migration of women on marriage

In both continents the migration of a high proportion of women on marriage does much to reduce the isolation of individual villages, and to create areas of close personal inter-communication within radii of some five to seven miles' walking distance, around each village. 'The geographical dispersal of women on marriage' was similarly patterned in both continents, in that – (a) the rate of migration to the nearby city was very low; (b) most women went to rural areas within (say) fifteen miles of their natal village – but see reference to removal of Anekal wives to Tamil Nadu below; and (c) migration to places distant more than (say) fifty miles away was extremely rare.

Marriage within the natal village

The incidence of marriage within the natal village area was higher for the two Hausa localities than for the Anekal villages. Over a half (57%) of Batagarawa wives[21] had been born within the Batagarawa Hamlet Area, and 60% of a sample of 324 Dorayi wives[22] had been born in that arbitrarily defined area of dispersed settlement. As for the Anekal villages, where it was often said that marriage outside the village is actively preferred by parents who arrange marriages, about a fifth[23] (22%) of a sample of 415 wives belonging to the Reddy, Gowda, Kuruba and Harijan (AK and AD) castes had been born in the village where they were still living – a further 10% having removed from natal villages which were very close; this proportion of one-fifth happened to apply both to the Reddy and the Harijan castes – the Gowda proportion being higher (35%) and the Kuruba lower (12%).

21. See Hill (1972), p. 96. 22. See Hill (1977), p. 80.

23. For south India this is a very low figure of 'village endogamy' if the statistics of Libbee *et al.*, which are based on census data, are reliable. See 'Marriage Migration in Rural India' by M. J. Libbee and D. E. Sopher, in Kosinski *et al.* (eds.), 1975, map on p. 354.

Migration from other nearby villages

About one-third (29%) of Batagarawa wives came from neighbouring hamlets within easy walking distance, the same proportion (30%) applying to Dorayi. In the case of the six Anekal villages,[24] 20% of wives (in addition to the 10% already mentioned above) came from other villages in Anekal Taluk, and 18% from villages in two other Taluks surrounding Bangalore city – Bangalore South and Bangalore North.

Migration from the cities

In the course of my work in Hausaland and the Anekal villages I have been constantly told that I underrate the extent of the socio-economic attachment of the rural communities to the nearby cities. One aspect of my reply to this taunt is to draw attention to the very small proportion of wives who came from the cities: the proportions were 2% from Katsina city in Batagarawa; 3% from Kano city in Dorayi; and 4% from Bangalore city in the six Anekal villages – a proportion which varied between 7% for the Gowda and 2% for the Reddy. (For the Anekal villages 12% of a sample of women who left their households on marriage went to Bangalore – the figures varying between 7% for the Reddy and 14% and 15% for the Harijans and Gowda respectively: such information was not collected in Hausaland.)

Kin marriages

In the Anekal villages, but not in Hausaland, high proportions of marriages involved close kin. For a sample of 240 marriages it was estimated that about a half (52%) of husbands married 'close kin', defined as father's sister's daughters (41% of all recorded kin marriages), mother's brother's daughters (39%) or sister's daughters (20%). The proportion of kin marriages appeared to be about as high for Harijans as for other castes.

Detailed dispersal

Considering the frequency of 'kin marriages' it might have been expected that the numbers of destinations and places of origin of wives would be fairly small relative to the number of marriages, as was not the case. For example, the 18 Harijan wives in our sample who were recorded as entering Hullahalli on marriage from other Anekal villages came from no fewer than 15 different villages; the corresponding figures for outgoing wives being 14 and 13 respectively. The same detailed dispersal also applied to the Reddy caste; thus, the 24 Reddy women who left Nanjapura for Bangalore South and Bangalore North Taluks went to as many as 17 different destinations. A sample of 63 Nanjapura marriages of members of the Reddy caste, involving places in Anekal, Bangalore South and Bangalore North Taluks, related to a total of 30 destinations or places of origin only – the corresponding number of

[24] The statistics for the Anekal villages all relate to the Reddy, Gowda, Kuruba and Harijans only.

places for 45 Harijan marriages being only 23. I am unable to explain such 'detailed dispersal'.

Migration from the Anekal villages to Tamil Nadu

Anekal Taluk borders the state of Tamil Nadu which lies no more than about ten miles south-east of Nanjapura. About 15% of women who left their households on marriage were recorded as having gone to Tamil Nadu, to destinations which it did not prove practicable to map, so that nothing is known about the dispersal of these women; the corresponding proportion for incoming wives was 11%.

APPENDIX X(2)

Statistics on migration into the Anekal villages

Table X(1). *Migrant householders by caste*

Caste	No. of migrants (1)	No. of migrants married in the village (2)	Col. (1) as a % of all householders in the villages (3)
Reddy	10	7	12
Gowda	10	4	20
Kuruba	7	6	12
Total dominant castes	27	17	14
Brahmin	3	1	38
Muslim	5	3	55
Other non-Scheduled	13	3	30
	21	7	35
Total non-Scheduled	48	24	19
Adikarnataka	21	19	16
Bhovi	7	3	28
Pichiguntala	6	3	16
Adidravida	4	3	22
Other Scheduled	3	–	27
Total Scheduled castes	41	28	18
GRAND TOTAL	89	52	19

Notes:

(a) The table relates to all the householders or their fathers who were known to have migrated into the six Anekal villages.

(b) Col. (2) relates to the number of migrants of each caste who married women belonging to the village in which they settled. (In some cases the wife may originally have joined the husband in his village and later have returned to her natal village with her husband.)

(c) Col. (3) shows the percentage of householders of each caste who were migrant.

APPENDIX X(3)

Hamlets established by recent migrants

None of the following hamlets is listed in the population census, each of them being enumerated with one of the five Anekal villages – see p. 86 above. (Throughout this book Srirampura has been denoted, for convenience, as one of the six Anekal 'villages', although it is more correctly a hamlet, being mainly inhabited by migrant Pichiguntala and being enumerated in the census with Kyalasanahalli.)

A. *Chattekerepalya* – see p. 87 above

Nearly all the inhabitants of this exceptionally large hamlet, which is enumerated with Hullahalli in the census, are members of the Bhovi caste, many of whose forebears migrated here around 1920 from a locality near Begur in Bangalore South Taluk, where they were landless. Having been promised land by the *jodidar*, they brought their cows, buffaloes and donkeys with them and built houses on sites which were alloted to them. When the *jodidar* was ultimately dispossessed, each cultivator was able to buy his land at around Rs 25 per acre – or sometimes less. The fact that most of the plots are still registered in the names of the deceased grandfathers or fathers who first cultivated them suggests that little farmland has been sold.

The migrants have prospered, mainly because most of the younger men work frequently (though not entirely regularly) in Bangalore, digging the foundations of buildings – a specialised occupation known as 'mudwork'. Some men commute daily by bus, others sometimes spend nights away in huts they have built in the city. As they attach importance to cultivation, daily-paid work suits them very well; thus, three sons of a widowed mother said that they all worked in Bangalore at times, but never simultaneously. Apart from the two shopkeepers who arrived recently, all householders are members of the Bhovi caste.

B. *Hamlet* (not named here)

The land was originally part of the estate of a rich Reddy farmer (not a *jodidar*) who failed to pay his land tax for many years, so that this portion was officially auctioned. Much, if not most, of the land was bought at the auction by a Muslim who lived in Bangalore, whose permanent labourers are said to have cheated him, so that he was obliged to sell his land.

The present inhabitants are strangers most of whom possibly bought their farmland from the Muslim in the decade after Indian Independence; although some 17 of the 22 householders belong to the Korama caste, they came from a variety of places – as specialist craftworkers (as well as cultivators) they make huge quantities of baskets from bamboo which is brought to them by traders. Members of three other castes inhabit the other houses.

C. *Krishnadoddi*

Situated about a mile from Mahantalingapura, this hamlet was established on land made available by a *jodidar*, which was subsequently bought by the migrants. In 1978 there were about 23 households, of seven castes, including 7 Bhovi, 5 Kuruba and 4 Viswakarma. On first arrival they worked as labourers and also collected firewood for sale. The migration probably started about 1950, the migrants coming in gradually from various directions. One of them is a blacksmith who claimed to live entirely on *mere* – i.e. he received between 10 and 25 *seers* of threshed *ragi* (and no cash) from each household in return for his work.

D. *Madappanododi*

Said to be one of 7 hamlets attached to Mahantalingapura, Madappanadodi bears the name of the ex-Patel of that village, who helped the migrants to settle when they first arrived in this remote, rocky area in the mid-1950s. (In 1978 Patel Madappa was invariably addressed by his former title.) There were two groups of migrants: landless Lambani (Banjara) who walked here from about 200 km away in Tamil Nadu (the distance being estimated on the basis of the bus fare in 1978 which was Rs 10) and members of a Kannada speaking caste, which could be found in no official list, who hailed from Kalanakuppe in Kanakapura Taluk, where they had insufficient land. Of the 7 or 8 original Lambani households, only one remains, the others having gone further or returned home; the other caste occupies some 22 households. The migrants were each granted at least 4 acres of official *darkast* land for which the land revenue is Rs 2 per acre. Although there was much poverty here, and most of the habitations were ill-thatched, some large *ragi* stacks were to be seen.

CHAPTER XI

Rural/Urban Relationships

In my next chapter I shall invert prevailing orthodoxy by insisting that rural stagnation in Hausaland and Karnataka results from the twentieth century *withdrawal from the countryside*; I shall show that the countryside,[1] which was once the matrix within which most economic activity in these regions was set, has now become a backwater – a forgotten land. When urban factories in both continents started[2] producing vast quantities of manufactures, such as textiles, which destroyed local craft industries, 'exploitation' was the key word; but just as that irreversible process is now 'defunct history' in this context, for no village lady wishes to wear a homespun sari, so we should examine contemporary rural/urban relationships without brooding on these homespun themes. Before starting the discussion I must briefly summarise some of my relevant conclusions up to this point.

First, we have conclusively shown (Chapter VI) that the essential basis of rural inequality is the ownership of farmland, which is very unevenly distributed between households. Second, it has been shown (Chapter V) that under-employment is one of the greatest scourges, which particularly affects poorer households. Third, it has been demonstrated (Chapter VII) that cultivators aspire to limit their dependence on dry grains by means of diversifying their farming and non-farming activities and that richer households do this very much more successfully than poorer households. Fourth, is our commonsense (though contentious) supposition, strongly developed in Chapter VIII, that the relationship between scale of production and yield is generally positive for dry grains – so that richer farmers have a greater capability of intensifying, as well as diversifying, their agriculture. Fifth, we have noted (Chapter IX) *both* that wealthier households are those most apt to have the best developed economic relationships with the wider world (rural as well as urban) *and* that the most impoverished people can seldom begin to improve their lot unless

[1] See Appendix XI(1) for a 'definition' of the countryside.

[2] Of course, in India cheap British manufactures had already done much to destroy local industry.

they, too, develop some degree of individual articulation with that world. Sixth, we have seen (Chapter X) that outward migration, most of which is to the countryside, seldom provides the most impoverished elements with a satisfactory means of escape from the village-induced poverty which resulted from a much earlier scramble for land.

With this background, I turn away from the causes and consequences of individual poverty to ask whether rural economies, *considered as corporate wholes*, are getting a fair deal in relation to the urban world. My argument will be that they are not and that owing to the escalating rate of inflation, which is city-generated, their situation is worsening all the time. In considering their situation I shall adopt a conventional balance of payments approach, each rural economy being seen as a small country with normal relations, involving imports and exports, with the outside world.

THE DEFINITION OF 'RURAL ECONOMY'

But using such an approach we are immediately up against the difficulty of defining the rural economy. As we know (Chapter III) there is apt to be a lack of correspondence, under our dry grain mode, between the village, considered as a residential unit, and the 'village land' in which it is set. There is no tract of land over which the residents of any particular village exert special cultivating rights – rights corresponding to those exerted by lineage members in West African societies where corporately owned tracts exist; and there is nothing to prevent residents in one village acquiring land in the 'village area' of another village. It was cautiously concluded that, in spatial terms, compact villages should be seen as residential clusters of farming households set in a sea of arable land; and village inter-dependence was, accordingly, stressed.

But does this, therefore, mean that in considering rural/urban relationships we need to take large areas, such as the whole of Anekal Taluk, with its population of c. 130,000 in 1971, rather than much smaller village units, such as the cluster comprising a Village Panchayat or even single villages? I fear that for some purposes this may be so. But for other purposes it is important that the individual village be considered the relevant rural unit, mainly because membership of a particular village still means so much in terms of the economic relationships between its members and also because individual villages vary in their relationship to the city, some of them being quite anomalous.[3]

[3] An extreme example was Shikaripalya, a Muslim village in Anekal Taluk, where nearly all the able-bodied younger men were obliged to work as stone-dressers in Bangalore, since they were short of land.

Certainly, one of the strongest justifications for treating individual villages as fundamental socio-economic units has all but vanished, for the erstwhile farm-slavery in Hausaland and paternalistic relationships between master and adult farm servant in Anekal Taluk (which are now very rare) both demanded residential propinquity – though the unfortunate untouchables had indeed to maintain a certain residential apartness in their 'ghettos'! The contemporary day-labourer, on the other hand, is free to wander about in search of work, and may even prefer to work outside his own village community – like older Hausa labourers who may be ashamed to be seen at work by their friends. Nor, nowadays, is there much in the way of communal village work.

However, there is a large range of economic dealings which most naturally involve people who know each other very well or who live very close together. Men and older children, but not women,[4] spend most of their daylight hours out of doors – or on their verandahs in south India – and the village streets are almost the equivalent of local market-places in terms of the transactions that are arranged and the information that is exchanged there. The importance of such surrogate market-places will be all the greater in the absence of convenient real market-places.

In none of our three research areas did actual market-places function as salient regular meeting grounds for men – let alone women,[5] who scarcely attended them; and I venture the suggestion that this might be a characteristic feature of our dry grain mode, which appears to be such that relatively little grain is retailed directly to consumers in open local market-places, unless a village is on a main road and happens to have a market which is frequented by grain traders from elsewhere.[6] In Batagarawa, where most grain required for immediate consumption is bought in houses, most men did no more than attend the nearest market-place, which was a few miles away, once a week in the evening; as for Dorayi men, they rarely went to market as buyers unless they had special requirements; and the ordinary village markets (shandies) in Anekal Taluk were both trivial assemblies and few and far between – there were only 6 markets in the Taluk, all on main roads and/or the railway, none being in our six villages. We may, therefore, say that there were no important institutionalised rural assembly places where men could rely on meeting their friends and making useful contacts

[4] Although, unlike the Hausa women, the Anekal women are not house-bound, they are apt to be indoors unless engaged in a specific task such as weeding, grazing cattle or drawing water.

[5] Anekal husbands are generally opposed to their wives going to market. As for Hausaland, the few women who attend markets are usually both old and husbandless.

[6] See Appendix XII(5).

on a day-to-day basis (though the commuters' bus[7] is a kind of substitute in Bangalore District) – and certainly none where influential outsiders might be encountered as, for instance, at the huge annual cattle fairs.

So villagers are necessarily thrown in on themselves – though in Anekal Taluk, unlike our Hausa areas, they are constantly refreshed by weekend visits from migrants. And just as it is more convenient to patronise a washerman in one's own village owing to the burdensomeness of the clothes, so there are many practical reasons why many types of relationship, such as paid housework by women, usually involve members of the same village – a conclusion which has particular application to rural credit-granting, as we shall see.

Accordingly, there seems to be sufficient reason for regarding the individual village, rather than the wider tract, or the village cluster, as the proper unit for our somewhat speculative discussion of rural balances of payments with the outside world.

URBAN EXPLOITATION

Individual village economies, considered as though they were small countries, or islands, have to export farm produce in order to pay for a great range of essential goods which they cannot produce themselves and must, therefore, import from the wider world – unless, of course, they have a sufficiently large net surplus on their invisible account to meet the deficit, which is highly unlikely in the case of our villages. It is a well-known fact that village prices of basic food grains in third world tropical countries fail to keep pace with inflation,[8] so that the prices which our villagers receive for their grains, which as we shall see are their chief exports, constantly fall relative to those of other goods.

Owing to the high degree of rural under-employment, and to the low grain prices received by their employers, the wages of farm labourers, which were very low before the advent of the great inflation,[9] constantly fall in real terms. In economists' jargon, the terms of trade between cities and countryside are bad, and constantly worsening, daily-paid labourers being among the chief victims of this vicious downward spiral.

[7] I suspect that a map of the 'location' of incoming and outgoing wives from the Anekal villages – see Appendix X(1) – would bear some relationship to local bus routes – since fathers often arrange marriages for their daughters with men they meet on buses.

[8] Thus, Lipton notes that 'Many governments in poor countries genuinely see measures to depress prices to the farm sector as protecting the very poor [urban-dwellers] by keeping down food costs.' *Why Poor People stay Poor: A Study of Urban Bias in World Development* by M. Lipton, 1977, p. 318.

[9] The great inflation started in the early 1970s in West Africa and has been much more severe there than in India up-to-date.

But the most remarkable paradox affecting these grain exports is not so much that they continue to flow despite the low price in real terms which they command, but that they represent supplies which are badly needed by the rural communities themselves. The millet and sorghum which is exported by Batagarawa and the *ragi* which is exported by the Anekal villages *is not grain which is surplus to the requirements of those communities*. I think it quite likely that in a normal year (by which I mean a year in which there has been no noteworthy failure of the rains) each of these communities is in the position that they produce less (dry) grain than they would wish to consume. Grain is exported because there is no other way of meeting the import bill, not because it is 'surplus'. So grain exportation is the direct cause of much hunger in these grain-deficit villages.

The universal assumption that grain exports necessarily represent grain surpluses partly derives from the belief that individual households never sell grain which they themselves need to satisfy their own appetites: in other words it reflects an entire insensitivity to the paradox of poverty which is such that people are often obliged to act in a way which, in the longer run, is adverse to their own interests. In Batagarawa it was quite likely that most of the grain that was sold immediately after harvest, when prices were lowest, came from the households of the very poor, who were obliged to dispose of grain which they badly needed, maybe immediately, in order to meet pressing debts and essential types of expenditure; later on, such households would be obliged to replace this grain by purchasing at higher seasonal prices. Of course, at later stages when seasonal prices had risen, some of the village grain exporters would be richer householders who produced more than sufficient for their own needs – but they might well have been in the minority.

On the basis of a number of heroic assumptions,[10] I estimate that *ragi* production in the Anekal villages might amount to little more than a half of total requirements for village consumption, *even if none were exported* – as it certainly is. (It is unfortunately impossible to evaluate *ragi* exports: all one knows is that large producers may export considerable quantities immediately after threshing, and that any other producer, however small-

[10] If the average yield of *ragi* per acre is put as high as 500 lb – higher than estimated in Appendix VII(1) – and if as much as 90% of the 1,500 acres of dry land known to be cultivated by villagers were under *ragi*, then annual production would be some 750,000 lb – in fact somewhat more as the acreage is certainly an under-estimate. In estimating village requirements of *ragi* I have followed convention in setting grain needs for a mixed population in the rural tropical world at 600 lb per head per year – see C. Clark and Margaret Haswell, *The Economics of Subsistence Agriculture*, 1964, p. 61; I have also assumed that about a quarter of the population is rice-eaters, only half of whose dietary grain would consist of *ragi*. On these assumptions, annual consumption needs would be some 1,400,000 lb of *ragi* – compared with estimated production of some 750,000 lb.

scale, may happen to be an exporter; as seasonal price fluctuations are much less severe in Karnataka than in Hausaland, there is less incentive to store grain for a seasonal price rise.)

The question then, is whether the villages are likely to be able to export sufficient produce to finance both the import of the 'missing grain', which might be worth the equivalent of some £30,000 at village prices (which in 1977–8 might have averaged about Rs 1.20 per kg) and the numerous essential imports. I am sure that this would be impossible and that the main sufferers are the Harijans, and other impoverished people, who go short on grain (and shorter on proteins) as well as lacking many ordinary things, such as blankets for cold nights, which others regard as necessities.

The two chief village exports are paddy and casuarina wood. Again, on various heroic assumptions,[11] I estimate that total paddy exports might be of the order of 140,000 lbs without affecting local consumption; if we assume the local price of paddy to have been Rs 2.50 per kg, then the value of these exports would be roughly £12,000. As for casuarina wood, if it is assumed that 10% of the dry land cultivated by villagers was under casuarina[12] and that the selling price of a seven-year-old wood was £700 per acre, then the value of casuarina exports would be some £11,500 – about equal to paddy exports. Even if other exports were worth as much as £6,500,[13] the total value of exports would do no more than finance the import of the 'missing grain', nothing being available for other essential imports. As 'invisible exports' (such, for instance, as the earnings of the travelling casuarina wood cutters of Srirampura) together with remittances from migrants (most of whom go to the countryside) are certain to be relatively small, the conclusion is obvious. *The villagers are being exploited both because they export much more* ragi *than they can spare*, going hungry as a consequence, *and because of the low price they receive.*

As these estimates are necessarily very rough (though I am convinced that they must be of the right order of magnitude), it is worth adding that there was, in fact, no evidence of large-scale grain importing to meet the

[11] I have assumed that the area of irrigated paddy land cultivated by villagers was 170 acres and that yields averaged 2,000 lb per acre, so that production ran at c. 340,000 lb annually. Annual consumption requirements of rice-eaters – see n. 9 – are put at 200,000 lb of paddy, leaving 140,000 lb for export.

[12] This would be compatible with the (rough) estimate of 90% of land under *ragi*, since the acreage of dry land carrying pure stands of other crops is negligible.

[13] The villages might conceivably be small net exporters of livestock – but no estimation is possible. As for exports of farm produce, such as vegetables, pulses, castor seed and sesame, they are certainly small.

'deficit'. The shopkeepers, without exception, work on a very small scale, usually selling no *ragi* (except, possibly, just before harvest), but only *jowar* (sorghum) flour; few householders, except possibly in Bukkasagara,[14] obtain supplies through a co-operative society; there is no evidence of purchase by householders in Bangalore city for resale from their houses;[15] and any quantities that are bought elsewhere by householders, for instance in the little market town of Jigani, are small enough to be transported by head or cycle – falling far short of whole sacksful.

So much for the evidence for the Anekal villages. In the case of Batagarawa, which is similar, I summarise my findings very briefly, more detail being elsewhere.[16]

For 1968 Batagarawa's full requirements of grain (bulrush millet and sorghum) for household consumption were estimated at about 400 tons (on the basis of 2 lb per head per day), compared with estimated production figures of 250 tons – on the rather optimistic assumption that yields were as high as a quarter of a ton per acre. (These figures are exclusive of production and consumption by the ruling class.) The value of the resulting grain deficit of 150 tons was put at £4,000. Batagarawa's chief export was groundnuts, estimated at £2,500[17] in 1968. It seemed unlikely that in that year Batagarawa would have been able to export a sufficient quantity of other goods to finance her necessary grain imports; but there was a very active market in grain imported by local traders – *'yan kwarami*. Since Hausa migrants commonly lose touch with their natal community, remittances were certain to have been small.

EXTERNAL BORROWING

So far no attention has been paid to the possibility that the grain deficit might be financed by external borrowing, for village economies resemble countries in having a capital, as well as a current, account with the outside world, being net creditors or debtors. (But their position is even more precarious than that of most countries, even small countries, since they are at the mercy of the extreme vagaries of the local climate, so that crop fluctuations may easily lead to a doubling or halving of the value of their main exports in successive years. One of their most crying needs, and one which they altogether lack, is the ability to borrow from the outside world just because times are exceptionally bad.)

Although in this chapter I conceive of village economies as though they

[14] There is a co-operative society at nearby Kalluballu.

[15] In other words, there are no counterparts of the *'yan kwarami* of Hausaland.

[16] See Hill (1972), pp. 196–7.

[17] The task of assessing the area of farmland under groundnuts had involved Alhaji Sabi'u Nuhu in estimating the extent of interplanting of groundnuts with grains on over 300 farm-plots. See Hill (1972), pp. 256–8.

were corporate wholes, I must not appear to be suggesting that they resemble small countries in being able to apply for loans from the International Monetary Fund, for, on the contrary, everything depends on individual initiative – it is the individual farmer who applies to a bank or other official credit-granting agency for a loan. But since official agencies are primarily interested in good-quality land as security for loans, and are uninterested in small holdings of dry land, the great bulk of the village population is unable to borrow on any sort of commercial basis outside their own community. Nor do richer potential borrowers, under our dry grain mode, necessarily find it at all easy to borrow the sums they might require to construct, say, a stone-lined irrigation well with an electric pumpset. They are likely to find it difficult to raise the large obligatory bribes,[18] that are the concomitant of all official transactions, as well as to overcome the resistance of potential creditors who do not consider dry land an attractive type of security, both because of its low yield in relation to its price and also because, when it comes to the crunch and the land is auctioned by the creditor[19] owing to default on the loan, the villagers are apt to gang up against him to ensure that he gets a low price. So borrowers are not so much exploited by the harsh terms which are offered[20] as by the obstacles that are put in their way in negotiating any satisfactory bank loan[21] – and they are likely to have to pay higher interest rates if they are successful in resorting to external private creditors.

Since, as a general rule, bigger creditors charge lower interest rates, from the point of view of the welfare of the village *considered as a corporate unit*, the more the richer members are able to borrow from big outside creditors the better, since some of this cash is bound to percolate down to poorer people, such as stone dressers and well diggers, or be re-lent to poorer people who would have no other access to funds. Of course these sub-borrowers would submit to harsher terms than the original borrowers – poorer people always pay more for goods and services than richer people – but they may still pay less than if they were wholly dependent on village-generated credit of a type which the bureaucrats have driven underground.

The richer village people have become only too well aware that their only hope of maintaining their living standards in the harsh, competitive, inflationary world is by exerting their superior power to borrow from the

[18] Villagers are often prepared to speak quite frankly about their efforts at bribery – whether successful or not.

[19] Needless to say, official agencies have no desire to take possession of the land.

[20] Indeed terms may be too lenient. 'Much rural lending by co-operatives and state-supported banks has been at rates too low even to keep up with inflation.' Lipton, 1977, p. 301.

[21] I am not here concerned with co-operative society loans which are much smaller than large bank loans. (Even so, poorer farmers seldom risk borrowing from a co-operative.)

urban world: owing to rising population densities and frightening inflation rates, this is a new and urgent situation. Whether or not such borrowing would enhance existent inegalitarianism must depend on the circumstances of the case;[22] and the question of whether, in a south Indian village, a higher total village income ever sufficiently compensates for greater economic inequality is a political question I cannot answer. But fortunately these questions have nothing whatsoever to do with the reality of urban exploitation. *The real urban exploitation*, in this context, *consists in the endeavour to suppress village-generated credit, which is all that is available to poorer people, while providing no one, not even the rich, with anything like sufficient to take its place.*

Why should officialdom be so opposed to village-generated credit? In south India[23] the reply lies on at least four levels. First, outsiders fail to comprehend the complexity of village credit systems or to realise that they can provide services which official agencies could never render. Second, and partly as a consequence, they caricature the actors concerned as either villains or innocent victims – this being an attitude which is in particular tune with our times but which is also inherited from the colonial obsession with debt.[24] Third, as tidy administrators they want to clean up an unfair system, taking the opportunity of granting a few loans that are larger than any that might be village-generated.[25] And, fourth, they are eager to avail themselves of the commissions attendant on the granting of every official loan.

RURAL CREDIT-GRANTING SYSTEMS

So I conclude this chapter with a brief survey of rural credit-granting systems in both continents, placing particular emphasis on 'the localisation of credit-granting' – on the need for creditor and debtor to be in day to day communication within the village, a situation which does not necessarily imply the existence of any patron/client relationship. My particular

[22] If the granting of additional loans for pump sets would result in the upsetting of the hydro-ecological balance (as in North Arcot where pump sets had proliferated, see Farmer (ed.), 1977, p. 337) the situation would indeed be clear. (In the 6 Anekal villages there were only 5 pump sets.)

[23] Officialdom adopts a similar attitude in Hausaland, denoting most village credit as usurous. In 1972 there was no official scheme for granting general loans to agriculturists.

[24] Throughout the colonial empire rural indebtedness was ignorantly, prudishly and invariably regarded as a moral problem, a sign that 'natives' lacked the virtues of thrift, self-reliance. . . . Village credit-granting was never seen as the converse of stultification or a sign of a lively economy. For an expression of this condescension see *Report regarding the Possibility of introducing Land Banks into the Madras Presidency* by F. A. Nicholson, Vol. 1, 1895, p. 4.

[25] It must be remembered that official agricultural banks were established in Mysore as long ago as in the 1890s.

purpose is to show up the errors in official thinking on this vital matter. It makes no more sense to attempt to suppress rural credit-granting than rural buying and selling – each is essential to the economic health of the rural community.

I start with a kind of savings group which does not meet with official disapproval – for that is usually reserved for the person of the creditor. The type of worldwide savings group[26] which is technically known as a rotating credit association is a good example of a club which is appropriately based on a village – or on closed occupational or ethnic groups in towns. Known as *adashi* in Hausaland and as *chiti* in Karnataka, this system involves all the members of a group, formed expressly for the purpose, in making regular cash contributions, perhaps weekly or monthly, into a common pool, one member taking the whole kitty on each occasion until each has had her turn. Unless the members who have already received their share can be relied on to continue to contribute the group will fail, so it is essential that they should know each other well and should respect the convener – as in Batagarawa where all the conveners, and very nearly all the members,[27] were women.

Such groups enable individuals to coagulate their short-term savings into small lumps of capital, perhaps for the purpose of buying a goat or a gown, the creditors and debtors respectively being those who receive their hand-out early or late. While they may appeal to the rich as well as to the poor, and certainly add some zest to life, it is certain that they do not account for more than a small proportion of the total village credit outstanding.

I turn now to consider the types of credit granted to poorer men within the village – men who lack the security to borrow from outsiders or official agencies (and who are reasonably terrified of the harsh action apt to be taken against defaulters by co-operative societies), and who, therefore, have to turn to those who trust them personally and/or can keep an informal eye on their activities.

In both continents an inability to borrow cash (as such), except in diminutive sums, is one of the hallmarks of severe impoverishment. In Hausaland the main way in which richer men and women help poorer people is by granting them non-cash credit which enables them to set themselves to work – to engage in a particular economic activity, from the proceeds of which they can repay the loan. Thus in Dorayi:

> Poor men often receive saleable local produce, such as henna, on credit, and pay for it after resale; donkeys are borrowed on credit, maybe in return for half the manure

[26] See Hill (1972), p. 203 – *adashi*.

[27] Members sometimes make contributions on behalf of others.

that is fetched [from the city]; payment for cornstalk is delayed until the [cornstalk] beds have been sold; grain is granted to farm labourers who repay in terms of work; payment for the use of a borrowed farm is made after harvest. When cash loans are made, these are usually very small and very short term, and related to particular activities: thus, small bridging loans granted for no more than a day, or even for a few hours, to enable particular transactions to be completed, are quite common.[28]

An example of a loan in kind, which has to be returned, is the *palu* system of cow-borrowing[29] in the Anekal villages, the debtor being rewarded with the first calf. The cow is an attractive type of loan to the debtor since if it dies when it is in his charge the debt is automatically extinguished; here, again, is a kind of 'localised debt' for, since the creditor needs to keep an eye on his cow to make sure she is flourishing, and not being underfed, he naturally prefers to lend her inside his village.

The question of borrowing on the security of farmland has already been discussed in Chapter VI where it was emphasised that mortgaging is all too often the prelude to (reluctant) selling – the debtor usually getting much less than the market price. But in the Anekal villages, as we know, a much more secure system involves lending a farm-plot of (say) half an acre for the planting of casuarina trees, in return for a loan of (say) Rs 500, the debt to be automatically liquidated from the borrower's agreed share of the wood when it is sold.

Since richer villagers sometimes act as agents for outside creditors, it may not be possible to estimate the extent to which locally-granted credit is actually generated locally. But it is a mistake to assume that local creditors *necessarily* stand near the bottom of a pyramidal structure of private credit-granting, with its apex in the city. Because some Hausa farm-produce buyers are agents for rich men in the city, it is mere vulgar urban bias to presume that rurally-based Hausa farm-produce buyers are seldom in a position to lend from their own resources. The casuarina wood contractors in Srirampura (see Chapter VII) were emphatic that the business men who financed their operations were independent creditors from other villages. Surprising as it may seem, in both continents examples were found of village creditors who were primarily interested in lending their own funds to wage-earners in the city,[30] at enormous interest rates, the money being compulsorily extracted on their behalf by the employers.

In the tropical third world generally, much secrecy usually surrounds village credit-granting which, in the absence of binding documents,[31] is a

[28] Hill (1977), p. 172. [29] See Appendix VII(2).
[30] For an example see p. 146 above.
[31] To one familiar with Ghanaian history, such documents seemed astonishingly rare in both Hausaland and Anekal Taluk.

species of personal relationship[32] which both parties are loath to discuss. So it is mistaken to attribute bashfulness to special circumstances such as fears of usury in Muslim Hausaland[33] or of the incomprehensible regulations designed to suppress private credit-granting in Karnataka – for instance, the Mysore Debtors Relief Act, 1966, which deals with the scaling down of debts in accordance with the debtor's means and with the ultimate transfer of the debt, if still unpaid, to a bank. In my experience the only type of credit-granting which is apt to be entirely above board involves the pledging (mortgaging) of farmland under conditions such that the property is usually (even automatically) redeemed by the debtor – a common situation among certain cocoa farmers of Ghana,[34] but uncommon in Hausaland and the Anekal villages where perennial crops (other than casuarina trees in the latter area) are unimportant. Nor is bashfulness peculiar to credit-granting. The extreme reticence about household grain-selling in both continents[35] shows that the nub of the matter, so far as both creditors and grain sellers are concerned, is the double-edged fear of being regarded as a rich man who is so vulnerable to the demands made on him by others that he is forced to neglect his own dependants.

Besides, reference to grain-selling is a reminder of the existence of a continuum running between the selling, the lending and the giving-out-free of grain, such that when the transaction occurs its nature is unclear, being any one of these possibilities.[36] The higher the chance the lender will soon pay for the grain, the greater the likelihood that the transaction amounted to selling. There are so many uncertainties. If a farmer 'lends' grain to a friend, but does not really expect it to be repaid, how soon is the 'debt' regarded as extinguished? Then, loans are often in kind, not cash, so valuation presents difficulty when prices fluctuate. As for 'rates of interest', they are commonly not rates at all, being timeless – the borrower of £*x*

[32] See Hill (1972), p. 211, for discussion of an elaborate contribution system (*biki*) under which partners assist each other, in rotation, over ceremonial expenditure.

[33] See Hill (1972), pp. 329–31, for the pathetic efforts often made by villagers to conform to Muslim law on indebtedness – pathetic, because much of the law is genuinely incomprehensible, even to experts, and because conformity is often impossible. 'Although it is arguable that the lifting of the "prohibition" on interest-taking would have little direct effect on rural economies, yet the present moral pretence stands as a barrier between officialdom and farmers, ensuring the continued irrelevance of legislation and official commands on such matters as pre-season crop-marketing and plough hiring and justifying the refusal to explore such fundamental problems of rural organisation as extreme poverty.' *Ibid.*, p. 331.

[34] See Hill (1956), Chapters V to VII, on the pledging of cocoa farms.

[35] The evasive attitude to questions about grain selling in south India was astonishingly familiar to a newcomer from West Africa.

[36] This is one of many reasons why all attempts to measure the volume of debt statistically are doomed to failure – see pp. 67–8.

being expected at some unspecified date (or at some date which, being specified, is not kept) to repay £$x+y$. In general, money interest on a monthly or annual basis (an interest *rate*) remains an alien concept in villages; similarly, where no interest is charged, creditors are commonly entitled to use the property, which has been pledged to them, for an indefinite period.

Since most creditors are also debtors; since borrowed funds are often re-lent; since the condition of being 'too poor to borrow'[37] is often worse than that of net indebtedness; as well as for a great many other reasons – in studying village credit-granting it is essential to think in terms of functions, types, conditions, terms and so forth, rather than examining the villainy or misery of the particular parties concerned. The unscientific attitude of blaming individual creditors *rather than the system as such* is unworthy of the successors of Marx and Lenin in their capacities as economists. On the one hand, as I keep on reiterating, credit is the life-blood of the village economy; on the other hand, it is of the nature of the system that poorer people borrow on harsher terms than richer. Official attempts to suppress village credit-granting are bound to fail – which is just as well; the only hope of controlling the worst excesses of a system which must necessarily continue to exist, is to prohibit (or to attempt to prohibit) certain obnoxious types of credit-granting, such as those which formerly tied indebted labourers to their employers for life, or which allow a mortgagee to grant loans on harsh terms, on the security of land, without any written documents.

Considering the degree to which village transactions in Karnataka are supposed to be regulated by a cobweb of legislation (relating to land reform, inheritance, indebtedness, bonded labourers, and so forth), it is surprising that this should overlook the mortgaging of farmland which, unlike renting, is entirely legal and unregulated – this being the one kind of borrowing which really arouses the anger of the Anekal Harijans and other insolvent victims whose lands, as they consider, are 'seized'. In the six Anekal villages I think[38] that there were no more than about 6 rich farmers whose fortunes had been much improved by the acquisition of land which had fallen in to them as mortgagees – and none of them cultivated more than about 30 acres.[39] (I doubt if there were more than a few outsiders who had acquired significant acreages in this way; although so much of the village farmland was owned by residents of nearby villages, large holdings were very rare.)

Under our dry grain mode economic life is much more seasonal than, for

[37] See p. 134 above.
[38] Profound secrecy made certainty impossible.
[39] Only one of these men (he a Harijan) had not inherited considerable acreages. (Mortgaging is a desperate act by those in a hopeless plight, and as such people usually own little land, the total volume of mortgaging is quite small.)

instance, in the forests of southern West Africa, where villagers do not depend on long-term storage[40] of grain and where there is a greater diversity of basic crops, particularly tubers and plantains, with varying harvesting dates. Because economic life is so seasonal, the need for short and medium term credit to tide people over the long dry season is particularly pronounced and many households (especially in Hausaland where household grain storage is so much better organised than in Karnataka) are obliged to borrow grain from richer households before harvest – under a system known as *dauke*[41] in Batagarawa, which is such that two bundles of grain are supposed[42] to be returned after harvest, when prices may have halved. Insofar as this type of borrowing involves many richer village farmers in lending to many poorer villages, I cannot see that it is to be condemned – indeed, it is far preferable to similar systems which involve villagers in borrowing directly from specialist traders who are non-residents. I think, indeed, that there are many circumstances in which ordinary village borrowers ought to be actively encouraged, as providing a cheaper and more competitive 'village service' than specialist outsiders. I, also, know that it is fallacious to suppose that the act of borrowing a bundle of grain from a fellow villager necessarily implies some kind of subservience in the short or long-term – this being another one of the great errors of our time.

So my earlier conclusion (p. 216) regarding the true nature of urban exploitation in terms of credit-granting, should be strengthened by adding that village-generated credit, of a small-scale variety, is often cheaper, as well as more convenient, than any alternative. Provided undesirable categories of village credit-granting are controlled, the authorities should endeavour to encourage not to suppress rural credit-granting in general – as well as to provide villagers with much better access to external credit.

APPENDIX XI(1)

The 'definition' of the countryside

Under our dry grain mode, as exemplified by northern Hausaland and south-eastern Karnataka, the only factor which prevents the bulk of householders in any

40 Maize is stored on the cob in open barns – but usually for relatively short periods. (Maize requires irrigation in northern Hausaland – none was grown in pure stands in Batagarawa and Dorayi – and is little grown in the Anekal villages.)

41 See Hill (1972), p. 223, where reference is also made to some of the other terms applied to various types of borrowing. (The Hausa vocabulary on this subject is most sophisticated.)

42 One of the main advantages of village credit-granting systems being their flexibility, it is impossible to say whether in fact two bundles are usually returned.

locality from being actual or aspirant cultivators is the lack of access to land resulting from the 'large size' of the town they inhabit. This being so, the only people who do not live in the countryside, as ordinarily understood in third world countries, are those who inhabit 'large towns', or cities, where an appreciable proportion of the population has no connection, actual or aspirant, with farming.

But what is the size of such large towns? If the average acreage of cultivated farmland per head of the population is put as high as 2 acres (a much higher figure than in any of our research areas), then a nucleated settlement with 5,000 inhabitants situated at the centre of a circle of cultivable farmland with a diameter of 3 miles (a convenient walking distance) would have access to much more than 2 acres per head,[43] and I think we would be justified in assuming that most householders would be cultivators unless their personal poverty prevented this – as it would be bound to do in many cases.

If a town be defined, in accordance with Indian census practice (with some exceptions), as having a population of 5,000 or more, then in 1971 there were only 13 such towns in Bangalore District, their total population of 211,975, comprising only 12% of that of the District exclusive of the city.[44] Even if the minimum size of a town were to be reduced to 3,000, the rural population would still be well over 80%.[45]

Unfortunately, reliable up-to-date statistics on settlement size are lacking in northern Nigeria.[46] Given that a high proportion of the population of Katsina and Kano Emirates is known, on the basis of such evidence as aerial photographs, to live dispersedly on the farmland; given, also, the extreme rarity of cities and the probability that towns with populations exceeding (say) 5,000 are nearly all situated on the relatively short mileage of motorable road, so that they are well-known names, being on all the maps – I think we are justified in assuming that now, as formerly, the proportions of settlements which have attained such a size are small. If this is correct, the very great proportion of the population in both of our regions lives in the countryside.

[43] If no allowance were made for house sites, grazing grounds, etc., the figure would be some 3½ acres.

[44] Bangalore city is so anomalously huge that it has to be excluded, especially as most of its immigrant population is not of local origin. (In 1971 only 11% of the total population of Karnataka lived in the ten cities with populations exceeding 100,000 – half of the city population being in Bangalore.)

[45] We cannot be sure of the precise proportion owing to the possible inclusion of many un-named hamlets with such towns – see p. 202.

[46] For technical defects in Nigerian population censuses and for town size in Kano Province in 1921 see Hill (1977), pp. 60–1 and p. 71.

CHAPTER XII

The Withdrawal from the Countryside

The discussion in this chapter is a fundamental element of my thesis regarding stagnation under our dry grain mode. In it I invert prevailing orthodoxy by insisting that rural backwardness in the dry grain zones in both continents results from a new-found contempt for country-dwellers who had previously commanded respect. Barrington Moore[1] has emphasised the apparently useful idea of 'a limited capitalist intrusion'[2] into the Indian countryside in this century, on the presumed supposition that any such advance into the countryside is something new. In this chapter I reverse this contention by emphasising the *withdrawal from the countryside* which has been particularly associated, during this century, with the ending of farm-slavery in Hausaland and with the abolition of the hereditary estate-holders (*jodidars*) in Karnataka – but which is also due to the final capitulation of rural crafts to city produced manufactures, particularly textiles, and to the development of motor transport, which is city-based. It is my insistence that forms of rural/urban communication that formerly flourished have now lapsed and that the countryside, which was once the matrix, has now become a backwater.

The word *matrix*, meaning womb, may be usefully applied to nineteenth century Kano Emirate, where the countryside was clearly the medium (womb water) within which economic enterprise flourished. The great bulk of the *entire* population of the Emirate then lived dispersedly on the farmland, just as the great bulk of the *rural* population still does today. As is well known,[3] Kano city was a great entrepot at that time, concerned mainly with 'international trade', extending as far as the north African littoral, and inhabited mainly, especially at certain seasons, by trading strangers from far away. On the other hand, long and medium distance

[1] *Social Origins of Dictatorship and Democracy: Lord and Peasant in the making of the Modern World.* By Barrington Moore, Jr, 1966, Penguin, 1977.

[2] *Ibid.*, p. 400. He mainly refers to recent anthropological works.

[3] The famous city, which was much the largest in the West African savannah, had been vividly described by Henry Barth in his book of 1857. See Hodgkin, 1975, for some useful excerpts from Barth.

trade, other than that which linked the northern savannah with far away regions close to, or across the Sahara, and with the partial exception of the kola[4] trade, was mainly rurally-based,[5] even though it ranged many hundreds of miles to southern Yorubaland and elsewhere. As for nucleated settlements within the countryside, the point was not so much that they were relatively few in number as that they usually emanated from the matrix – not *vice versa* as the early colonialists invariably supposed.[6] 'Urban bias' is an illness with much deeper and more insidious roots than is commonly realised.

Until about 1920, when farm-slavery was clearly on the verge of collapse, the Kano countryside was still the matrix: although the infants to which she (the enormous mother) had given birth, had achieved a certain viability, they still took much of their sustenance from her, partly because rich merchants and princes, who did not permanently reside in areas of dispersed settlement, cultivated large estates with the labour of farm slaves. Also, the urban-based leaders of trade caravans were largely dependent on transport donkeys, reared and maintained in the countryside – until, very gradually, in the 1920s and 1930s the lorry began to oust them, a process which is still far from complete.[7]

When farm-slavery ended the rich city merchants, and most of the princes, lost interest in their estates (which in some cases might even have been denoted plantations), to the point that they sold them off, gave away portions to their ex-slaves or simply abandoned them altogether.[8] From their viewpoint the daily-paid farm labourers who had replaced the slaves were so relatively inefficient, and so tiresome to supervise and recruit, that there would have been little prospect of making a profit from cultivation – and, besides, much of their original satisfaction had derived from the status of being a slave owner.[9] Perhaps things would have been different had there been any lucrative perennial crops, like cocoa or kola in southern forest country: but rich city merchants found millets and sorghum, even

[4] While the members of the exceptionally large kola trade caravans may usually have assembled in cities, many of them ordinarily lived in the countryside.

[5] See Appendix XII(1).

[6] See Hill (1977), p. 44, on the inability of colonial officials in Hausaland to escape from the belief that each hamlet had originally been attached to a larger nearby unit – a belief that is implicitly shared by census-takers in India today.

[7] Whereas in southern Ghana in the 1920s most lorries were probably owned by cocoa farmers, who thus continued to assert themselves in relation to townsmen, the relatively large lorries of northern Nigeria have always been urban-based. It is mainly owing to the ill-developed rural road network that medium-distance donkey-trading, involving farm produce, still continues in the savannah.

[8] Thus in Dorayi by 1972 the descendants of all the erstwhile private non-local slave owners (with a single exception) had wholly abandoned their land.

[9] See *Baba of Karo* by Mary Smith, 1954.

when tempered with groundnuts,[10] humdrum crops – especially when there were no slaves or other retainers to whom they could be freely issued.

Such members of the urban elite as had originally emanated from the countryside usually found little difficulty in contracting out of it altogether, because, pursuing our metaphor further, they had forgotten their infancy and, like most Hausa migrants today, had not been at pains to re-establish their links with their erstwhile mother. Postponing consideration of the deep questions of political organisation which endorse, or reflect, such a denial of origins – a denial which enhances the hiatus between urban and rural values – I return to my criticism of the seminal ideas of Moore and to the withdrawal of the elite from the countryside in the dry zones of south-eastern Karnataka. I do so in the spirit of agreeing with Moore that:

> As one tries to grapple with the details of contradictory and fragmentary evidence, either of two things may happen. The certainty may evaporate into a chaos of ill-assorted facts, or else the evidence may be selected to produce an argument that runs too smoothly to be true. There is not much that any author can do about this situation that would persuade a really convinced sceptic.[11]

Moore's starting point (and it must be remembered that he was writing before the Green Revolution) was the truth of the familiar platitude that India belongs to two worlds: while India, as a 'political species' belongs to the modern world, 'economically it remains in the pre-industrial age'.[12] He considered that the powerful obstacles to modernisation which had existed prior to the British conquest were reinforced by the British presence, which ensured (for reasons which will be discussed) that economic stagnation continued throughout the British era until now:

> Crops and ways of growing them were very much the same in Akbar's time [1555–1606] as they still are today over wide sections of India.[13]

For south India, Moore dismissed any technical advances that might have been fostered by those feudal landlords the *zamindars* by assuming, like virtually everyone else at that time,[14] that *ryotwari* (individual) tenure was universal there. He claimed that in the Madras area 'there were no

[10] The great expansion in groundnut exporting did not occur until the mid-1920s, when slavery was collapsing. In the case of Hausaland our thesis of the withdrawal from the countryside must not overlook the great drain of groundnuts for export overseas which reached a peak of over a million tons in the 1960s – and which has now totally collapsed. The expatriate buying firms in the 1920s and 1930s did themselves penetrate the more accessible parts of the Kano countryside.

[11] Moore, 1966, p. 356. [12] *Ibid.*, p. 314. [13] *Ibid.*, p. 330.

[14] The seminal importance of C. J. Baker's work on the large south Indian estates, starting with 'Tamilnad estates in the twentieth century', 1976, is only just beginning to be appreciated. And, see Chapter XIV below, there were also many hereditary estate owners in Mysore.

zamindars with whom to effect a settlement' and that this situation had come about

> mainly because the local chieftains made the mistake in this area of opposing the British, who destroyed them while pensioning off a few.[15]

It is even clear that Moore regarded post-Independence Indian villages as having been virtually 'pre-capitalist', for one of his reasons for concluding that Nehru's agrarian programme was 'an out-and-out failure' was that he had 'failed to introduce a market economy or a workable substitute to get food from the peasants to the city'.[16] He saw relevance in the dubious conclusion[17] of an official report that 'more than three-quarters of India's food production never reached the market'.[18]

This notion of the existence of non-market economies in modern rural (Hindu) south India lacks all historical depth – what had happened to the rural market-places of former times? Was Moore unaware of the astonishment, amounting almost to elation, which had been experienced by Western explorers or observers, notably Buchanan, Clapperton,[19] Barth,[20] Morel[21] and even Lugard,[22] when faced with the sophistication of certain south Indian and West African[23] agricultural systems? He is indeed wrong in stating that 'throughout Buchanan's reports there runs the same theme of inefficient cultivation and low productivity'[24] – and when he denigrates mixed cropping as an inefficient substitute for crop rotation! The fact is that Buchanan was obliged to include so much fascinating technical and economic detail about elaborate cultural practices that his three-volume work resembles a contemporary encyclopaedia (which is, of course, unrivalled) – as well as being a monument to unchangingness.[25]

When E. D. Morel visited Northern Nigeria in 1910–11 he considered that:

> Instead of wasting money with the deluded notion of 'teaching modern methods' to the Northern Nigerian farmer we should be better employed in endeavouring to find an answer to the puzzling questions of how it is that land which for centuries has been yielding enormous crops of grain, which in the spring is one carpet of green, and in November one huge cornfield 'white unto harvest', can continue to do so.[26]

15 Moore, 1966, p. 347. 16 *Ibid.*, p. 395.
17 Admittedly, Moore himself is partly critical of the report.
18 *Report of India's Food Crisis and Steps to meet it*, 1959, cited in Moore, 1966, p. 395.
19 Clapperton, 1829. 20 See n. 3 above.
21 Morel, 1911. 22 Lugard, 1904.
23 Of course Moore's book is not concerned with Africa.
24 Moore, 1966, p. 332.
25 See Appendix XII(2) for some relevant citations from Buchanan.
26 Morel, 1911, pp. 115–16.

Nor did 'modernity' apply only to cultural practices, such that land could be manured and cultivated year after year without any decline in yield. Thus Clapperton, for example, was astonished by the great clay granaries of northern Hausaland in which grain could be safely stored for two or three years – perhaps eight to ten tons in one 'urn'.[27]

We should not wonder at the surprise expressed by Buchanan in Mysore, but we do so because the backwardness of British agriculture in many regions at that time is nowadays usually forgotten. In West Devonshire in 1796 it was reported that:

> Twenty years ago, there was not a 'pair of wheels' in the country; at least not upon a farm; and nearly the same may be said at present.[28]

But the existence of cattle-drawn seed drills in Mysore in 1800 proves nothing about the presence of 'market economies'. Our knowledge that such was, indeed, the appropriate term for rural economies in both Hausaland and Mysore at that time has to do *inter alia* with the extent to which cash had evidently insinuated itself into the interstices of these economies, regulating or mediating the relationship between individuals or classes, being used to pay day labourers in Mysore, and serving as a medium of exchange in market transactions and long-distance trade. Ordinary farmers (not necessarily members of any urban elite) themselves bought farm slaves at market-places, and elsewhere, for cash (cowry shells) as though they were a species of plough oxen. In Kano Emirate farm slaves, who had the right of self-ransom, were not automatically assimilated into their owners' households so that as chattels they, and their children, represented a store of value which could be accumulated and immediately converted into cash if required.[29] As a matter of fact farm slaves as a store of wealth were superior to any form of agrarian capital in Hausaland today (with the exception of the farmland itself), the stock being self-reproducing.

What is the basis for the prevailing belief, which was shared by Moore, that these nineteenth century rural economies were necessarily 'non-market' – as, indeed, many other tropical rural economies were at that time? I think that this orthodox belief – which has been both intentionally

[27] The distinguished potter M. Cardew, in 'Gobir Granaries', *Nigeria Magazine*, 1960, was impressed by the accuracy of Clapperton's observations.

[28] *The Rural Economy of the West of England including Devonshire and parts of Somersetshire* . . . by W. Marshall, Vol. I, 1796, reprinted 1970. The list of farm implements then in use was very short and included a 'dung sledge' and old-fashioned wooden ploughs; there was no mention of seed drills.

[29] See Chapter XIII below.

and unintentionally disseminated by many anthropologists[30] – stems from the vague idea that 'everything started in the cities', so that if new ideas about agronomic practices, technologies and so forth do not percolate out properly the countryside is bound to remain backward. Those who believe that village economies ought now, *for the first time*, to start shedding their 'pre-market practices' and modes of thought, are not necessarily contemptuous of villagers – indeed, like Moore himself, they may go out of their way to deny that:

> the unpredictability of natural forces has made the Indian peasant passive and apathetic and prevented the transition to intensive peasant agriculture.[31]

Perhaps, like Moore, many believe that the root of the trouble lies in the caste system which 'arranges life effectively in the specific locality', thus making central goverment an 'excrescence'?[32] But how, then, can one explain *stagnation* (which is, after all, the main subject of this book) in non-caste societies like rural Hausaland? No, the difficulty is simply ahistoricity: a failure to realise that most important changes occurred *before* the base, or starting, date.

A curious feature of Moore's argument stems from his conviction that India is (or was in 1966) an 'agrarian state', such that the countryside is failing to generate a 'surplus' which could be used for industrial growth.[33] But since the industrial sector is closely linked with international capitalism, surely the obligation to create a surplus which could be used for rural development falls upon it? However this may be, we have already seen in the last chapter that this obligation is not honoured but reversed under our dry grain mode, the countryside suffering from a grain deficit which is aggravated by grain exportation to urban areas.

It is now necessary to effect some reconciliation between the metaphor of the original life-giving rural (female) matrix and that of the stern commanding (male) centralised state – for both Mysore and the Kano and Katsina Emirates were ruled by hereditary maharajas[34] or by emirs who resembled kings. How, in other words, could country people have been the source of so much economic originality when the central bureaucracy's main concern was to extract as much taxation from them as possible, without detriment to crop production,[35] other sources of revenue being seriously deficient?

[30] Epstein recently stated explicitly that 'Wangala's economic system changed from subsistence to cash about twenty years ago.' 'A Sociological Analysis of Witch Beliefs in a Mysore Village', in Middleton, 1967, p. 145.

[31] Moore, 1966, p. 331. [32] *Ibid.*, p. 339. [33] *Ibid.*, p. 385.

[34] It is not without significance for our further argument that when the British ousted the Mysore Maharaja for as long as forty years in mid-century the effect was unremarkable.

[35] For particulars of the taxation system in pre-colonial Kano see Appendix XII(3).

The reply to this question is quite straightforward: it is to the effect that the colonial governments (or the emirs in pre-colonial Nigeria) would have been able to extract far more revenue from the countryside had they made any serious effort, in the words of Moore, to reach 'out into the countryside to stimulate productivity or transform rural society'.[36] In both continents the bureaucracies were only too well aware that they were giving hardly anything (not even law and order which did not have to be forcibly imposed) in return for the taxes they forcibly extracted – this having been particularly true later on in Northern Nigeria where colonial indirect rule was virtually equivalent to rural non-rule.[37] It was partly because the Mysore Government's tentacles scarcely extended beyond taluk headquarters that it found itself virtually powerless to relieve the agonies of the great famine[38] of 1876–8 which may have killed between a quarter and a third of the population in south-eastern Mysore – for by that date the profound fear of tampering with free market forces, which had dominated British thinking at the time of the Irish potato famine, had slightly lessened.

The structure and strength of authority within centralised states are so exceedingly variable as to make the dichotomy 'centralised/acephalous' much less valuable than anthropologists formerly supposed. Both Mysore and Kano were examples of centralised states which were run by bureaucracies headed by kings who had appointed few princes or peers to reside in the 'hinterland': nor had the rural people themselves elected their own chiefs from below. In Mysore the chief executive agents of the central bureaucracy in the countryside were minor non-hereditary Indian officials, nowadays usually called *tahsildars* (formerly more often *amildars*), one for each taluk; in pre-colonial Kano Emirate there were no resident local officials – only travelling emissaries whom the British later mistakenly dubbed 'messengers',[39] supposing they merely moved about collecting revenue, somewhat like those who read gas meters today. While it is true that the Mysore *tahsildars* delegated the task of tax collection to large numbers of local headmen (*patels*) and accountants (*shanbhogs*), these pseudo officials, whose offices were hereditary,[40] also resembled petty pseudo-chiefs – they were expert at the art of feathering their own nests

36 Moore, 1966, p. 385. (It happens that Moore is here referring to the years after Indian Independence.)

37 See Hill (1977).

38 See Appendix XII(4).

39 See Appendix XII(3) on the *jakadu*.

40 Such was the importance of these offices that for about 25 years from about 1880 a large proportion of the series of official *Proceedings* of the Mysore Government was taken up with cases relating to appeals regarding the appointment, dismissal, etc., of these officials – particularly *shanbhogs* (Karnataka State Archives). (Much of this material is of great historical interest.)

while keeping things running smoothly, but had no special influence outside their own tiny villages, which often had a population of two or three hundred only. Unlike the position in China where 'the imperial bureaucracy gave cohesion to the society',[41] the central bureaucracies in Mysore and Kano Emirate were irrelevancies to countryfolk, however impressed or awed they might be by the personal image of the king and his high court officials. It is no wonder that many Anekal villagers today have little idea of the number of years that has elapsed since Indian Independence.

As a consequence of the weakness of this bureaucratic articulation, the kinds of economic hierarchies which are often regarded as necessary features of centralised states were lacking in both Kano Emirate and Mysore. Hierarchical spatial marketing structures, of the kind which have been made so familiar to us by the writings of G. W. Skinner on China,[42] were altogether lacking;[43] the government's role in the maintenance of tank-irrigation systems in Mysore was fairly limited; and there were few laws which impinged on the individual countryman. So the salient forms of communication between countryside and urban centres mainly involved influential individuals who straddled the gap between the two worlds in their capacities as large-scale farmers and businessmen. Therefore when, owing to the dissolution of the large estates, these men removed from the countryside, rural/urban articulation (such as it was) was transformed into dislocation, and it was the countryside which became irrelevant – for the first time.

Although nowadays the symbols of civilisation, such as electricity (which hardly anyone can afford) and postal services (which carry few letters) exist in every village in Anekal Taluk, as they do not in most of the Kano Close Settled Zone where, in 1972, little had changed since Clapperton's day;[44] and although Karnataka's rural bus service is widespread, cheap, businesslike (albeit, uncomfortable and overcrowded), it is yet true that Karnataka villagers have been more devastated by the contemporary rural/urban dislocation than their Hausa counterparts for the very strong reason that they are almost wholly dependent on outside traders. Whereas the rural Hausa, both men and women, have trading in their blood,

[41] Moore, 1966, p. 339.

[42] 'Marketing and Social Structure in Rural China' by G. W. Skinner, Parts I to III, *The Journal of Asian Studies*, 1964 and 1965.

[43] See Appendices XII(5) and XII(6).

[44] In 1972 the population of Dawakin Tofa District, which may have been nearly half a million, lived almost entirely dispersedly on the farmland, there being hardly any roads; yet it was not geographically remote, lying just north-west of Kano city. See Hill (1977), p. 63.

Karnataka villagers tend either to show an abject dependence on outside traders or hastily to dump all their grain on the city themselves at the time, immediately after threshing, when prices are lowest. While one may find fault with Moore's narrow concept of 'the market', which would seem to exclude all local transactions which are conducted outside market-places proper, he must be seen as astute when he observed that 'the grain that did reach the market was usually sold to local traders at depressed harvest-time prices'.[45]

Such an analysis goes a long way to explain contemporary backward technology under our dry grain mode. Just as the Mysore seed drills[46] which so impressed Buchanan in 1800 were designed and constructed by local craftsmen, and did not (presumably) emanate from cities, so there is no proper urban tradition of designing, manufacturing and issuing appropriate modern technology for unpromising dry grain areas like Anekal Taluk. Village blacksmiths, despite their poor technology,[47] are expert at copying and even modifying modern implements such as metal ploughs (which were, of course, originally introduced by the British in both continents); yet it is no one's function to assist these skilled men by providing them with suitable instructions and blueprints for new implements – or if it is, they are not to be seen in the Anekal villages. Since farm tools and equipment need constant, urgent repair by village craftsmen, and since smithing is a craft which does not benefit from factory conditions, village smiths should be fostered and encouraged – yet they are wholly neglected. The failure of Gandhi's concept of Panchayat Raj, which he would weep to behold, is connected with his use of a spinning wheel, not a forge, as his symbol of rural regeneration.

In this chapter, with its slim time depth, I have not of course been concerned with such fundamental questions as whether 'work that we usually consider rural . . . originated in the countryside'[48] or in cities: my initial discussion of the countryside as the matrix related to Hausaland as recently as the nineteenth century. But whatever the relevance of Jane Jacob's work to nineteenth century northern Nigeria and south India, her conclusion that

> city economies create new kinds of work for the rural world, and by doing so also invent and reinvent new rural economies[49]

[45] Moore, 1966, p. 395. [46] See Fig. II(1), p. 78 above.

[47] The equipment of both Hausa and Karnataka blacksmiths is much inferior to that in use in rural southern Ghana.

[48] *The Economy of Cities* by Jane Jacobs, 1970, p. 1. (Jacobs found herself in entire opposition to what she regarded as the prevailing orthodoxy of 'agricultural primacy'.)

[49] *Ibid.*, p. 39.

has much contemporary relevance – and, like myself, she pours scorn on the idea that urban development *ought* to be financed by the agrarian sector. Whether or not cattle-drawn seed drills, like McCormick's horse-drawn reaper, were originally invented in a city, they were, as I have said, unlikely to have been manufactured there, and the time has now arrived for seed drills and hundreds of other simple, but improved, tools and implements to be produced in factories[50] – preferably situated in rural areas for otherwise dry grain agriculture will lag further and further behind. The village blacksmith's importance, as a kind of local garage, servicing and repairing agricultural tools and equipment, designed with his capacities in mind, would then be greatly enhanced.

In both continents the withdrawal from the countryside is now so extreme that things are bound to get much worse before, if ever, they get any better. Although this book is in no wise concerned with policy, for once I allow myself to draw three humdrum conclusions, one negative, two positive – the former being an insistence that old-fashioned rural craft industries are a basic irrelevance in rural south India[51], which makes it all the more unfortunate that rural economic development is so commonly supposed, at least in India, to necessitate the establishment of 'cottage industries'. On the positive side it is certain that until many more influential people somehow get their fortunes tied up with the 'dry grain countryside' the urban/rural hiatus will widen[52] – here, indeed, is so delicate a political issue that no more need be said! It is also certainly necessary that in Karnataka, in particular, rural-dwellers should be enabled to show far more enterprise as traders, in both intra-rural and rural/urban capacities.

APPENDIX XII(1)

Why are Hausa countrymen traders?

Throughout this book, and especially in Chapter VII, I have emphasised that Hausa villagers (women as well as men) have trading in their blood, as Karnataka villagers

[50] There is an embarrassing kind of colonial ethos adhering to the superficial context of 'intermediate technology' – a neglect of its social and political context.

[51] Except rarely, as in the cases of sericulture and the Kerala coir industry.

[52] It is already quite old. 'In England we consider that the townsmen are very much divorced from agriculture, but I do not think that they are nearly as much divorced as they are in Western India.' 'My own belief is that the intelligensia do not take any real interest at all in rural economics.' Both these citations are from evidence taken by the Royal Commission on Agriculture in India, 1926–8. The first view is that of Dr Harold H. Mann (Vol. II of *Evidence*), the second of Sir K. V. Reddy Nayudu (Vol. III).

have not. Given the need for diversification under our dry grain mode, as well as the importance of improving rural/urban terms of trade (Chapter XI), the Karnataka villagers must be seen to be at a considerable disadvantage compared with their Hausa counterparts. Why should this be?

The question of women traders is dealt with elsewhere.[53] Here I suggest that the eagerness of so many Hausa farmers nowadays, as in the past, to participate in trade of numerous different types might be associated with the following historical factors among others. First, was the fact that they owned most of the donkeys which were the main pack animals used by the long-distance caravans which flourished until the advent of the lorry.[54] Second, was the high incidence of slavery, for farm slaves were useful donkey-drivers and trade caravan porters. Third, was the fact that most of the wares that were carried southwards to forest country were of rural origin or manufacture – thus, much of the famous 'Kano cloth', which was carried all over the western Sudan and into the Sahara and north Africa, must have been woven and dyed in the countryside.[55] Fourth, was the great length of the dry season when many men were obliged to travel in search of work. Fifth, was the generally mobile outlook of Hausa men, who were apt to wander about far and wide for many purposes, perhaps in search of famous Koranic teachers – some of them even making the great overland journey by foot to Mecca, which lasted at best several years. Sixth, was the fact that villagers were obliged to store most of the grain which was ultimately consumed in urban areas for many months, since the process of threshing, which was done without the help of animals, necessarily took a long time – and if they were the grain storers, it was natural for them to be the traders as well. Seventh, was the importance of intra-rural trade; even in pre-colonial times there were some densely populated localities which had to buy grain for their own consumption from elsewhere.

Karnataka farmers have no such tradition.[56] Of particular significance was the fact that they owned no pack animals corresponding to the Hausa donkeys, for the pack-oxen were owned by specialist transporters who were employed by urban-based merchants.[57] Even if trade goods, such as good quality cloth, were produced in a village, outside assistance would usually have been required to market the wares. Livestock traders, particularly cattle traders, nowadays abound in the villages, but in general, trading is considered a specialist occupation unfit for cultivators – and the carts, which are relatively few in number, move very slowly and inefficiently on the roads, being designed for farm work.

[53] See pp. 147–8.

[54] See p. 36 above. Many ordinary farmers joined these dry-season trading expeditions, travelling with their own and maybe other men's donkeys. Many hundreds of people, with their loads, might have travelled together. Special donkeys might have had to have been used for carrying the cowry shells – the all-too-heavy and bulky currency. See Hill (1972), pp. 243 *et seq.*

[55] See Hill (1977), pp. 12 *et seq.*

[56] See p. 149 above.

[57] See Buchanan, 1807, Vol. I, pp. 205–6, for a general account of bullock transport; he noted that the carriers were responsible for any accident so that the merchant had to send a representative to accompany them. Asses (donkeys) were generally despised, though sometimes used by low-caste transporters of salt and grain and by sellers of brass utensils and glass bangles – Vol. I, p. 7.

APPENDIX XII(2)

Two excerpts from Buchanan's book on his travels in south India[58]

N.B. Italicised words are italicised in the original

The cultivation of ragi

After the first showers until about the 5th of June:

> the field is ploughed from four to six times. . . . The dung is then given. . . . When the rains begin to be heavy, the seed is sown broadcast, and covered by the plough. The field is then smoothed with the *Halivay*, which is a harrow, or rather a large rake drawn by two bullocks. . . . Next day, single furrows are drawn throughout the field, at the relative distance of six feet. In these is dropt the seed of either *Avaray*[59] or *Tovary*,[60] which are never cultivated by themselves; nor is *Ragy* ever cultivated, without being mixed with drills of these leguminous plants . . . . According to the quantity of rain, the *Ragy* ripens in from three to four months. The *Avaray* and *Tovary* do not ripen till the seventh month.[61]

He explains that if the *ragi* dies the leguminous plants resist the drought and are ripened by the dews, which are strong in autumn. When the *ragi* succeeds, the leguminous plants are oppressed by it; when it fails they spread wonderfully.

Ragi threshing

> At any convenient time within three months, it [the *ragi* stack] is opened, dried two days in the sun, and then trodden out by oxen. The seed, having been thoroughly dried in the sun, is preserved in straw *Mudies*.[62] The remainder is put into pits, or *Hagays*:[63] where, if care has been taken to dig the pit in a dry soil, it will keep in perfect preservation for ten years.[64]

Manuring

On manuring see citation from Buchanan[65] on p. 178 above.

[58] See p. 34 above.
[59] I.e. *avare* or cow beans.
[60] I.e. *togari* or red gram.
[61] Vol. I, p. 101.
[62] *Mude* or *mute*, a straw bundle containing grain seed.
[63] I.e. *hagevu* – large underground granaries.
[64] Vol. I, p. 102.
[65] Vol. I, p. 122.

APPENDIX XII(3)

Pre-colonial taxation in rural Kano Emirate

After the British had finally completed their conquest of Kano Emirate in 1903,[66] they were at once resolved to reform the elaborate and sophisticated rural taxation system which they found there; most economic activity being rurally-based, the bulk of the revenue which supported the Emir and his administration was naturally raised from country-dwellers. But as the British failed to understand the indigenous system; as their administration was grossly understaffed; as the District Heads (*hakimai*) were most resistant to pleas that they should leave the capital and reside in their own territories; as 'the resident town and village chiefs had had hardly any power'[67] over their people; as well as for numerous other reasons – nearly twenty years elapsed before the range of different taxes on cultivators was (more or less) effectively replaced by one consolidated tax.[68] Known as *haraji*, this tax varied slightly with the 'wealth' of the taxpayer – it was not a land tax.[69]

The list of pre-colonial taxes had included a general 'farm tax';[70] taxes on farms planted with special crops such as groundnuts and cassava as well as on irrigated farms; a Koranic grain tithe which was collected most haphazardly; and a cattle tax. Some of the tax collectors (*jakadu*) were agents of the Emir, others of the District Heads; the British abused these functionaries while being at a loss, owing to the weakness of local administration, to see who should undertake their work.

It is indeed consistent with the withdrawal from the countryside that rural taxation, having been the mainstay of the pre-colonial state, should now be in course of final abolition.

APPENDIX XII(4)

The south Indian famine of 1876–8

The awful south Indian famine of 1876–8, which resulted from the failure of the *ragi* and paddy harvests in 1875–7, was particularly severe in the dry uplands of south-eastern Karnataka. Between 1871 and 1881 the recorded populations of Anekal Taluk, Bangalore District (exclusive of Bangalore city) and Tumkur

66 See, for example, 'The British Conquest of Kano, 1903', Chapter IV of *The Kano Civil War and British Over-rule, 1882–1940* by A. M. Fika, 1978.

67 *Ibid.*, p. 171. See, also, Hill (1977), Chapter II.

68 See Hill (1977), Appendix II(1).

69 See Hill (1972), pp. 312–13 and Fika (1978), pp. 182 *et seq.*, on the introduction of a land tax in 1909 in a few districts – this never succeeded as had been hoped and was ultimately abandoned altogether in the 1950s.

70 The tax was payable in cowry shells. See Hill (1977), pp. 50 *et seq.*, for a list of pre-colonial taxes.

District fell by 20%, 25% and 34% respectively,[71] and the population of Bangalore District in 1901 was only 3% higher than in 1871. Many villages were abandoned, and it is probable that all the uninhabited villages (*becharkh*) listed in the census reports up to the present day[72] lost their populations in the great famine. It was reported that 70,000 cattle died between April and July 1877 in the Nandydroog Division – which comprised Bangalore, Kolar and Tumkur Districts.

In July 1877 it was reported[73] that about 500 starving people were entering Bangalore daily, many of them from Kolar District where many relief kitchens had been closed. The Viceroy himself visited Mysore in September 1877 and was so shocked by what he saw that he placed the Famine Department in his personal charge.[74]

A Famine Commission was appointed by the Government of India in 1878: reporting in 1880, 'it advised the Government as a general principle to abstain from interference with private trade for the supply of food to any tract but they admitted that in exceptional cases Government might find it necessary to intervene'.[75] But the Commission did at least recommend the formation of Agricultural Departments, the first 'agricultural expert', Dr Voelcker, arriving in India as late as 1889. However, it was not long before he suffered official rebuke for his premature efforts in the direction of agricultural improvement.[76]

Whereas it is possible to argue that the terrible famine in Northern Nigeria in 1914 marked the beginning of the withdrawal from the countryside (owing to the abscondment of many famished farm slaves), the same was not necessarily true of the south Indian famine of 1876–8 for we do not know if the Mysore *jodidars* began to lose heart as soon as that.[77] But one can well believe that the coffee planter R. H. Elliot was right when he argued[78] in 1872 that the restricted development of communications was 'sufficient to drain the countries in the interior of their grain', but not to bring it back again in sufficient quantities in time of famine.

[71] According to a Census Report on Mysore (1901 Census, Vol. XXIV), some poorer castes had suffered much more than the average, judging by population falls between 1871 and 1881. Whatever the reliability of these figures, one may certainly believe a report from Tumkur (Mysore *Proceedings*, 16 January 1877) that the *thotis*, in particular, were in great want, being unable to abandon their villages.

[72] See p. 85, n. 17 above.

[73] Mysore *Proceedings*, 26 July 1977.

[74] *The History of Indian Famines and Development of Famine Policy (1858–1918)* by H. S. Srivastava, 1968, p. 139.

[75] *Ibid.*, p. 163.

[76] This was reported in Appendix I, p. 27, of *Proceedings of the Agricultural Conference*, Calcutta, Government Printer, 1894.

[77] For severe famines had occurred in south India in 1799–1800, 1804–7, 1811–12, 1824 and 1833–4. 'Integration of the Agrarian System of South India' by B. Stein in *Land Control and Social Structure in Indian History* ed. R. E. Frykenberg, 1969, p. 197.

[78] In evidence he gave to the India Finance Committee of the House of Commons in 1872. See Elliot, 1894, p. 11.

APPENDIX XII(5)
The lack of a market hierarchy

The literature on Karnataka markets, as on Indian rural periodic markets generally,[79] is very weak – the most useful descriptions again being provided by Buchanan (1807). So my conclusions (p. 230 above) relating to the lack of an hierarchical marketing structure with its apex in the city, in both regions, is consequently somewhat speculative – more so for Karnataka than for Kano Emirate. But it is a matter which has to be considered in relation to our thesis of a recent withdrawal from the countryside, since had such a structure existed before that withdrawal occurred the economic isolation of the countryside would nowadays be less extreme.

Several factors, some of them interrelated, accounted (and still account) for the lack of marketing structures in both regions, such as are often taken for granted in third world countries;[80] I discuss some of them here.

First, is the fact that local village markets have 'une grande autonomie',[81] perhaps for the very good reason that all the sellers are producers and all the buyers are consumers of the goods they handle. These markets mainly serve producers who have an urgent need to sell small quantities of crops other than basic grains (which they can sell from their houses) and consumers who need to buy ingredients, such as vegetables, for the next few meals. In Anekal Taluk such markets are much smaller and less numerous than in Hausaland – perhaps mainly because they are unimportant social gatherings where, incidentally, few if any small livestock are sold. Local village markets are not, therefore, the lowest level of any hierarchy – they stand right outside it, as G. W. Skinner himself noted.

However, this is not to decry the importance of rural markets as such, some of which, in both regions, are very large on any standards, even though they are not necessarily well articulated with any city market. In regions where most medium or long-distance trade was formerly based on pack animals (donkeys in Hausaland and pack-oxen in south India[82]) which followed recognised trade routes, large 'relay markets' might arise where these routes crossed, irrespective of the size of the settlement there. Having noted the general lack of small markets in Mysore,[83] Buchanan referred to a huge relay market at Gubi, a small town 'frequented by merchants from great distances', being 'an intermediate mart for the goods passing

[79] This is noted by R. J. Bromley in *Periodic Markets, Daily Markets and Fairs: A Bibliography*, Monash University Publications in Geography, No. 10, 1974.

[80] Thus, G. W. Skinner wrongly regards them (1964, Part I, p. 3) as 'characteristic of the whole class of civilizations known as "peasant" or "traditional agrarian" societies'.

[81] Cited from an unpublished work on markets in the Niger Republic by G. Nicolas in Hill (1972), p. 293.

[82] See n. 57, p. 233, above. Donkeys owned by washermen were sometimes used for transporting grain and salt.

[83] *Ibid.*, p. 40.

through the peninsular'.[84] As the countryside was the matrix within which most trade flowed and flourished, so the trade routes did not necessarily centre on the cities.

My third point is that important cultivators in both regions usually tended to bypass the marketing system when selling basic crops, so that it was quite unusual for farm produce to pass through a chain of markets. Writing about Tanjore District in Madras in 1880 to 1920, Washbrook noted that the large landlords, the *mirasidars*, traded directly from their estates so that:

> Towns built around the rail-heads and ports remained only geographical points along the path of produce movents. They did not come to serve as markets at which crops from a dispersed hinterland were collected, assembled and processed for further marketing.[85]

In Tanjore, at that time, 'there was no obvious rural/urban dichotomy'.

Fourth, is the question of the ownership of transport animals. In Hausaland ordinary village cultivators not only owned most of the donkeys in the long-distance trade caravans which plyed southwards, but were also apt to be caravan members themselves; this gave them a general interest in types of trading which bypassed markets – which has served them well until the present day. In south India the transport cattle were not owned by village cultivators but by members of specialist transporter castes; even if most of the merchants involved were townsmen, it did not follow that wares would be less likely to pass directly from one merchant to another than through a chain of markets.

Finally, it is worth noting that some of the most famous city markets in Hausaland, such as those in the old city at Kano and at Katsina, are not apical in relation to rural periodic markets; they handle little basic farm produce, most grain being sold by wholesalers from city sheds, and are mainly concerned with provisioning city residents and handling imported goods.

APPENDIX XII(6)

Cattle fairs in Karnataka

It is indeed significant that the only Karnataka assemblages comparable in size to the largest rural periodic market-places of West Africa should be the immense annual cattle fairs (*jathre*) which are held at varying dates between about January and April, usually being associated with a local festival. I have found no literature on these fairs, other than paltry references in reports in the State Archives and in Epstein (1962) – who mentions that villagers travel to them from far and wide.

So huge are these fairs apt to be that estimates of the attendance of men and animals, during the week or more for which they last, are useless unless based upon

84 Vol. II, p. 31. Gubi (Gubbi) lies some twenty miles west of Tumkur on a route to Shimoga in the west.

85 'Political Change in a Stable Society: Tanjore District 1880 to 1920' by D. A. Washbrook, in C. J. Baker and D. A. Washbrook (eds.), 1975, p. 24.

hard figures such as the total yield of the tax levied. Certainly the attendance of men, not all of whom are potential buyers or sellers, usually runs into several (if not many) tens of thousands; cattle sales may be considerably lower, many potential buyers and sellers returning home disappointed, many attenders being there out of curiosity.

Given the lack of literature, I summarise some of my findings when I attended the colossal *jathre* near the village of Hennagara, some three miles from Vabasandra, on 24 January 1978. The hurly-burly, noise, dust, wind, blown sand, dirt and vast size of the remote high open space, near a pond for watering, where the fair was held, made observation difficult, especially as potential sellers spend nearly all their time sitting patiently by their animals waiting for something to happen.

Most sales are conducted with the help of unlicensed brokers, men from far and wide who receive a small fee from both parties; they promote and regulate bargaining and notify the seller if any defect is found in an animal within three days of its purchase. Prices are secretly negotiated by means of fingers inside a cloth held by the broker, earnest witnesses attending for consultations. The procedure may be very slow: one seller of a small bullock started at Rs 560, reduced to Rs 535 and finally agreed to Rs 500 after twenty minutes of hard bargaining.

The main animals displayed were bullocks, some of very superior quality; a few cows and pigs were seen but no buffaloes or sheep. Some people buy for quick resale at a profit at the same fair; many sell one animal and buy another; some exchange their animals, any price discrepancy being met in cash; some of the buyers of the skinnier animals are butchers; many people come from a hundred miles away or more and sleep the night there; cooked foods, fruit, coffee, bangles, etc., are on sale and primitive shelters are erected; cobblers mend shoes and sandals; there is, of course, a temple.

Before the fair opens officials call for tenders from men interested in running the fair and collecting the tax (of half a rupee per bullock); and the animal dung is auctioned when all is over.

CHAPTER XIII

Agrestic Servitude

I employ 'agrestic servitude' to cover both farm-slavery proper, which existed in Hausaland in 1900, but not (of course) in south-eastern Mysore, and the bonded farm-labouring system of Mysore, which had no counterpart in rural Hausaland. Nowadays, as we know, there are very few household heads in either region who are prevented, *by bonds of agrestic servitude alone*, from being free cultivators.

CONTRACT LABOURERS IN KARNATAKA

Defining contract labourers in south-eastern Karnataka as those not employed on the usual daily basis, but for longer periods, our first question is whether significant proportions of such labourers in earlier times were likely to have been bonded labourers proper – i.e. men tied by debt to their masters.

The literature on the history of contract labourers in south-eastern Mysore is very weak – indeed, it would be virtually non-existent were it not for Buchanan. Sources on south Indian bonded labouring, such as Hjejle,[1] usually refer almost exclusively to the Madras Presidency, partly because Mysore, as a princely state, was backward in record keeping. Even so, I think it is significant that I could find hardly any references to contract labouring in south-eastern Mysore in the Karnataka State Archives, references to day labourers being numerous. Nor has recent fieldwork been of much help. In the Anekal villages a careful distinction is always made between daily-paid labourers (*kuli*) and full-time farm servants, who are very rare, but everyone seemed to have his own definition of such euphemistic Kannada words as *sambalagara, jitadalu, alugalu, batigaru*, all of which refer to labourers on some kind of contract basis. Perhaps the multiplicity of words still vaguely recollected reflects the former existence

[1] 'Slavery and Agricultural Bondage in South India in the Nineteenth Century' by Benedicte Hjejle, *The Scandinavian Economic History Review*, XV, 1 and 2, 1967.

of different systems in different localities? Perhaps systems were everywhere adaptable?

Fortunately, Buchanan was scrupulous in distinguishing daily-paid and other farm labourers.

> The hire of farmers' labourers at *Seringapatam*, and generally within two miles from the city [Mysore], when employed throughout the year is 10 *Sultany Fanams*, or 6s 8½d a month. The servant lives in his own house; and it is customary for the master, on extraordinary occasions, such as marriages, to advance the servant money. This is not deducted from his wages by gradual instalments; but is considered as a debt, that must be repaid before the servant can leave his place. In case of the servant's death, his sons are bound to pay the debt, or to continue to work with their father's master. . . . In harvest, the daily hire of a man is six *Seers of Paddy*. A woman transplanting rice gets daily ¼ of a *Sultany Fanam*, or about two-pence.[2]

But, unfortunately for the categorising sociologist, practices varied. On his return journey, when south of Bangalore, Buchanan noted that the money that was advanced to servants was:

> repaid by instalments out of the wages that are given in cash; for the people here are not anxious to keep their servants in bondage, by a debt hanging over them.[3]

The usual vernacular word for non-daily labourers employed by Buchanan was *batigaru* – whom he sometimes denoted 'servants employed in agriculture' or 'yearly servants'. At one point,[4] he says that the *batigaru* were of all castes save Brahmins and Muslims, which seems unlikely, not only because a few pages further on[5] he states that the Vodda (Bhovi) were never prepared to work in this capacity. The likelihood is that the great majority of *batigaru* in south-eastern Karnataka at that time belonged to the untouchable caste he called Whallia (Holeya), now known as Adikarnataka. Many members of this caste were *batigaru*, but some of them wove coarse cloth and smelt iron ore.[6] The less numerous Madiga (the leather workers now known as Adidravida) were also apt to be *batigaru*.

But the number of such labourers clearly varied in different localities. When south of Bangalore Buchanan noted that while most labour was performed by household members:

> A few rich men hire yearly servants; and at seed-time and harvest additional daily labourers must be procured. There are no slaves. A ploughman gets annually . . . £1 7s 5½d.[7]

[2] Buchanan, 1807, Vol. I, p. 124.
[3] Vol. III, p. 455. [4] Vol. I, p. 298. [5] Vol. I, p. 310.
[6] Vol. I, p. 314. [7] Vol. III, p. 454.

This reference to ploughmen is interesting, for it is possible that annual labourers were particularly apt to work in this capacity – as was suggested to me by Harijans in the Anekal villages. Owing to the seasonality of ploughing, would there have been many cultivators in Buchanan's time who would have been rich enough to employ such permanent labourers? Here we come up against the curious fact that Buchanan ignored the existence of those landed gentry the *jodidars*, who sometimes held hereditary rights over the farmland of 'whole villages'. It seems likely that they were the main employers of bonded labourers in south-eastern Karnataka.

Like other fieldworkers in south India, I became convinced that hereditary relationships between ordinary farmers and bonded labourers had been rare (in the Anekal villages) within living memory – I postpone consideration of those who might have been employed by *jodidars*. I met no old men with a history of life-long bondage, and the following case was rather exceptional.

A very old Adidravida man in Bukkasagara – he wore ear-rings and had an old fashioned appearance – said that both he and his brother had worked as *sambalagaras* for about 20 years before their marriages, having received meals, clothes and Rs 20 annually; they had not only succeeded in paying off a debt owed by their father, who like himself had been a carpenter, but he had bought a fair acreage of land for Rs 350, which he had cultivated with the aid of a plough and bullocks lent to him by his employer who was a potter. Permanent labouring, he reflected, had been very hard work, especially when the moon was full, and one had no house of one's own. Nowadays he lives with his married son in a five-roomed house and owns 3 cows, a metal plough and a poor-quality cart. His position is far from hopeless.

Harriss, when reporting on a village in Tamil Nadu, is emphatic that:

> The kind of hereditary relations between Peasant farmer families and Untouchable labourer families . . . which guaranteed the labourers a minimum subsistence while permitting the cultivators to profit greatly from the relationship in good years, have not existed within living memory in Randam.[8]

In a village in Mysore over thirty years ago Srinivas found there were 58 *jita* servants, most of whom were probably boys or youths, whose temporary relationship, lasting for two or three years, he denoted 'contractual' to distinguish it from the 'traditional servantship' of former times.[9]

[8] 'Implications of Changes in Agriculture for Social Relationships at the Village Level: the case of Randam' by J. Harriss, in Farmer (ed.), 1977, p. 236.

[9] See 'The Social System of a Mysore Village' by M. N. Srinivas, in Marriott, 1955, pp. 23–8, and Srinivas, 1976, p. 13.

Epstein found small numbers of 'contract servants' in one of two Mysore villages (and none in the other), most of whom were temporarily employed outsiders.[10] The conclusion must, unfortunately, be that contemporary fieldwork throws hardly any light on former 'traditional relationships', though it does suggest that the incidence of bonded labouring has been low within living memory.

As we have seen (Chapter X) the incidence of outward migration from the Anekal villages varies little with caste, and I therefore think it reasonable to suppose that the present-day distribution of Harijans between villages in Anekal Taluk is fairly similar to that in 1901, for which no statistics are available. Furthermore, the ratio of Harijans to non-Harijans is likely to be much the same today as in 1901 considering that in Bangalore District (exclusive of the city) they made up almost exactly a fifth of the population in 1901, 1911 and 1971, according to the Census figures.[11]

If most Harijans had been tied labourers in, say, 1901, it would be reasonable to assume that the ratio of the Harijan to the non-Harijan population would tend to have been fairly constant as between villages, but the evidence is that in 1971, and therefore presumably in 1901, there was considerable variation, as Table XIII(1) shows. Nor does this ratio show any consistent variation with the proportion of wet land in the village – land which is more labour intensive.[12]

Whatever allowance is made for the fact that some labourers live in one village and work in another,[13] and for variations in the proportions of AKs and ADs, I think that these figures provide strong support for the idea that high proportions of Harijans in many villages would not have been hereditary labourers in 1901.

Another approach is in terms of the proportion of cultivators whose holdings were large enough to justify the employment of one or more full-time adult labourers. Unfortunately, I have little confidence in official

[10] See, for example, Epstein, 1973, p. 137.

[11] The figures were, respectively, 22%, 21% and 21% – the latter relates to rural Bangalore District and excludes a few towns as well as the city. (The 1971 figure for rural Anekal Taluk was 29%, but I could find no corresponding figures for 1901 or 1911 for the Taluk or for villages.)

[12] For the 77 Anekal villages for which statistics are provided in Table XIII(1) I found no significant correlation between the proportions of irrigated land and of Scheduled castes, as recorded in the 1971 census. (This is inconsistent with Mencher's assertion in 'The Caste System Upside Down', *Current Anthropology*, December 1974, p. 474, that 'in Tamil Nadu the highest percentage of untouchables is to be found in the biggest rice-producing regions'.)

[13] It was to reduce the effect of this variable that I omitted all villages which necessarily had populations less than 500.

Table XIII(1). *Proportion of Harijans by village, 1971, Anekal Taluk*

% of Harijans	Villages	
	No.	%
Under 10	2	3
10+	15	19
20+	29	38
30+	19	25
40+	6	8
50+	3	4
60+	–	–
70+	3	4
	77	100%

Notes:

(1) The table relates to 77 villages in Anekal Taluk with recorded populations of 500 or more in 1971 – it will be remembered that actual populations in many cases would have been lower owing to the inclusion of un-named hamlets.

(2) The average proportion of Harijans in these villages was 27%.

(3) Although in this book I usually find it convenient to employ 'Harijan' to include members of the AK and AD castes only, this table necessarily relates to all Scheduled castes, as totals only are given in the Census; as members of the Scheduled Bhovi caste never worked as contract labourers their omission would have been appropriate – though impossible. However, there is every reason to believe that the AKs and ADs make up a high proportion of all members of the Scheduled castes in most villages.

statistics relating to the size distribution of farm-holdings,[14] but anyway I could find no published statistics for Anekal Taluk and those for Bangalore District in the *Mysore Gazetteer* of 1929 have no attached notes and are quite suspect.[15] They show that there were only about 1,700 holdings above 50 acres in 1924–5 (some 1.2% of the total), but the number above, say, 20 acres, which might have been large enough to justify the employment of a bonded labourer, cannot be estimated since the 10–50 acre size-group is undivided. (It is also unfortunate that wet and dry acreages were lumped together.)

[14] See pp. 55 *et seq.*

[15] See Vol. V of the *Mysore Gazetteer* ed. C. Hayavadana Rao, 1929, p. 53. The statistics which relate to the five years 1920–1 to 1924–5, are badly presented with no notes or commentary whatsoever, and are unconvincingly erratic.

In 1901 the recorded population density in Anekal Taluk was as high as 316 per sq mile. If we assume that the total cropped area was then about a half of the total area (compared with 65% in 1971[16]), then the average cropped area per head of population was of the order of only about one acre. I would argue that such a high density was then incompatible with the existence of many large estates, other than those owned by the *jodidars* (which were largely rented out) and by a few absentee farmers – it will be remembered that, later on, no Anekal holdings were large enough to be affected by land reform legislation. Nowadays there are few landless households belonging to the Vokkaliga, Kuruba, Lingayat and Brahmin castes, which probably accounted for about 40% of total households in Anekal Taluk in 1901; assuming that average household size was much the same then as today (it is now 5.7 persons in the six villages) and that then, as today, it varied little with caste, the average holdings of households of these high castes might have been of the order of 10 acres (or nearly 2 acres per head) which would have allowed for some land ownership by members of other castes. In Anekal Taluk in 1901 it is likely that the very great majority of all heads of the higher caste farming households were working farmers, as they are today – only 3% of the population were Brahmins. Nor would cultivation have been beneath the dignity of most household members. We may, therefore, presume that many of the richer households would have dispensed with labourers altogether, except at seasons of peak labour intensity, such as harvesting, when they would have engaged day labourers.

In Chapter XV I shall argue that high, though variable, proportions of Harijans were wholly unattached persons in (say) 1901 – non-cultivators who somehow managed to scrape up a living in the interstices of the rural economy. This is not to say that 'loose' (unattached) labourers or weavers, for instance, never enjoyed paternalistic relations with richer men who would support them in emergencies and bestow largesse on ceremonial occasions; nor is it to suppose that the corporate village community would ever permit any of its members to starve; but it is to insist that most Harijans, other than the village servants (*thotis*) who, as we shall see, were not numerous, could not count on such 'maintenance' for their *basic* livelihood, but had to fight for themselves.

The whole ideology of this issue has suffered both from 'delta bias' (particularly since the publication of Gough's influential 'Caste in a Tanjore Village',[17] which relates to an area where, as long ago as 1906, wet

[16] Information from the Tahsildar of Anekal Taluk. (For most villages the cropped area is a much higher proportion, the lower total figure being mainly explained by a large wild westerly tract, which includes a forest reserve.)

[17] In *Aspects of Caste in South India, Ceylon and North-West Pakistan*, ed. E. R. Leach, 1960.

paddy cultivation occupied three-quarters of the arable land) and from a failure to realise that there were simply not enough rich households in impoverished dry grain areas, with their low crop yields, who could afford to play a significant part in maintaining a large body of Harijans in partial idleness. Even in Buchanan's day there is no evidence that in our dry grain zone rich landlords were ever, as it were, *compelled* to support lowly farm servants. In short, the arithmetic supporting the views expressed in the following citation got out of hand much longer ago than is there suggested – there were far too many Harijans in relation to the small number of rich farmers before the 'recent rapid increase' in population.

> The low castes suffer economically not because they are low *castes* but because present conditions have turned them into an unemployed working-*class*. What has put them in this position is not their caste but the recent rapid increase in population, coupled with the fact that the caste rules which formerly compelled (*sic*) the high-status landlords to support their low-status servitors have been progressively destroyed by arbitrary acts of 'liberal' legislation extending over the past 150 years.[18]

In south-eastern Karnataka the recent reduction in the small number of male bonded labourers who existed in, say, 1901, is due rather to the abolition of the *jodidars*, who were the main employers, than to Mrs Gandhi's Twenty Points Programme of 1975 for, after a year or two, her 'declaration' that bonded labourers were forthwith abolished, was apt to be ignored – sometimes collusively, destitute ex-labourers begging their former employers to reinstate them. The profound poverty of the masses, rather than the diminutive incidence of adult bonded labouring in this particular part of the world,[19] is the real problem: to concentrate on the latter rather than the former, is to flee from reality by adopting an over-institutionalised approach.

But the question of the contemporary boy labourers, the *sambalagaras*, whose fathers pledge them to work for a short term, such as two years, in return for a loan which they demand from the employer, has to be faced. Since most of these boys are drawn from exceptionally poor Harijan households which have difficulty in feeding them properly; since the loan (it ought not to be called a debt) is automatically and rapidly liquidated by service rendered; since a father who is dissatisfied with one employer is usually in a position to free his son by borrowing from another employer; since the poor fathers may start to raise themselves a little, by such means as buying a heifer with the loan they receive – for these and other reasons I

[18] *Ibid.*, p. 6. From the Introduction by E. R. Leach.

[19] Of course there are other regions (though none of them is likely to be in the dry grain zone of south India) where bonded labouring is a very serious problem.

hold the practical view that the institution should not necessarily be found politically shocking, even though one's inclination is to condemn it outright. I provide additional facts in Appendix XIII(1) so that readers may judge for themselves.

In Chapter XV I shall argue that (say) a century ago the Holeyas and Madigas of south-eastern Karnataka (with the exception of the *thotis*) effectively formed a landless class which cultivated no tank-irrigated land and very little dry land; owing to their difficulties in picking up a living in the interstices of the rural economy, members of this class were eager to work as daily-paid labourers with cultivators who were rich enough to employ them – they were a ready-made, resident rural proletariat such, as we shall see, had no counterpart in West Africa at that time. As members of this class were even occasionally prepared to face the possibility of falling into hereditary servitude, there was no need at all for the richer cultivators, most of them *jodidars*, to recruit their bonded servants from far afield, as did the coffee planters in the Western Ghats.

FARM-SLAVERY IN KANO EMIRATE

In Kano Emirate, on the other hand, as in West Africa generally, farm slaves were nearly always strangers in origin,[20] men and women who had been captured elsewhere in war or kidnapped in armed raids and had been placed on sale on the open market, probably mainly by specialist slave-brokers, though the literature is weak on this question.[21] (However, since most men and women farm slaves had slave spouses and since in Kano Emirate the children of slaves were not in process of assimilation as free men[22] – there having been no status intermediate between slavery and freedom[23] – it followed that considerable, though varying, proportions of

[20] They were 'institutionalised outsiders' – to use an expression employed in the best of all introductions to Africa slavery, viz. *Slavery in Africa: Historical and Anthropological Perspectives* eds. Suzanne Miers and I. Kopytoff, 1977, which has a long introductory chapter by the two editors.

[21] A number of European travellers in Hausaland in the nineteenth century described the revolting spectacle of the shackled captives on display in markets.

[22] This assertion is elaborately justified in Chapter XIII, 'From Slavery to Freedom', of Hill (1977). For reasons which I cannot understand, and which are never stated, M. G. Smith's contrary findings in Zaria Emirate continue to be regarded as typical of Hausaland, though I am sure that they cannot be owing to anomalous conditions of land tenure there. (It is relevant to note that the generalised belief that in West Africa 'slaves never reproduce themselves' necessitates the assumption of invariable assimilation, such as did not occur in Kano Emirate.)

[23] The question of clients (*barori*) is entirely separate; in the countryside they were not the ex-slaves of their masters, but temporarily attached strangers who were in process of settling down as free men.

the farm slaves in old-established farming localities happened to have been born where they worked.)

The likelihood is that the proportion of farming households in the Kano Close Settled Zone which owned farm slaves in 1900 was much higher than the corresponding proportion of households in the Anekal villages which had bonded labourers, partly because the farm slaves, unlike the labourers, were partially self-supporting; also, owing to the lack of systems of contractual or daily-paid labouring and the likelihood that most free women were not cultivators,[24] farm-slavery was the only means of supplementing the (essentially male) family labour force. Although the general incidence of farm-slavery in Kano Emirate must remain forever unknown, fieldwork has certainly established that it was high in some localities: thus, although most slave-descendants removed from over-populated Dorayi in the 1920s and 1930s, yet as many as 26% of married men there in 1972 were recorded as being of slave descent in the male line.[25]

This is not the place to review the vast literature on West African or even Hausa farm-slavery.[26] I say no more than that in pre-colonial West Africa, with the exception of some of those rare societies which stood detached from the cash economy, slavery existed in some form; that most slaves were strangers in origin; that there were few societies which were wholly dependent on servile labour for production; and that 'control over people' was sought for many more reasons than that they were mere 'units of labour in farming or elsewhere'.[27] In the broadest terms, Miers and Kopytoff suggest that a necessary, but far from sufficient, condition for the emergence of slavery was the preference for acquiring men and women 'to be used and controlled as total persons, rather than merely to use their specific services'.[28]

However, my limited concern here is with the 'specific services' rendered by Hausa farm slaves, taking the general background of West African servile institutions for granted. While it is true that the existence of West African slavery cannot be interpreted 'in terms of the economics of the classic triad of labour, land and capital',[29] but must be sought in the total social and political economy of a society, my present limited concern is

[24] It is commonly surmised that this was connected with the fact that such a high proportion of farm slaves were women.

[25] Hill (1977), p. 216.

[26] Another general survey is *L'esclavage en Afrique précoloniale*, ed. C. Meillassoux, 1975; it relates to slavery in former French colonies. Some of the notable historical sources on Hausa slavery are listed in Hill (1976), p. 396, n. 6. Among the most notable recent publications are *Baba of Karo* by Mary Smith, 1954, which is the recorded autobiography of a Hausa woman who had vivid childhood memories of slavery, and M. G. Smith, 1955.

[27] Miers and Kopytoff, 1977, p. 69.

[28] *Ibid.*, p. 69.

[29] *Ibid.*

primarily economic. While slave owners were often motivated by considerations of status when acquiring additional farm slaves, I am here concentrating on the way in which such slaves were put to work.

But first a few words about the Colonial Office's attempt to control slavery in Northern Nigeria when faced with Lugard's revelations that compulsory emancipation was necessarily quite impracticable.[30] A 1901 Proclamation prohibited slave-raiding, abolished the legal status of slavery, and declared that all those subsequently born of slave parents would be free; but it did not prohibit slave-holding as such, for given the existence of ancient and flourishing slavery systems, which probably involved several million slaves, it would have been quite beyond the power of the understaffed colonial administration to have enforced any policy of immediate emancipation – and this quite apart from the sympathy which Lugard felt for slave owners as a class. Subsequent Proclamations prohibited all transactions in slaves,[31] but slave-holding was never legally prohibited. Nor, in the longer run, was there any need for this, for after flourishing for the first twenty years, or so, of colonial rule, slavery rapidly collapsed, dying a natural death by about 1930, owing both to the diminished slave stocks and to the changed attitudes of the times. In Dorayi in 1972 I knew only two old men of slave parentage who had been born before 1901; but the institution of slavery was, of course, a living memory among older people of free descent, a few of whom were happy to talk about it freely, to the extent of identifying all those in the community who were of slave descent in the male line.[32]

Hausa farm-slavery is readily comprehensible today as the slaves were in *gandu* in the same way as married sons are nowadays. Slaves and sons toiled alongside each other on the *gandu* farmland, maybe under the authority of a slave 'foreman' and had similar rights and obligations. The main obligations of the *gandu* head (the slave owner or father) were similar to those outlined in Appendix IV(1) above. Hausa farm slaves thus enjoyed much more economic freedom than their Karnataka counterparts, the bonded labourers – except that it seems that if the labourers lived separately from their master, their wives and children, unlike the slaves' dependants, were entirely free. This superior freedom was partly due to the slaves' opportunities of using their spare time productively, whether as cultivators, artisans, traders, transporters, etc.; it was greatly to the advantage of slave owners to encourage their slaves to produce grain for themselves or to

30 See Hill (1977), Chapter XIII, for more detail.

31 This led to the closure of the slave markets but not to the end of local selling.

32 Such information is far easier to obtain in societies where slaves are not assimilated into local lineages so that there is much less secrecy about origins.

earn money, so that their Koranic obligations to provide them with adequate maintenance were reduced – and because contented slaves are less likely to abscond. More fundamentally, the condition of total economic subordination, whether of sons, wives or servile persons, was (and is) far more socially acceptable in Karnataka than in Hausaland.

Cultivators bought slaves in market-places, or directly from dealers or other slave owners; they paid cash, i.e. cowry shells, the price, as with other forms of agrarian capital, such as donkeys, being determined by supply and demand. Females were valued more highly than males, presumably because they were the potential procreators of additional slave capital, for the children of a slave-couple usually belonged to the mother's owner.

Depending on 'quality', sex, age and so forth, prices of adults may commonly have ranged from about 150,000 to 300,000 cowries, or the equivalent of about £3 10s to £7 – sums which have some meaning when compared with the value of an adult's annual grain requirements, which in 1900 was possibly of the order of £1 to £2.[33]

In Kano Emirate farm slaves never enjoyed immunity from sale, however long they or their forebears had been in the service of their master;[34] however, it was considered socially reprehensible to break up slave families if at all avoidable. But slaves were not chattels in the full legal sense for under Muslim law they had the right of being ransomed by themselves or others; in the former case a slave was entitled to enter into an agreement with his owner to cease working for him for a period so that he might earn the redemption money, which was a somewhat notional doubling of his putative market value. Here again, we see that it was owing to his potentially superior earning ability, as a temporarily liberated man, that a Hausa slave might have had more control over his destiny than a Karnataka hereditary labourer.

A father's obligation to assist a son-in-*gandu* was paralleled by a farm slave's right to marry and to demand that his owner should help him to obtain a slave wife. In great contrast to ancient Greece and Rome, where there were few women slaves in the countryside, nearly half of all Hausa farm slaves may have been female. Most slaves owned by private farmers, whether or not they had the same owner, lived *en famille* with their dependants; richer male slaves were apt to be polygynous.

Most free cultivators in Kano Emirate were probably not rich enough to acquire farm slaves or had insufficient farmland on which to set them to work. There are no reliable data on the distribution of farm slaves among slave owners, and the numbers owned by outstandingly wealthy farmers

[33] Hill (1977), p. 208.

[34] This is my insistence – see n. 22 above.

are always liable to exaggeration; but field enquiries suggest that many private farmers owned no more than, say, two to four (male and female) slaves and that few private owners had more than about ten to fifteen. They also reveal that some slave owners were women.

The primary economic function of Hausa farm slaves, as of Karnataka bonded labourers, was usually to increase the production of basic grains, which might either have been for household consumption or sold. In Hausaland, more often than in Karnataka, agrestic servitude enabled free men and their sons to travel more widely, for instance as long-distance traders,[35] than if they had been dependent on family labour alone.

In this brief discussion of agrestic servitude in the two regions I have not been concerned with the aristocrats, city-based merchants and other absentee owners of large estates who depended on farm slaves or bonded labourers for much of their cultivation. But in the next chapter I shall deal with the abolition of the large estates in both regions – with the slave-run estates owned by stranger farmers in Hausaland and with the *jodidars* of Karnataka. In this chapter it remains to consider the transition from slavery to freedom from the point of view of the farm slaves themselves.

Most farm slaves were not formally freed, as was legally possible, but either ran away or lapsed into freedom. From about the time of the great famine[36] of 1914 it became abundantly clear to all concerned that the institution of farm-slavery would soon be moribund, so that increasingly large numbers of slaves must then have absconded, if only to avoid panic-selling by slave owners whose main type of agrarian capital would soon lose all value. Gradually the institution of daily-paid farm-labouring began to replace slavery. If the labourers were ex-slaves or men of slave descent (and many of them were of free descent), then in Kano Emirate they were no more apt to work with their former slave owner than with anyone else – and, as we know, most day labourers work for many different employers.

The main initial disability suffered by the ex-slaves and their descendants was that they owned very little manured farmland: indeed, most of them would have owned none had it not been that some of their owners gave them plots[37] – small plots, maybe, but not necessarily diminutive. Land hunger must have resulted in much migration, which was presumably mainly to the countryside since the urban population was still relatively very small and not yet showing a strong tendency to increase. Whether

[35] They might have needed to set off before their harvest had been brought in.

[36] This terrible famine in northern Hausaland was caused by a drought in 1913. See Hill (1972), p. 284 under *Malali.* (Many slaves ran away at that time.)

[37] Strangers who were obliged to stop farming when slavery ended were among those particularly apt to give land to their slaves.

much migration was prompted by the urge to look like a man of free descent we cannot tell; but the likelihood is that relatively few ex-slaves endeavoured to return to their homeland, with which they would usually have lost touch.[38]

As for the ex-slaves, and their descendants, who did not migrate, did they suffer from disabilities such that they might be compared to contemporary Harijans in south India? The reply to this question is 'emphatically no' – if only for the very strong reason that they were not an endogamous group. Their exogamous behaviour had two aspects, one positive, the other negative: on the one hand they were clearly not motivated by any wish to preserve the (non-existent) purity of their group,[39] on the other hand, men of free descent had few prejudices about marrying women of slave-descent.[40] Nor were any demeaning occupations – with the possible exception of butchering – pursued only by those of slave-descent. So, with the lapse of over half a century since slavery ended, the matter of whether a person is of slave-descent has ceased to be of any particular interest, except sometimes to the very old; and younger people are often unaware of their origins.

Lugard misunderstood Hausa land tenure to the point that he supposed that slaves could be prevented from absconding by denying them access to land – whereas, as we know, the plain fact of the matter was that authorities with the power to allocate land to individuals were lacking. Men of slave-descent had as much right as any other resident to appropriate uncultivated land for themselves: insofar as they found it necessary to abscond, this had nothing to do with land tenure but everything to do with fear of recapture. So when the slaves found that they were free men, they were as much entitled to convert themselves into ordinary cultivators as anyone else.

In less densely populated areas it is probable that men of slave-descent are nowadays no poorer, on average, than anyone else: one mentions this in passing, despite one's contempt for that kind of arithmetic. But in densely populated Dorayi elaborate enquiries showed that the incidence of extreme poverty among slave descendants was somewhat higher than for other men – the incidence of 'riches' being somewhat lower. Interested readers may turn to the detailed statistics: here I merely record that the incidence of landlessness among fatherless married men was 17% for those of slave

[38] This was true for numerous reasons including the fact that many second, third, etc., generation slaves were ignorant of their 'origin' – which, owing to marriages of slaves of different origins, was often a meaningless concept.

[39] As are Harijans. See *An Untouchable Community in South India: Structure and Consensus* by M. Moffatt, 1979.

[40] Insofar as the converse prejudice was once significant this is probably no longer so. See Hill (1972), Table XIII.2, p. 179.

origin compared with 11% for those of free origin, and that for the age group of 55 years and upwards the proportions of 'rich men' were 15% for those of slave origin against 22% for those of free origin. It is by means of this kind of indirect arithmetic that we can see that the contemporary agrarian system in Dorayi has, as it were, forgotten its recent dependence on farm-slavery – which makes its resemblance to the Anekal system the less surprising.

APPENDIX XIII(1)

The young bonded labourers in the Anekal villages

The householders of the six Anekal villages reported that 46 of their sons were working as bonded labourers (always known as *sambalagaras*) either in their natal village (26 of them) or in nearby villages. Although we did our best to check the figures, they are certainly a significant under-estimate, especially for Hullahalli where only 6 cases were reported despite the large Harijan population. Nearly all these labourers were well under twenty years old and unmarried; half of them were from one village (Nanjapura), where the Harijans were notably poor; and 40 (87%) of them belonged to the AK or AD castes. As many as 16% of all AK households were known to have placed one or more of their sons in this work – the proportion for Nanjapura being as high as one-third. About a fifth of all Reddy households were known to employ such labourers. It seemed that there were no *sambalagaras* in, or from Srirampura – members of the Pichiguntala caste do not favour this system.

The conditions of employment were fairly standard, except that some of the boys lived at home, others with their employer. I think that few of them were bonded for more than two years; that virtually all the fathers had demanded loans before they would release their sons; that annual cash wages varied between about Rs 100 (for a young boy) and about Rs 250; that food, clothing and other benefits were always provided; that loans varied and were not accurately reported; that the debt was almost always automatically liquidated by services rendered, even though there were seldom any documents recording the agreed terms; and that the demand for employment of this type was less than the potential supply.

The motives of the impoverished fathers who released their sons were easy to understand: the loans were extremely welcome and the sons were probably always better fed and clothed than if they had depended on irregular daily-paid work. The great majority of the fathers involved had found positions for no more than one unmarried son.

So far as I could ascertain, all the debt involved was new: in other words, fathers did not place their sons with employers to whom they were already indebted, but rather demanded new loans from the employers on the security of the work to be performed over the next year or two.

CHAPTER XIV

The Inevitable Dissolution of the Large Estates

In Chapter XII I examined the *withdrawal from the countryside* which has occurred during this century in both continents, stressing its association with the ending of farm-slavery in Hausaland and with the legal abolition of the hereditary estate-holders (*jodidars*) in Karnataka. In this brief chapter I discuss the inevitability of the dissolution of the large estates.

HAUSALAND

In pre-colonial Hausaland all the aristocratic and absentee owners of large estates, which were often holdings which were widely dispersed, were almost wholly dependent on the labour of their male and female slaves, which was supervised by slave foremen. Ordinary private slave owners, who were much more numerous, would usually have had their resident sons working alongside their slaves. Given that few free women worked on the land at that time, it is likely that most private farmers with holdings above, say, 50 acres[1] would have owned farm slaves, for systems of farm-labour employment were lacking and communal labour was no more than a stop-gap for private farmers.

The large estate owners (I refer to the aristocratic and absentee owners as such) might have survived the collapse of farm-slavery had the system of daily-paid farm-labouring, which replaced it, been properly adaptable to their purposes – as it was not. As we know, this system has many inherent defects, which essentially reflect the spasmodic nature of farming activity during the farming season; two, at least, of these defects proved fatal to the estate owners, namely the constant effort of recruiting new workers at short notice and the need to supervise all the labourers' work. In the harsh conditions of northern Hausaland, where the short rainy season usually lasts for some four to five months only, the employment of annual

[1] Owing to polygyny household heads may have many sons, making it difficult to suggest a maximum.

labourers, corresponding to the farm servants of south India, would have been out of the question, even for rich farmers, as they would have been largely unoccupied for over half the year, not even having the care of cattle in the dry season. The slaves had been another matter since they had been partly responsible for maintaining themselves.

In Kano Emirate the only large estates which did not collapse when slavery ended were owned by the Emir himself or his very close kinsmen, or by a very small number of high office-holders such as the Chief Blacksmith. Such very high dignitaries were in a unique position to persuade the slaves' descendants to remain on their estates indefinitely, in a capacity which resembled that of tenants,[2] for they were free to leave, though they could not sell their land. But by 1972 such royal estates comprised but a tiny portion of all the Emirate land.

With the aid of our farm maps, based on aerial photographs, we were able to show[3] that each of the non-office-holding outsiders who were known to have owned slave-run holdings in the Dorayi area ultimately sold, or gave away, all their land there. One of the very few colonial Tax Assessment Reports to have mentioned slavery[4] – and then only in retrospect in 1932 – noted that farms on the end of the main route from Zaria to Kano city, which ran down the western boundary of Dorayi, had been prized by 'wealthy merchants' who owned farm slaves:

> The abolition of slavery threw these estates . . . out of cultivation. The original owners are dead . . . Yet the estates still remain, owned by aged widows and small traders who exist in the ruined mansions of their husbands and fathers which line the road.[5]

A decade or two later, when all the aged widows had departed, the estates would have vanished too.

Probably most of the land was sold on the open market by the ex-slave owners or their sons; but some of it was given away, or sold on easy terms, to the owner's ex-slaves or their descendants – as in the case of a woman slave owner, a salt trader, three of whose male slaves had as many as 26 married male descendants living in Dorayi in 1972.

As for the local farmers who had owned considerable numbers of slaves

[2] See Hill (1977) on the Dorayi estates owned by the Emir and the Kano Chief Blacksmith. I also visited a number of other former royal estates, including one south of Kano city, near the Challawa river, where the slaves' descendants, who constantly referred to themselves as such, called their inalienable farms *gayauni*, i.e. plots allocated by the *gandu* head. These men were responsible for recruiting and supervising daily-paid labourers for the main farm.

[3] See Hill (1977), p. 215.

[4] Understandably, officials preserved extreme reticence about their (genuine) inability to suppress slavery during the first quarter-century of British rule.

[5] Source given on p. 215 of Hill (1977).

– it seemed that in Dorayi about three local men may have owned some fifteen slaves or more – they did not necessarily need to dispose of any of their farmland since they would anticipate its imminent division between their sons. On the one hand, the inexorable forces of inheritance have necessarily diminished the size of all these holdings; on the other hand, the largest owners did not seek to maintain their original size of holding by land purchase, owing to dissatisfaction with the farm-labouring system.

I think that the only contemporary cultivators, other than the diminutive number of 'royals' and other high city dignitaries, who may have the power of insulating themselves from the rigours of the labouring system are first the District Heads (of whom there were only 25 in the vast Kano Emirate in 1972), second a few Village Heads of important towns, and third a new type of city industrialist or contractor some of whom can afford to employ full-time foremen – and to apply chemical fertilisers.[6]

Mallamawa, the District Head of Batagarawa, was altogether superior to any of his people in 1967 in terms of the scale and dispersal of his farming. This was not because he had a large official farm attaching to his office – that was a mere 7 acres – but because he and his forebears had acquired farms in about ten other Hamlets[7] in his District, which were in the charge of the Village Heads. Whereas, for reasons of supervision or inspection, the ordinary cultivator dislikes owning farms more than (say) 2 to 3 miles from home, Mallamawa's high status enabled him to rely on others to supervise and recruit his labourers; it also meant that he was able to persuade other plough owners to render communal labour[8] (*gayya*) on his land. The Batagarawa Village Head, whose father had been the late District Head, had no official farms, but he operated on a fairly large scale with the help of his paid farm servants (*bara*,[9] pl. *barori*), who were attached only to members of the ruling family. The only other exceptional farmer was Mallamawa's senior son, whose farms were widely dispersed; he relied heavily on his power to 'call *gayya*', to the extent that on one day in July 1968 as many as 103 men worked on his farms outside the Batagarawa area, three donkey loads of cooked food being provided there.[10]

So emotive is the question of the car-bound stranger-farmers, so inadequate the supply of hard facts on their numbers and activities, that I can do no more than express the opinion that their importance is always apt to be inflated by urban bias[11] and that outside very recently irrigated areas,

[6] They are usually interested only in accessible land near motor roads.

[7] See Hill (1972), p. 28.

[8] See Hill (1972), p. 286 and pp. 251–2.

[9] See p. 247, n. 23 above.

[10] See Hill (1972), p. 208.

[11] Urban-based farmers are those whom most visitors happen to meet.

with which I am here not concerned,[12] they will remain entirely insignificant in comparison with their former counterparts who owned slave-run estates, at least until there are vast improvements in the miserably inadequate road network and in grain yields and prices – and probably not even then. Although in 1972 the farmland which lined the road running through Dorayi to the Challawa river was quite exceptionally attractive to city farmers owing to the closeness of the city, as well as to modern developments (including the expansion of the nearby university) which justified speculative buying, only 65 acres had so far been acquired by thirty-two city men with no former connection with Dorayi.

KARNATAKA ESTATES

Outside such official papers as are available in the Karnataka State Archives, there appears to have been little mention of the former large estates in Karnataka, except in the two official *Gazetteers* and the *Mysore Revenue Manual*.[13] On my first arrival in one of the Anekal villages (Hullahalli) I did not, therefore, understand the significance of the *jodidar*, who had been legally expropriated, with compensation, under the Inams Abolition Act of 1955, much of his land having been permanently acquired by those villagers who had previously rented it, some having been sold to villagers and outsiders.[14] I did not then know that owing to much dissatisfaction with the conditions and prospects of the tenants of such estate-holders, a series of official committees[15] from as long ago as 1915 onwards had examined their position, but that it was not until 1950 that the Committee for the Revision of the Land Revenue System in Mysore had finally recommended their abolition – the 1955 Act ultimately solving a problem which had exercised officials and politicians for many years.

The confusing Muslim term *inam*,[16] as applied to official land, relates to any official grant made by the government for religious or charitable purposes or to individuals in respect of services rendered or for any other reasons. A list of 'types of land inams' contained in a report[17] of 1901 ran to as many as 91 headings, including the grants made to the village *thotis*. Fortunately, however, if we are dealing in terms of whole villages we need

[12] There is, so far as I know, no reliable sociological literature on the recent large-scale irrigation schemes which were not in operation when I was in Hausaland.

[13] The *Gazetteers* are by B. Lewis Rice Vol. I, 1897 and C. Hayavadana Rao, 1929. The last edition of the *Mysore Revenue Manual* was published in 1938.

[14] The *jodidar*'s heir had retained none of the farmland as would have been legally possible.

[15] See *The Mysore Gazette*, 19 Oct. 1933, for the report of the committee appointed in 1932, which refers to earlier committees and to a commission appointed in 1918.

[16] This Muslim word has replaced the earlier *manya*.

[17] See Appendix XIV(1) below.

only distinguish three types of land grant: viz. free grants (*sarvamanya*); grants made on easy terms (*jodi* – the estate-holder being the *jodidar*); and grants mainly in depopulated or under-populated villages, on a fixed permanent (tax) assessment (*kayamgutta*). Since a high proportion of the first type was temple land; since *jodi* was the most common type of grant to individuals; and since *kayamgutta* is sometimes hard to distinguish – I have chosen to follow the villagers themselves who generally denote the former holders of large estates as *jodidars*, not, incidentally, as *zamindars*, as in Tamil Nadu and north India.

Although the literature is so official and so scanty, this is not because the *jodidars* owned but little land. In 1891 as many as 12% of all Mysore villages were recorded[18] as 'alienated'; the corresponding figure for Bangalore District was 22%, where as many as 27% of all the alienated villages in Mysore were situated. In Anekal Taluk 17% of all the 223 villages[19] listed in the census were alienated,[20] 34 of the total of 37 being classified as either *jodi* or *kayamgutta* The importance of these villages was far greater than these figures suggest if, as is commonly supposed, alienated land included an unusually high proportion of excellent irrigated land.

In 1881 all the owners of whole *inam* villages in the State received a title deed. Thereafter, owing to incessant complaints from interested parties and politicians the position underwent constant, though inconclusive, examination until in 1950 officialdom finally got its way. Meanwhile many of the *jodidars* had greatly neglected their irrigation tanks and were neglectful in other ways:

> There was a general complaint that the inamdars were not keeping proper accounts, were not issuing pattas [cultivation papers] and were not giving proper receipts for kandayam [tax] paid. In many villages there were no shanbhogs and patels and in some instances the shanbhogs were not on amicable terms with the inamdars. Some inamdars would be continuously absent from their villages, would allow arrears to accumulate for years, and then suddenly demand from the tenants the entire amount. In some villages there was no assignment of gomal [grazing ground], the tanks were in a neglected condition and remissions of assessment [tax] were not allowed by the inamdars as in Government villages.[21]

The government refused to agree with the 1933 committee that each *jodidar* should have a government-appointed accountant and headman.

[18] *Census of India, 1891*, Vol. XXV, Part I.

[19] *Mysore Gazetteer*, 1897, Vol. II, p. 29. The total number of villages (see p. 236 above) was equal to that in the 1971 census!

[20] They accounted for 24% of the total area of village land.

[21] 'Report of the committee established in 1932 for examining the existing conditions and prospects of tenants in inam and jodi villages', *The Mysore Gazette*, 19 Oct. 1933, p. 921.

But 'permanent tenancy rights' were thereafter established by twelve, rather then the previous twenty years of occupation.

As I had searched in vain in the Karnataka State Archives for material throwing light on the inevitability of the break-up of the large estates, it seems suitable to cite the excellent and sophisticated article by C. Baker 'Tamilnad estates in the twentieth century',[22] especially as it has reference to our general theme of the withdrawal from the countryside, virtually all the estates lying in the 'dry tract' of Tamilnad – 'that is, the area which depended on the meagre rainfall and small irrigation works, rather than major river systems'.[23] (But it must be borne in mind that some of the enormous Tamilnad estates were very much larger than any in the little state of Mysore; and that the average size, also, was very much greater.)

As a result, first, of the great increase in the production of cotton and groundnuts and then of the great depression which took grip in the early 1930s, the Madras Government, the politicians, and even many of the estate owners themselves, all favoured the abolition of the estates. Many *zamindars*, just as much as prominent farmers, were distracted away from the 'insular relationships' upon which estate administration had depended and were 'tempted into new opportunities in commerce, industry and politics'[24] in the towns. The *zamindar* of Bagalur, owner of nearly 12,000 acres, 'gave up his rather harsh realities of upcountry Salem'[25] for the bright lights of Bangalore. One observer in 1938, looking back nostalgically to the 1870s, when the *zamindars* had resembled heads of large families, noted that they 'began to lead a new modern life'.[26] In the estates, *zamindars* and their tenants fought bitterly to divide the reduced income from the land. In the late 1930s many 'beleaguered zamindars'[27] wanted their estates taken off their hands. Such was the relief at the withdrawal from the declining countryside, that one of the grandest estate owners of all – he owned nearly 400,000 acres – 'was quite pleased when after independence the Congress government relieved him of the burden of his estate'.[28] When the Congress revenue minister introduced the *zamindari* abolition Bill in 1948 he remarked that the system had

> led to a loss of contact between the Government and the actual cultivator and has acted as a brake in regard to agricultural improvement. . . . The zamindari system in force in the Province has outlived its usefulness.[29]

No doubt it had. But what happened to the 'agricultural improvement' which the government supposed would follow?

[22] *The Indian Economic & Social History Review*, Vol. XIII, 1, 1976. (I cite from this article since the author's *The Tamilnad Countryside* is unpublished at the time of writing.)
[23] *Ibid.*, p. 14. [24] *Ibid.*, p. 23. [25] *Ibid.* [26] *Ibid.*
[27] *Ibid.*, p. 31. [28] *Ibid.*, pp. 33–4. [29] Cited in *ibid.*, p. 43.

JODIDARS IN ANEKAL TALUK

At the time of the abolition of the Karnataka estates we do not know whether most of the *jodidars* were Brahmins, since even if this had been so in earlier times many of them might meanwhile have sold or otherwise disposed of their estates to non-Brahmins.[30] Of the six *jodidars* in Anekal Taluk for whom I happened to obtain a few particulars,[31] 4 were Brahmins, one a Muslim and one a member of the Ganiga caste. The legislation permitted the expropriated estate-holders to retain small acreages of different categories of land for their own use.[32] Some of them took advantage of this, some cleared out altogether – and in one case the final intention was unclear since the formalities of transfer were not quite complete in 1978. Unlike land reform legislation, which came later, this change was a great success in reflecting the wishes of nearly everyone concerned, including the villagers, the administration, the politicians and maybe the *jodidars* themselves; and, as already emphasised, the Harijans in an ex-*jodidar* village like Hullahalli are considerably better off than those in Nanjapura, where there had been no *jodidar*, as a direct result of the transfer of lands to them.

As usual in the countryside, the legislation says one thing and the people do another, so I shall relate a little of what I learnt from the Harijans and others in Hullahalli rather than trying to interpret the intricacies of the legislation. In Hullahalli I was told that the *jodidar*'s agent started selling dry land to those already occupying it at the very low price of some Rs 15–25 per acre, the price of wet land having been about Rs 2,000 per acre. Most of the wet land had been directly cultivated by the *jodidar* and not let out; he had employed 'bonded ploughmen' (*jeetadalu*) as well as day labourers, many of whom were permitted the use of small plots. Many outsiders bought land from the *jodidar*, some of them with the deliberate intention of reselling it at a profit.

Most Harijans seemed to be satisfied with the price they paid for their small plots in the early stages. But later on, when prices of dry land rose to (say) Rs 100 per acre (still very cheap on normal standards), they were sometimes obliged to raise the sums involved by temporarily pledging the services of their unmarried sons as *sambalagaras*. However, the chief beneficiaries of the dispossession were first local members of the dominant Reddy and Gowda castes, who were able to raise the large sums required to

[30] See Appendix XIV(1).

[31] Only three of them had land in any of the six villages.

[32] For details of the complicated legislation see para. 6 of the Mysore (Personal and Miscellaneous) Inams Abolition Act, 1955.

buy the wet land previously cultivated by the *jodidar*, and second some twenty outsiders who bought such land.[33]

Some Anekal *jodidars* lived in their villages in large houses which have since been sold; others lived mainly in Bangalore, visiting their estates, of which they might have had several, quite frequently. During the past half century there has been so much change in the political, though not in the economic atmosphere, that it is hard to believe that there are still many in Hullahalli who remember the *jodidar* arriving from Bangalore in his horse-drawn carriage.

APPENDIX XIV(1)

The Mysore inam *villages*

As there appears to be no literature, other than reference material, on the history of the Mysore *inam* villages I append the following notes:

According to the *Mysore Revenue Manual*,[34]

> The origins of inams dates prior to 1800 from antiquity. Under the orders of Dewan Purnaiya [1799 to 1812], a survey was made of all inam land. This survey was neither accurate nor perfect; still, the results were of some use for purposes of inam settlement[35] . . . [The upshot of this settlement] appears roughly to have been the confirmation of inams of the value of about eight lakhs of rupees, with a jodi, however, of about three lakhs. . . . A number of inams were also created during the period 1811 to 1831 [under Maharaja Krishnaraja Wadiyar III] . . . and large alienations were made in addition to which a good many villages were granted on *khayamgutta*.

A searching investion into *inam* tenure was conducted in 1863 when it was found that many types of agreement existed. Such documents as were extant (and sometimes there were none) ranged in date from the fifteenth to the nineteenth centuries. An Inam Commission was organised in 1866, and under the Inam Rules of 1868 it was laid down that when grants had been made by a Maharaja and conveyed full powers of alienation and were hereditary they should be registered as such, but in other cases rents were charged.[36] In 1881 final title deeds were issued for all the 2,080 'whole inam villages in the State'.

A Report[37] of 1901 which considered the operations of the Inam Commission since its commencement stated (p. 5) that during the Maharaja's administration from 1811:

33 About a third of the 74 acres of wet land in Hullahalli was owned by outsiders, nearly all villagers.

34 1938, Vol. I. Government Press, Bangalore, p. 273.

35 The survey was in terms of *bijavari* – the amount of seed required.

36 See *Mysore Gazetteer*, 1929, Vol. IV, p. 156.

37 *Report of the Operations of the Inam Commission from the Commencement*. By J. P. Grant, 1901, Karnataka State Archives.

> large alienations were recklessly made, chiefly of whole, and the very best villages, while other villages were conferred on favourable kayamgutta or permanent tenure, the administrations being so lax that even the subordinate officers made other alienations without authority. . . . The grants made by the British Government since 1831 . . . were few and were moreover for useful purposes such as the maintenance of topes,[38] tanks and avenue trees[39] and the upkeep of chattrams.

This report[40] classified 91 types of 'land inam' in six groups:

(1) *religious* (40 types, including special settlements for the maintenance of Brahmins);
(2) *personal* (20 types);
(3) *miscellaneous service* (15 types, including grants for hereditary chief revenue accountants of a District or group of villages);
(4) *village service* (4 types, namely *shanbhog, patel, 'tulwar'* – village watchmen – and *thotis*);
(5) *village artisans* (6 types, being the *nirgunti* and others 'for regulating the discharge of water to village irrigated lands', village blacksmiths, carpenters, potters, washmen and barbers[41]);
(6) *miscellaneous* (a mixed bag of 6 types including (a) the 'village cobbler and scavenger',[42] (b) 'grants of land or of a share of the produce for the up-keep of tanks or other irrigation works constructed or restored by private individuals', (c) 'for the up-keep of wells dug by private individuals for the irrigation of Government lands', (d) *kayamgutta* villages 'which were mostly depopulated and granted to influential persons and court favourites by the Maharaja on a fixed permanent assessment').[43]

Some *inamdars* held many lands. Thus a 1920 report mentioned a man, with religious connections, who was *inamdar* of 7 villages in 7 taluks with an area of 19,552 acres, and another who owned 10 villages in various taluks.

At that time the last word seemed to lie with an *inamdar* who expressed the following sentiments,[44] for, as we know, it was not until 1950 that the abolition of *inam* villagers was recommended:

> The Government in its far fetched and liberal views and thoughts brought different portions of the country under agriculture by granting and creating Inams in favour of military fighters, men of gigantic capacity and intellect men (*sic*) who did yeoman's service to the country and for the salvation and happy repose of the departed souls who as administrators and rulers of this state enlarged the limits of the state by making additional improvements to the state. In this view and in memory of these great personages the Inams created and granted by those great authorities must be protected by affording all reasonable facilities.

The only reference I could find to the Mysore estate-holders in Francis Buchanan's book reads as follows:

38. Groves, gardens or orchards.
39 The beautiful huge trees still lining some of the main roads running out of Bangalore were established by means of land grants to those who cared for them.
40 p. 30 *et seq.*
41 There is no evidence that grants of land had ever been made to the last five types of artisan during living memory in the Anekal villages.
42 The same note applies as with other artisans.
43. *The Inam Commission Mysore 1919–20*, Bangalore, Karnataka State Archives.
44 *Ibid.*, p. 84.

When a rich man undertakes at his own expense to construct a reservoir for the irrigation of land, he is allowed to hold in free estate (*Enam*),[45] and by hereditary right, one fourth part of the lands so watered; but he is bound to keep the reservoir in repair. Such a proprietor is called *Caray-cuttu Codigy*.[46] The *Tanks* to which there is a person of this kind are notoriously kept in better repair, than those which the government supports. . . . The reason assigned for this by the natives is perfectly satisfactory. They say, that they can compel the holder of the free estate to perform his duty; but the state has no master.[47]

45 Viz. Inam.

46 Presumably these words are a rendering of *kayamgutta kodigi* – *kodigi* having been a type of tenure, based on the upkeep of tanks, which would be abolished in 1875.

47 Buchanan, 1807, Vol. III, pp. 453–4.

CHAPTER XV

How did the Weakest Elements formerly Survive in the Anekal Villages?

Unlike all but one (Chapter XVI) of the other chapters in this book, this chapter is almost entirely concerned with one of the continents only – namely with the question of how the erstwhile untouchables, and other near-destitute people, managed to survive in south-eastern Karnataka in (say) 1900.

We idealise our childhoods, the long summer afternoons of yesteryear – and the conditions of the weakest elements of rural tropical communities in 'earlier times'. We share the common conviction that rural poverty today is not merely more intense (as, indeed, it may be owing to the unprecedented rate of growth of the population as well as to inflation), but somehow different in kind owing to greater 'individual', i.e. household, insecurity. Whereas the past is seen as ordered, rigorous and harmonious, the present is regarded as chaotic and disorderly. Of course all the dates get mixed so that 'disorder' may be attributed to the arrival of the British, to increasing urbanism, to the decline of rural crafts, to the sale of land, to the degradation of the soil, to increased monetisation – and so forth. However this may be, the condition of the weakest elements today is always seen as essentially more precarious than formerly. I am sure that this is a serious fallacy and that unless we come to understand that *the poverty of the present springs directly from the poverty of the past*[1] we shall make no intellectual progress.

Certain ardent colonialists, among them Lugard in Northern Nigeria, were at once very sensitive to the dangers of destroying 'natural harmony' and very insensitive to the existence of 'natural poverty'. Many of the false presuppositions with which they bolstered their ideology, such as that Northern Nigerian *natives* did not really sell land, went so strongly into circulation that they are still natural presuppositions today – ideological decolonisation is far from complete and occurs in the most unexpected places. Lugard was so muddled over land tenure (the most emotive of all

[1] 'There was never . . . an egalitarian golden age in Maharashtra'. Charlesworth in Dewey and Hopkins (eds.), 1978, p. 103.

colonial economic topics) that he sincerely believed that a class of 'free peasants', i.e. non-aristocrats who owned their land, came into existence *for the first time* as slavery declined. The institution of farm-slavery was wrongly presumed to have owed its existence to the 'unavoidable security' enjoyed by all free farmers in conditions of 'land surplus', none of whom would have been prepared to work as farm labourers for others – though many of them actually did so in the 1920s, even before slavery had ended. It was because he wrongly believed that farmland was harmoniously allocated to individual cultivators by 'chiefs' who reflected the wishes of their people, whereas it was effectively appropriated by individuals, who were simply careful not to trespass on existent rights, that he supposed that fugitive slaves could somehow be formally denied land rights.[2] His fears of destabilisation largely stemmed from the awful (though misunderstood) lesson of Indian colonialism; he did not realise that in West African conditions his policy of indirect rule amounted to rural non-rule.[3]

JAJMANI

It is necessary to provide a very brief summary of the most recent Indian attempt to 'harmonise the past' by means of the *jajmani*[4] system, which was first 'observed' by W. H. Wiser,[5] an American missionary, in a village in Uttar Pradesh some time before 1930. Some twenty-five years later Dumont explained:

> It has become common practice to apply the term 'the *jajmani* system' to the system corresponding to the prestations and counter-prestations by which the castes as a whole are bound together in the village, and which is more or less universal in India.[6]

That the system had much in common with earlier formulations of harmony is made entirely clear, for the passage continues:

> To a large extent it is a question of natural as opposed to monetary economy. It is also a question of the closed economy of the Indian village in which essential goods and especially services are found, or used to be found, either on the spot or in the immediate vicinity: this fact corresponds, therefore, to what has long been called the 'village community' in the economic sense of the phrase.

Answering the question as to 'the principle behind' *jajmani*, Dumont replies[7] that it makes use of hereditary personal relationships to express the

[2] Hill (1977), p. 210. [3] See Hill (1977), Chapter II.
[4] This Hindi word is unknown, in this sense, to Karnataka villagers.
[5] *The Hindu Jajmani System*, 1936.
[6] Dumont, 1970, p. 97. [7] *Ibid.*, p. 98.

division of labour and that 'it regulates prestations and counter-prestations in a way which accords with custom'. His exposition at this point is insufficiently explicit, partly because there is too much 'vague harmony' in an explanation that 'each family has a family of specialists at its disposal for each specialized task', and also because the non-specialists are disregarded. However, it is unnecessary to linger long on this as Dumont himself later criticises Wiser's concept of *jajmani* by emphasising that the latter idealised:

> not only security for the poor, but also, by stressing the middle orders, a sort of egalitarian harmony, which accords ill with the whole, but is somewhat reminiscent of the idyllic picture of the 'village community' painted by the romantic civil servants of the beginning of the nineteenth century.[8]

Perhaps the most cogent critic of *jajmani* has been Gough who found fault[9] with Beidelman's comparative analysis of the system,[10] which he dubbed 'feudalistic', mainly on the grounds of his failure to realise that the socio-economic relationships between castes had been *defined by law* in the pre-British period.[11] But I am not inclined to follow her argument further here since it is impossible to believe that in dry, upland, impoverished localities like Anekal Taluk:

> the several castes in the village establishment were *all* vested with hereditary, differential rights, caste-bound and prescribed by law, either in plots of land or in the produce of the village land.[12]

As much of the literature on *jajmani* is very technical and concerned with religious, not economic aspects, I conclude with a passing reference to the most recent critical contribution by J. P. Parry. He concludes that in present-day Kangra, which lies in the far north of India beyond the Punjab plains, *jajmani* is 'economically peripheral', even if 'conceptually central'.[13] It is the villagers themselves who are over-attracted by their 'ideal model', projecting the 'harmonised past' into the present like the rest of us:

> To the extent, then, that the people themselves (and derivatively their ethnographers) represent the empirical economy of the village in terms of *jajmani* relations and the division of labour between castes, they misrepresent it.[14]

The principal weakness of the *jajmani* system of ideas for present

[8] *Ibid.*, pp. 102–3.
[9] 'The Hindu Jajmani System' by Kathleen Gough, *Economic Development & Cultural Change*, 1960.
[10] *A Comparative Analysis of the 'Jajmani' System* by T. O. Beidelman, 1959.
[11] Gough, 1960, p. 90. [12] *Ibid.*, p. 87.
[13] Parry, 1979, p. 82. [14] *Ibid.*, p. 83.

purposes is its imprecision on the position of non-specialist, non-owner-cultivators like the general run of Harijans – a subsidiary weakness being the concentration on the village as a secluded entity. In a situation where, as may be realistically supposed,[15] 30% of a village population in 1900 consisted of Harijans, few of whom (as we know) were bonded labourers or specialist artisans, is there any reason to believe that the richer households of the dominant landholding caste(s) would *necessarily* have been in a position to offer sufficient maintenance to such a large unattached population? I suggest that in densely populated localities such as Anekal Taluk, where less than a tenth of the cultivated land was irrigated from tanks; where the average yield of the basic crop *ragi* was very low; where the area of 'garden land' irrigated from wells was quite small; and where many non-Harijan cultivators were consequently too poor to offer much help to others except in emergencies or on ceremonial occasions – I suggest that in such circumstances it would be sheer sentiment to postulate an automatic correspondence between 'the need for help' (on the part of poor Harijans) and 'the power to help Harijans' (on the part of richer households).

MISCELLANEOUS OCCUPATIONS

Such an arithmetical argument may seem superficially persuasive, but to be convincing it is necessary to consider the means by which the great mass of the Harijan population might have managed to scrape up a living by their own largely, though not entirely, unaided efforts. I take it for granted (matters which I shall soon discuss) that most Harijans were not cultivators on their own account or village servants (*thotis*); I also assume that, as today, the demand for daily-paid labour, which must have been very seasonal,[16] was usually considerably below the potential supply. In such circumstances is it conceivable that other remunerative occupations might have filled the yawning 'maintenance gap'?

At first glance such an idea *is* inconceivable, since in rural Karnataka so many of the occupations open to poor men in rural West Africa were either reserved for specialist artisan, trading or transporting castes, or were largely the preserve of urban-dwellers. But persistence is necessary considering (as we know) that the opportunities open to Harijans remain unimpressive today, although their population is apparently increasing about as fast as other people's. Indeed, in one particular respect, there may

[15] See p. 244 above.

[16] Then, as today, the tanks were so apt to be in partial disrepair that it is likely that a single crop only was taken from most paddy land.

have been a serious deterioration since (say) 1900 if one is right in thinking that Harijans formerly owned many more cattle per household – and also benefited from the generally higher ratio of cattle to people.[17] No doubt many of the animals were of very inferior quality and the cows produced even less milk than today, but they represented a tangible form of agrarian capital, which Harijans now so often lack. The rearing and maintenance of cattle and the collection of dung from the land would have involved more paid labour per head of the population than today, much of which would have devolved on Harijans. Then landless Harijans might more often have received extra wages for hiring themselves out as ploughmen with their own cattle.

Buchanan has made it abundantly clear that cash circulated freely in the villages in 1800; the villages, as such, were cash economies, the distinction between grain and money being unimportant to Harijans who then, as now, hardly participated in trade, other than in livestock, outside their own villages. (Indeed, there is not really any evidence that contemporary agricultural labourers are any more apt to be paid in cash than in grain (*ragi*) than in 1800, for *ragi* is often preferred for its greater convenience and because it tends to be under-valued in the transaction.)

Unfortunately, little has been recorded on lowly types of non-farming occupation. While Buchanan is hardly an exception,[18] he does mention the weaving of coarse cloth by Harijans – the production of fine cloth having been a caste-bound occupation. He stated that the weavers of poor-quality cloth got 1s 8d for weaving, in 4 to 5 days, a piece worth 5s 4½d.

> The Whalliaru [now Adikarnataka] make a coarse, white, strong cloth called *Parcalla*. Weavers of this kind live scattered in the villages, and frequently hire themselves out as day-labourers to farmers, or other persons who will give them employment.[19]

The fact is that owing to the British (and pre-British) obsession with land revenue, as well as to delta bias, we are much too apt to regard such rural economies as those of the dry uplands of south-eastern Karnataka as having been essentially arable,[20] thus ignoring the extent to which local

17 My surmise that cattle (though not necessarily water buffaloes) were formerly more numerous is not based on archival statistics, which are certain to lack reliability, but on oral information from old Harijans, on our knowledge that grazing grounds (*gomal*) were formerly much more extensive and on remembered low cattle prices.

18 Though he is careful to mention women labourers, including house servants – Buchanan, 1807, Vol. I, p. 125.

19 *Ibid.*, Vol. I, p. 218. Elsewhere (Vol. I, p. 313) Buchanan refers to the Morasu Whalliaru, the highest endogamous sub-caste, as 'cultivators of the ground, weavers and smelters of iron ore'.

20 I am grateful to C. J. Baker for this idea.

people generally were regularly engaged in such activities as pastoralism, collecting (forage, firewood, etc.), construction (houses, temples, wells, tanks, roads, etc.), porterage and non-specialist craft work such as coarse weaving and rough carpentry.

While I am far from satisfied with the completeness of the following list of paid occupations pursued by Harijan men and youths in the Anekal villages today (which is more detailed than Table VIII(1) above), it provides a fair indication of the range of opportunities that was available in 1900. The list excludes all occupations necessitating commuting to urban areas, all factory work (e.g. in the brick factory near Bukkasagara), all 'paid work' connected with ceremonies, etc., and all duties, such as the removal of dead animals, which the *thotis* are obliged to perform. I employ 'Harijans' in this context as relating essentially to the AK and AD castes, omitting the specialist mud workers, the Bhovi.

Classification of the various paid occupations pursued by Harijan men and boys in the Anekal villages today

(1) *Farm-labouring*: ploughing, sowing, transplanting, weeding, harvesting, irrigating, etc. – usually daily-paid
(2) *Other labouring*: including road work, house-building and brick-making
(3) *Mud work*: including repairing the bunds of paddy fields
(4) *Repair and maintenance of irrigation tanks*
(5) *Well-digging*
(6) *Collection* of 'free goods' such as firewood, bamboo, cow dung, fodder (including grass and leaves), edible wild plants, etc.
(7) *Porterage* of water, milk, crops, crop residues, manure and loads of many other kinds
(8) *Grazing* of animals
(9) Miscellaneous work on *threshing yards*, including building of stacks of unthreshed grain and of straw
(10) *Watchmen* at threshing yards, gardens, etc.
(11) *Fishing and hunting*
(12) *The cutting of casuarina plantations*
(13) *Rock-cutting* at local quarries and *stone-dressing* for well linings, village paving, etc.
(14) *Manufacture of miscellaneous craft goods*: a short list including leather goods (ADs only), ropes, mats, baskets, brooms, sewn leaf plates, incense sticks and a few others
(15) *Other skilled craftsmen*: including blacksmiths, masons, carpenters, etc.
(16) *Production of building components*: thatches, bricks, etc.
(17) *Traders*
(18) *Miscellaneous services for other Harijans*: barbering, etc.

Notes

(1) Certain of these occupations, such as transplanting and harvesting, are more commonly pursued by women.

(2) I cannot judge the extent to which road work was formerly done by unpaid communal labour; nowadays it is undertaken by licensed village contractors who hire men.

(4) Radical repair work might have been undertaken by immigrant Bhovis.

(5) While there are few specialist well diggers, the construction of wide-diametered stone-lined irrigation wells requires many general labourers for earth-digging and carrying – fair proportions of whom are apt to be women.

(6) Firewood and twigs may be freely collected and cut from uncultivated and marginal land, but a licence is required for cutting in Forest Reserves. As for cow dung, it is said to be permissible, though only in the dry season, to collect droppings from any privately owned field. Cattle are often hand-fed.

(7) As many households did not (and do not) own carts; as cart owners are reluctant to hire out; and as there were (and are) no pack animals in the villages (other than the washermen's donkeys) – human porterage, much of it by females, is far more important than in rural Hausaland.

(8) When animals are out grazing they are usually closely supervised, except on large official grazing grounds; old men, women and children are those most apt to conduct single, roped cows and bullocks onto small patches of waste land and the verges of footpaths, tanks, etc.

(9) Much of this work is rewarded with food, on the spot, and with grain when the threshing is complete.

(10) In the Anekal villages there is no fishing, except in tanks on official licences granted to very few men.

(12) Wood-cutting must have provided much less employment in 1900 than today.

(13) In (say) 1900 most quarry workers and stone dressers may have been Bhovis and Muslims, as at Mahantalingapura today.

(14) The few types of goods listed are those which are not necessarily made by members of skilled artisan castes – see notes on Table VII(2). The cutting of tiny bamboo sticks, for sale to factories making incense sticks, is nowadays a new 'industry' in one village only. Judging from village survey reports[21] in the Karnataka State Archives, village crafts were no more flourishing in (say) 1900 than today.

(15) However, most blacksmiths are members of the (non-Harijan) Viswakarma caste. There is (and was) much work for carpenters, including the making of doors, window frames, etc., wooden ploughs, wooden farming equipment such as seed drills, tool handles, cattle 'yokes', etc. – some of which is done by the Viswakarma.

(16) Now that factory-made tiles roof most houses, thatching provides much less work than formerly. (Thatching materials, such as grass and sugar cane leaves, are of poor quality, so that constant replacement and repair would have been necessary; long straw is lacking.)

(18) However, these services are often rendered free as between friends.

Turning to female occupations, it has to be emphasised that Harijan women, like those of many other castes, undertake much heavy labouring, porterage, etc., and commonly assist men builders, brick-makers, well-diggers, etc. They are actually involved in all the occupations (1) to (10) in the above list. As for the other occupations in the list, the opportunities for Harijan women are much inferior to those for men, though they sometimes

[21] Made in connection with the revision of land revenue assessments, they were published in the official Mysore *Proceedings*.

crack rocks for road-making, occasionally make craft goods for sale and may sell eggs, small livestock and vegetables. Additionally, Harijan women are often part-time house servants.

The general conclusion of this detailed discussion is that, except in localities where there were formerly many Harijan weavers, the Harijans' opportunities of picking up a living for themselves in the interstices of the village economy would have been much the same in 1900 as today. Then, as now, it is likely that most Harijans basically fought their own battles for survival. Struggle, not harmony, was the order of the day, and there must have been many who fell by the roadside.

LAND OWNERSHIP

This whole discussion has been based on the supposition that Harijans, with the exception of the hereditary village *thotis*, owned little land in 1900: as we know, there is no reason to believe that they have lost land, on balance, by sale or mortgage, to richer castes during this century. On the contrary, small-scale land ownership is more common than formerly, especially in some villages. Nowadays, see Table VI(2) above, it may be that about three-quarters of all Harijans own between 2 and 5 acres, about a fifth being landless. This is bad enough, in all conscience, but the likelihood is that in 1900 the only significant Harijan land owners were the *thotis*, at least nine out of ten households being landless.

Contrary to popular belief, which tends to explain landlessness in terms of deprivation or loss, this is not because the Harijans had in some sense been denied access to land – for had this been so, the *thotis* would scarcely have been rewarded with *inamti* land for their services or permitted to acquire additional land for themselves. In Anekal Taluk a free market for land has certainly existed since at least the middle of the last century,[22] and any corporate power possessed by the dominant castes was not of a type which would have prevented their members from selling farmland to

[22] The weakness of the literature on south Indian land selling may be another aspect of delta bias if, as seems likely, transactions in farmland were much more common in densely populated dry areas than in wet areas. As already noted (p. 120), many socio-economic studies fail to mention land-selling at all; and when it is mentioned, naive surprise at its occurrence is often expressed. It is, therefore, worth recording that a Mysore Circular on Revenue Procedure, 1864–5, in the Karnataka State Archives (L.R. 1863, file 2) stated that land was 'freely sold and mortgaged by the ryots in most Talooks' – with and without the permission of the government. Official stamp paper (*chapakadaga*) for use for land sales had been issued in Mysore as early as the 1860s, and I found reference in an unregistered file in the Karnataka State Archives to a *shanbhog* of as many as 11 villages, who before 1866 had sold half of his land. In evidence before the Indian Famine Commission (III, Cd 3086, 1881, p. 417) it was stated that good dry land in Mysore fetched prices averaging about Rs 35 per acre.

members of other castes – as in some regions of south India. The plain fact was that few Harijans would have been able to afford the open market price for dry land of (say) Rs 35 per acre in the 1880s after the great famine, when much land was for sale: and those few men who had the money would usually have lacked the other resources needed.

Relevant historical material relating to land transactions in south-eastern Karnataka being so scanty, it is necessary to range round more widely geographically, even though few clues can be found.[23] Nor is this the accident that Dumont suggests:

> *It so happens* [my italics] that the question of rights over the land, whilst amply discussed in the nineteenth and twentieth centuries, has scarcely ever been related to the caste system.[24]

It was rather, as Hjejle puts it, that:

> The slaves and the untouchables of India did not belong to the group of people about whom full information is available in the records. The British officers hardly ever got in direct contact with them, and one therefore has to handle the information in the official records with considerable care.[25]

Abbé J. A. Dubois, who was regarded by Max Müller as 'a trustworthy authority on the state of [south] India from 1792 to 1823',[26] wrote as follows about the 'Pariahs':

> In a few districts they are allowed to cultivate the soil on their own account, but in such cases they are almost always the poorest of their class. Pariahs who hire themselves out as labourers earn, at any rate, enough to live on. . . . But those who are their own masters, and cultivate land for themselves, are so indolent and careless that their harvests, even in the most favourable seasons, are only sufficient to feed them for half the year.[27]

Ignoring the Abbé's prejudiced references to indolence and carelessness (for might he not equally well have cast doubt on the Pariahs' ability to apply sufficient manure to their fields?), is this not evidence that the Harijans were apt to be too poor to farm effectively, labouring being a superior alternative?

Even Buchanan is weak on sociological aspects of land tenure, whilst providing detail of unsurpassed richness on agricultural economics and techniques. Official ethnographic surveys were also feeble:

[23] But see Kessinger's statement that in a village in the Punjab land had been sold since at least 1849. Kessinger, 1974, p. 131.

[24] Dumont, 1970, p. 156. [25] Hjejle, 1967, p. 74.

[26] From p. vii of Müller's introduction to *Hindu Manners, Customs and Ceremonies* by the Abbé J. A. Dubois, 1906.

[27] *Ibid.*, p. 50.

> Some Madigas [now ADs] have taken to agriculture. They hold lands either in their own right or cultivate others' lands on *Vara* or other tenure. But most of them are either day labourers or hired servants under raiyats on annual contracts.[28]

Since richer farmers were often very dependent on casual labourers it might sometimes have been to their advantage to obstruct Harijans' access to land in order to assure themselves adequate supplies of labour.[29] But, as I have already insisted, this would not have happened in dry grain areas of Mysore, where there had been a free market in land for so long.[30] Unfortunately the official sources on land-selling do not distinguish wet and dry land. But as much wet land (and no dry land) was let out directly by the Mysore government on *batayi*[31] tenure, which persisted for much longer during the nineteenth century than official sources were ready to admit, it is possible that a high proportion of selling involved dry land, for *batayi* land was inalienable.

So there is, I am sure, no escape from the conclusion that in Anekal Taluk Harijans were as much entitled to acquire farmland, which was freely bought and sold, as members of any other caste, but that, with the possible exception of richer *thotis*, they were almost always too poor to do so.

THE *THOTIS*

Finally, I must add a note on those indispensable hereditary village officers, the *thotis*,[32] whose significance has been so strangely neglected in the literature. I suggest that it was because these men were partly rewarded for their services by a share of the grain at the threshing yard,[33] that it is

[28] *The Ethnographical Surveys of Mysore* Vol. XVII, *Madiga Caste*, 1909, p. 23.

[29] The anthropologist J. H. Hutton in his introduction to the 1931 Census of India mentioned that the Kallars of Ramnad (Madras) had propounded eleven prohibitions against depressed castes in 1931, among them the following: 'They must sell away their own lands to Mirasdars of the village at very cheap rates, and if they don't do so, no water will be allowed to them to irrigate their lands. Even if something is grown by the help of rain-water, the crops should be robbed away, when they are ripe for harvest.' Hutton added that it was not suggested that these injunctions would be taken very seriously by anyone other than the Kallars themselves. *Census of India, 1931*, Vol. I, p. 485.

[30] In reference to the period 1811–31, Rice, whose reliability I cannot assess, stated that there were 'ryots' who had held their lands by long descent from generation to generation, who were in the habit of transferring it to others, by sale or mortgage, etc. *Mysore Gazetteer*, 1897, Vol. I, p. 618.

[31] Under this tenurial system, which probably applied to irrigated land only, the government was entitled to a half share of the crop.

[32] See Appendix XV(1).

[33] Buchanan provides a detailed description of the grain allocation system, specifying the shares received by the *thotis*, along with other village functionaries and artisans. Buchanan, 1807, Vol. I, p. 389.

12 A 'village servant' (*thoti*) by an irrigation tank

sometimes vaguely presumed that Harijans in general were necessarily entitled to such maintenance.[34] But in localities, such as Anekal Taluk, where the Holeyas (now AKs) were commonly the largest caste in a village, only a small proportion of Holeya households belonged to the *thoti* lineages, members of other Holeya households having no chance of benefiting from the perquisites of office.

The *thotis* nowadays tend to be better off than other members of their caste partly because of the *inamti* land that was officially granted to them, which they still usually retain.[35] It is a matter of great political significance that, whereas in Sri Lanka an 'influential and prosperous local person' was the official responsible for controlling and allocating water from irrigation tanks,[36] in Karnataka such functions fell (and still fall) on the humble *thoti* – then often known as *nirganti*. The members of the 1950 Committee for the Revision of the Land Revenue were, therefore, quite wrong in concluding that:

> the abolition of posts of thotis would free these village servants, who are

[34] Thus it is quite common in historical sources to find *thoti* (or *toti*) treated as though it were a caste name.

[35] The original grant was divisible on inheritance between sons, and constantly diminished in size.

[36] Farmer (ed.), 1977, p. 351.

mostly Harijans, from the virtual feudal bondage in which they are now and would facilitate Harijan uplift.[37]

APPENDIX XV(1)

The village thotis

Although the principle of abolishing hereditary village officers in Mysore had been officially agreed as long ago as 1935, it was not until 1961 that the Mysore Village Offices Abolition Act was passed – it related to the *patel* (headman), the *shanbhog* (accountant) and to those dubbed 'inferior village officers'. In due course the superior officers lost their positions, the appointed Panchayat Secretary replacing the *shanbhog* and the elected Panchayat Chairman partially filling the gap left by the departing headmen. But the 'inferior village officers', usually known as *thotis* in south-eastern Karnataka, quietly continued to perform their functions.

Among the many functions of these Harijan officials, who are usually derogatorily termed 'village servants' in the literature, were: regulators of the irrigation water, watchmen of growing crops, general assistants to higher officers in connection with revenue collection, etc., festival functionaries, town criers, cattle scavengers, grave-diggers, messengers and assistants to strangers – like myself. In the Anekal villages a distinction was made between the 'village' and the 'field' *thotis* – the latter being rewarded with paddy (as he was concerned with the regulation of irrigation water) the former with *ragi*. Like the higher officers, the *thotis* could retain their *inamti* land indefinitely under the Abolition Act. It is mainly owing to these land grants that, as we have seen, the *thotis* tend to enjoy slightly higher living standards than other members of the AK caste.

In the Anekal villages the *thotis* belong to certain AK lines only; if a *thoti* has no son, his daughter's son may succeed; if the line dies out, an outsider may be invited to take up the post. Individuals hold office for a year in rotation, the system being agreed among themselves. Field *thotis*, who often carry a long staff, have various special perks, such as the right to cut grass for fodder from the bunds of irrigation tanks. Formerly the *thotis* were entitled to receive considerable quantities of grain from each cultivating household; whether these obligations were more honoured in the breach than in the observance one cannot say, but it is certain that the amounts given are now much reduced and are regarded as 'voluntary'.

Although similar villager officers who are nearly always Harijans, exist in many Indian regions, having many different titles, the literature seems to be scanty. But see Moffatt[38] on the Vettiyans in a village in southern Tamil Nadu, and Mencher[39] who states that certain of these officers are now salaried. See, also, Wade[40] on salaried 'common irrigators' in a canal-irrigated district of Andhra Pradesh.

[37] *Report* of the Committee in Karnataka State Archives, pp. 193–4.

[38] Moffatt, 1979, p. 193. [39] Mencher, 1974, p. 473.

[40] 'The Social Response to Irrigation: an Indian case study' by R. Wade. *The Journal of Development Studies*, Oct. 1979, p. 7.

CHAPTER XVI

The Lack of an Agrarian Hierarchy in Pre-colonial West Africa

This chapter is concerned with a grand inter-continental contrast, namely the general lack of an agrarian hierarchy in pre-colonial Anglophone West Africa,[1] such as is rightly taken for granted in south India in (say) 1900. Following Béteille, I define the mutual relationship between 'landlords, owner-cultivators, tenants, sharecroppers and agricultural labourers' as constituting 'the heart of what may be described as the agrarian hierarchy'.[2] At the same time I agree with Béteille that these categories derive from a conceptual framework which is not very suited to dry grain cultivation; and that in the hands of statisticians they tend to create 'a strait jacket which grossly distorts the realities of social life in rural India'.[3]

The agrarian hierarchy in south-eastern Mysore in 1900 was not elaborate. Most 'landlordism' involved the hereditary estate-holders, the *jodidars* – in other words, there were few ordinary village cultivators who let out land on any scale. Then, there seems to have been hardly any share-cropping proper, a system which must be distinguished from straightforward renting since it involves the landlord in providing certain inputs, such as plough animals or seeds, in addition to farmland.[4] Bonded labourers, other than those employed by the *jodidars* were, as we know, rare. But daily-paid labourers, both male and female, abounded.

The idea that landlordism was absent from pre-colonial Africa was recently discussed by J. R. Goody[5] who asserted that African land tenure was unlike that which obtained in much of Eurasia generally, 'as it had to do with the means of production rather than with productive relations:

Basically Africa is a land of extensive agriculture.[6] The population is small,

[1] Exclusive of the Sahel, a zone which borders the Sahara desert – and which is largely Francophone.

[2] *Studies in Agrarian Social Structure* by A. Béteille, 1974, p. 32. [3] *Ibid.*, p. 46.

[4] In Karnataka the question of whether or not the rent consists of a portion of the crop or of cash is often of little significance. Share-cropping is not a distinct category of relationship between landowner and tenant unless it is conventionally defined as I have indicated.

[5] *Technology, Tradition and the State in Africa*, 1971.

[6] In a footnote this statement is almost contradicted by qualifications.

> the land is plentiful and the soils are relatively poor. Moreover, one fundamental invention that spread throughout the Eurasian continent never reached Africa south of the Sahara, with the exception of Ethiopia . . . I am referring to the Bronze Age invention, the plough.[7]

In addition, the absence of the wheel in pre-colonial Africa 'limited the possibilities of water control'[8] for agriculture and meant that animal power was not used for any form of traction. So there was 'nothing equivalent to estates in land of the European kind'.[9]

I first consider the plough and Goody's belief that it increases 'the area of land a man can cultivate', thus stimulating the move away from 'shifting agriculture' and increasing the value of land.[10] (He also believes, though this is irrelevant to the question of landlordism, that women's agricultural role is far less important in plough than in hoe economies[11] – an idea which is oddly inapplicable to south India where, as we know, women may represent nearly half of the agricultural labour force.)

The difficulty with the concept of *plough* is that it suggests a rather elaborate implement replete with coulter, winged share, ground wrest and mould-board. But the south Indian wooden plough, which did not begin to be very slowly replaced by the iron plough until this century,[12] is (at least in Anekal Taluk) one of the simplest implements ever devised for harnessing to animals – a mere wooden point with one handle, knocked up from a single piece of wood by a village carpenter. There is no evidence that such an implement was 'more efficient' in terms of man-days per acre of dry land, than the immense metal hoe, the *galma*, which has for long[13] been in use in Hausaland for ridging prior to sowing, especially as ploughing always has to be repeated several, if not many, times.[14] Certainly, modern metal ploughs have transformed the agricultural landscape in some, though not all, districts of northern Hausaland during the past few decades.[15] But it

[7] *Ibid.*, p. 25. [8] *Ibid.*, p. 27.

[9] This is modified by: 'save only in some places and under limited conditions', *ibid.*, p. 33.

[10] *Ibid.*, p. 25. [11] See Goody *et al.*, 1973. [12] See p. 77.

[13] Clapperton (1829, p. 221) described the *galma* as having 'a short bent handle, with a large head', for use 'in all the heavy work instead of a spade'. It is 'perforated', being made of metal stripes attached to a strong iron frame – see Hill (1972), Plate 16.

[14] Although the actual number of times depends on many factors including type of crop, nature of land, weather and other exigencies, outside observers are far too apt to 'fix' a standard figure for 'their' localities.

[15] See Hill (1972), pp. 307–9 on the introduction of the metal plough, which is still usually owned by a minority of farmers in any locality. Unfortunately, there is little information on ploughing in *Agricultural Ecology of Savanna: A Study of West Africa* by J. M. Kowal and A. H. Kassam, 1978; this repeats (p. 340) the indestructible myth about the large minimum size of farm-holding that justifies plough ownership, which is based on the false belief that ploughs are seldom hired out – see Hill (1972).

is doubtful if wooden ploughs would have replaced the *galma* in pre-colonial Hausaland, even had the necessary trained cattle been available.

Nor, in the case of pre-colonial Hausaland, can I accept the argument that the use of the plough would have hastened the switch away from shifting cultivation, considering that much of the farmland in the more densely populated localities was (as we know) under permanent cultivation – manured and cultivated every year. As a matter of fact, systems of shifting cultivation were generally rare. Involving the movement of people and their habitations, they should not be confused with the much more common systems of bush fallow, such that sedentary populations allow their farmland to be rested for a term of years long enough to establish the regrowth of secondary vegetation, before it is recultivated.[16] As for the vague idea that the population of pre-colonial Africa was 'small' so that land was 'plentiful', this takes no account of the high population density in some important and populous regions of pre-colonial West Africa, including large parts of Yorubaland and Iboland, as well as of Hausaland.

The thesis I am presenting here is more generalised than Goody's. It is that where differential and transmittable rights over farmland (or certain categories of superior farmland) exist *or* where significant proportions of households are prevented by poverty from actually undertaking cultivation, then agrarian hierarchies are likely to occur, as in south India – but that *neither of these conditions was usually satisfied in pre-colonial West Africa*. As a general rule in pre-colonial West Africa an individual's right to cultivate derived either from his membership of a corporate land-holding lineage (whether matrilineal or patrilineal) or from his position as a resident member of a rural community, whether a nucleated village or a locality of dispersed settlement.

Corporate land-holding descent groups were both a device for *suppressing individual ownership*, by ensuring that any land which a man had appropriated for himself, for instance by clearing forest, would evolve into lineage land, usually on his death if not earlier; and a *social security system* which guaranteed each member of the localised descent group the right to cultivate land for himself on a usufructurary basis. Usufructurary rights might have been so impermanent that land was reallocated each year;[17] but

16 Goody, like many other writers, confuses these two systems – Goody, 1971, p. 30. P. C. Lloyd in *Yoruba Land Law*, 1962, defines shifting cultivation as follows, adding that it is not practised in Yorubaland: 'A system where a large body of people, an entire tribe perhaps, slowly gyrates within its tribal area, individual villages being abandoned every few years and their people founding new ones in unfarmed areas; the land is cultivated for a few seasons and then abandoned without any intention on the part of the cultivators that they should one day return to the same area' (p. 73).

17 An example is given by Lloyd, *ibid.*, p. 73.

even if individuals were never dislodged from their farmland during their lifetime, their sons (or other heirs as the case might be) would have been unlikely to have inherited the land unless perennial crops were grown there. The famous principle, which C. K. Meek asserts has existed all over the world from ancient times, 'that he who clears land establishes rights of a permanent character',[18] should not be thought to imply that such rights were necessarily transmittable or could never be lost owing to failure to recultivate after fallow, when the bush had regenerated sufficiently. Nor, as Lloyd points out,[19] was the lack of permanent rights necessarily a feature of sparse settlement, for it was in densely populated areas that periodic reallocation of land might make particular sense, ensuring that individuals did not hold large areas of uncultivated fallow.

In southern forest country trypanosomiasis prevented (and still prevents) cattle-keeping, so that there was no possibility of manuring the land and planting the same annual crop year after year; permanent transmittable rights were associated with the cultivation of perennial crops. But in pre-colonial times there were few perennial crops, not even kola nuts, which were cultivated in pure stands, so that there were often special rules governing the ownership of economic trees as distinct from the land on which they stood. However, in south-eastern Ghana there had been oil palm *plantations* as early as the middle of last century, and it is no accident that land-selling first developed there;[20] in eastern Nigeria, on the other hand, the pure stands of wild palms were apt to be communally exploited. As for cocoa farming, which started in earnest in both southern Ghana and Nigeria in colonial times, just before 1900, this had the most profound effect on land tenure, soon leading to the creation of permanent, transmittable rights over land.

Turning to the situation where the right to cultivate followed automatically from residence in the 'village community', it is unlikely that permanent transmittable rights over dry farmland ever existed unless the land was manured and cultivated every year. Even though Hausaland was certainly exceptional[21] in having a special category of saleable manured farmland, we still need to ask why this did not lead to the formation of an agrarian hierarchy there? All we can say is that despite the great rise in population density since pre-colonial times, and the increased proportions

[18] *Land Law and Custom in the Colonies* by C. K. Meek, 1949, p. 23.

[19] Lloyd, 1962, p. 73.

[20] As early as about 1861 the Krobo, of south-eastern Ghana, organised themselves in 'companies' for the purpose of buying land outside their homeland for cultivating oil palms. See Hill (1963), pp. 72 *et seq.*

[21] Owing both to exceptionally high population densities, and to the close relationship between Hausa cultivators and (manure-providing) Fulani pastoralists – see Appendix I(1).

both of land under permanent cultivation and of landlessness, no tenancy system has yet evolved in Kano Emirate.[22] Although landlessness must have been common in Dorayi in 1900, there were yet no daily-paid farm labourers there at that time. The landless did not stand, any more than the farm slaves, at the bottom of the conventional agrarian hierarchy as earlier defined – they lay outside it. Nor were the large plantation owners appropriately dubbed 'landlords' because they were dependent on slave labour. Differential rights over farmland did not exist there.

As is well known, strong and elaborated agrarian hierarchies in south India were particularly associated with irrigated farmland. But in pre-colonial West Africa community-controlled, permanent irrigation systems, involving channels fed from rivers or irrigation tanks, did not exist. I think that the only permanently irrigated farmland was riparian or estuarial, the actual area of which was severely limited owing to climatic factors;[23] and the extreme inefficiency of the sole water-lifting device, the *shaduf*,[24] meant that its use was only justified for the cultivation of especially valuable crops, such as onions.

Insofar as households managed to irrigate any land, for instance the gardens around their homesteads, this was their own affair and not because they were the fortunate owners of any special category of irrigable community farmland. Scattered throughout the literature, though never collated so far as I know, are minor references to petty, individually owned, irrigation systems, based on networks of tiny leats, which are linked by a main channel fed by well water.[25] Drinking-water wells abounded in many savannah regions of pre-colonial West Africa, and some of them were very deep indeed;[26] presumably it was mainly because the water was inefficiently lifted by humans (mainly women) unassisted by animals, that so little of it was used for crop cultivation.[27]

In pre-colonial West Africa most rice was grown on riverain, estuarial and coastal swampland or flood plains, in the Francophone south-west

[22] See pp. 57–8.

[23] Thus, in the savannah most rivers, other than the great waterways like the Niger and the Sokoto, are dry at all times except immediately after a storm.

[24] This is the familiar Biblical-style device consisting of a pole working on a pivot, with a water container at one end and a weight at the other, which usually requires two men to operate it effectively. (It is not true, as stated by Goody (1971, p. 27), that these devices were found only as far north as the 'Saharan fringe': by 1900 they had already penetrated much further south.) See Fig. II(2), p. 79 above.

[25] See p. 154 above.

[26] Especially in north-eastern Nigeria, where expertly dug wells exceeding 100 ft in depth were common.

[27] An exception being the famous shallot beds at Angola in Eweland in south-eastern Ghana which represent some of the most intensive agriculture in the world – and where agrarian hierarchies did develop. See Hill (1970), Chapter 3.

region (now Senegal, Guinée and Mali) and the Sahel. Very commonly swampland rice was inefficiently cultivated by overworked women, as a secondary crop, and there 'was small attention to transplanting or hydraulic controls until recent decades'.[28] As a general rule in Nigeria and Ghana richer farmers never derived the bulk of their livelihood from scarce wet land, such as the marshland (*fadama*) of Hausaland, so that rich and poor cultivators alike depended mainly on dry crops. Accordingly, there was no agrarian hierarchy based on the ownership of wet land.

I turn now to the second possibility mentioned above: that agrarian hierarchies might have arisen where the condition of 'too poor to farm' was common. Here again the fact that *men had not harnessed animals to work for them* (except as transporters of themselves or their loads) was highly relevant, for it meant that few men were prevented by lack of agrarian capital from establishing themselves as cultivators, as commonly in the Anekal villages today.

Such considerations sufficiently account for the lack of conventional tenancy and share-cropping systems in pre-colonial West Africa and thus for the fact that few cultivators were at the mercy of private landlords. But it is perhaps necessary to touch on a peripheral matter – that of the pledging, or pawning, of farms (like other forms of property) to a creditor, which was an ancient practice in much of the forest zone of Nigeria and Ghana, and which commonly involved plots planted with a mixture of perennial and other crops. As has been widely reported, the property was never supposed to pass permanently to the creditor – 'debt dies, but never rots' was one of many aphorisms – who, himself or his heirs, was obliged to return it to the debtor, or his heirs, when the debt was liquidated. As most pledgors probably retained part of their 'portfolio' of farm-plots, they could devote part of their farming income to debt repayment, so that the principle that pledged farms were never lost was more realistic than might be supposed. Pledging was almost the inverse of conventional tenancy in the way it automatically protected the weak from the rapacity of the strong;[29] for this and other reasons it has but slight relevance to the question of a pre-colonial agrarian hierarchy. (But a very different situation developed with the rapid expansion of cocoa growing in colonial times.)

Finally, I turn to the lack of the lowest level of the agrarian hierarchy in pre-colonial West Africa – the farm labourer. The literature on past, and

[28] *Economic Change in Precolonial Africa: Senegambia in the Era of the Slave Trade* by P. D. Curtin, 1975, p. 29.

[29] It was often very short term, the debtors being rich and poor alike. Usufructural rights only were pledged – and the debt was often automatically liquidated by the usufruct.

present, farm-labouring systems is still very weak, mainly, I think, because such systems have seldom been regarded as an aspect of land tenure, a subject which has given rise to such an unimaginably[30] vast and respectable volume of writings – legal, anthropological, political, administrative, historical, but not so much economic. And the refusal to face the facts has increased recently owing to the false contemporary belief that, as in India, dependence on family labour is necessarily 'more progressive' than other systems.

So economic historians have paid scant attention to the development of farm-labouring systems during this century – or to the circumstances in which they failed to develop. We know from Buchanan that in south India free farm labourers, both men and women, were employed on a daily basis in 1800. Why did such systems not develop in parts of pre-colonial West Africa, especially where currency circulated? Maybe the practice of paying free people for particular services rendered was an ancient one, but yet there was no day-labouring – no hiring of labourers to undertake general agricultural tasks on a time, as distinct from a piece,[31] basis.

I suggest that M. I. Finley's statement that the institution of wage-labour was 'a sophisticated latecomer' in the ancient world has relevance to West Africa:

> Historically speaking, the institution of wage-labour is a sophisticated latecomer. The very idea of wage-labour requires two difficult conceptual steps. First it requires the abstraction of a man's labour from both his person and the product of his work. When one purchases an object from an independent craftsman . . . one has not bought his labour but the object, which he had produced in his own time and under his own conditions of work. But when one hires labour, one purchases an abstraction, labour-power, which the purchaser then uses at a time and under conditions which he, the purchaser, not the 'owner' of the labour-power determines. . . . Second, the wage-labour system requires the establishment of a method of measuring the labour one has purchased, for purposes of payment, commonly by introducing a second abstraction, namely labour-time.'[32]

In the ancient world, as in pre-colonial West Africa, the need to mobilise manpower to supplement family labour forces commonly involved compulsion – 'by force of arms or by force of law and custom'.[33]

[30] Especially unimaginable to Indian historians, who have taken relatively little interest in the actual principles of land tenure and inheritance, as distinct from the legal principles of land revenue (taxation).

[31] An example of piece-work having been the hiring of young men to climb coconut palms to pick the nuts.

[32] *The Ancient Economy* by M. I. Finley, 1973.

[33] *Ibid.*, p. 66.

> Free hired labour was casual and seasonal, its place determined by the limits beyond which it would have been absurd to purchase and maintain a slave force, most obviously to meet the exceptional short-term needs of harvesting in agriculture.[34]

So, on the assumption that it was the *concept* of wage-labour which was lacking, it is not true that 'the use of slave rather than wage-labour was a matter of deliberate choice on the part of African employers'[35] or that 'slaves were preferred because the costs of acquiring and maintaining them were less than the cost of hiring labour'.[36] The system was certainly not 'based on an elementary but broadly accurate, cost-benefit analysis',[37] for cultivators had no means of weighing up their options like that.

As we know, the prime functions of Karnataka land reform were to reduce the size of the largest holdings and to limit the scope of the agrarian hierarchy by prohibiting renting – the main landlords, the *jodidars*, having been expropriated some years earlier. In such circumstances the concept of an agrarian hierarchy has lost its usefulness there, this being one of the main explanations for the convergence of the agrarian systems in the two regions under our dry grain mode. In both regions there are four categories of 'farming household': owner-cultivators who sometimes employ labourers; owner-cultivators who never employ labourers; owner-cultivators who sometimes work as labourers; and landless labourers. For many reasons which have been discussed above, these categories do not form a genuine hierarchy: it is just that 'landless labourers' stand below everybody else.

[34] *Ibid.*, p. 73.
[35] *An Economic History of West Africa* by A. G. Hopkins, 1973, p. 24.
[36] *Ibid.*, p. 25. [37] *Ibid.*, p. 26.

CHAPTER XVII

A Dry Grain Mode: Some Conclusions

In this concluding chapter I lack the space to summarise the many features of our dry grain mode which have been discussed above. So I mainly confine myself to emphasising some of the conclusions which seem to be particularly at variance with 'prevailing general orthodoxy' – by which I mean orthodoxy which tends to appeal to those of all political complexions, for nowadays Right and Left often find themselves in an unholy embrace. I take the conclusions in a somewhat arbitrary order, under a number of headings.

A. THE NATURE AND ORIGINS OF RURAL STAGNATION: THE WITHDRAWAL FROM THE COUNTRYSIDE (CHAPTER XII)

It is my contention that contemporary stagnation in the dry grain zones, which is particularly expressed in terms of low grain yields and lack of agricultural and other forms of diversification, is basically due to a withdrawal from the countryside rather than to urban 'capitalist intrusion' – as is so commonly supposed. Formerly having been the medium, or matrix, within which most economic enterprise flourished, the dry grain countryside has now become a backwater which is increasingly ignored by urban-dwellers – the process of withdrawal, which is very long term, having been hastened by the necessary collapse of the large estates owned by influential outsiders and aristocrats which has resulted from the ending of farm-slavery in Hausaland and the legal dispossession of the *jodidars* in Karnataka.

Partly owing to the weakness of the centralised bureaucracies in relation to the countryside in each of our three research areas, hierarchical marketing structures, with their apices in the cities, which are often supposed to be a characteristic feature of centralised states, have always been lacking there. Long-distance transporters, in the pre-railway and pre-lorry age, largely bypassed markets and, especially in Karnataka, rural traders are nowadays stultified by the inadequacies of markets linking city and countryside, particularly since the withdrawal of the *jodidars* who straddled the gap between the two worlds as estate owners-*cum*-businessmen.

Those who believe that these village communities are stagnant owing to a refusal to shed their 'pre-market practices and modes of thought' are ahistorical: they fail to realise that such shedding occurred before their own thoughts were born – or, more prosaically, before their base dates. (But the lack of any proper urban tradition of designing and producing simple modern technology suitable for impoverished dry grain areas *is* a serious deficiency.)

B. FACTORS ACCOUNTING FOR THE CONTEMPORARY CONVERGENCE OF THE AGRARIAN SYSTEMS

(i) *The end of agrestic servitude* (Chapter XIII)

In both continents agrestic servitude (farm-slavery in Hausaland and bonded labouring in south-eastern Karnataka) has largely given way to daily-paid farm-labouring. In Kano Emirate this replacement is complete for the contemporary agrarian system has entirely forgotten its dependence until the 1920s on farm-slavery, which makes its resemblance to the Anekal system the less surprising. In an impoverished dry grain area like south-eastern Karnataka the change has been far less significant for there were rather few rich men, other than the erstwhile *jodidars*, whose holdings had been large enough to enable them to maintain full-time labourers throughout the year. *The profound poverty of the masses*, rather than the diminutive incidence of adult bonded labouring *was, and is, the real problem*: to emphasise the latter rather than the former is to limit one's outlook by lingering on unimportant institutional matters rather than on huge human issues. (Although bonded labouring has been technically illegal since 1975, there has been a recent rapid increase in the number of Harijan fathers who have raised loans from employers on condition that their sons work as full-time labourers for two or three years, after which they are automatically released.)

(ii) *The inevitable dissolution of the large estates* (Chapter XIV)

In Kano and Katsina Emirates the ending of farm-slavery resulted in the collapse of all the large estates, many of which were owned by non-villagers, except for a very small number owned by emirs, their close kinsmen and a few high officials; this was because the system of daily-paid farm-labouring, which replaced farm-slavery, had serious drawbacks which were intolerable to large estate owners – and because the slaves had been partly responsible for maintaining themselves.

In Karnataka, where the large, mainly hereditary, estate-holders (*jodidars*) were dispossessed, with compensation, following an Act of 1955, there had been much official dissatisfaction over the conditions and prospects of their tenants for many decades – and many of the estate-holders themselves had become disheartened by the increasing socio-economic stagnation in the dry zones.

As for ordinary private farmers hardly any of them nowadays would care to operate on a scale exceeding some 40 acres (even if they could), owing to the practical difficulties of supervising the work of numerous daily-paid labourers.

(iii) *The lack of an agrarian hierarchy in pre-colonial West Africa* (Chapter XVI)

It is my contention that: where there were differential and transmittable individual rights over farmland, or certain categories of superior farmland; or where significant proportions of households were prevented by poverty from actually undertaking cultivation, although there was surplus land; or where there were elaborated irrigation systems – that then agrarian hierarchies were likely to occur. Such hierarchies therefore existed in south India but not, in general, in pre-colonial West Africa, so that Hausaland resembled most other West African regions in lacking landlords, tenants, share-croppers and daily-paid farm labourers in pre-colonial times – none of these categories, with the exception of day labourers, having meanwhile developed there.

Accordingly, one of the main factors accounting for the contemporary convergence of hitherto divergent agrarian systems in the two continents is the weakening of the agrarian hierarchy in south-eastern Karnataka, which has mainly resulted from the ousting of the *jodidars* and the reduction in the size of the largest holdings of village farmers as a result of rapid population growth, so that the landlord class has been virtually eliminated. (Land reform legislation – see Appendix II(2) – which was effectively concerned with suppressing the agrarian hierarchy, came too late to have any significant effect, except that some tenants were ousted by their landlords in anticipation of the Act.)

C. INDIVIDUAL VILLAGERS HAVE NO SPECIAL RIGHTS OVER THEIR 'VILLAGE LAND' (CHAPTER III)

In both continents there is a lack of correspondence between the village considered as a residential unit and the 'village land'. As there are no restrictions on the sale of the land pertaining to any village to outsiders, it follows that there is a strong tendency for a considerable proportion of 'village land' to be owned by non-residents, most of them from nearby villages. In diagrammatic terms, nucleated villages should be seen as residential clusters of farmers who own decreasing proportions of the farmland in each successive concentric ring as one moves over the boundary away from the village. (This is one reason – a very strong one – why *villages are not isolates but parts of a general matrix, the countryside*; another is the pronounced tendency for many women, in both continents, to remove some distance away from their natal community on marriage, thus creating wide kinship networks over broad tracts of countryside.)

D. THE NATURE OF URBAN EXPLOITATION (CHAPTER XI)

(i) *Grain 'exports' are not necessarily 'surpluses'*

The paradox of poverty is such that the poorest people are often obliged to act in a way which is adverse to their own medium or longer term interests – thus, the poorest cultivators are those who sell grain immediately after harvest (or after threshing in Karnataka) not because it is surplus to their requirements but because they have urgent debts and consumption needs. From the angle of the rural community as a whole, 'grain exporting' to the outside world is necessary in order to finance the 'import' of a great range of essential goods, notably cloth, for there are few other important types of export. For both these reasons, *grain sales should not be equated with grain surpluses* – as they invariably are. Indeed, insofar as supplies of grain consumed in the cities are drawn from very densely populated localities, such as our research areas, they resemble a compulsory levy on hungry communities which cannot afford to 'import' sufficient replacement supplies at a higher average seasonal price than they have themselves received.

(ii) *The adverse terms of trade between urban and rural areas*

Owing to inflation the terms of trade between cities and countryside, which have been bad for a long time, are constantly worsening, daily-paid agricultural labourers being the chief rural victims of this malign spiral, involving the low price of basic grains. (The poorest households in the rural third world are among those worst affected by the worldwide inflation.)

(iii) *The official endeavour to suppress village-generated credit*

Because economic life is so especially seasonal under our dry grain mode, with its prolonged non-farming season, there is a pronounced need for short and medium term credit, of a kind which would not normally be granted by banks or other official agencies, but which has to be rurally-generated. Urban exploitation consists in the endeavour to suppress village-generated credit (under the false pretence that it is usurous in Hausaland), which is all that is anyway available to poorer people, while providing no one, not even the rich, with anything like sufficient non-village credit for their needs. It makes no more sense to attempt to suppress rural credit-granting than rural buying and selling; each is essential to the economic health of the rural community – there being, in any case, a continuum running between the selling, the lending and the giving-out-free of grain by particular individuals. Of course poorer people commonly borrow on harsher terms than the rich because the risk is greater, their security is weak or non-existent, their needs are urgent and their loans small; this is an inescapable fact of life which has no necessary overtones in terms of the morals of the parties involved. (It is no accident that professional money lenders are uninterested in setting themselves up in impoverished dry grain zones.)

E. THE CONSEQUENCES OF HIGH AND INCREASING POPULATION DENSITY

(i) *Under-employment* (Chapter V)

The volume of employment offered by richer farmers, whose holdings are constantly diminishing in size, is quite insufficient to meet the demand for paid agricultural work. The labour market is in a chronic state of disequilibrium, the miserably low wage rates bearing no relationship either to minimum needs or to the productivity of labour. Since the basic problem is under-employment, minimum wage legislation, were it ever enforceable, would only exacerbate the situation. Hardly any agricultural work, other than manure collection and preparation, is undertaken in the long dry season in Hausaland, which lasts for more than half the year, and many households with empty granaries are then dependent on ill-paid non-farming occupations which are hard to find; although there are two monsoons in Karnataka, the non-farming season is nearly as long there as in Hausaland since little land bears two successive crops. (The daily-paid farm-labouring systems in the two continents are remarkably similar – other systems of labour employment being relatively unimportant.)

(ii) *The stultification of the land market* (Chapter VI)

Contrary to general belief, there was an active market in farmland in the more densely populated localities in both continents a century, or more, ago. For many decades the richest households in such areas were able to buy land to compensate, at least in part, for the reduction in holding size resulting from division on inheritance – though the property of rich polygynous Hausa farmers, with many sons, was peculiarly apt to be dissipated on death. Nowadays, however, all this has changed, for the recent rise in land prices has made everyone, including the poorest landowners, reluctant to sell their land. On the one hand, our statistics show the uneven distribution of farmland between households to be the fundamental basis of economic inequality; on the other hand, the pattern of land distribution has become more inflexible than at any time within living memory – though some of the poorest landowners fail to redeem their mortgaged land.

(iii) *Despite low yields, dry land is increasingly coveted* (Chapter VI)

The price of dry land being so remarkable high in relation to the low yield, and value, of basic grains, which take up a high proportion of the total area, why should it be increasingly coveted? One reply to this question is that in both continents high status is achieved by no one who disdains or neglects farming as a way of life. And since it is the ambition of every significant land owner, however multifarious his non-farming activities, to retire into farming in due course, land (which is becoming increasingly scarce) is as necessary as sons to assure a man's comfort and security in his later years. (While for this and other reasons 'landlessness' is a condition of 'economic disenfranchisement', it is mistaken to suppose that impoverished men necessarily attach particular significance to owning small holdings – so that a concept of 'near landlessness' (say 2 acres or less) is useful in some contexts.)

Among the numerous other reasons why dry land is coveted are: first, that its very existence provides many men with the basis for hoping that, sooner or later, their yields might be increased by agricultural intensification – involving, for instance, new crops or varieties, chemical fertilisers, the construction of wells, or merely the cultivation of transplanted *ragi*, with its higher yield; second, that land is far and away the best form of security for raising loans from banks and other official agencies – and there are none who are so rich as to disdain the opportunity of borrowing; third, that land is a reliable store of capital the value of which is bound to increase over the years – even if a man has no intention of selling the family heirloom, it is good to know that it is there; and fourth, that the chances of ultimately enjoying the prestige associated with being the head of a joint household are much increased by ownership of a fair acreage.

(iv) *The increased need for agricultural and non-agricultural diversification and intensification* (Chapter VII)

Partly because it is so well known that rural craft goods, notably textiles, have been superseded by urban manufactures, the extent of the dependence of rural communities on arable farming is apt to be greatly exaggerated. On the one hand, *farming does come first in the sense that there is no other vocation whose neglect automatically leads to loss of status*; on the other hand, there are many households, from the richest to the poorest, which are more dependent economically on their non-farming occupations than on cultivation and/or labouring – and their number is growing as land scarcity increases.

It is a mistake to regard the two forms of activity as in any sense alternatives: each promotes the other and there is no rule as to which has priority when it comes to investing the profits – if any. Nor, considering the low yield of basic grains and the low wages of farm labourers, should one necessarily regard most non-farming occupations as poorly remunerated – thus, the firewood-cutters of Dorayi were very much better off than farm labourers. On the whole, the trouble with these occupations is that they provide insufficient work: many more young men would be firewood cutters in Dorayi if there were more firewood to cut. So, again, we should regard 'under-employment' as the great scourge, which is one reason why the *revivification of the countryside* requires the establishment of proper rural industries which would provide regular employment, in factories or brickworks for example. With the exception of sericulture, which is an important home industry in many rural localities in south-eastern Karnataka (but not, as it happens, in the Anekal villages), the types of enterprise which particularly demand official encouragement in rural south India should not be dubbed 'cottage industries' – as they invariably are there.

Owing to the low yield of basic grains, agricultural diversification and intensification must be the aim of all ambitious farmers – though this is subject to the qualification that richer farmers, in particular, have inherited a kind of moral obligation, which some may find anachronistic, to produce considerable quantities of basic grains. *For over a century* economic conditions in our research areas have been such that cash has circulated as a 'village currency'; crops, of all types, have been saleable; and land, at least of certain categories, has freely entered the market. In such circumstances the age of 'cash crop revolutions' has long since passed – if it ever occurred. But this is not say that new crops, such as the casuarina tree in Karnataka, may not be of great economic importance to individuals and communities alike.

F. THE SUPERIOR CAPACITY OF RICHER HOUSEHOLDS TO DIVERSIFY AND INTENSIFY THEIR ECONOMIC ACTIVITIES (CHAPTERS VII AND VIII)

That farming and non-farming activities nourish each other is clearly indicated by the very close association between scale of farming and type of occupation – all the really lucrative occupations being followed by the largest farmers. In rural Hausaland short to medium distance trading in farm produce (grain, locust beans, groundnuts, etc.) is one of the most rewarding occupations followed by richer farmers who alone can afford to invest in stocks which they, or the growers whom they finance, will store for a seasonal price rise. (In Dorayi, where this particular occupation was followed by only about 10 of the 717 married men there, there were hardly any other traders, numerous though they were, who were wholly unrestricted by local limitations of demand and supply. As for the Dorayi craftsmen, only the 13 blacksmiths enjoyed unlimited demand for their wares.)

In Hausaland every able-bodied man aspires to follow at least one 'occupation'. The multiplicity of ill-paid, part-time occupations ensures that few impoverished men become a burden on the community – but virtually landless men have long resembled a rural proletariat the members of which, like their counterparts in the cities, waste much time searching the interstices of the economy for odd jobs. The range of opportunities open to impoverished men in the Anekal villages is narrower than in Hausaland; but the care and maintenance of cattle involves much work, especially as they are often hand-fed. (*Cattle are strictly economic assets; there are no ageing cows in the Anekal villages, all of them being sold before they become too decrepit for work or breeding.*)

The prevailing belief in an inverse relationship between the scale of household farming and crop yield (per acre) is very strong in relation to India. In stating my general objections to this belief, *in relation to this dry grain mode only*, I have paid little attention to the likelihood that richer farmers have superior opportunities of diversifying their dry farming, since my argument stands up on its own without this additional prop. I would replace the 'inverse relationship law' with one which states that *poorer farmers necessarily receive a lower reward per unit of effort than richer men* – so much so that some of them abandon all attempts at cultivation, prefering to rent out their land. (The main ideology behind the prevailing orthodoxy appears to be the beliefs that poverty induces people to cultivate with more enthusiasm and meticulousness and that family labour is necessarily superior to hired labour. It ignores such a fact as that the work of daily labourers is always closely supervised.) Under our dry grain mode there are so few farmers who own so much land that they have passed the point of decreasing returns, that the institution of landlordism (which formerly existed in Karnataka but not in Hausaland) has now virtually collapsed in its old form. Most of the new-style 'landlords' are widows and other small land-holders, who are better remunerated by rents than they would be by their own inefficient cultivation.

G. LAND OWNERSHIP BY HARIJANS (CHAPTERS VI AND XV)

Until recently very few Harijans, other than *thotis*, were landowners. So, contrary to fairly popular (though not universal) belief, there is no reason to believe that the main Harijan castes lost any significant amount of land to the richer castes during the period when land-selling was common, for they had hardly any to lose. I would regard the Harijans of south-eastern Karnataka as an *old-style* rural proletariat – my findings being at variance with those expressed by Leach in the citation on p. 246 above. During the past century they enjoyed little paternalistic support from rich men, such as is implied by the term *jajmani*, if only because they were far too numerous; jobs as full-time labourers also being scarce, most men and women were obliged to pick up a living as best they might, by undertaking odd jobs for payment in cash or grain. It follows that the Harijans have long closely resembled the impoverished free men of Hausaland.

H. THE RURAL COMMUNITIES ARE INNATELY INEGALITARIAN

Rural economic inequality does not derive from the outside world though it is often enhanced by it.

J. POVERTY AS A CONDITION OF INDIVIDUAL IMPASSE

(i) *A poverty threshold* (Chapter IX)

Although, on the one hand, the proportion of rich men shows a strong tendency to increase with the age of the household head, on the other hand the incidence of severe poverty shows little age variation – in other words, a certain threshold of poverty must be overcome by a householder in his middle years, when he has working sons, if he is to make any progress in life and not be dragged down by increasing decrepitude.

(ii) *Poverty is the natural condition of younger household heads* (Chapter IX)

With the notable exception of members of the rich Reddy caste in the Anekal villages, it is a general rule that younger household heads are impoverished. In Hausaland, in particular, many younger householders who had had rich fathers do not prosper – especially if their fathers had died before meeting their marriage expenses.

(iii) *Penurious men cannot prosper failing direct contract with the outside world* (Chapter IX)

The numerous victims of extreme indigenous poverty under our dry grain mode can seldom hope to extricate themselves from their plight without developing some direct relationship with the outside world (rural or urban), other than that which involves the mere 'export' of basic grains. (In some Anekal villages an official endeavour had been made to allot 2 acres of marginal land to some landless men: this was a mere sop.)

(iv) *But outward migration is no automatic panacea* (Chapter X)

The poorest people are those who are most strongly impeded from migrating by lack of finance; they are never able to afford to migrate to less densely populated areas for farming – though, like many Harijan migrants, they may join relatives there – and few of them venture to seek their fortune in cities. (Our research areas are typical of many third world regions in that the great proportion of the population continues to live in the countryside; the very rapid expansion of city populations, is therefore, entirely compatible with very low rates of outward migration to cities from villages – see p. 197, n. 8 above.)

K. THE RELATIONSHIP BETWEEN FATHERS AND SONS (CHAPTERS IV AND IX)

Under our dry grain mode, population density has increased to the point that it is often very difficult for fathers to allot land to their married sons, who are usually unable to buy it for themselves owing to the sluggishness of the land market and high prices. Married sons therefore find it increasingly difficult to establish themselves as farmers on their own account, which may very well mean that the 'incidence of joint households' is not decreasing, as is commonly supposed – it may even be increasing. Though fathers often encourage some of their sons to separate, few fathers, in either region are abandoned by all their sons and few richer householders enter the conventional phase of economic decline in their later years. Fathers are faced with the insoluble problem of maintaining family property intact while giving the younger generation of men a fair deal. Most sons show a considerable reluctance to solve the problem by migrating and, especially in Hausaland, seek to persuade their fathers to retire early from farming, handing over responsibility to them.

Although, in principle, equal division of property among sons on the father's death is the rule, in practice division is necessarily rough and ready in both continents, this being one of several reasons for the notable degree of 'inequality of (fatherless) brothers'. Although the position will soon be reached where 'rich forebears' (whether alive or dead) are a necessary condition for economic success, they are certainly not a sufficient condition. Thus, in Dorayi only 8 out of 27 sons of rich retired fathers were themselves rich.

I conclude by discussing a general matter – namely *the confusion between crisis and stagnation*. The condition of economic *stagnation* under our dry grain mode often lies beyond that commonly denoted *crisis*, and is more permanent. I illustrate this assertion with citations from the influential bimonthly *Rain*.[1]

In part of an article entitled 'Societies in Acute Crisis',[2] Frances D'Souza, referred to her recent observations of certain valley communities in north Pakistan which had previously been wheat exporters. In the past 15 years or so there had been unprecedented population growth and reduced migration. Increased pressure on resources had resulted in 'severe economic stratification'[3] such that within any of the valleys there were but few

[1] Otherwise *Royal Anthropological News*.

[2] *Rain*, 43, April 1981, pp. 7–13. The article reported the findings of a recent conference with the same title, D'Souza being Director of the International Disaster Institute.

[3] This citation, and those that follow, are all on *ibid*., p. 9.

wealthy families who produced considerable food surpluses. However, most people managed 'to provide sufficient food for their own families and to market a small surplus'. But there was also a 'significant section' of each valley which lived on 'the threshold of acute crisis':

> that is small families who have only small, poorly-located and ill-drained fields and cannot produce a surplus to market or accumulate even the small amount of capital necessary to irrigate virgin land should it be available.

The agrarian systems of these valley communities do not conform to our dry grain mode: most people managed to produce sufficient food for household consumption, *whereas in northern Hausaland and the Anekal villages this applies only to a minority of households.*[4] Households described by D'Souza as 'in crisis' are not landless – their difficulty is that they cannot produce a 'marketing surplus'. Under our dry grain mode, *the majority of households are either virtually landless or are obliged to sell grain which they badly need to consume themselves* – they are beyond the point of crisis as defined by D'Souza.

Under our dry grain mode increasing population pressure does *not* result in increased concentration of resources in the hands of a few rich households as in this instance: on the contrary, the richest farmers constantly operate on a decreasing scale.[5] Certainly, the population of effectively landless people (say 2 acres or less) constantly increases; but most of these households find themselves stagnating in a familiar, though horrible manner – not facing a crisis with which they cannot cope. *The ability of impoverished third world households to withstand extreme hardship without panicking* is not appreciated by the world outside.

POSTSCRIPT

Many people have urged me to provide a list of other regions to which this tropical dry grain mode might be expected to apply, but owing to lack of published information I cannot do this. I would only say that as population densities increase, and as more and more land is manured and kept under permanent cultivation with no fallow, there will soon be many tens of millions[6] of people in widely flung world

[4] See, for example, the first pages of Chapter VII above.
[5] See, for example, the first pages of Chapter VI above.
[6] Haswell, 1975, pp. 151–2, cites Cummings (1974) on the unirrigated semi-arid tropics of the world which are inhabited by some 400 million people, whose staple diet is commonly 'sorghums and millets, supplemented by limited amounts of pulses and other high protein foods'. He insists that there have been 'no significant breakthroughs in production techniques in those regions'.

regions, who will find themselves enduring agrarian conditions similar to those outlined here, unless the acreages under non-grain crops and/or irrigation systems are greatly extended.

My chief difficulty is uncertainty as to the list of basic grains to which this mode applies – in this book I have tentatively defined it as involving millets and sorghum only. I do not know whether there are any tropical regions which are as dependent on maize,[7] as their basic crop, as south-eastern Karnataka is on *ragi* – if so, their agrarian systems are unlikely to conform to our dry grain mode, since maize is one of the highest yielding of all grain crops.[8] As for wheat, this is often considered to be a temperate crop, although it is widely grown in north India.[9]

I now append a few notes on the geographical distribution of millets and sorghum. Bulrush millet (*Pennisetum typhoides*) is very widely grown in the West African savannah and is said to be a useful cereal (known as *bajra*) in the drier areas of India which are unsuited for finger millet. In West Africa it is often interplanted with sorghum.

On the distribution of finger millet (*Eleusine coracana*) see Appendix VII(1).

Sorghum, often known as guinea corn in West Africa, is the fourth cereal in the world after wheat, rice and maize. It is the chief crop of 'the plains of India'[10] – India being the second largest world producer after China. Like bulrush millet, it has a very wide distribution in savannah West Africa.[11]

It is impossible to estimate the extent to which, in different regions of the world, millets and sorghum are grown year after year on the same manured plots, without any fallowing, as under our dry grain mode. As this practice is probably usual in the dry zones of south India and is becoming increasingly common in the more densely populated regions of the West African savannah, the population involved in these two regions alone must surely run into several tens of millions.

Finally, it is worth stressing that our dry grain mode does not apply to densely populated dry grain communities, such as the Tallensi of northern Ghana, who do not sell their land.[12]

[7] In southern West Africa, where maize is widely grown, it is usually one of several crops, including root crops, in any area.

[8] See Purseglove, 1972, p. 329.

[9] Purseglove, *ibid.*, p. 293, comments that the bulk of Indian wheat is grown outside the tropics.

[10] *Ibid.*, p. 270.

[11] See Morgan and Pugh, 1969, pp. 107–9.

[12] See 'The Economic Basis of Tallensi Social History in the Early Twentieth Century' by K. Hart, 1978, p. 211, where it is stated that commercial land transfers are still almost non-existent in this society which was so well studied by Fortes in the 1930s. (Hart's fascinating analysis of a lineage-organised society, such that a half of all males are usually absent in urban areas at any time, provides an extraordinary contrast to our dry grain mode.)

References

Indian official Publications

(Nearly all the references to official material in this book relate to India to which this list is confined; for references to Nigerian archival material see Hill (1977).)

Census of India, 1891. Vol. XXV, Part I

Census of India, 1901. Vol. XXIV

Census of India, 1931. Vol. I

Census of India, 1961. Village Survey Monographs. Various dates

Census of India, 1971. Mysore. *District Census Handbook, Bangalore*, Parts X-A and X-B.

Ethnographical Survey of Mysore. See Nanjundayya, H. V.

Indian Famine Commission. Vol. III. Cd 3086, HMSO, London, 1881

Karnataka Legislation:

Mysore (Personal and Miscellaneous) Inams Abolition Act, 1955

Karnataka Village Panchayats and Local Boards Act, 1959

Mysore Village Offices Abolition Act, 1961

Karnataka Land Reforms Act 1961 (as amended)

Karnataka Prevention of Fragmentation and Consolidation of Holdings Act, 1966

Mysore Agricultural Debtors Relief Act, 1966

Karnataka Bonded Labour System (Abolition) Ordinance, 1975

Karnataka State Archives:

Mysore Circular on Revenue Procedure, 1864–5 (L.R. 1863, file 2)

Proceedings of the Chief Commissioner (later Government) of Mysore. Numerous dates

Report of the Operations of the Inam Commission from the Commencement. By J. P. Grant, 1901

Report of the Inam Commission Mysore, 1919–20

Report on the Administration of the Village Panchayats for 1928–29

Committee for the Revision of the Land Revenue System in Mysore. 1950.

Mysore Gazetteers. See Rice (1897) and Rao (1929)

Mysore Revenue Manual. Government Printer, Bangalore, 1938

Nanjundayya, H. V. *The Ethnographical Survey of Mysore*. Vol. XVII. *Madiga Caste*. Government Press, Bangalore, 1909

Nicholson, F. A. *Report regarding the possibility of introducing Land Banks into the Madras Presidency*. Vol. I. Government Press, Madras, 1895. Reprinted 1960

Proceedings of the Agricultural Conference. Government Printer, Calcutta, 1894

Rao, C. Hayavadana. *Mysore Gazetteer*. Vols. I to V. Government Press, Bangalore, 1929

'Report of the Committee for examining the existing conditions and prospects of tenants in Inam and Jodi Villagers'. *The Mysore Gazette*, 19 Oct. 1933

Report on the 4th Census of Livestock and Agricultural Implements. Government of India Press, 1936

Report of the Karnataka Backward Classes Commission (Havanur Report). Vol. II: *Population and Education Particulars*. Government of Karnataka, Bangalore, 1975

Report of India's Food Crisis and Steps to Meet It. Ministry of Food and Agriculture, Delhi, 1959

Rice, B. L. *Mysore: A Gazetteer compiled for Government*. Vols. I and II. London, 1897

Royal Commission on Agriculture in India. Vol. II: *Evidence taken in the Bombay Presidency*; Vol. III: *Evidence taken in the Madras Presidency*. HMSO, London, 1927

(All India) Rural Labour Enquiry, 1963–5. Final Report. Government of India. No date, preface dated 1973

Thurston, E. and Rangachari, K. *Castes and Tribes of Southern India*. Vol. III. Government Press, Madras, 1909

United Nations

Food and Agricultural Organisation. *Agricultural Development in Nigeria, 1965–1980*. Rome, 1966

Books and other publications

Ajayi, J. F. A. and Crowder, M. (eds.) *History of West Africa*, Vol. I. Longman, London, 1971

Andrews, D. J. 'Plant Density and Grain Yield of Nigerian Sorghums'. *Savanna*, June 1976

Arnold, D., Jeffrey, R. and Manor, J. 'Caste Associations in South Asia: a comparative analysis'. *Indian Economic & Social History Review*, XIII, 3, 1976

Baker, C. J. 'Tamilnad Estates in the Twentieth Century'. *Indian Economic & Social History Review*, XIII, 1, 1976

Baker C. J. and Washbrook, D. A. *South India: Political Institutions and Political Change, 1880–1940*. Macmillan, Delhi, 1975

Barber, W. J. *British Economic Thought and India, 1600–1858*. Clarendon Press, Oxford, 1975

Barth, H. *Travels and Discoveries in North and Central Africa, 1849–1855*. Vols. I to V. London, 1857. Reprinted in 3 volumes, Cass, London, 1965

Bauer, P. T. and Yamey, B. S. *The Economics of Under-Developed Countries*. Cambridge, 1957

Beals, A. R. 'Interplay among Factors of Change in a Mysore Village' *in* Marriott (ed.), 1969

Beattie, J. M. and Lienhardt, R. G. (eds.) *Essays in Memory of E. E. Evans-Pritchard*. Oxford, 1975

Beck, Brenda E. F. *Peasant Society in Konku: A Study of Right or Left Subcastes in South India*. University of British Columbia Press, Vancouver, 1972

Beidelman, T. O. *A Comparative Analysis of the 'Jajmani' System*. Monographs for the Association of Asian Studies VIII, New York, 1959

Berry, R. A. and Cline, W. R. *Agrarian Structure and Productivity in Developing Countries*. The Johns Hopkins University Press, Baltimore and London, 1979

Béteille, A. *Caste, Class and Power: Changing Patterns of Stratification in a Tanjore Village*. University of California Press, Berkeley, 1965

Béteille, A. *Studies in Agrarian Social Structure*. Oxford University Press, 1974

Bloch, M. (ed.) *Marxist Analyses and Social Anthropology*. Association of Social Anthropology Studies, Malaby Press, London, 1975

Bromley, R. J. *Periodic Markets, Daily Markets and Fairs: A Bibliography*. Monash University Publications in Geography, No. 10, 1974

Buchanan, F. *A Journey from Madras through the Countries of Mysore, Canara and Malabar*. Vols. I to III. London, 1807

Buckley, Joan. *See* Goody, 1973

Bujra, Janet M. (ed.) *See* Caplan (ed.), 1978

Burnell, A. C. *See* Yule, 1886

Caldwell, J. C. and Okonjo, C. (eds.) *The Population of Tropical Africa*. Longman, London, 1968

Caplan, Patricia and Bujra, Janet M. (eds.) *Women United, Women Divided: Cross-cultural perspectives on female solidarity*. Tavistock Publications, London, 1978

Cardew, M. 'Gobir Granaries'. *Nigeria Magazine*, 67, 1960

Cassen, R. H. *India: Population, Economy, Society*. Macmillan, London, 1978

Chambers, R. 'Rural Poverty Unperceived: problems and remedies'. *World Development*, Jan. 1981

Chambers, R., and Harriss, J. 'Comparing Twelve South Indian Villages: in search of practical theory' *in* Farmer (ed.), 1977

Charlesworth, N. 'Rich Peasants and Poor Peasants in late Nineteenth-century Maharashtra', *in* Dewey and Hopkins (eds.), 1978

Charlesworth, N. 'Trends in the Agricultural Performance of an Indian Province: The Bombay Presidency, 1900–1920', *in* Chaudhuri *et al.* (eds.), 1979

Chaudhuri, K. N. and Dewey, C. J. (eds.) *Economy and Society: Essays in Indian Economic and Social History*. Oxford University Press, Delhi, 1979

Chayanov, A. V. *The Theory of Peasant Economy*, 1925, translated D. Thorner *et al*, Irwin, for American Economic Association, 1966

Clapperton, H. *Journal of a Second Expedition into the Interior of Africa*. 1829. Reprinted Cass, London, 1966

Clark, C. and Haswell, Margaret. *The Economics of Subsistence Agriculture*. Macmillan, London, 1964

Crick, B. Review of *Politics and History* by R. Aron, *The Observer*, 22 April 1979

Crowder, M. (ed.) *See* Ajayi (ed.), 1971

Cummings, R. W. 'Expectations for developments in sorghums, millets and legumes'. Paper presented at Conference on Science and Agribusiness in the 'Seventies. London, 1974

Curtin, P. D. *Economic Change in Precolonial Africa: Senegambia in the Era of the Slave Trade*. University of Wisconsin Press, Madison, 1975

Dalton, G. (ed.) *Research in Economic Anthropology: an Annual Compilation of Research*. Vol. I. 1978

Dewey, C. J. (ed.) *See* Chaudhuri, 1978

Dewey, C. J. and Hopkins, A. G. (eds.) *The Imperial Impact: Studies in the Economic History of Africa and India*. University of London, The Athlone Press, 1978

Dharampal. *Indian Science and Technology in the Eighteenth Century: some Contemporary European Accounts*. Impex, Delhi, 1971

Dubois, Abbé J. A. *Hindu Manners, Customs and Ceremonies*. Ed. H. K. Beauchamp, 3rd edn, Oxford, 1906

Dumont, L. *Homo Hierarchicus: The Caste System and its Implications*. Weidenfeld & Nicolson, London, 1970

Dupire, Marguerite. *Organisation sociale des Peul: étude d'ethnographie comparée*. Librairie Plon, Paris, 1970

Dushkin, Lelah. 'Scheduled Caste Politics' *in* Mahar (ed.), 1972

Elliot, R. H. *Gold, Sport and Coffee Planting in Mysore*. London, 1894

Epstein, T. Scarlett. *Economic Development and Social Change in South Asia*. Manchester University Press, 1962

Epstein, T. Scarlett. 'A Sociological Analysis of Witch Beliefs in a Mysore Village' *in* Middleton (ed.), 1967

Epstein, T. Scarlett. *South India: Yesterday, Today and Tomorrow*. Macmillan, London, 1973

Farmer, B. H. (ed.) *Green Revolution? Technology and Change in Rice-Growing Areas of Tamil Nadu and Sri Lanka*. Macmillan, London, 1977

Fika, A. M. *The Kano Civil War and British Over-rule, 1882–1940*. Oxford University Press, Ibadan, 1978

Finley, M. I. *The Ancient Economy*. Chatto & Windus, London, 1973

Fortes, M. 'Strangers' *in* Fortes, M. (ed.), 1949

Fortes, M. 'Introduction' to Goody (ed.), 1958

Fortes, M. (ed.) *Social Structure: Studies presented to A. R. Radcliffe-Brown*. Clarendon Press, Oxford, 1949

Fortes, M. and Patterson, Sheila (eds.) *Studies in African Social Anthropology*. Academic Press, London, 1975

Foster, G. M. 'Peasant Society and the Image of Limited Good'. *American Anthropologist*, April 1965

Fricke, W. *Cattle Husbandry in Nigeria*. Geographical Institute of Heidelberg University, 1979

Frykenberg, R. E. (ed.) *Land Control and Social Structure in Indian History*. University of Wisconsin Press, Madison, 1969

Gambling, T. *Societal Accounting*. Allen & Unwin, London, 1974

Geertz, C. *Agricultural Involution: The Processes of Ecological Change in Indonesia*. University of California Press, Berkeley, 1963

Goody, J. R. *Technology, Tradition and the State in Africa*. Oxford University Press, 1971

Goody, J. R. and Buckley, Joan. 'Inheritance and Women's Labour in Africa'. *Africa*, XLIII, 2, 1973

Goody, J. R. and Tambiah, S. J. *Bridewealth and Dowry*. Cambridge, 1975

Goody, J. R. (ed.) *The Developmental Cycle in Domestic Groups*. Cambridge, 1958

Goody, J. R. (ed.) *Changing Social Structure in Ghana*. International African Institute, London, 1975

Gough, Kathleen. 'The Hindu *Jajmani* System'. *Economic Development & Cultural Change*. 1, Oct. 1960

Gough, Kathleen. 'Caste in a Tanjore Village' *in* Leach (ed.), 1960

Hall, A. D. *Fertilizers and Manures*. Murray, London 1909; 3rd edn. 1929

Harris, D. R. (ed.) *Human Ecology in Savanna Environments*. Academic Press, London, 1980

Harris, M. 'The Cultural Ecology of India's Sacred Cattle'. *Current Anthropology*, Feb. 1966

Harriss, J. 'Implications of Changes in Agriculture for Social Relationships at the Village Level: the Case of Randam' *in* Farmer (ed.), 1977

Harriss, J. and Chambers, R. *See* Chambers, R., 1977

Hart, K. 'The Economic Basis of Tallensi Social History in the Early Twentieth Century' *in Research in Economic Anthropology*, Dalton (ed.), 1978

Haswell, Margaret. *Economics of Agriculture in a Savannah Village*. Colonial Research Studies, No. 8, HMSO, London, 1953

Haswell, Margaret. *The Nature of Poverty: A case-history of the first quarter-century after World War II*. Macmillan, London, 1975

Haswell, Margaret and Clark C. *See* Clark, 1964

Heston, A. 'An Approach to the Sacred Cow of India'. *Current Anthropology*, April, 1971

Hill, Polly. *The Gold Coast Cocoa Farmer*. Oxford University Press, 1956

Hill, Polly. *The Migrant Cocoa-Farmers of Southern Ghana*. Cambridge, 1963

Hill, Polly. 'Notes on the Occupations of Former Schoolboys: the case of a Hausa Village'. *Nigerian Journal of Economic & Social Studies*, July 1969

Hill, Polly. 'Hidden Trade in Hausaland'. *Man*, Sept. 1969

Hill, Polly. *Studies in Rural Capitalism in West Africa*. Cambridge, 1970
Hill, Polly. *Rural Hausa: A Village and A Setting*. Cambridge, 1972
Hill, Polly. 'The West African Farming Household' *in* Goody (ed.), 1975
Hill, Polly. *Population, Prosperity and Poverty: Rural Kano, 1900 and 1970*. Cambridge, 1977
Hill, Polly. 'Comparative Agrarian Relations in Karnataka (South India) and Hausaland (Northern Nigeria)'. *Indian Economic & Social History Review*, XVI, 3, 1979
Hill, Polly. 'Joint Families in Rural Karnataka, South India'. *Modern Asian Studies*, 14, 1, 1980.
Hindess, B. and Hirst, P. *Pre-capitalist Modes of Production*. Routledge & Kegan Paul, London, 1975
Hirst, P. *See* Hindess, B., 1975
Hjejle, Benedicte. 'Slavery and Agricultural Bondage in South India in the Nineteenth Century'. *The Scandinavian Economic History Review*, XV, 1 and 2, 1967
Hobson, Sarah. *Family Web: A Story of India*. Murray, London, 1978
Hodgkin, T. *Nigerian Perspectives: An Historical Anthology*. Oxford University Press, 2nd edn 1975
Hogendorn, J. S. 'The Vent-for-Surplus Model and African Cash Agriculture to 1914'. *Savanna*, June 1976
Hogendorn, J. S. *Nigerian Groundnut Exports: Origins and Early Development*. Ahmadu Bello University Press and Oxford University Press, 1978
Hopkins, A. G. *An Economic History of West Africa*. Longman, London, 1973
Hopkins, A. G. (ed.) *See* Dewey (ed.), 1978
Horton, R. 'Stateless Societies in the History of West Africa' *in* Ajayi (ed.), 1971
Iliffe, J. *A Modern History of Tanganyika*. Cambridge, 1979
Jacobs, Jane. *The Economy of Cities*. Cape, London, 1970
Jameson, J. D. (ed.) *Agriculture in Uganda*. Oxford University Press, 1970
Jeffrey, R. *See* Arnold (ed.), 1976
Jevons, W. S. *The Theory of Political Economy*. Macmillan, London, 1871
Jones, R. *An Essay on the Distribution of Wealth and on the Sources of Taxation*. London, 1831
Kassam, A. H. *See* Kowal, 1978
Kessinger, T. G. *Vilyatpur 1848–1968: Social and Economic Change in a North Indian Village*. University of California Press, Berkeley, 1974
Keynes, J. N. *The Scope and Method of Political Economy*. Macmillan, London, 1890
Kidron, M. (ed.) *See* Robinson (ed.), 1970
Kirk-Greene, A. and Rimmer, D. *Nigeria since 1970: A Political and Economic Outline*. Hodder & Stoughton, London, 1981
Kolenda, Pauline. *Caste in Contemporary India: Beyond Organic Solidarity*. Benjamin/Cummings Publishing Co., Menlo Park, California, 1978
Kopytoff, I. *See* Miers, 1977

Kosinski, L. A. and Prothero, R. M. (eds.) *People on the Move: Studies on Internal Migration*. Methuen, London, 1975

Kowal, J. M. and Kassam, A. H. *Agricultural Ecology of Savanna: A Study of West Africa*. Clarendon Press, Oxford, 1978

Kumar, Dharma. *Land and Caste in South India: Agricultural Labour in the Madras Presidency during the Nineteenth Century*. Cambridge, 1965

Kumar, Dharma. 'Landownership and Inequality in Madras Presidency: 1853–4 to 1946–47'. *Indian Economic & Social History Review*. July–Sept. 1975

Lamb, P. H. 'Agriculture in Hausaland, Northern Nigeria'. *Bulletin of the Imperial Institute*. XI, 1913

Law, R. 'Wheeled Transport in Pre-colonial West Africa'. *Africa*. 3, 1980

Leach, E. R. (ed.) *Aspects of Caste in South India, Ceylon and North-West Pakistan*. Cambridge, 1960

Lenin, V. I. *Collected Works*. Vol. 3. *The Development of Capitalism in Russia*. Lawrence & Wishart, London, translation of 2nd edition of 1918

Lenin, V. I. *The Agrarian Question and 'Critics of Marx'*. Progress Publishers, Moscow, 1976

Libbee, M.J. and Sopher, D. E. 'Marriage Migration in Rural India' *in* Kosinski, *et al.* (eds.), 1975

Lienhardt, R. G. (ed.) *See* Beattie (ed.), 1975

Lipton, M. *Why Poor People stay Poor: A Study of Urban Bias in World Development*. Temple Smith, London, 1977

Lloyd, P. C. *Yoruba Land Law*. Oxford University Press, 1962

Lugard, F. D. (Lord) 'Northern Nigeria'. *The Geographical Journal*, XXIII, 1904

Mahar, J. M. (ed.) *The Untouchables in Contemporary India*. University of Arizona Press, Tucson, 1972

Mann, H. H. *Land and Labour in a Deccan Village*. Series no. 1. Oxford University Press, 1917

Mannheim, K. *Ideology and Utopia*. Kegan Paul, London, 1936

Manor, J. *See* Arnold, 1976

Marriott, M. (ed.) *Village India: Studies in the Little Community*. University of Chicago Press, 1955, reprinted 1969

Marshall, W. *The Rural Economy of the West of England including Devonshire and parts of Somersetshire, Dorsetshire and Cornwall*. Vol. I, 1796. Reprinted David & Charles, Newton Abbot, 1970

Marx, K. *Capital: A Critique of Political Economy*, Vol. III, Book III. 1894. Progress Publishers, Moscow, 1971

Marx, K. *Theories of Surplus Value*, Part III. Progress Publishers, Moscow, 1971

Meek, C. K. *Land Law and Custom in the Colonies*. Oxford University Press, 1957

Meillassoux, C. (ed.) *L'esclavage en Afrique précoloniale*. François Maspero, Paris, 1975

Mencher, Joan P. 'The Caste System Upside Down'. *Current Anthropology*, Dec. 1974

Mencher, Joan P. *Agricultural and Social Structure in Tamil Nadu: Past Origins,*

Present Transformations and Future Prospects. Allied Publishers, Delhi, 1978

Middleton, J. (ed.) *Magic, Witchcraft and Curing*. The Natural History Press, New York, 1967

Miers, Suzanne and Kopytoff, I. (eds.) *Slavery in Africa: Historical and Anthropological Perspectives*. University of Wisconsin Press, Madison, 1977

Moffatt, M. *An Untouchable Community in South India: Structure and Consensus*. Princeton University Press, 1979.

Moore, B. Jr. *Social Origins of Dictatorship and Democracy: Lord and Peasant in the making of the Modern World*. 1966. Reissued Penguin, London, 1977

Morel, E. D. *Nigeria: Its Peoples and its Problems*. London, 1911, reprinted Cass, London, 1968

Morgan, W. B. and Pugh, J. C. *West Africa*. Methuen, London, 1969

Mortimore, M. J. 'Land and Population Pressure in the Kano Close-Settled Zone, Northern Nigeria'. *The Advancement of Science*, April 1967

Mortimore, M. J. 'Population Distribution, Settlement and Soils in Kano Province, Northern Nigeria, 1931–1962' *in* Caldwell (ed.), 1968

Myint, H. 'The "Classical Theory" of International Trade and the Underdeveloped Countries'. *Economic Journal*, June 1958

Myint, H. *The Economics of the Developing Countries*. Hutchinson, London, 1964

Myrdal, G. *Asian Drama: An Inquiry into the Poverty of Nations*. Vols. I to III. Penguin, London, 1968

Nadel, S. F. *A Black Byzantium: The Kingdom of Nupe*. Oxford University Press, London, 1942

Norman, D. W. 'Labour Inputs of Farmers: a case study of the Zaria Province of the North-Central State of Nigeria'. *Nigerian Journal of Economic & Social Studies*, II, 1, 1969

Norman, D. W. 'Crop Mixtures under Indigenous Conditions in the Northern Part of Nigeria' *in* Ofori (ed.), 1973

Ofori, E. D. (ed.) *Factors of Agricultural Growth in West Africa*. University of Ghana, Legon, 1973

Okonjo, C. *See* Caldwell (ed.), 1968

Paden, J. N. *Religion and Political Culture in Kano*. University of California Press, 1973

Parry, J. P. *Caste and Kinship in Kangra*. Routledge & Kegan Paul, London, 1979

Patterson, Sheila. *See* Fortes, M., 1975

Payne, W. J. A. *See* Williamson, 1959

Protherto, R. M. *See* Kosinski (ed.), 1975

Pugh, J. C. *See* Morgan, 1969

Purseglove, J. W. *Tropical Crops; Monocotyledons*, Vol. I. Longman, London, 1972

Raaij, J. G. T. van. *Rural Planning in a Savanna Region: the case of Fulani Pastoralists in the North Central State of Nigeria*. University of Rotterdam, 1974

Raj, K. N. 'Investment in Livestock in Agrarian Economies: an analysis of some issues concerning "Sacred Cows" and "Surplus Cattle"'. *Indian Economic Review*, IV, 1, April 1969

Raj, K. N. *In* Robinson (ed.), 1970

Raj, K. N. 'India's Sacred Cattle: theories and empirical findings'. *Economic & Political Weekly*, 13, 27 March 1971

Rimmer, D. *See* Kirk-Greene, 1981

Robinson, E. A. G. and Kidron, M. (eds.) *Economic Development in South Asia* (Proceedings of a Conference held by the International Economic Association.) Macmillan, London, 1970

Roxborough, I. *Theories of Underdevelopment*. Humanities Press, New Jersey, 1979

Rudra, A. and Sen, A. 'Farm size and Labour Use: analysis and policy'. *Economic & Political Weekly*, Annual Number, 1980

Sahlins, M. *Stone Age Economics*. 1972. Reprinted Tavistock Publications, London, 1974

Sen, A. *See* Rudra, 1980

Shah, A. M. *The Household Dimension of the Family in India: A Field Study in a Gujarat Village and a Review of other Studies*. University of California Press, Berkeley, 1973

Shanin, T. *Peasants and Peasant Societies*. Penguin, London, 1971

Sharma, Ursula. 'Segregation and its Consequences in India: rural women in Himachal Pradesh' *in* Caplan, 1978

Skinner, G. W. 'Marketing and Social Structure in Rural China'. Part I. *Journal of Asian Studies*, Nov. 1964

Slater, G. *Some South Indian Villages*. Oxford University Press, 1918

Smith, Mary. *Baba of Karo: A Woman of the Muslim Hausa*. Faber, London, 1954

Smith, M. G. *The Economy of Hausa Communities of Zaria*. Colonial Research Series No. 16, HMSO, London, 1955

Sopher, D. E. *See* Libbee, 1975

Sopher, D. E. 'Indian Civilization and the Tropical Savanna Environment' *in* Harris (ed.), 1980

Sopher, D. E. (ed.) *An Exploration of India: Geographical Perspectives on Society and Culture*. Longman, London, 1980

Srinivas, M. N. 'The Dominant Caste in Rampura'. *American Anthropologist*, LXI, 1959

Srinivas, M. N. 'The Social System of a Mysore Village' *in* Marriot (ed.), 1969

Srinivas, M. N. 'The Indian Village: Myth and Reality' *in* Beattie (ed.), 1975

Srinivas, M. N. *The Remembered Village*. University of California Press, Berkeley, 1976

Srivastava, H. S. *The History of Indian Famines and Development of Famine Policy (1858–1918)*. Agra, Sri Ram Mehra, 1968

Stein, B. 'Integration of the Agrarian System of South India' *in* Frykenberg (ed.), 1969

Tambiah, S. J. 'Dowry and Bridewealth and the Property Rights of Women in South Asia' *in* Goody, 1975

Voelcker, J. A. *Report on the Improvement of Indian Agriculture*. London, 1893

Wade, R. 'The Social Response to Irrigation: an Indian case study'. *Journal of Development Studies*, 16, 1, Oct. 1979

Washbrook, D. A. 'Political Change in a Stable Society: Tanjore District 1880 to 1920' *in* Baker, 1975

Whewell, W. (ed.) *Literary Remains: consisting of lectures and tracts on Political Economy of the late Rev. Richard Jones*. London, 1859

Wilks, M. *Historical Sketches of the South of India*. Vol. I, London, 1810

Williamson, G. and Payne, W. J. A. *An Introduction to Animal Husbandry in the Tropics*. Longman, London, 1959

Wiser, W. H. *The Hindu Jajmani System*. Lucknow Publishing House, India, 1936

Yamey, B. S. *See* Bauer, 1957

Yule, H. and Burnell, A. C. *Hobson-Jobson: A Glossary of Anglo-Indian Colloquial Words and Phrases*. London, 1886

Index